Student Study Guide

for use with

ESSENTIALS OF UNDERSTANDING PSYCHOLOGY

Sixth Edition

Robert S. Feldman
University of Massachusetts—Amherst

Prepared by
Barbara L. Radigan
Community College of Allegheny County

With ESL Sections prepared by
Sheryl M. Hartman
Miami Dade Community College

Boston   Burr Ridge, IL   Dubuque, IA   Madison, WI   New York   San Francisco   St. Louis
Bangkok   Bogotá   Caracas   Lisbon   London   Madrid   Mexico City
Milan   Montreal   New Delhi   Santiago   Seoul   Singapore   Sydney   Taipei   Toronto

The **McGraw·Hill** Companies

Student Study Guide
for use with
Essentials of Understanding Psychology

Published by McGraw-Hill, an imprint of The McGraw-Hill Companies, Inc., 1221
Avenue of the Americas, New York, NY 10020. Copyright 2005 by
The McGraw-Hill Companies, Inc. All rights reserved.

1 2 3 4 5 6 7 8 9 0 QPD/QPD 9 0 9 8 7 6 5 4

ISBN 0-07-296505-3

www.mhhe.com

Table of Contents

Preface

This *Student Study Guide* has been prepared with several very important student concerns in mind, primarily: (1) the students' needs for a comprehensive guide that is meant to supplement Robert Feldman's *Essentials of Understanding Psychology, Sixth Edition* in such a way as to take advantage of the many features in the book that support effective study habits; and (2) the students' need for practice and drill work that focuses on the full content of each module and presents practice questions that are similar to those provided in the instructor's *Test Bank*. Key term definitions in the text were used to develop the key term drills found throughout the study guide in the *Evaluate* sections. Three practice tests have been created for each set of modules. The first two tests consist of questions that are primarily factual in nature. The third test consists of difficult factual, applied, and conceptual questions. A complete set of answer explanations for both the right and wrong answers to all of the multiple-choice questions is available at the end of each set of modules.

You will also find three practice essay questions for each set of modules. These questions are intended to provide opportunities for you to practice writing and critical analysis skills. In each module's answer key, a list of points that should be covered in your answer to each question has been provided. These questions are meant to be difficult and to require you to draw on both conceptual and factual knowledge. Some questions require that you apply concepts to situations, whereas others may require that you compare several ideas. New in this edition, students will discover the "Keys to Excellence: Study Skills" section and counterpart end-of-module sections called "Spotlight on Terminology and Language—ESL Pointers" for readers who may be less experienced in American usages of the English language.

The introduction explains the organization of the *Study Guide* and offers tips on how to use the features of the *Study Guide* to improve your study skills and make your time spent with the text more effective.

SUPPLEMENTS

Online Learning Center (ISBN 0-07-296507-X)
The Student Online Learning Center houses an array of module-by-module study tools, including detailed module outlines, learning objectives, keywords, self-quizzes, short-answer questions, activities and projects, answers to selected *Rethink* questions from the textbook, interesting Web links, and interactive exercises. Visit us at www.mhhe.com/feldmanup7.

NEW! *PsychInteractive* CD-ROM (ISBN 0-07-296504-5)
This exciting new CD-ROM for students contains a unique library of electronic interactivities with conceptually based quizzes, designed specifically to help students master the set of basic learning objectives laid out in the book. Using the assessment tools provided for every exercise, including a self-test and a concept quiz, both students and instructors can track progress in attaining these objectives. Students can also create and print a personalized study page after completing each interactivity, giving them an excellent tool for reviewing the learning objectives.

ACKNOWLEDGMENTS

Developing this *Student Study Guide* has proved to be a challenging and quite exciting project. I wish to thank the team at McGraw-Hill—particularly Kirsten Stoller and Louis Swaim. I am especially indebted to Robert Feldman, for without a high-quality text, a student study guide would be meaningless. His contribution to the introduction is one of many examples of his concern for students. The *Keys to Excellence: Study Skills* and *Spotlight on Terminology and Language—ESL Pointers* sections were prepared by psychologist Sheryl Hartman, who teaches remedial courses and introductory psychology to non-native English-language speakers at Miami Dade Community College. Her contribution, which is fundamental in aiding non-native speakers of English in understanding and retaining key course content, makes the *Student Study Guide* one of the best resources for student success. Finally, I would like to thank Michael Garrison, whose exemplary work on the fourth edition of this *Study Guide* left me with a solid base of well-written material to revise.

Barbara L. Radigan
Community College of Allegheny County
Pittsburgh, Pennsylvania

Introduction

Using *Essentials of Understanding Psychology:* Strategies for Effective Study

Essentials of Understanding Psychology has been written with the reader in mind, and it therefore includes several unique features that will help you maximize your learning of the concepts, theories, facts, and other kinds of information that make up the field of psychology. To take advantage of these features, you should take several steps when reading and studying the book. The *Student Study Guide* was designed to help the student take full advantage of the features in the textbook, and the steps recommended for the text have been incorporated into this *Study Guide*. By following these steps, you will not only get the most from reading and studying *Essentials of Understanding Psychology*, but you will also develop habits that will help you study other texts more effectively and think critically about material you are learning. Among the most important steps are the following:

Familiarize yourself with the logic of the book's structure. Begin by reading the Table of Contents. It provides an overview of the topics that will be covered and gives a sense of the way the various topics are interrelated. Next, review the Preface, which describes the book's major features. Note how each module is a self-contained unit; that provides logical starting and stopping points for reading and studying. Also note the major highlights of each set of modules: a topic-opening outline, a Prologue, a Looking Ahead section that includes module objectives, and a P.O.W.E.R. learning system, which will include module goals, the organizational format, a Work section, an Evaluate section, and a Rethink section to help you increase your ability to learn and retain information and to think critically. At the end of each set of modules, three tests are provided so you can review and evaluate the skills you have acquired while studying each set of modules. Answers to all of the work and evaluation sections are located at the end of each set of modules, along with answers to the practice tests. Because every module is structured in the same way, you are provided with a set of familiar landmarks as you chart your way through new material, allowing you to organize the module's content more readily. This study guide is designed to lead you through each of these steps.

Title Bars. Each module is divided by title bars like the one shown below, and each title bar provides recommendations for what can be done with the material provided.

Practice Questions	

Test your knowledge of the material in each set of modules by answering the **Multiple-Choice Questions**. These questions have been placed in three Practice Tests. The first two tests consist of questions that will test your recall of factual knowledge. The third test contains questions that are challenging and primarily test for conceptual knowledge and your ability to apply that knowledge. Check your answers and review the feedback using the Answer Key at the end of each chapter of the *Study Guide.*

The new ***Keys to Excellence: Study Skills*** and ***Spotlight on Terminology and Language—ESL Pointers*** sections are intended to facilitate the comprehension and retention of the text material by non-native speakers of English, focusing on 490-plus key terms and concepts in ***Essentials of Understanding Psychology, Sixth Edition***. The *Keys to Excellence: Study Skills* section in the front of the Study Guide provides tips to identifying in-text language cues and organizing study materials accordingly. The *Spotlight on Terminology and Language—ESL Pointers* sections in each set of modules provide clarification of many content-specific idiomatic phrases by defining them in context.

The new edition of the ***Essentials of Understanding Psychology Student Study Guide*** provides students with the option of using *P.O.W.E.R. Learning*, a systematic approach to learning and studying based on five key steps (*P*repare, *O*rganize, *W*ork, *E*valuate, and *R*ethink). Based on empirical research, *P.O.W.E.R. Learning* systematizes the acquisition of new material by providing a learning framework. The system stresses the importance of learning objectives, self-evaluation, and critical thinking. The elements of the *P.O.W.E.R. Learning* system can also be used in conjunction with other learning systems, such as *SQ3R*. Specifically, use of the *P.O.W.E.R. Learning* system entails the following steps:

- ***Prepare.*** Before starting any journey, we need to know where we are headed. Academic journeys are no different; we need to know what our goals are. The *Prepare* stage consists of thinking about what we hope to attain from reading a particular section of the text by identifying specific goals we seek to accomplish. In your ***Essentials of Understanding Psychology Student Study Guide,*** these goals are presented in the form of broad questions that start each major section.

- ***Organize.*** Once we know what our goals are, we need to develop a route to accomplish those goals. The *Organize* stage involves developing a mental roadmap of where we are headed. The ***Essentials of Understanding Psychology Student Study Guide*** highlights the organization of each upcoming section. Read the outline to get an idea of what topics are covered and how they are organized.

- ***Work.*** The heart of the *P.O.W.E.R. Learning* system entails actually reading and studying the material presented in the book. In some ways, *Work* is the easy part, because if you have carried out the steps in the preparation and organization stages, you'll know where you're headed and how to get there. Of course, it's not so simple—you'll need the motivation to conscientiously read and think about the material presented in the chapter. And remember, the main text isn't the only material you need to read and think about. It's also important to read the boxes, the marginal glossary terms, and the special sections in order to gain a full understanding of the material, so be sure to include them as part of the *Work* of reading the module and then use the *Work* section of your study guide to support your text reading.

- **Evaluate.** The fourth step, *Evaluate*, provides you with the opportunity to determine how effectively you have mastered the material. The ***Essentials of Understanding Psychology Student Study Guide*** has matching tests following each *Work* section that permits a rapid check of your understanding of the material. Evaluating your progress is essential to assessing your degree of mastery of the material.

- **Rethink.** The final step in *P.O.W.E.R. Learning* involves critical thinking, which entails reanalyzing, reviewing, questioning, and challenging assumptions. It provides the opportunity to look at the big picture by thinking about how material fits with other information you have already learned. Every major section of ***Essentials of Understanding Psychology, 7/e,*** ends with a *Rethink* section that contains thought-provoking questions. Answering them will help you understand the material more fully and at a deeper level.

If you want to maximize your potential to master the material in ***Essentials of Understanding Psychology, 7/e***, use *P.O.W.E.R. Learning*. Taking the time and effort to work through the steps of the system is a proven technique for understanding and learning the material.

Supplementing *P.O.W.E.R. Learning* with *SQ3R*

Although *P.O.W.E.R. Learning* is the learning strategy that is built into the book and consequently easiest to use, it is not the only system compatible with the book. For example, some readers may wish to supplement the *P.O.W.E.R. Learning* system with the *SQ3R* method, which includes a series of five steps, designated by the initials *S-Q-R-R-R*. The first step is to *survey* the material by reading the module outlines, module headings, figure captions, recaps, and Looking Ahead and Looking Back sections, providing yourself with an overview of the major points of the module. The next step is to *question*. Formulate questions about the material, either aloud or in writing, before actually reading a section. The queries posed in the *Prepare* sections and the *Evaluate* and *Rethink* questions are also good sources of questions.

The next three steps in *SQ3R* ask you to *read, recite,* and *review* the material. *Read* carefully and, even more important, read actively and critically. While you are reading, answer the questions you have asked yourself. Critically evaluate material by considering the implications of what you are reading, thinking about possible exceptions and contradictions, and examining underlying assumptions. The *recite* step involves describing and explaining to yourself (or a friend) the material you have just read and answering the questions you have posed earlier. Recite aloud; the recitation process helps identify your degree of understanding of the material you have just read. Finally, *review* the material, looking it over, reading the Looking Back summaries, and answering the in-text review questions.

Final Comments

Find a location and time. The last aspect of studying that warrants mention is that *when* and *where* you study are in some ways as important as *how* you study. One of the truisms of the psychological literature is that we learn things better, and are able to recall them longer, when we study material in small chunks over several study sessions, rather than massing our study into one lengthy period. This implies that all-night studying just before a test is going to be less effective—and a lot more tiring—than employing a series of steady, regular study sessions.

In addition to carefully timing your studying, you should seek out a special location to study. It doesn't really matter where it is, as long as it has minimal distractions and is a place that you use *only* for studying. Identifying a special "territory" allows you to get in the right mood for study as soon as you begin.

Use a study strategy. Although we are expected to study and ultimately to learn a wide array of material throughout our schooling, we are rarely taught any systematic strategies that permit us to study more effectively. Yet, just as we wouldn't expect a physician to learn human anatomy by trial and error, it is the unusual student who is able to stumble on a truly effective studying strategy.

The *P.O.W.E.R. Learning* system (as well as *SQ3R)* provides a proven means of increasing your study effectiveness. Yet you need not feel tied to a particular strategy. You might want to combine other elements into your own study system. For example, learning tips and strategies for critical thinking will be presented throughout **Essentials of Understanding Psychology**, such as in Module 20 when the use of mnemonics (memory techniques for organizing material to help its recall) are discussed. If these tactics help you successfully master new material, stick with them.

By using the proven *P.O.W.E.R. Learning* system, you will maximize your understanding of the material in this book and will master techniques that will help you learn and think critically in all of your academic endeavors. More important, you will optimize your understanding of the field of psychology. It is worth the effort. The excitement, challenge, and promise that psychology holds for you is immense.

Robert Feldman   ***Barbara Radigan***

Keys To Excellence: Study Skills

The following study strategies will help you think deeply and critically about what you read. Non-native speakers of English should find this section especially helpful.

Words are the instruments of communication, learning, and thinking. Use keywords to trigger your consolidation of material. One keyword can initiate the recall of a whole cluster of ideas. A few keywords can form a chain from which you can reconstruct an entire lecture.

Learning involves digesting what you read and actively using the information, as follows:

- *Digesting*: Give yourself time for a thinking pause after you finish a paragraph and summarize it. The thinking pause will provide time for the main idea to sink in and connect with information you already know.

- *Using New Information*: Consciously rehearse what you've learned. Repetition can often be the key to remembering. Always strive to link what you learn to what you already know. Reinforce new ideas by associating them with the things close to you in your own life.

Recognizing Patterns of Organization

Organizational patterns help organize a reader's thoughts and help you better comprehend key concepts. As your brain works to make sense of the world around you, it tries to fit everything into a recognizable shape and pattern that has meaning for you. Placing work into reasonable blocks of information makes it easier for your brain to understand and remember information.

There are four basic approaches, or *patterns*, that writers use in presenting concepts:

- Describing the concept in the form of a generalization
- Explaining the similarities and/or differences of the concept as compared to other concepts
- Using cause and effect to show the active relationship of the concept to other concepts and to a bigger picture (e.g., a theory)
- Including a series of events or steps, breaking the concept down into digestible pieces

Familiarize yourself with the organizational pattern the text author is using. By recognizing the structure of the author's writing style, you will be better prepared to organize your studying and note-taking strategy. Recognizing patterns helps you anticipate information that is coming and incorporate and assimilate it within your existing knowledge base. You become more involved in your own learning process by focusing on the presentation of the material. You can think of yourself as a partner with the author as you learn this new information.

Use Signal Words to Organize Reading

Words can be used as obvious indicators of the direction of a writer's thoughts. These signal words for patterns can also be referred to as *transitional words*. Writers use these words to mark the shifts and turns in their thinking. Following these signal words, readers can identify when the writer is moving from one idea to the next. Using signal words and phrases imposes a recognizable order on ideas, facts, and details.

Different kinds of signal words can alert you to what type of material is to follow. For example, the following ***comparison and contrast*** signal words and phrases can be used to explain similarities and/or differences:

- However
- Although
- Rather
- Conversely
- Different from
- In contrast
- Instead
- More than

- But
- While
- Yet
- Less than
- On the other hand
- One difference
- Unlike
- Another major difference

When you read sentences, use signal words and organizational clues. If you see "on the one hand," watch for the words "on the other hand," which introduces the other side of the argument.

The following are ***cause and effect*** signal words and phrases that call attention to a concept's connection to other concepts and its role in an overriding theme:

- Therefore
- As a result
- Accordingly

- Consequently
- Because

Sequencing signal words help you notice important events and the logical progression of material. Sequence word and phrase examples are:

- Near
- Until
- First
- For the next
- Then
- Finally

- After
- Last
- While
- Later
- Before
- The following

Signal words that are used to add ***emphasis***, and in doing so distinguish important points to take note of, are:

- Most important
- Remember that
- Pay attention to
- Above all
- A key (component, feature, etc.)

- The main idea
- Of primary concern
- Most significant
- In conclusion

Creating Study Cards

Use three-by-five-inch notecards to learn your vocabulary words by recitation and repetition. Select a word you want to remember and write the word on the front of a card. On the back of the card, write the complete sentence in which the word occurs in the text. Then, write the same word in a meaningful context that is familiar to you. This process will reinforce your use of the term and help you incorporate it more fully into your current vocabulary base.

To study the word, always look first at the front of the card. Pronounce the word. Think about the word and how you would define it. Put the word in a new sentence, and then check the use and definition of the word on the back of the card. The best part about using these study cards is that you can take them just about anywhere and use them for review in your spare time.

Understanding and Applying the Steps of Marking a Text

The purpose of making marks in a text is to create your own personal roadmap to make navigating through the material easier. Marking a textbook will help you accumulate information in an orderly and systematic way. You can underline important words and sentences and make notes in the margins about them. Paraphrase important statements in the top and bottom margins of your text to simplify concepts into kernels of important information. Circle words, phrases, and theorists' names where they appear, or rewrite them in the margin if they seem meaningful or are difficult to grasp. Seeing these words stand out on the page will draw you back to review them. Use memory-jogging abbreviations to stimulate your recall of information. Circle numbers that indicate a series of arguments, facts, or ideas—either main or supporting. Develop visual diagrams of the concepts when you can. Consider all blank spaces as flexible note-taking areas. By marking your book, you are turning your textbook into your own custom-made study guide. Referring back to your marginal notes, you will be able to review the essential material at a glance just by flipping back through the pages.

Using special marks and colors, you can highlight and differentiate between different types of material. By creating a key of marks and colors, you can easily identify where certain types of information can be found. You might choose to highlight key terms in yellow marker or draw squares around theorists' names. One successful method of marking is to star (*) the beginning of a sentence, paragraph, questions, and so on that you believe your instructor may quiz you on. Instructors may suggest, through their emphasis in class, that certain information is likely to appear on an exam. Finding the coverage of this material in your text and starring it will distinguish it as a potential test question. Then, when you revisit your text, you can better focus your studying time.

Vocabulary

Knowing the meaning of prefixes, roots, and suffixes can unlock the meaning of unfamiliar words. Common word parts are building blocks used in forming many English words. Increasing your awareness of these basic word parts helps unlock the meaning of unfamiliar words.

- **Root.** A root is a basic word part to which prefixes, suffixes, or both are added.
- **Prefix.** A prefix is a word part added to the beginning of a word. Following is a list of some common prefixes with their meanings.
- **Suffix.** A suffix is a word part added to the end of a word. Although a suffix may affect a word's meaning slightly, it is more likely to affect how the word is used in a sentence.

PREFIX	MEANING
• A-	in, on, at
• Ab-	from, away
• Ad-, a-	to, toward
• An-, a-	not, without
• Ambi-, amphi-	around, both
• Ana-	back, opposite
• Ante-	before
• Anti-	against, opposite
• Cata-	break down
• Circum-	around
• Con-	with, together
• Contra-	against
• Dia-	through
• Dis-	apart
• Dys-	ill
• Extra-	beyond
• Fore-	before
• Hyper-	over, beyond
• Hypo-	under
• Inter-	between
• Intra	within
• Para-	beside
• Post-	after
• Re-	before
• Retro-	backward
• Sub-	under
• Super-	over
• Trans-	across
• Ultra-	beyond
• Un-	not

*For an online audio glossary, go to www.mhhe.com/feldmanup7.

Introduction to Psychology

1: Psychologists at Work
2: A Science Evolves: The Past, the Present, and the Future
3: Research in Psychology
4: Research Challenges: Exploring the Process

Overview

Module 1 defines psychology as the scientific study of behavior and mental processes. The diversity of the field of psychology is illustrated by listing several of the subfields of psychology. This is followed by samples of questions that each psychological subfield attempts to answer. A portrait of psychologists illustrates both the types of psychologists along with the educational requirements necessary for those who choose careers in the field of psychology. The module goes on to examine the different positions that are available to psychologists in today's workplace.

Module 2 presents the historical roots of psychology with attention to the roles that women have played in the development of the discipline. The module then goes on to trace the events that led to the five basic perspectives in psychology today: neuroscience, psychodynamic, cognitive, behavioral, and humanistic. This is followed by a discussion on the role that psychology plays in the study of violence.

The five key issues in psychology today are discussed next and include nature versus nurture, conscious versus unconscious causes of behavior, observable behavior versus internal mental processes, free will versus determinism, and individual differences versus universal principles. These key issues are used to understand how culture, ethnicity, and race influence behavior.

Module 3 examines the ways in which psychologists reach conclusions about the unknown. The scientific method is discussed in detail, focusing on the development of theories as the framework for understanding relationships, and is followed by a discussion about how hypotheses are used to test theories. A description of the way in which psychologists develop suppositions and test theories is also presented. Consideration is then given to the specific means that researchers use in doing research. These include archival research, naturalistic observation, survey research, case studies, correlational research, and experimental research. Next, the major techniques used in carrying out research are discussed, and the benefits and limitations of each type of research are listed.

Module 4 discusses the ethics of doing psychological research, both on humans and animals. The treatment of subjects is examined, and a discussion on when it is and is not appropriate to design experiments using human subjects and/or animals is presented. Finally, because none of us can turn on the television, listen to the radio, or pick up a newspaper or magazine without being bombarded with ideas about how to gain happiness and bliss, improve our lives, our work, and our futures, questions are posed that help the consumer scrutinize thoroughly what is valid and what is not in psychological research and the ways that we can become knowledgeable and critical consumers of research findings.

To further investigate the topics covered in this chapter, you can visit the related Web sites by visiting the following link: www.mhhe.com/feldmanup6-01links.

Prologue: Seven Became One
Looking Ahead

Module 1:
Psychologists at Work

The Subfields of Psychology: Psychology's Family Tree
Working at Psychology

Psychology at Work: Carolyn Copper, Government Analyst

- ■ *What is the science of psychology?*
- ■ *What are the major specialties in the field of psychology?*
- ■ *Where do psychologists work?*

Psychologists at Work

[a] _____ is defined as the scientific study of behavior and mental processes. Psychologists investigate what people do as well as their thoughts, feelings, perceptions, reasoning processes, and memories. They also investigate the biological foundations of these processes. Psychology relies on the scientific method to discover ways of explaining, predicting, modifying, and improving behavior. The study of behavior and mental processes involves examining animal as well as human subjects to find the general laws that govern the behavior of all organisms.

Contrary to the mistaken view held by many people that psychology is interested only in abnormal behavior, psychologists examine a wide array of behaviors and mental processes. The specialty areas are described in the order in which they appear throughout the text.

[b] _____ explores the relationship between fundamental biological processes and behavior. The study is focused on the brain and the nervous system, and both diseases and healthy functions are examined for their contribution to the understanding of behavior.

[c] _____ *psychology* is both a specialty and a task undertaken by most psychologists. The scientific work of psychology requires experimental methods to be applied wherever possible. **[d]** _____ *psychology* is a specialty within experimental psychology that focuses on higher mental functions such as thought, language, memory, problem solving, reasoning, and decision making, among other processes.

Emerging areas of psychology include: **[e]** _____, an area that seeks to identify behavior patterns that are a result of our genetic inheritance; **[f]** _____, which unites the areas of biopsychology and clinical psychology. It focuses on the relationship between biological factors and psychological disorders. This specialty area has led to promising new medications to treat psychological disorders; **[g]** _____, the study of how physical environments influence behavior; **[h]** _____ is the study of law and psychology. It has changed many of the methods and techniques used in the criminal justice field today; **[i]** _____ is the branch investigating applications of psychology to sports and athletic activity.

Psychologists are employed in a variety of settings. Most doctoral-level psychologists are employed by **[j]** _____ or are self-employed. Others work in hospitals, mental health clinics, schools, etc. About **[k]**_____ of all psychologists are found in the United States and about half of all psychologists are women. **[l]**_____ is one of the great concerns among today's psychologists. Racial and ethnic minorities are underrepresented in the field, and only 6 percent of all psychologists are members of a minority.

Most psychologists have a **[m]**_____, which requires four or five years of work after a bachelor's degree. About one-third of those in the field have two to three years of schooling after their bachelor's degree and have **[n]**_____ degrees. Both students and current members of the field share a common desire to improve the human condition.

The most common area of employment for students who receive a bachelor's degree in psychology is in the**[o]** _____ field, providing direct care.

Evaluate

_____ 1.   health psychology

_____ 2.   clinical psychology

_____ 3.   counseling psychology

_____ 4.   educational psychology

_____ 5.   school psychology

a.   The branch of psychology that explores the relationship of psychological factors and physical ailments or disease.

b.   The branch of psychology devoted to assessing children in elementary and secondary schools who have academic or emotional problems and to developing solutions to such problems.

c.   The branch of psychology that focuses on educational, social, and career adjustment problems.

d.   The branch of psychology that deals with the study, diagnosis, and treatment of abnormal behavior.

e.   The branch of psychology that considers how the educational process affects students.

Rethink

1-1   Why might the study of twins who were raised together and twins who were raised apart be helpful in distinguishing the effects of heredity and environment?

1-2   Suppose you know a seven-year-old child who is having problems learning to read and you want to help. Imagine that you can consult as many psychologists as you want. How might each type of psychologist approach the problem

1-3   Do you think intuition and common sense are sufficient for understanding why people act the way the do? In what ways is a scientific approach appropriate for studying human behavior?

Spotlight on Terminology and Language—ESL Pointers

Psychologists at Work

Page 4 "Social psychologists would examine the reasons for the **outpouring** of support for the astronauts' families after their deaths."

Outpouring of support suggests strong positive emotions of support. There has been an **outpouring** of support for Private First Class Jessica Lynch after she was rescued from being a POW in 2003. Her community worked together to build her a house she could navigate with her injuries, and her town welcomed her return with parades and well wishes. The community worked together to try to take care of her financially, psychologically, and physically.

Page 4 "Can people change their **dysfunctional** behavior?"

Dysfunctional behavior is not performing in a way that is normally expected. When you counsel a **dysfunctional** family, perhaps the siblings and the parents are not communicating at all, or behaviors of a family member are very different than would be expected for their age and culture.

Page 5 "A month after losing his arm in an industrial accident, Henry Washington sits with his eyes closed as Hector Valdez, a research psychologist who studies the **perception** of touch, dribbles warm water on his cheek."

Perception involves using your senses to acquire information about your environment. In psychology, **perception** involves any of the neurological processes of acquiring and mentally interpreting information from the senses. A **perception** can be an idea, a feeling, an impression, or a thought.

Page 5 "The **sensation** is so strong that he checks to be sure that the arm is still missing."

Sensation is a physical feeling. Sometimes it can be a vague or general feeling not attributable to an obvious cause. You have a **sensation** when one or more of your sense organs are stimulated.

Page 5 "By comparing twins who have lived together **virtually** all their lives with those who have been separated from birth, Poirier is seeking to determine the relative influence of heredity and experience on human behavior."

Virtually means that for all practical purposes, these twins have lived together. If there is a time when they haven't lived together, it's a very brief period.

Page 5 "**Methodically**—and painfully—**recounting** events that occurred in his youth, the college student **discloses** a childhood secret that he has revealed previously to no one."

Methodical means in a systematic, organized manner. The college student arranged the way he told his story, so that he told it in a systematic and orderly method. He told it **methodically**.

To **recount** is to review, call to mind, and tell the particular details of this secret. **Recounting** is to tell about an event, to report or describe the event. When you **recount** and narrate an event, people now know about it.

Disclose is to reveal or confess. As it is **disclosed**, he has revealed his secret. Are there some events in your life that you have **recounted methodically** as you have **disclosed** them?

Page 5 "Although the last scene might be the only one that fits your image of the practice of psychology, each of these episodes describes work carried out by **contemporary** psychologists."

To be **contemporary** is to be modern; to be up-to-date. Health psychologists, developmental psychologists, cognitive psychologists, clinical neuropsychologists, evolutionary psychologists, and clinical psychologists are just a few of the major subfields of psychology of a **contemporary** psychologist.

Page 5 "This **breadth** is reflected in the definition of the field: Psychology is the scientific study of behavior and mental processes."

Breadth has to do with the comprehensive quality of definition of the science of psychology.

Page 5 "Should the field **encompass** the study of such diverse topics as physical and mental health, perception, dreaming, and motivation?"

To **encompass** is to include. What are some of the diverse topics you expect to find the field of psychology including?

Page 5 "Most psychologists have answered these questions with the argument that the field should be **receptive** to a variety of viewpoints and approaches."

Receptive means interested in the ideas and theoretical approaches.

Page 8 "For example, they may examine the link between specific sites in the brain and the muscular **tremors** of people affected by Parkinson's disease or attempt to determine how are emotions are related to physical sensations."

When your body shakes as a result of physical weakness or emotional stress, this is an involuntary **trembling**, or quivering, of muscle. These **tremors** vary in intensity and duration.

Page 8 "If you have ever wondered why you are susceptible to **optical** illusions, how your body registers pain, or how you can study with the greatest effectiveness, an experimental psychologist can answer your questions."

Anything **optic** pertains to the eye or vision. An **optical** illusion is a misleading image presented to the vision.

Page 8 "Our complex networks of social **interrelationships** are the focus of study for a number of subfields of psychology."

The prefix **inter-** means between, among, in the midst of something. When we talk about **interrelationships**, we mean carried on between groups, occurring between and shared by the groups. What are some of the social **interrelationships** you have as part of your lifestyle?

Page 9 "Candidates must have the ability to establish a **rapport** with senior business executives and help them find innovative, practical, and psychologically sound solutions to problems concerning people and organizations."

When you establish **rapport** with someone, you develop a relationship with that person. Psychologists need to be able to establish **rapport** with a patient so the patient has confidence in the psychologist. Establishing **rapport** is an important initial component of successful psychotherapy.

Page 10 "First, the field of psychology is **diminished** by a lack of the diverse perspectives and talents that minority-group members can provide. Furthermore, minority-group psychologists serve as role models for members of minority communities, and their lack of representation in the profession might **deter** other minority-group members from entering the field."

To **diminish** is to decrease. The lack of representation of minority psychologists in the field of psychology subtracts from the authority of the field. It also **deters**, and may discourage or inhibit, minority-group members from entering the field of psychology. Have you have felt **deterred** from certain activities because you have not observed people like you doing them?

Page 12 "Because undergraduates who specialize in psychology develop good **analytical** skills, are trained to think critically, and are able to **synthesize** and evaluate information well, employers in business, industry, and the government value their preparation.

A student who has good **analytical** skills is able to separate an event into its component parts or ingredients. Can you analyze, or carefully determine, the procedures you use to check your competence in learning the psychology text material?

You are **synthesizing** the material learned from your psychology textbook as you use your skills of reasoning to learn the general principles and apply them to your understanding of particular situations. You **synthesize** the information as you combine it and use it to understand psychological circumstances.

Module 2: A Science Evolves: The Past, the Present, and the Future

The Roots of Psychology
Today's Perspectives
Psychology's Key Issues and Controversies

Applying Psychology in the 21st Century:
Psychology and the Reduction of Violence

Psychology's Future

- ■ *What are the historical roots of the field of psychology?*
- ■ *What are the major approaches used by contemporary psychologists?*

A Science Evolves: The Past, the Present, and the Future

The era of scientific psychology is usually dated from the establishment of an experimental psychology laboratory by Wilhelm Wundt in 1879.

The perspective associated with Wundt's laboratory is called **[a]** _____. It focused on the elements, or building blocks, that constitute the foundation of perception, thinking, and emotions. Structuralism utilized a technique called **[b]** _____ to examine these elements. Introspection required the subject to report how a stimulus was experienced. A perspective called **[c]** _____ replaced structuralism, and instead of focusing on the structure of mental elements, it focused on how the mind works and how people adapt to environments. William James was the leading functionalist in the early 1900s, and one of the leading educators, John Dewey, took a functionalist approach in his development of school psychology. **[d]** _____ was another reaction to structuralism that developed in the early 1900s. The gestalt approach examines phenomena in terms of the whole experience rather than the individual elements, and gestalt psychologists are identified with the maxim "the whole is greater than the sum of the parts."

Several early female contributors to the field of psychology were Leta Stetter Hollingworth, known for her focus on **[e]** _____ and for an early focus on women's issues, and June Etta Downey, who studied personality traits in the 1920s. Also among the early contributors were Karen Horney, who focused on the social and cultural factors behind the development of **[f]** _____, and Anna Freud, whose contributions were in the field of abnormal behavior.

8

Contemporary psychology is now dominated by five major conceptual perspectives. The **[g]** _____ perspective is focused on the study of the relationship between biological processes and behavior. The **[h]** _____ perspective views behavior as motivated by inner and unconscious forces over which the individual can exert little control. The psychodynamic perspective, developed by Sigmund Freud in the early 1900s, has been a major influence in twentieth-century thinking and continues to have an influence in the treatment of mental disorders. The **[i]** _____ perspective has evolved the structuralists' concern with trying to understand the mind into a study of how we internally represent the outside world and how this representation influences behavior. This includes how we think and how we understand. The **[j]** _____ perspective began as a reaction to the failure of other early perspectives to base the science of psychology on observable phenomena. John B. Watson developed behaviorism as a study of how environmental forces influence behavior. He suggested that observable behavior, measured objectively, should be the focus of the field. His views were shared by B. F. Skinner, probably the best-known psychologist. The newest perspective, the **[k]** _____ perspective, rejects the deterministic views of the other perspectives and instead focuses on the unique ability of humans to seek higher levels of maturity and fulfillment and to express **[l]** _____. All of the major perspectives have active practitioners and continuing research programs.

The field of psychology is more unified than one might expect. Psychologists agree on the key issues of psychology. And psychologists, no matter what their area of specialization, rely on one of the five major perspectives.

Few psychologists identify exclusively with one perspective. However, not every branch can utilize any perspective equally well. Neuroscience is far more focused on the biological perspective than on others. Social psychologists are more likely to find the cognitive perspective to be more useful than the biological perspective.

Major issues and questions form a common ground for psychology. The question of **[m]** _____ places perspectives that focus on the environmental influences on behavior against the perspectives that focus on inheritable traits. The perspective to which a psychologist subscribes determines the view taken concerning this issue. The question of whether behavior is determined by **[n]** _____ forces also separates psychological perspectives. The psychodynamic perspective interprets behavior as influenced by unconscious forces, whereas the cognitive perspective may attribute abnormal behavior to faulty (conscious) reasoning. The issue of observable behavior versus internal mental processes places the behavioral perspective against the cognitive perspective. The controversial question of free choice versus **[o]** _____ raises such issues as whether abnormal behavior is a result of intentional choice. Some psychologists rely on the behavioral perspective. Their contention is that only **[p]** _____ is a legitimate source of information. The focus of the final issue is to determine how much of our behavior is a consequence of our unique and special qualities and how much is **[q]** _____.

Interests in individual differences conflict with the desire to find universal principles. These five key issues should not be viewed in an either-or manner, but instead they should be understood as creating a continuum along which psychologists would place themselves.

Psychology will become increasingly specialized as the knowledge base grows. As our understanding grows, more and more psychologists will focus on [r] _____ of psychological disorders rather than treatment. The study of issues of [s] _____, such as violence, prejudice, poverty and technological disasters, will allow psychologists to make important contributions toward their resolution.

Racial, ethnic, and [t] _____ issues will also become more critical to psychologists as the population becomes more diverse and as the socioeconomic decisions we anticipate making become more universal.

Evaluate

PART A

_____ 1. neuroscience perspective

_____ 2. psychodynamic perspective

_____ 3. cognitive perspective

_____ 4. behavioral perspective

_____ 5. humanistic perspective

a. The psychological perspective that suggests that observable behavior should be the focus of study.

b. The psychological perspective that views behavior from the perspective of biological functioning.

c. The psychological perspective based on the belief that behavior is motivated by inner forces over which the individual has little control.

d. The psychological perspective that suggests that people are in control of their lives.

e. The psychological perspective that focuses on how people think, understand, and know the world.

PART B

_____ 1. Nature versus nurture

_____ 2. Free will versus determinism

_____ 3. Observable behavior versus internal mental process

_____ 4. Conscious versus unconscious behavior

_____ 5. Individual differences versus universal principles

a. How much of our behavior is produced by forces we are aware of and how much is a result of unconscious activity?

b. Should psychology focus on behavior that can be observed by outside observers, or should it focus on unseen thinking processes?

c. How much of our behavior is unique and how much reflects the culture and society in which we live?

d. How much behavior is choice by the individual and how much is produced by factors beyond our control?

e. How much behavior is a result of heredity and how much is a result of environment?

Rethink

2-1   How might today's major perspectives of psychology be related to the earliest perspectives, such as structuralism, functionalism, and gestalt psychology?

2-2   Focusing on one of the five major perspectives in use today (i.e., neuroscience, psychodynamic, cognitive, behavioral, or humanistic), can you describe the sorts of research questions and studies that researchers using that perspective might pursue?

2-3   How do some of psychology's key issues relate to law enforcement and criminal justice?

Spotlight on Terminology and Language—ESL Pointers

A Science Evolves: The Past, the Present, and the Future

Page 15 "Franz Josef Gall, an eighteenth-century physician, argued that a trained observer could **discern** intelligence, moral character, and other basic personality characteristics from the shape and number of bumps on a person's skull."

To **discern** means to be able to detect, usually with senses other than vision. Can you discern an unfamiliar odor in a room? Are you capable of **discerning**, revealing insight and understanding, when you are in an uncomfortable situation?

Page 15 "Psychology's roots can be traced back to the ancient Greeks and Romans, and philosophers argued for hundreds of years about some of the questions psychologists **grapple** with today."

To **grapple** is to struggle and to work to come to grips with. As we **grapple** to understand what we are reading, we cope with the new knowledge and deal with needing to understand it by working to make sense of it—by synthesizing and analyzing the new information.

Page 16 "These drawbacks led to the **evolution** of new approaches, which largely **supplanted** structuralism."

Evolution is often progressive development, a process of continuous change as we acquire more complex knowledge.

To **supplant** is to replace. Structuralism was **supplanted** with the **evolution** of new approaches to understand the fundamental elements of the mind.

Page 17 "Instead of considering the individual parts that make up thinking, gestalt psychologists took the opposite **tack**, concentrating on how people consider individual elements together as units or wholes."

When you take the opposite **tack**, you move in a different direction, or shift your focus. Generally, when you are experimenting with a new method of action, you are trying a new **tack**.

Page 17 "Their **credo** was 'The whole is different from the sum of its parts,' meaning that when considered together, the basic elements that compose our perception of objects produce something greater and more meaningful than those individual elements alone."

When you have a **credo**, you have a belief system that you use to guide your actions and achievements. Many psychologists have a **credo** of usefulness to society. What is the **credo** of gestalt psychologists?

Page 18 "She collected data to **refute** the view, popular in the early 1900s, that women's abilities periodically declined during parts of the menstrual cycle."

Refute is to disprove, to prove false. Who is the psychologist that collected this data?

Page 18 "Karen Horney focused on the social and cultural factors behind personality, and June Etta Downey **spearheaded** the study of personality traits and became the first woman to head a psychology department at a state university."

To **spearhead** means to be the leading element, to take a leading role. Often, the person who **spearheads** an activity is the leader and the leading force. Have you **spearheaded** any efforts to improve your community or your academic institution?

Page 19 "**Proponents** of the psychodynamic perspective believe that behavior is motivated by inner forces and conflicts about which we have little awareness or control."

A **proponent** is an advocate, someone who argues in favor of something, such as a legislative measure or a doctrine. Are you a **proponent** of one specific psychological perspective?

Page 19 "In fact, Watson believed rather optimistically that it was possible to **elicit** any desired type of behavior by controlling a person's environment.

Elicit means to bring out, to draw forth a behavior. Do some learning environments **elicit** different behaviors from you as a student?

Page 20 "As we will see, the behavioral perspective crops up along every **byway** of psychology."

A **byway** is generally a secondary aspect. The behavioral perspective is used to explain much of how people learn behaviors, and in designing programs to implement change.

Module 3: Research in Psychology

- *What is the scientific method?*
- *How do psychologists use theory and research to answer questions of interest?*
- *What are the different research methods employed by psychologists?*
- *How do psychologists establish cause-and-effect relationships in research studies?*

Research in Psychology

A major aim of research in psychology is to discover which of our assumptions about human behavior are correct. First, questions that interest psychologists must be set into the proper framework so that a systematic inquiry may be conducted to find the answer to the question.

Psychologists use an approach called the **[a]** _____ to conduct their inquiry. The scientific method has three main steps: (1) identifying questions of interest; (2) formulating an explanation; and (3) carrying out research designed to support or refute the explanation.

[b] _____ are broad explanations and predictions about phenomena that interest the scientist. Because psychological theories grow out of the diverse models (presented in Chapter 1), they vary in breadth and detail. Psychologists' theories differ from our informal theories by being formal and focused. Latané and Darley proposed a theory of *diffusion of responsibility* to account for why bystanders and onlookers did not help Kitty Genovese.

After formulating a theory, the next step for Latané and Darley was to devise a way of testing the theory. They began by stating a **[c]** _____, a prediction stated in a way that allows it to be tested. Latané and Darley's hypothesis was "The more people who witness an emergency situation, the less likely it is that help will be given to a victim." Formal theories and hypotheses allow psychologists to organize separate bits of information and to move beyond the facts and make deductions about phenomena not yet encountered.

Research is systematic inquiry aimed at the discovery of new knowledge. It is the means of actually testing hypotheses and theories. In order to research a hypothesis, the hypothesis must be stated in a manner that is testable. **[d]** _____ refers to the translation of a hypothesis into specific, testable procedures that can be observed and measured.

If we examine scientific methods closely, we can then make more critically informed and reasoned judgments about everyday situations.

[e] _____ requires examining existing records and collecting data regarding the phenomena of interest to the researcher. Latané and Darley would have begun by examining newspaper clippings and other records to find examples of situations like those they were studying.

[f] _____ involves the researcher observing naturally occurring behavior without intervening in the situation. Unfortunately, the phenomena of interest may be infrequent. Furthermore, when people know they are being watched, they may act differently.

In **[g]** _____, participants are chosen from a larger population and asked a series of questions about behavior, thoughts, or attitudes. Techniques are sophisticated enough now that small samples can be drawn from large populations to make predictions about how the entire population will behave. The potential problems are that some people may not remember how they felt or acted at a particular time, or they may give answers they believe the researcher wants to hear. Also, survey questions can be formulated in such a way as to bias the response.

When the phenomena of interest is uncommon, psychologists may use a

[h] _____, an in-depth examination of an individual or small group of people. Insight gained through a case study must be done carefully because the individuals studied may not be representative of a larger group.

[i] _____ examines the relationship between two factors and the degree to which they are associated, or "correlated." The correlation is measured by a mathematical score ranging from +1.0 to -1.0. A positive correlation says that when one factor _increases_, the other correlated factor also _increases_. A negative correlation says that as one factor _increases_, the other negatively correlated factor _decreases_. When little or no relationship exists between two factors, the correlation is close to 0. Correlation can show that two factors are related and that the presence of one predicts another, but it cannot prove that one causes the other. Correlation research cannot rule out alternative causes when examining the relationship between two factors.

Experiments must be conducted in order to establish cause-and-effect relationships. A formal

[j] _____ examines the relationship of two or more factors in a setting that is deliberately manipulated to produce a change in one factor and then to observe how the change

affects other factors. This **[k]** _____ allows psychologists to detect the

relationship between these factors. These factors, called **[l]** _____, can be behaviors, events, or other characteristics that can change or vary in some way. The first step in developing an experiment is to operationalize a hypothesis (as did Latané and Darley). At least

two groups of participants must be observed. One group receives the **[m]** _____,

the manipulated variable, and is called the **[n]** _____. The other group is called the

[o] _____ and is not exposed to the manipulated variable.

Latané and Darley created a bogus emergency and then varied the number of bystanders present, in effect creating several different treatment groups.

In order to be assured that some characteristics of the participant do not influence the outcome of an experiment, a procedure called **[p]** _____ must be used to assign participants to treatment or control groups. The objective of random assignment is to make each group comparable.

Evaluate

PART A

_____ 1. scientific research

_____ 2. hypothesis

_____ 3. theories

a. A prediction of future behavior that is based on observations and theories.

b. Careful observation of a phenomenon, statement of theories, hypotheses about future behavior, and then a test of the hypotheses through research.

c. Broad explanations and predictions concerning phenomena of interest.

PART B

_____ 1. naturalistic observation

_____ 2. survey research

_____ 3. independent variable

_____ 4. operational definition

_____ 5. experimental group

a. The group in an experiment that receives the independent variable.

b. A precise definition that allows other researchers to replicate an experiment.

c. The study of behavior in its own setting, with no attempt to alter it.

d. The variable manipulated by a researcher to determine its effects on the dependent variable.

e. Assignment of experimental participants to two or more groups on the basis of chance.

_____ 6. random assignment

_____ 7. correlation coefficient

_____ 8. experimental research

_____ 9. case study

f. A research method that involves manipulating independent variables to determine how they affect dependent variables.

g. An in-depth study of a single person that can provide suggestions for future research.

h. A number ranging from +1.00 to -1.00 that represents the degree and direction of the relationship between two variables.

i. A research method that involves collecting information from a group of people who represent a larger group.

Rethink

3-1   Starting with the theory that diffusion of responsibility causes lack of responsibility for helping among bystanders, Latané and Darley derived the hypothesis that the more people who witness an emergency situation, the less likely it is that help will be given to the victim. How many other hypotheses can you think of based on the same theory of diffusion of responsibility?

3-2   Can you describe how a researcher might use naturalistic observation, case study methods, and survey research to investigate gender differences in aggressive behavior at the workplace? First state a hypothesis, then describe your research approaches. What positive and negative features does each method have?

3-3   Tobacco companies have frequently asserted that no experiment has ever proved that tobacco use causes cancer. Can you explain this claim in terms of the research procedures and designs discussed in this chapter? What sort of research would establish a cause-and-effect relationship between tobacco use and cancer? Is such a research study possible?

Spotlight on Terminology and Language—ESL Pointers

Research in Psychology

Page 27 "As illustrated in Figure 1, it consists of three main steps: (1) identifying questions of interest, (2) formulating an explanation, and (3) carrying out research designed to lend support to or **refute** the explanation."

To **refute** is to be able to prove something is false. In the courtroom, evidence and proof are used to **refute** statements. Psychological research is often used to **refute** assumptions that people believe are true.

Page 27 "If you have ever asked yourself why a particular teacher is so easily annoyed, why a friend is always late for appointments, or how your dog understands your commands, you have been **formulating** questions about behavior."

You **formulate** hypotheses in psychology as you state your observations or questions that you can test statistically.

Page 28 "Psychologists Bibb Latané and John Darley, responding to the failure of **bystanders** to intervene when Kitty Genovese was murdered in New York, developed what they called a theory of **diffusion** of responsibility (Latané and Darley, 1970)."

A **bystander** is someone who is present but not taking part in an event. He or she would be a spectator.

Diffusion means to spread out and make more widespread. When there is a **diffusion** of responsibility among a group of people, it means that so many people are witness to an event that each feels a lesser responsibility to report the event or to act on it because they can tell themselves the next person will do this. Have you experienced the phenomenon of **diffusion** of responsibility on a crowded road following an accident?

Page 29 "Hypotheses stem from theories; they help test the underlying **validity** of theories."

When a hypothesis has **validity**, the way the hypothetical prediction has been stated makes this statement capable of measuring, predicting, or representing what it has been designed to measure.

Page 29 "In the same way that we develop our own broad theories about the world, we also **construct** hypotheses about events and behavior."

To **construct** is to build, to create. As we observe behaviors, we construct hypotheses to begin to determine the patterns we are witnessing.

Page 29 "These hypotheses can range from **trivialities** (such as why our English instructor wears those weird shirts) to more meaningful matters (such as what is the best way to study for a test)."

A **triviality** is something that's really not important, or an event that is insignificant. Sometimes we are tempted to focus on **trivia** instead of on the larger picture.

Page 29 "For one thing, theories and hypotheses allow them to make sense of unorganized, separate observations and bits of information by permitting them to place the pieces within a structured and **coherent** framework."

When you are told you are thinking **coherently**, your thinking has logical consistency and an order to it. As you learn the psychological theories, you have a structured and **coherent** framework for explaining behavior.

Page 29 "In this way, theories and hypotheses provide a **reasoned** guide to the direction that future investigation ought to take (Howitt & Cramer, 2000; Cohen, 2003)."

A **reasoned** guide is a logical, rational direction for your thinking.

Module 4: Research Challenges: Exploring the Process

The Ethics of Research

Exploring Diversity: Choosing Participants Who
Represent the Scope of Human Behavior

Should Animals Be Used in Research?
Threats to Experiment Validity: Experimenter and Participant Expectations

Becoming an Informed Consumer of Psychology:
Thinking Critically About Research

- *What major issues confront psychologists conducting research?*

Research Challenges: Exploring the Process
There are issues other than the quality of research that are of concern to psychologists. The ethics of certain research practices come into question when there exists a possibility of harm to a participant. Guidelines have been developed for the treatment of human and animal participants, and most proposed research is now reviewed by a panel to assure that guidelines are being met.

The concept of **[a]** _____ has become a key ethical principle. Before participating in an experiment, participants must sign a form indicating that they have been told of the basic outlines of the study and what their participation will involve. Following their

participation, they must be given a **[b]** _____ in which they are given an explanation for the study. For proper and meaningful generalizations of research results, a selection of participants that reflects the diversity of human behavior is necessary. Also, ethical guidelines call for assurance that animals in experiments do not suffer as a consequence of being participants in the experiment.

Researchers must all address the issue of **[c]** _____, the factors that distort the experimenter's understanding of the relationship between the independent and

dependent variables. **[d]** _____ *expectations* occur when the experimenter unintentionally conveys cues about how the participants should behave in the experiment.

[e] _____ *expectations* are the participant's expectations about the intended goal of the experiment. The participant's guesses about the hypothesis can influence behavior and thus the outcomes. One approach is to disguise the true purpose of the experiment. Another is to use a **[f]** _____ with the control group so that the participants remain unaware of whether they are being exposed to the experimental condition. The *double-blind procedure* guards against these two biases by informing neither the experimenter nor the participant about which treatment group the participant is in.

Psychologists utilize statistical procedures to determine if the results of a research study are significant. A **[g]** _____ means that the results of the experiment were not likely to be a result of chance.

Evaluate

_____ 1. bias

_____ 2. placebo

_____ 3. informed consent

_____ 4. representative sample

a. A written agreement by the researcher in an experiment that is signed by the subject after receiving information about the researcher's specific procedures.

b. A sample that is selected to reflect the characteristics of a population the research is interested in studying.

c. Beliefs that interfere with a researcher's objectivity.

d. In drug research, the positive effects associated with a person's beliefs about a drug even when it contains no active ingredients.

Rethink

4-1 A pollster studies people's attitudes toward welfare programs by circulating a questionnaire via the Internet. Is this study likely to accurately reflect the views of the general population? Why or why not?

4-2 A researcher believes that college professors in general show female students less attention and respect in the classroom than male students. She sets up an experimental study involving the observation of classrooms in different conditions. In explaining the study to the professors and students who will participate, what steps should the researcher take to eliminate experimental bias based on both experimenter expectations and participant expectations?

Spotlight on Terminology and Language—ESL Pointers

Research Challenges: Exploring the Process

Page 41 "We turn to the most fundamental of these issues: **ethics**."

Ethics are a basic and necessary component of psychological research, relating to and affecting the integrity of the research work.

Page 41 "Put yourself in the place of one of the participants in the experiment conducted by Latané and Darley to examine the helping behavior of bystanders, in which another "bystander" simulating a seizure turned out to be a **confederate** of the experimenters (Latané & Darley, 1970)."

A **confederate** is an ally, or an accomplice involved and aware of the plot. Can you name any reality TV shows in which they employ the use of **confederates**?

Page 41 "How would you feel when you learned that the supposed victim was in reality a paid **accomplice**?"

An **accomplice** is somebody who is part of the plot or conspiracy. They knowingly help someone to commit an act considered morally wrong, or an undesirable act or an activity that involves breaking the law. Can you identify any recent news cases in which the **accomplice** has been named?

Page 41 "Although you might at first experience relief that there had been no real emergency, you might also feel some resentment that you had been **deceived** by the experimenter."

When you have been **deceived**, you are intentionally being misled. Can you suggest why **deception**—or the practice of deliberately making a research subject believe things that are not true—might be important in conducting some psychological research?

Page 41 "You might also experience concern that you had been placed in an embarrassing or **compromising** situation—one that might have dealt a blow to your self-esteem, depending on how you had behaved."

A **compromising** situation is a situation in which it is likely you will be exposed to disgrace or humiliation.

Page 42 "In fact, college students are used so frequently in experiments that psychology has been called—somewhat **contemptuously**—the "science of the behavior of the college sophomore" (Rubenstein, 1982)."

When you do something with **contempt**, you are suggesting that you have no respect or regard for it. **Contempt** here refers to disrespect for the research results conducted with the college sophomore research population. Persons point out **contemptuously** that the college student population is a contained and limited grouping that is easy to involve in the research conducted at educational institutions.

Page 43 "Because psychology is a science that purports to explain human behavior in general, something is therefore **amiss**."

When something is **amiss**, there is a problem with it. In the case of scientific explanations for human behavior, something is faulty or **amiss** when a significant proportion of the population is not included in the sample population used to draw conclusions. This problem may produce research results that are not useful.

Page 43 "Research using animals has provided psychologists with information that has **profoundly** benefited humans."

Animal research has helped psychologists to penetrate and understand problems. The resulting valuable knowledge and insight has had a **profound** and significant impact on human lives and lifestyles. Do you think animal research involving cloning will have a **profound** effect on the societal perception of family?

Page 44 "Even the best-laid experimental plans are **susceptible** to experimental **bias**—factors that distort the way the independent variable affects the dependent variable in an experiment."

When something is **susceptible**, it has the capacity for being acted on and impressed. Some young adults are **susceptible** to the behavior of the leaders in their group.

Bias is a prejudice. When you have a **bias** you have a tendency or an inclination toward something. Have you ever found yourself having expectations for the difficulty of a class based on a professor's dress, reputation, or lecturing style? If so, you are exhibiting a **bias** because you have made prejudgments.

Page 45 "People often jump to conclusions on the basis of incomplete and inaccurate information, and only rarely do they take the time to **critically** evaluate the research and data to which they are exposed."

Critically does not need to mean to criticize or to see unfavorably. When you think **critically** about research, you are able to weigh all of the factors involved and use careful judgment and judicious evaluation skills.

Page 45 "Because the field of psychology is based on an **accumulated** body of research, it is crucial for psychologists to **scrutinize** thoroughly the methods, results, and claims of researchers."

When you have **accumulated** a body of research, you have a mass of research, a high quantity of research. **Accumulate** suggests an increasing quantity, which is why the research must be **scrutinized**, or examined closely. To **scrutinize** is to inspect and to evaluate.

Practice Tests

Test your knowledge of these modules by answering these questions. These questions have been placed in three Practice Tests. The first two tests consist of questions that will test your recall of factual knowledge. The third test contains questions that are challenging and primarily test for conceptual knowledge and your ability to apply that knowledge. Check your answers and review the feedback using the Answer Key on the following pages of the *Study Guide*.

PRACTICE TEST 1:

1. Observing future trends in the field of psychology,
   a. the future trend will be to encourage psychologists to be generalists rather than specialists.
   b. new theoretical models are unlikely to develop.
   c. psychologists will likely become less involved in broad public issues.
   d. psychological treatment will continue to become more accessible.

2. A cognitive psychologist would be most interested in:
   a. the learning process.
   b. our perceptions of the world around us.
   c. dreams.
   d. the functioning of the brain.

3. Which of the following sources of evidence would be the least acceptable to behaviorist like John B. Watson?
   a. Evidence gathered using introspection
   b. Evidence from intelligence tests
   c. Evidence regarding emotional growth and development
   d. Evidence from perception and sensation experiments

4. Dr. Gaipo is investigating the influence of inherited characteristics on behavior. This would be a focus on the:
   a. cognitive perspective.   c. behavioral perspective.
   b. psychodynamic perspective.   d. biological perspective.

5. "The whole is greater than the sum of the parts" is a postulate of:
   a. structuralism.   c. gestalt psychology.
   b. functionalism.   d. behaviorism.

6. Which of the following techniques distinguishes the kind of inquiry used by scientists from that used by professionals in nonscientific areas such as literature, art, and philosophy?
   a. intuitive thought   c. common sense
   b. scientific methods   d. construction of new theoretical models

7. Which of the following psychological specialty areas would be considered a model?
   a. psychodynamic psychology   c. experimental psychology
   b. cross-cultural psychology   d. counseling psychology

8. The problem that psychology faces of losing its diversity as a discipline can best be corrected by:
   a. social psychologists becoming more active trainers of psychologists.
   b. more studies in cultural psychology based on demonstrating the importance of diversity.
   c. increasing the ethnic sensitivity of counseling and clinical psychologists.
   d. increasing the number of minorities in the profession.

9. One of the steps in _____ is formulating an explanation.
   a. naturalistic explanation   c. an ethics review panel
   b. experimenter bias   d. the scientific method

10. Theories tend to be _____, whereas hypotheses are _____.
    a. general statements; specific statements c. provable; impossible to disprove
    b. specific statements; general statements d. factual; based on speculation

11. Scientific research begins with:
    a. formulating an explanation.   c. identifying a research question.
    b. beginning the data-collection exercise. d. confirming or disconfirming a hypothesis.

12. Operationalization requires that:
    a. data always be useful.   c. variables are correctly manipulated.
    b. procedures are followed exactly. d. predictions be made testable.

13. When researchers obtain information by using the survey method, results are most likely to be inaccurate when:
    a. nearly everyone surveyed is willing to give a response.
    b. people are asked about socially sensitive subjects.
    c. questions about attitudes are included.
    d. only a few thousand people are surveyed to predict what millions think.

14. Researchers sometimes have the opportunity to conduct an in-depth interview of an individual in order to understand that individual better and to infer about people in general. This research method is called a:
    a. focused study.   c. case study.
    b. generalization study.   d. projection study.

15. Dr. Bianchi listed the strength of a relationship between length of time children spent in day care and the child's vocabulary level at age four by a mathematical score of +.87. This score means we are dealing with a:
    a. dependent variable.   c. correlation.
    b. manipulation.   d. treatment.

16. Although it is usually more expensive and time consuming, researchers like to do experiments whenever feasible because experiments:
    a. impress the public that psychology is really scientific.
    b. identify causal relationships.
    c. permit the application of statistical analyses to the data.
    d. are required in order for the study to get government funding.

17. Maura was part of an experiment and assigned to a group in a weight loss program that received no treatment. This program had several other groups that did receive treatment. Maura was:
    a. a control.   c. an independent variable.
    b. a case.   d. a measured variable.

18. In an experiment, the event that is measured and expected to change is the:
    a. dependent variable.   c. control variable.
    b. independent variable.   d. confounding variable.

19. The document signed by the participant in an experiment that affirms that the participant knows generally what is to happen is called:
    a. "in loco parentis."   c. informed consent.
    b. participant expectations.   d. experimenter expectation

20. Ingrid was part of an experimental drug research program and was given a pill without any significant chemical properties. The pill used in this experiment was called:
    a. a control.   c. a dependent variable.
    b. a placebo.   d. an independent variable.

21. When the results of a study cannot be replicated, then:
    a. the claimed effect is regarded with skepticism.
    b. cheating by the experimenter should be presumed.
    c. psychics have probably worked mischievously against the research.
    d. the data have probably been analyzed incorrectly.

_____ 22. scientific method

_____ 23. theories

_____ 24. hypothesis

_____ 25. research

_____ 26. operationalization

_____ 27. introspection

_____ 28. functionalism

_____ 29. structuralism

a. Systematic inquiry aimed at discovering new knowledge.

b. The assignment of participants to given groups on a chance basis alone.

c. A prediction stated in a way that allows it to be tested.

d. The process of translating a hypothesis into specific testable procedures that can be measured and observed.

e. The process of appropriately framing and properly answering questions, used by scientists to come to an understanding about the world.

f. Broad explanations and predictions concerning phenomena of interest.

g. The ability to describe one's own mental images and emotional reactions.

h. Early approach Wundt hoped would help clients analyze images and sensations as basic elements of perception.

i. Emphasized the function or purpose of behavior.

30. Describe the perspective—or conceptual model—that best fits your current understanding of why people behave the way they do. Be sure to explain why you selected this particular perspective. Which perspectives do you reject? Why?

PRACTICE TEST 2:

1. The relationship of experimental psychology and cognitive psychology might best be described as:
   a. only experimental psychology conducts experiments.
   b. cognitive psychology is not interested in studying learning.
   c. cognitive psychology is a specialty area of experimental psychology.
   d. experimental psychology is a specialty of cognitive psychology.

2. Although their interests are diverse, psychologists share a common:
   a. concern for applying their knowledge to social situations.
   b. interest in mental processes or behavior.
   c. respect for the ideas of psychoanalyst Sigmund Freud.
   d. interest in the study of animals' behavior.

3. Dr. Phil's new TV show will include a panel of obese women whose average weight is 450 pounds. This program may be especially interesting to:
   a. forensic psychologists.
   b. social psychologists.
   c. cognitive psychologists.
   d. health psychologists.

4. During legislative hearings to review the state's child care bill, lawmakers are likely to seek the advice of:
   a. social psychologists.
   b. counseling psychologists.
   c. clinical psychologists.
   d. forensic psychologists.

5. While psychologists are employed in all of the following areas, the largest proportion of psychologists are employed:
   a. privately at their own independent practices.
   b. in hospitals or mental institutions.
   c. at colleges or universities.
   d. in private businesses or industries.

6. The proportional representation of women in psychology is expected to _____during the next 15 years.
   a. decrease.
   b. remain about the same.
   c. increase, with the number of women still trailing the number of men.
   d. increase, with women eventually outnumbering men.

7. "Slips of the tongue" are seen by _____ psychologists as revealing the unconscious mind's true beliefs or wishes.
   a. cognitive
   b. psychodynamic
   c. biological
   d. humanistic

8. Which of the following types of psychologists would be most interested in the "unconscious" side of the conscious versus unconscious determinants of behavior issue?
   a. a behavioral experimental psychologist
   b. a humanistic psychologist
   c. a psychodynamic clinical psychologist
   d. a sport psychologist

9. Authors who write self-help books that promote quick cures for psychological problems should be doubted because:
   a. if the procedures worked as stated, they would already be applied widely.
   b. only medically based therapies are fast.
   c. the American Psychological Association would suppress any procedures that would cut back on the income earned by therapists.
   d. the books' authors are overqualified to write on those topics.

10. If you decide that love is measured by the amount of touching that a couple engages in, then you have _____ love.
    a. archived
    b. operationalized
    c. theorized
    d. correlationalized

11. While shopping at the mall, Maria and her friends are often stopped by what they call "clipboard stalkers," who are questioning large numbers of shoppers to gather information concerning their views on a variety of different products and services. This method of gathering information is called
    a. case study research.
    b. survey research.
    c. experimental research.
    d. archival research.

12. Dr. Radigan, a psychology professor, joined the circus and got a position working with the elephants in order to study the treatment of animals in the circus. Which research method is being applied?
    a. archival research
    b. correlational research
    c. naturalistic observation
    d. experimentation

13. Omar's task was to establish groups for the smoking cessation study. In order for proper assignment of participants to be made to the conditions in the experiment, the assignments had to be determined by:
    a. someone who does not know the participants.
    b. chance.
    c. someone who does know the participants.
    d. factors relevant to the experiment.

14. Neither the doctor nor the participants in the flu shot study are told which of the syringes have the real vaccine and which have only saline solution in order to:
    a. keep the confederate from influencing other participants.
    b. eliminate dependent variables.
    c. control the placebo effect.
    d. eliminate participant and experimenter expectations.

15. When a researcher reports that a study's outcome was statistically significant, this suggests that:
    a. efforts to replicate the results will succeed.
    b. a theory has been proven true.
    c. the results will have a noticeable social impact.
    d. the results were unlikely to have happened by chance.

_____ 16. Sigmund Freud   a. The first laboratory

_____ 17. Descarte   b. Functionalism

_____ 18. Franz Josef Gall   c. Hollow-tubed nerves

_____ 19. Wilhelm Wundt   d. Psychoanalysis

_____ 20. William James   e. Phrenology

_____ 21. experimental manipulation   a. The variable that is manipuated in an experiment.

_____ 22. experimental group   b. The experimental group receiving the treatment or
                                           manipulation.

_____ 23. control group
                                       c. The manipulation implemented by the experimenter
_____ 24. independent variable   to influence results in a segment of the experimental
                                           population.
_____ 25. dependent variable
                                       d. The variable that is measured and is expected to
                                           change as a result of experimenter manipulation.

                                       e. The experimental group receiving no treatment.

26. Select two of the key issues for psychology and describe how the resolution of these issues one
     way or the other would change the way you view yourself and others, your goals, and your
     immediate responsibility for your own success.

PRACTICE TEST 3: Conceptual, Applied, and Challenging Questions

1. Professor Bianchi has identified a trait he calls persistence, and he has begun to conduct research
    on the consistency of this trait in various situations. Professor Bianchi is most likely:
    a. a social psychologist.   c. an educational psychologist.
    b. a cross-cultural psychologist.   d. a personality psychologist.

2. Aaron falls when coming down the escalator and drops his packages and injures his leg. Which
    type of psychologist would be most interested in whether other shoppers offered assistance?
    a. a social psychologist   c. a clinical psychologist
    b. an environmental psychologist   d. an industrial-organizational psychologist

3. Ed Smith, an architect interested in designing an inner-city apartment building that would not be
    prone to vandalism might consult with:
    a. a clinical psychologist.   c. a forensic psychologist.
    b. a school psychologist.   d. an environmental psychologist.

4. The procedure for studying the mind, in which structuralists train people to describe carefully, in
    their own words, what they experienced upon being exposed to various stimuli, is called:
    a. cognition.   c. perception.
    b. mind expansion.   d. introspection.

5. The major distinction between educational and school psychology is that:
   a. educational psychology is devoted to improving the education of students who have special needs, and school psychology is devoted to increasing achievement in all students.
   b. school psychology is devoted to improving the schooling of students who have special needs, and educational psychology is devoted to better understanding of the entire educational system.
   c. school psychology attempts to examine the entire educational process, and educational psychology looks at individual students.
   d. educational psychology attempts to examine the entire educational process, and school psychology is devoted to assessing and correcting academic and school-related problems of students.

6. When the drug manufacturers claim that a new sleeping aid is a safe drug and present studies that they paid to have done to support their claims, to what does this bear a strong resemblance?
   a. Self-help experts who claim that their system is best
   b. The self-help program that will solve major problems with a very low cost
   c. The expectation that there exists a universal cure for each major problem
   d. The view that the creators of an idea know best because they were expert enough to have the original idea

7. Studies of violence that suggest a cycle of violence, which is violence in one generation is correlated with violence in the next generation, support which of the following sides in the key issues examined by psychology?
   a. determinism
   b. nature
   c. individual differences
   d. conscious control of behavior

8. Professor Cheetham is particularly interested in explanations of an individual's ability to make decisions based on free choice. She is exploring several factors that may influence or determine choices, but she is very hopeful that she can demonstrate that some nondetermined choices can be demonstrated. Which of the following combinations best represents the two perspectives that would be supported by her research?
   a. the psychoanalytic and biological perspectives
   b. the behavioral and the humanistic perspectives
   c. the humanistic and cognitive perspectives
   d. the cognitive and behavioral perspectives

9. The method of sampling the attitudes of a small group of persons to use the information to predict those of the general population is called:
   a. situational research.
   b. archival research.
   c. survey research.
   d. experimentation.

10. Ashid used data he had collected on the previous incidence of cancer in the New York state community surrounding the Love Canal to see if there were patterns in the frequency of occurrence. This method of research is called:
    a. delayed naturalistic observation
    b. a case study.
    c. a survey.
    d. archival.

11. In-depth examinations of the psychological aspects of the personalities of Ted Bundy and patterns of serial killers uses a method of research that relies on the use of:
    a. case studies.
    b. correlational data.
    c. dependent variables.
    d. naturalistic observation.

12. A prospective executive may undergo intensive interviews and extensive psychological testing. The executive may also have to provide references from previous and current occupational and personal sources This process is most similar to:
   a. a survey.
   b. an experimental study.
   c. naturalistic observation.
   d. a case study.

13. A researcher finds a positive correlation between the amount of alcohol that pregnant women report drinking and the birth weight of their babies. This correlational finding means:
   a. drinking alcohol can cause lower birth weights.
   b. moms who drink less give birth to babies who have higher birth weights.
   c. drinking alcohol and birth weight are somewhat related, so one can be roughly predicted from the other.
   d. drinking alcohol gives babies a disadvantage over the babies whose moms don't drink.

14. Dr. Slocum has been studying the effects of music on the ability to sooth infants. Each experiment varies the conditions slightly, but usually only one factor is altered each time. Dr. Slocum is most likely trying to:
   a. develop a new statistical test.
   b. operationalize her hypothesis.
   c. formulate a new hypothesis.
   d. test the limits of her theory.

15. A graduate class in the School of Public Health has analyzed the death rates reported in several studies of SARS. They have compared the statistical results from each study and have been able to create a summary analysis. To complete their analysis, they most likely used:
   a. significant outcomes.
   b. meta-analysis.
   c. correlational research.
   d. experimental techniques.

16. Professor Krishniah uses a different tone of voice while speaking to groups of subjects in a problem-solving study: She speaks encouragingly to students in a class for the gifted and with a discouraging voice to a remedial class. This shows the experimental bias of:
   a. experimenter expectations.
   b. the double-blind procedure.
   c. randomization.
   d. the placebo effect.

17. Dr. Kent, a leading researcher in the area of voter behavior, is convinced that his theory claiming that voters are more easily influenced by negative campaign messages is correct. Which of the following would be his first step in demonstrating the theory to be correct?
   a. Dr. Kent must find ways to measure the negativity of messages and voter behavior.
   b. Dr. Kent must define the correlation coefficients.
   c. Dr. Kent must collect data about voters and campaigns.
   d. Dr. Kent must select the appropriate statistical analyses to utilize.

18. Which of the following statements requires the least modification in order to produce testable predictions?
   a. Decreases in physical exercise are associated with higher rates of heart-related diseases.
   b. Intelligence declines dramatically as people age.
   c. Disgruntled employees are likely to steal from their employers.
   d. Smiling can make you feel happy.

19. In an experiment, participants are placed in one of several rooms, each with a different color scheme. In each setting, the participants are given a problem-solving task that has been shown to be challenging and often results in increased tension while the problem solver attempts to solve the problem. Researchers have hypothesized that some colors may reduce stress and improve problem solving. In this study, the color schemes of the rooms would be considered:
   a. irrelevant.
   b. the independent variable.
   c. the dependent variable.
   d. the confounding variable.

20. In the previous study (number 13), the levels of stress experienced by the participants would be considered:
    a.   a combination of the problem and the color schemes.
    b.   the confounding variable.
    c.   the independent variable.
    d.   irrelevant.

21. In the previous study (number 13), the time required for each participant to solve the problem could be used as:
    a.   the control condition.   c.   the dependent variable.
    b.   the independent variable.   d.   the confounding variable.

22. After participating in the university weight loss study, study participants are invited to receive a _____, where they will receive an explanation of the study and the part they played in it.

23. When scientists use animals in research, they must strive to avoid physical discomfort to the animals and to promote their _____ well-being.

24. Occasionally, researchers argue that the use of _____ is sometimes necessary to prevent participants from being influenced by what they think the true purpose of the study might be.

25. Explain how you would respond to the comment that psychology is just common sense. Define critical thinking and demonstrate how it is used in psychological research.

■ ANSWER KEY: MODULES 1, 2, 3, AND 4

Module 1:	Module 2:	Module 3:	Module 4:
[a] Psychology	[a] structuralism	[a] scientific method	[a] informed consent
[b] Biopsychology	[b] introspection	[b] Theories	[b] debriefing
[c] Experimental	[c] functionalism	[c] hypothesis	[c] experimental bias
[d] Cognitive	[d] Gestalt psychology	[d] Operationalization	[d] Experimenter
[e] evolutionary psychology	[e] adolescent development	[e] Archival research	[e] Participant
[f] clinical neuropsychology	[f] personality	[f] Naturalistic observation	[f] placebo
[g] environmental psychology	[g] biological	[g] survey research	[g] significant outcome
[h] forensic psychology	[h] psychodynamic	[h] case study	
[i] sport and exercise psychology	[i] cognitive	[i] Correlational research	Evaluate
[j] academic settings	[j] behavioral	[j] experiment	1. c
[k] two-thirds	[k] humanistic	[k] experimental manipulation	2. d
[l] Diversity	[l] free will	[l] variables	3. a
[m] doctorate	[m] nurture	[m] treatment	4. b
[n] master's degree	[n] unconscious	[n] experimental group	
[o] social services	[o] determinism	[o] control group	
	[p] observable behavior	[p] random assignment to condition	
Evaluate	[q] universally human		
1. a	[r] prevention	Evaluate	
2. d	[s] public interest	Test A Test B	
3. c	[t] cultural diversity	1. b 1. c	
4. e		2. a 2. i	
5. b	Evaluate Evaluate	3. c 3. d	
	Part A Part B	4. b	
	1. b 1. e	5. a	
	2. c 2. d	6. e	
	3. e 3. b	7. h	
	4. a 4. a	8. f	
	5. d 5. c	9. g	

Selected Rethink Answers

1-1 Twins share a similar genetic makeup. If they do not share the same environment, questions can be explored about whether behavior is nature (heredity) or nurture (behavioral characteristics that are created and maintained by the environment).

1-2 List those psychologists (e.g., biological, school, developmental, cognitive, behavioral, etc.) that you believe may study issues (e.g., poor nutrition, lack of maturity, inability to perceive the written word correctly) related to a seven-year-old's inability to read. State the viewpoint/perspective that each would have about a seven-year-old's inability to read. Discuss how each would identify and correct the problem.

2-1 List the basic ideas early researchers had when developing structuralism, functionalism, and gestalt psychology. List the five major psychological perspectives in psychology (i.e., behavioral, cognitive, psychodynamic, humanistic, biological) and describe the basic tenets of each perspective. Note the similarities in the approaches.

2-2 Identify a psychological perspective (e.g., the biological perspective, the study of the relationship of the mind and the body). Research questions are then based on this mind-body connection. Are issues such as alcoholism, aggression and violence, and shyness determined by things such as genetics, diet and nutrition, amount of sleep, exercise, etc.? Studies to address this might include experiments that manipulate a certain group's daily diet, sleep, or exercise habits. Other studies/surveys might look at family histories of alcoholism, aggression, etc. Also, studies that look at the use of drugs to manipulate the behaviors that have been mentioned would all be areas that might be pursued by a researcher with a biological perspective.

2-3 Law enforcement and the criminal justice field both work to identify the causes of criminal behavior. They study people's conscious and unconscious motivations for committing offenses. They are also interested in whether people are born (nature) with certain personality traits or live in environments (nurture) that support criminal behaviors. Researchers in these fields try to find ways to both understand and change certain behaviors. Each of the five contemporary psychologists would have their own approach

3-1 Define the theory of diffusion of responsibility. Think about other explanations for why the people did not give assistance (e.g., people only help people like themselves or older people are afraid of younger people).

3-2 State an operational definition for what you would consider aggression in the workplace. In naturalistic observation, researchers could get jobs at the workplace being studied in order to experience, or not, the aggression. In a case study, a thorough and detailed history of the situation could be taken from a selected few people who had experienced this behavior. Design a survey to gather information from a wide group of people. List the positive and negative features of each. Which would you select and why?

4-1 The general population does not use the Internet; only a select portion of citizens fall into this survey group. Information gathered here would have to be presented as "People who use the Internet and filled out an attitude survey on welfare" had the following views on the topic. Your sample must reflect characteristics of the population being studied.

Practice Test 1:

1. d   mod. 2 p. 24
a. Incorrect. Psychologists continue to become more specialized.
b. Incorrect. New conceptual perspectives are unlikely.
c. Incorrect. Psychologists are among the most politically and socially involved academics.
*d. Correct. Of course, HMOs and managed care may alter the way this kind of treatment is delivered.

2. a   mod. 1 p. 8
*a. Correct. The learning process would be of interest to cognitive psychologists.
b. Incorrect. While not central, the perceptions are of interest to psychodynamic psychologists.
c. Incorrect. Because dreams reflect the activity of the unconscious elements of the mind, they would be of great interest to psychodynamic psychologists.
d. Incorrect. While not central, the functioning of the brain has been of some interest to some psychodynamic psychologists.

3. a   mod. 2 p. 20
*a. Correct. Above all things, Watson abhorred the use of information derived from consciousness and other unobservable phenomena.
b. Incorrect. If gathered through observable events, this is acceptable.
c. Incorrect. See answer b.
d. Incorrect. See answer b.

4. d   mod. 2 p. 19
a. Incorrect. The cognitive model focuses on understanding thought processes.
b. Incorrect. The psychodynamic model focuses on understanding the role of unconscious motivation and primitive forces in behavior.
c. Incorrect. The behavioral model focuses on understanding how behavior is conditioned and modified by stimuli and reinforcements.
*d. Correct. The neuroscience model examines the role of genetics in all aspects of human behavior.

5. c   mod. 2 p. 18
a. Incorrect. This statement is completely associated with gestalt psychology.
b. Incorrect. See answer a.
*c. Correct. This statement reflects the gestalt view that the mind organizes perceptions as it adds information to them.
d. Incorrect. See answer a.

6. b   mod. 3 p. 27
a. Incorrect. Intuitive thought describes something other than an approach to collecting data, referring perhaps to thinking about intuitions.
*b. Correct. Scientists refer to their systematic methods for collecting and analyzing data as the scientific method.
c. Incorrect. Common sense is an approach available to all and does not necessarily have the qualities of systematic and rigorous data collection and analysis associated with science.
d. Incorrect. Literature, art, and philosophy often construct theories of interpretation or truth, or may utilize theories to account for evil, and so on.

7. a   mod. 2 p. 19
*a. Correct. Psychodynamic psychology follows a coherent conceptual perspective.
b.   Incorrect. Cross-cultural psychology involves a collection of approaches.
c.   Incorrect. Experimental psychology involves a collection of theoretical approaches, although all utilize experimental methods.
d.   Incorrect. Counseling psychology involves a wide range of approaches.

8. d   mod. 1 p. 10
a.   Incorrect. The effort must involve more than social psychologists.
b.   Incorrect. Studies demonstrating the importance of cultural diversity may help, but they will not remedy the situation.
c.   Incorrect. Being sensitive to ethnic origins of one's clients is important, but it will not remedy the problem.
*d. Correct. The only way to solve the problem of too little diversity is to recruit more individuals from diverse backgrounds.

9. d   mod. 3 p. 27
a.   Incorrect. Naturalistic observation (not explanation) does not have a prescribed step of formulating an explanation.
b.   Incorrect. Experimenter bias is a phenomena related to unintended effects of the experimenter's expectations.
c.   Incorrect. The ethics review panel reviews proposed studies to ensure that they do not violate the rights of animal or human subjects.
*d. Correct. The scientific method follows three steps according to the text, and the formulation of an explanation is the second step.

10. a   mod. 3 p. 27-28
*a. Correct. Typically, theories are general statements about the relationships among the phenomena of interest, while hypotheses are specific statements about those relationships.
b.   Incorrect. This is opposite the general trend.
c.   Incorrect. All theories are potentially provable, but hypotheses can be disproved.
d.   Incorrect. If it were a fact, it would not be a theory.

11. c   mod. 3 p. 27
a.   Incorrect. This would come second.
b.   Incorrect. This would follow formulating an explanation.
*c. Correct. First, one must identify what shall be studied.
d.   Incorrect. The hypothesis can only be confirmed after data is collected.

12. d   mod. 3 p. 30
a.   Incorrect. Much data collected by science is not useful to anyone.
b.   Incorrect. Good scientific practice suggests that procedures be followed exactly, but this is not what is meant by operationalization.
c.   Incorrect. See answer b.
*d. Correct. Operationalization means that the hypothesis and its prediction have been put in a from that can be tested.

13. b   mod. 3 p. 31
a.   Incorrect. In almost every case, everyone is willing to give a response.
*b. Correct. Further research has indicated that sensitive issues result in least accurate responses.
c.   Incorrect. Surveys can be used to gather accurate information about attitudes
d.   Incorrect. At about 1,500 participants, surveys become as accurate as possible for predicting behavior of a population, even millions of people.

14. c   mod. 3 p. 31
a.   Incorrect. This is not a term in psychology, except as it may refer to the way students should study for exams.
b.   Incorrect. Perhaps a learning theorist may conduct a study to test the generalization of stimuli or responses, but such would not fit the definition given.
*c. Correct. This definition describes a case study.
d.   Incorrect. This is not a term in psychology.

15. c   mod. 3 p. 32
a.   Incorrect. A dependent variable changes as a result of changes in the independent variable.
b.   Incorrect. The experimenter manipulates variables during an experiment.
*c. Correct. This defines a correlation.
d.   Incorrect. The manipulation of variables is sometimes called a treatment.

16. b   mod. 3 p. 33
a.   Incorrect. The public is unlikely to be impressed by such a move.
*b. Correct. Experiments are the only procedures that provide a definitive account of causal relationships.
c.   Incorrect. Statistical methods can be applied to nonexperimental procedures.
d.   Incorrect. Government funding is not contingent on experiments, only sound research practices.

17. a   mod. 3 p. 34
*a. Correct. The experiment must compare the behavior of one group to that of another to demonstrate that a specific variable caused the difference. The group receiving no treatment is one in which the variable should not change.
b.   Incorrect. A case may refer to one instance of the event.
c.   Incorrect. An independent variable is changed in order to be "treated."
d.   Incorrect. All variables should be measured, even those in the "no treatment" group.

18. a   mod. 3 p. 35
*a. Correct. The dependent variable changes as a result of a change in the independent variable.
b.   Incorrect. The independent variable is manipulated by the experimenter, and it causes the change in the dependent variables.
c.   Incorrect. The control involves a group that does not receive the treatment, and the dependent variable is not expected to change.
d.   Incorrect. A confounding variable causes change in the dependent variable unexpectedly.

19. c   mod. 5 p. 41
a.   Incorrect. This refers to someone who legally serves as a parent in absence of an actual parent.
b.   Incorrect. Subject expectations may result in the subjects behaving as they think the experimenter wants them to behave, thus spoiling the experiment.
*c. Correct. The subject signs the informed consent to indicate that he or she has been fully informed about the experiment, what to expect, and that he or she can withdraw at any time.
d.   Incorrect. When an experimenter accidentally reveals his or her expectations, thus gaining the compliance of the subjects and invalidating the outcome.

20. b   mod. 5 p. 45
a.   Incorrect. The control is the group that does not receive the treatment.
*b. Correct. This is the term for a pill or any other event that has an effect only because the recipient thinks it should.
c.   Incorrect. The dependent variable changes as a result of a change in the independent variable.
d.   Incorrect. The independent variable is manipulated by the experimenter, and it causes the change in the dependent variables.

21. a   mod. 4 p. 38
*a. Correct. The ability of others to repeat a study is critical to its conclusions being accepted by the scientific community.
b.   Incorrect. Cheating is rare in the scientific community precisely because of the need to be able to replicate results.
c.   Incorrect. Not in this lifetime.
d.   Incorrect. The data are probably suspect.

22. d   mod. 3 p. 27
23. e   mod. 3 p. 27
24. b   mod. 3 p. 28
25. a   mod. 3 p. 27
26. c   mod. 3 p. 29

27. a   mod. 2 p. 16
28. b   mod. 2 p. 17
29. c   mod. 2 p. 15

30.
- Identify the key principle of the perspectives you have chosen. For instance, in the psychodynamic perspective, one of the key principles is unconscious motivation. For the biological perspective, the focus is on the physiological and organic basis of behavior.
- Offer a reason, perhaps an example, that illustrates why you like this perspective. Asserting that you just "liked it" or that "it makes the most sense" is not a sufficient answer.

Practice Test 2:
1.   c   mod. 1 p. 7
a.   Incorrect. Experiments are conducted by almost every major specialty of psychology.
b.   Incorrect. Cognitive psychology is interested in studying learning and any other process related to mental life.
*c. Correct. Cognitive psychology began as a subspecialty of experimental psychology, although it is now a specialty in its own right.
d.   Incorrect. It is the other way around.

2.   b   mod. 1 p. 5
a.   Incorrect. Not all psychologists seek to apply their knowledge to social situations.
*b. Correct. Mental processes and behavior constitute the area of study of psychology.
c.   Incorrect. Few psychologists appear to respect the ideas of Freud.
d.   Incorrect. Only special areas of psychology are interested in animal behavior.

3. d   mod. 1 p. 8
a. Incorrect. Forensic psychologists study legal issues.
b. Incorrect. Social psychologists study social behavior.
c. Incorrect. Cognitive psychologists study how we understand the world and solve problems.
*d. Correct. Health psychologists are focused on health issues such as obesity.

4. a   mod. 1 p. 8
*a. Correct. Social psychologists are interested in the child care laws of the state.
b. Incorrect. Counseling psychologists are not interested in the child care laws of the state.
c. Incorrect. Clinical psychologists are not interested in the child care laws of the state.
d. Incorrect. Forensic psychologists study legal issues and behavior.

5. c   mod. 1 p. 10
a. Incorrect. Figure 1–1 shows 22% self-employed.
b. Incorrect. Figure 1–1 shows 9% in private not-for-profit institutions.
*c. Correct. Figure 1–1 shows 33% in colleges or universities.
d. Incorrect. Figure 1–1 shows 19% in private for-profit institutions.

6. d   mod. 1 p. 10
a. Incorrect. See answer d.
b. Incorrect. See answer d.
c. Incorrect. See answer d.
*d. Correct. There are currently more women than men students in graduate psychology programs.

7. b   mod. 2 p. 19
a. Incorrect. Cognitive psychologists would view these as information-processing errors.
*b. Correct. Psychodynamic psychologists are interested in issues of the unconscious.
c. Incorrect. Biological psychologists would be more interested in the tongue itself.
d. Incorrect. Humanistic psychologists would want the person to accept the conscious intent of the slip of the tongue.

8. c   mod. 2 p. 19
a. Incorrect. Behavioral experimental psychology has little interest in the unconscious whatsoever.
b. Incorrect. The humanistic perspective has little interest in the unconscious whatsoever.
*c. Correct. The psychodynamic approach explores the unconscious in order to understand behavior.
d. Incorrect. A sports psychologist may have some interest in how subconscious influences performance, but the role is not significant.

9. a   mod. 3 p. 45
*a. Correct. Inexpensive solutions would be self-extinguishing!
b. Incorrect. Few therapies are fast, and medical therapies are not typically among that group.
c. Incorrect. This action would be unethical.
d. Incorrect. More likely, the authors are less qualified than practitioners.

10. b   mod. 3 p. 29
a. Incorrect. "Archived" means to store in a secure place.
*b. Correct. "To operationalize" is to make something measurable and thus testable.
c. Incorrect. "To theorize" is to speculate about causal or other relationships.
d. Incorrect. This is not a word.

11. b   mod. 3 p. 30
a. Incorrect. A case study focuses on one or a few individuals to gain an in-depth description of a given phenomena.
*b. Correct. This is one technique of surveyors.
c. Incorrect. An experiment utilizes more exacting controls and would probably not use this technique.
d. Incorrect. Archival research involves the researchers using information that has been stored in a library, in an electronic form, or in some other form of data storage.

12. c   mod. 3 p. 30
a. Incorrect. Archival research involves searching records and libraries.
b. Incorrect. Correlational research involves a statistical analysis of pairs of data sets.
*c. Correct. One means of naturalistic observation is to blend into the situation and be unnoticed.
d. Incorrect. An experiment requires careful subject selection and control of variables.

13. b   mod. 3 p. 35
a. Incorrect. Not knowing the subjects does not mean that potential biases resulting from other factors would not influence the selection.
*b. Correct. Only a selection by chance will ensure proper assignment of subjects.
c. Incorrect. Knowing the subjects may result in biased assignment to groups.
d. Incorrect. The factors of the experiment should not influence the assignment of subjects to a condition.

14. d   mod. 4 p. 44
a. Incorrect. Often it is the goal of a confederate to influence subjects in an experiment.
b. Incorrect. An experiment must have dependent variables, otherwise it would not be an experiment.
c. Incorrect. The placebo effect can occur under many conditions, even the double-blind procedure.
*d. Correct. This is the only procedure that will guarantee that both subject and experimenter expectations are eliminated.

15. d   mod. 3 p. 38
a. Incorrect. The results can be analyzed as significant, even if the study cannot be replicated.
b. Incorrect. The hypothesis may have been confirmed or disconfirmed, but the theory may still be up for grabs.
c. Incorrect. Statistical significance does not imply social importance.
*d. Correct. Statistical significance judges the probability that the results occurred due to chance.

16. d   mod. 2 p. 17
17. c   mod. 2 p. 16
18. e   mod. 2 p. 16
19. a   mod. 2 p. 15
20. b   mod. 2 p. 17

21. c   mod. 3 p. 34
22. b   mod. 3 p. 34
23. e   mod. 3 p. 34
24. a   mod. 3 p. 35
25. d   mod. 3 p. 35

26. For this answer, "freedom of choice versus determinism," is used as the example.
  ▪ The selection of the freedom of choice side of this answer reflects how most people would choose. However, it suggests that all of our actions are thus our responsibility—even our boredom and our mistakes. We should be unable to attribute any causes for our behavior to others than ourselves.
  ▪ Should the issue be resolved in favor of determinism, then we should be able to understand all of human behavior as flowing from some root cause. Many religions have this kind of view, and some theorists and philosophers believe that science should be able to find causes. For psychology, this view is most compatible with behaviorism and psychoanalysis.

Practice Test 3:
1. d   mod. 1 p. 8
a. Incorrect. A social psychologist does not study traits directly, but may be interested in the role of groups as they may influence such a trait.
b. Incorrect. The only interest that a cross-cultural psychologist may have is whether the trait was common to more than one cultural group.
c. Incorrect. An educational psychologist would probably be interested in whether the trait could be acquired for learning purposes.
*d. Correct. The study of traits is specifically the domain of personality psychologists.

2. a   mod. 1 p. 8
*a. Correct. The helping behavior studied by social psychologists is called prosocial behavior.
b. Incorrect. An environmental psychologist may be remotely interested in determining whether the climatic conditions influence prosocial behavior.
c. Incorrect. This would not be of interest to a clinical perspective.
d. Incorrect. This would not be of interest to an I/O psychologist.

3. d   mod. 1 p. 7
a. Incorrect. A clinical psychologist could not offer this kind of consultation.
b. Incorrect. A school psychologist conducts assessment and recommends corrective measures for students.
c. Incorrect. A forensic psychologist is more interested in the legal system than in the hall system.
*d. Correct. Environmental psychologists examine factors like crowding and architectural design to understand the influences they may have on behaviors like aggression.

4. d   mod. 2 p. 16
a. Incorrect. Cognition is a specialty area of psychology and refers to how we perceive, process, and store information; it is not a method of investigation.
b. Incorrect. Although it may lead to some kind of "mind expansion," such is not the psychological research technique.
c. Incorrect. Perception refers to any processing of sensory stimuli.
*d. Correct. This defines the concept of introspection and the way that Tichener sought to utilize the procedure.

5. d   mod. 1   p. 7
a. Incorrect. This responses has the two types switched.
b. Incorrect. The school psychologist does more than promoting the needs of special students.
c. Incorrect. The difference is not one of a group versus the individual, as this option suggests.
*d. Correct. Both halves of this statement are true, and they reflect the broadest formulation of the goals of the two areas.

6. a   mod. 3   p. 44
*a. Correct. Like the self-help experts, the drug companies have much to gain when the tests are in their favor.
b. Incorrect. Because such a self-help program would have little financial benefit, the comparison is fairly weak.
c. Incorrect. This view goes well beyond the current analogy.
d. Incorrect. This view lacks the necessary critical element, but includes the element of bias of self-interest, since the claim can be made by others who have nothing to gain from the outcome.

7. a   mod. 2   p. 24
*a. Correct. This is one of the ways that a behavior may be determined, that is, by its passage from one generation to the next.
b. Incorrect. This would suggest that something genetic was at work here, affecting more family members.
c. Incorrect. If individual differences were key here, then violence would not be passed from one generation to another, instead appearing without regard to family influence.
d. Incorrect. If conscious control of behavior were at work, then this generational violence would not be as likely.

8. c   mod. 2   p. 20-21
a. Incorrect. These two perspectives are both highly deterministic.
b. Incorrect. The behavioral approach is highly deterministic, whereas the humanistic approach is focused on free choices.
*c. Correct. Both of these approaches would accept self-determination in decision making.
d. Incorrect. Although the cognitive approach would allow for free will, the behavioral approach is highly determined.

9. c   mod. 3   p. 30
a. Incorrect. Situational research is not a formal method of research.
b. Incorrect. Archival research involves searching through records.
*c. Correct. This example describes a survey.
d. Incorrect. An experiment requires control over variables.

10. d   mod. 3   p. 29
a. Incorrect. There is no such thing as "delayed" naturalistic observation.
b. Incorrect. A case study would involve in-depth analysis of one incident of cancer.
c. Incorrect. A survey requires living participants.
*d. Correct. The psychologist is searching "archives" and thus conducting archival research.

11. a   mod. 5   p. 31
*a. Correct. Case studies involve in-depth examinations of an individual or a group of individuals.
b. Incorrect. Correlational data are used to make comparisons between two variables.
c. Incorrect. Dependent variables are found in experiments, not case studies.
d. Incorrect. Because the examinations took place in the setting of therapy, this could not be considered naturalistic observation.

12. d   mod. 5   p. 31
a. Incorrect. A survey involves many subjects.
b. Incorrect. An experimental study would require greater controls and randomly selected subjects.
c. Incorrect. Naturalistic observation would require that the executive be observed in his or her natural setting (perhaps, during actual work).
*d. Correct. The collection of in-depth information is most like a case study.

13. c   mod. 3   p. 32
a. Incorrect. Correlations cannot demonstrate causal relationships.
b. Incorrect. The factors of additional experiences were not included in the statement of the correlation.
*c. Correct. The presence of one factor predicts the likelihood of the other factor being present too.
d. Incorrect. This conclusion is beyond the evidence of the correlation.

14. d   mod. 3 p. 34
a.   Incorrect. No statistical test was mentioned or suggested in this scenario.
b.   Incorrect. The amount of music and the levels of stress would need to be operationalized from the beginning.
c.   Incorrect. A hypothesis would already need to be in place for this series of studies to have any meaning.
*d. Correct. Often researchers will repeat their studies with slight variations as they test the limits of their theories.

15. b   mod. 3 p. 38
a.   Incorrect. Significant outcomes would have been reported in the studies, but so would results without significance.
*b. Correct. The use of other studies is the foundation for the procedure known as meta-analysis.
c.   Incorrect. True, correlational data would be used, but as a part of the procedure known as meta-analysis.
d.   Incorrect. Experimental techniques require controlled situations.

16. a   mod. 4 p. 44
*a. Correct. The experimenter's anticipation of favorable results can lead to subtle (and not-so-subtle) clues like those just described.
b.   Incorrect. In this procedure, she would not know which group of participants was before her.
c.   Incorrect. Randomization applies to participant selection.
d.   Incorrect. The placebo effect is a participant bias, not an experimenter bias.

17. a   mod. 3 p. 28
*a. Correct. The first step after one has formulated a theory is to create a testable hypothesis.
b.   Incorrect. One does not define correlation coefficients for specific studies.
c.   Incorrect. True, but before collecting the data, it is necessary to define what data needs to be collected.
d.   Incorrect. This will come after the data has been defined and collected.

18. a   mod. 3 p. 29
*a. Correct. Both the amount of physical exercise and the decline in heart-related disease can be measured and recorded.
b.   Incorrect. "Dramatically" is not very well defined.
c.   Incorrect. "Disgruntled" needs careful definition.
d.   Incorrect. "Happy" is not well defined.

19. b   mod. 3 p. 35
a.   Incorrect. If colors are a key to problem solving, then they must be relevant.
*b. Correct. The hypothesis suggests that color scheme influences tension, so varying the schemes would serve as the independent variable.
c.   Incorrect. The level of tension is the dependent variable.
d.   Incorrect. A confounding variable would be some factor not found in the design of the experiment.

20. a   mod. 3 p. 35
*a. Correct. Tension would depend on both the color scheme and the challenge of the problem.
b.   Incorrect. A confounding variable would be some factor not found in the design of the experiment.
c.   Incorrect. The color scheme is the independent variable.
d.   Incorrect. Levels of stress are quite relevant to the hypothesis.

21. c   mod. 3 p. 35
a.   Incorrect. The control would be something like a neutral color scheme.
b.   Incorrect. The color scheme is the independent variable.
*c. Correct. Time would indicate the amount of tension and how it impedes the solving of the problems.
d.   Incorrect. A confounding variable would be some factor not found in the design of the experiment.

22. debriefing   mod. 4 p. 42
23. psychological mod. 4 p. 43
24. deception   mod. 4 p. 41

25. Give examples of things that we believe are "common sense" or that you believe are intuition:
   ▪ Critical thinking is the ability and willingness to assess claims and make objective judgments on the basis of well suported reasons.
   ▪ Next, define the scientific approach. Explain how stating a hypothesis and then gathering information/facts to support the hypothesis through careful, methodical scientific methods will elicit a more exact measure of what is being studied.

Neuroscience and Behavior

Overview

This set of modules focuses on the biological structures of the body that are of interest to biopsychologists.

Module 5 discusses nerve cells, called neurons, which allow messages to travel through the brain and the body. Psychologists are increasing their understanding of human behavior and are uncovering important clues in their efforts to cure certain kinds of diseases through their growing knowledge of these neurons and the nervous system.

Module 6 offers a review of the structure and the main divisions of the nervous system. This is followed by a discussion on how the different areas work to control voluntary and involuntary behaviors. The chapter also examines how the various parts of the nervous system operate together in emergency situations to produce lifesaving responses to danger. Finally, the chemical messenger system of the body, the endocrine system, is examined.

Module 7 presents a discussion of the brain and explains neural activity by examining the brain's major structures and the ways in which these affect behavior. The brain controls movement, senses, and thought processes. It is also fascinating to focus on the idea that the two halves of the brain may have different specialties and strengths, so this area is discussed and the research presented.

To further investigate the topics covered in this chapter, you can visit the related Web sites by visiting the following link: www.mhhe.com/feldmanup6-03links.

Prologue: A Tiny Movement, But a Big Step
Looking Ahead

Module 5: Neurons: The Basic Elements of Behavior

The Structure of the Neuron
How Neurons Fire
Where Neurons Meet: Bridging the Gap
Neurotransmitters: Multitalented Chemical Couriers

- *Why do psychologists study the brain and nervous system?*
- *What are the basic elements of the nervous system?*
- *How does the nervous system communicate electrical and chemical messages from one part to another?*

Neurons: The Basic Elements of Behavior

Psychologists' understanding of the brain has increased dramatically in the past few years.

Neuroscientists examine the biological underpinnings of behavior, and **[a]** _____ explore the ways the biological structures and functions of the body affect behavior.

Specialized cells called **[b]** _____ are the basic component of the nervous system. Every neuron has a nucleus, a cell body, and special structures for communicating with other neurons. **[c]** _____ are the receiving structures and **[d]** _____ are the sending structures. The message is communicated in one direction from the dendrites, through the cell body, and down the axon to the

[e] _____ . A fatty substance known as the **[f]** _____ surrounds the axons of most neurons and serves as an insulator for the electrical signal being transmitted down the axon. It also speeds the signal. Certain substances necessary for the maintenance of the cell body travel up the axon to the cell body in a reverse flow. Amyotrophic lateral sclerosis (ALS), or Lou Gehrig's disease, is a failure of the neuron to work in reverse.

The neuron communicates its message by "firing," which refers to its changing from a

[g] _____ to an **[h]** _____ . Neurons express the action potential following the **[i]** _____ law, that is, firing only when a certain level of stimulation is reached. Just after the action potential has passed, the neuron cannot fire again for a brief period. The thicker the myelin sheath and the larger the diameter of the axon, the faster the action potentials travels down the axons. A neuron can fire as many as 1,000 times per second if the stimulus is very strong. However, the communicated message is a matter of how frequently or infrequently the neuron fires, not the intensity of the action potential, which is always the same strength.

The message of a neuron is communicated across the [j] _____ to the receiving neuron by the release of [k] _____. The synapse is the small space between the terminal button of one neuron and the dendrite of the next. Neurotransmitters can either excite or inhibit the receiving neuron. The exciting neurotransmitter makes

[l] _____ and the inhibiting neurotransmitter makes [m] _____. Once the neurotransmitters are released, they lock into special sites on the receiving neurons.

They must then be reabsorbed through [n] _____ into the sending neuron or deactivated by enzymes.

About 100 chemicals have been found to act as neurotransmitters. Neurotransmitters can be either exciting or inhibiting, depending on where in the brain they are released. The most common neurotransmitters are *acetylcholine (ACh)*, *gamma-amino butyric acid (GABA)*, *dopamine (DA)*, *serotonin*, *adenosine triphosphate (ATP)*, *glutamate*, and *endorphins*.

Evaluate

Part A

_____ 1. neurons

_____ 2. dendrites

_____ 3. axon

_____ 4. terminal buttons

_____ 5. myelin sheath

a. Specialized cells that are the basic elements of the nervous system that carry messages.

b. Small branches at the end of an axon that relay messages to other cells.

c. A long extension from the end of a neuron that carries messages to other cells through the neuron.

d. An axon's protective coating, made of fat and protein.

e. Clusters of fibers at one end of a neuron that receive messages from other neurons.

Part B

_____ 1. acetylcholine (ACh)

a. Affects movement, attention, and learning.

_____ 2. glutamate

b. Similar to painkillers, they often produce euphoric feelings.

_____ 3. gamma-amino butyric acid (GABA)

c. Transmits messages to skeletal muscles.

_____ 4. dopamine

d. Plays a role in memory.

_____ 5. serotonin

e. Inhibitory transmitter that moderates behaviors from eating to aggression.

_____ 6. endorphins

f. Regulates sleep, eating , mood, and pain.

Rethink

5-1   Can you use your knowledge of psychological methods to suggest how researchers can study the effects of neurotransmitters on human behavior?

5-2   In what ways might endorphins help produce the placebo effect: Is there a difference between _believing_ that one's pain is reduced and actually _experiencing_ reduced pain? Why or why not?

Spotlight on Terminology and Language—ESL Pointers

Neurons: The Basic Elements of Behavior

Page 53 "Neurons are physically held in place by glial cells, which provide nourishment and **insulate** them (Bear, Connors, & Paradiso, 2000; Vylings, 2002)."

The glial cells **insulate** the neurons by shielding and protecting them. To **insulate** is to place in a detached situation or in isolation.

Page 54 "The myelin sheath also serves to increase the **velocity** with which electrical impulses travel through axons."

Velocity is speed. The myelin sheath increases the rapidity of movement.

Page 57 "When a nerve impulse comes to the end of the axon and reaches a terminal button, the terminal button releases a chemical **courier** called a neurotransmitter."

The chemical **courier**, the neurotransmitter, carries messages. One of the most common neurotransmitters is acetylcholine. This neurotransmitter transmits messages related to our skeletal movement.

Page 57 "Like a boat that ferries passengers across a river, these chemical messengers move toward the **shorelines** of other neurons."

Shorelines suggest a zone of contact.

Page 57 "In the same way that a jigsaw puzzle piece can fit in only one specific location in a puzzle, each kind of neurotransmitter has a distinctive **configuration** that allows it to fit into a specific type of receptor site of the receiving neuron."

Configuration has to do with the relative disposition or arrangement of parts—in this case, the structure of the neurotransmitter.

Page 57 "**Excitatory** messages make it more likely that a receiving neuron will fire and an action potential will travel down its axon."

Excitatory messages are likely to induce action.

Page 57 "**Inhibitory** messages, in contrast, do just the opposite; they provide chemical information that prevents or decreases the likelihood that the receiving neuron will fire."

Inhibitory messages tend to reduce or suppress the activity of the receiving neuron.

Page 58 "To solve this problem, neurotransmitters are either **deactivated** by enzymes or—more frequently—**reabsorbed** by the terminal button in an example of chemical recycling called reuptake."

When neurotransmitters are **deactivated**, they are made inactive or ineffective. Your body is basically deprived of the chemical activity that would be occurring.

When neurotransmitters are being **reabsorbed**, they are being reused.

Page 58 "Like a vacuum cleaner sucking up dust, neurons reabsorb the neurotransmitters that are now **clogging** the synapse."

When the synapse is being **clogged**, activity is restricted or halted.

Page 61 "Endorphins also may produce the **euphoric** feelings that runners sometimes experience after long runs."

Euphoria is a feeling of well-being or elation. What physical activities do you do that activate feelings of **euphoria**?

Module 6: The Nervous System and the Endocrine System: Communicating within the Body

The Nervous System
The Endocrine System: Of Chemicals and Glands

- *In what way are the structures of the nervous system tied together?*
- *How does the endocrine system distribute its messages?*

The Nervous System and the Endocrine System: Communicating within the Body

The nervous system is divided into the **[a]** _____—composed of the brain and the spinal cord—and the peripheral nervous system. The **[b]** _____ is a bundle of nerves that descends from the brain. The main purpose of the spinal cord is as a pathway for communication between the brain and the body. Some involuntary behaviors, called **[c]** _____, involve messages that do not travel to the brain but instead stay entirely within the spinal cord. **[d]** _____ neurons bring information from the periphery to the brain. **[e]** _____ neurons carry messages to the muscles and glands of the body. **[f]** _____, a third type of neuron, connect the sensory and the motor neurons, carrying messages between them. The spinal cord is the major carrier of sensory and motor information. Its importance is evident in injuries that result in *quadriplegia* and *paraplegia*. The **[g]** _____ branches out from the spinal cord. It is divided into the **[h]** _____, which controls muscle movement, and the **[i]** _____, which controls basic body functions like heartbeat, breathing, glands, and lungs.

The role of the autonomic nervous system is to activate the body through the **[j]** _____ and then to modulate and calm the body through the **[k]** _____. The sympathetic division prepares the organism for stressful situations, and the parasympathetic division calms the body to help the body recover after the emergency has ended.

The branch of psychology known as **[l]** _____ attempts to provide answers concerning how our genetic inheritance from our ancestors influences the structure and function of our nervous system and influences everyday behavior. The new field known as

[m] _____ studies the effects of heredity on behavior.

The **[n]** _____ is a chemical communication network that delivers

[o] _____ into the bloodstream, which, in turn, influence growth and

behavior. Sometimes called the "master gland," the **[p]** _____ gland is the major gland of the endocrine system. The hypothalamus regulates the pituitary gland.

Evaluate

_____ 1.   peripheral nervous system

_____ 2.   somatic division

_____ 3.   autonomic division

_____ 4.   sympathetic division

_____ 5.   parasympathetic division

a.   The part of the autonomic division of the peripheral nervous system that calms the body, bringing functions back to normal after an emergency has passed.

b.   All parts of the nervous system *except* the brain and the spinal cord (includes somatic and autonomic divisions).

c.   The part of the nervous system that controls involuntary movement (the actions of the heart, glands, lungs, and other organs).

d.   The part of the autonomic division of the peripheral nervous system that prepares the body to respond in stressful emergency situations.

e.   The part of the nervous system that controls voluntary movements of the skeletal muscles.

Rethink

6-1   How might communication within the nervous system result in human consciousness?

6-2   In what ways is the "fight or flight" response helpful to organisms in emergency situations?

Spotlight on Terminology and Language—ESL Pointers

The Nervous System and the Endocrine System: Communicating within the Body

Page 63 "As you can see from the **schematic** representation in Figure 1, the nervous system is divided into two main parts: the central nervous system and the peripheral nervous system."

When you see a **schematic**, you are seeing a diagram or a drawing that is being used to help illustrate what the author is discussing. It is important to look at all of the **schematics** and review them.

Page 63 "However, the spinal cord is not just a communications **conduit**."

A **conduit** is a passage within or between parts.

Page 63 "Actor Christopher Reeve, who was injured in a horse-riding accident, suffers from **quadriplegia**, a condition in which voluntary muscle movement below the neck is lost."

Quadriplegia is paralysis of both arms and both legs.

Page 64 "In a less severe but still debilitating condition, **paraplegia**, people are unable to voluntarily move any muscles in the lower half of the body.

Paraplegia is paralysis of the lower half of the body with involvement of both legs, usually caused by disease of, or injury to, the spinal cord.

Page 65 "In contrast, the **parasympathetic** division acts to calm the body after the emergency situation has been resolved."

The **parasympathetic** division is the division of the autonomic nervous system that oversees digestion, elimination, and glandular function. It is the resting and digesting subdivision.

Page 68 "Its job is to **secrete** hormones, chemicals that circulate through the blood and affect the functioning or growth of other parts of the body."

Secreting is the process of producing a substance from the cells and fluids and discharging it.

Module 7: The Brain

Studying the Brain's Structure and Functions: Spying on the Brain

Applying Psychology in the 21st Century: Robot Rats and Wired Brains: Harnessing Brainpower to improve Lives

The Central Core: Our "Old Brain"
The Limbic System: Beyond the Central Core
The Cerebral Cortex: Our "New Brain"
Mending the Brain
The Specialization of the Hemispheres: Two Brains or One?

Exploring Diversity: Human Diversity and the Brain

The Split Brain: Exploring the Two Hemispheres

Becoming an Informed Consumer of Psychology:
Learning to Control Your Heart—and Mind—through Biofeedback

- *How do researchers identify the major parts and functions of the brain?*
- *What are the major parts of the brain, and for what behaviors is each part responsible?*
- *How do the two halves of the brain operate interdependently?*
- *How can an understanding of the nervous system help us find ways to alleviate disease and pain?*

The Brain

Important advancements have been made that now allow a more precise examination of the brain than the traditional autopsy investigations of the past. Scanning techniques, such as the

[a] _____ , which records the electrical activity of the brain; the [b]

_____ , which uses a computer to construct an image of the brain's structures;

and the [c] _____ , which provides a detailed three-dimensional image of the brain, have greatly improved both research and diagnosis. Activity at the neural level can now be

monitored by **[d]** _____, which monitors magnetic fields, and by **[e]**
_____, which records biochemical activity.

Because it evolved very early, the **[f]** _____ of the brain is referred to as the old brain. It is composed of the *medulla*, which controls functions like breathing and heartbeat; the *pons*, which transmits information helping to coordinate muscle activity on the right and left halves of the body; and the **[g]** _____, which coordinates muscle activity. The **[h]** _____ is a group of nerve cells extending from the medulla and the pons that alert other parts of the brain to activity. The central core also includes the **[i]** _____, which transmits sensory information, and the **[j]** _____, which maintains *homeostasis* of the body's environment. The hypothalamus also plays a role in basic survival behaviors like eating, drinking, sexual behavior, aggression, and child-rearing behavior.

The **[k]** _____ is a set of interrelated structures that includes pleasure centers, structures that control eating, aggression, reproduction, and self-preservation. Intense pleasure is felt through the limbic system. The limbic system also plays important roles in learning and memory. The limbic system is sometimes called the "animal brain" because its structures and functions are so similar to those of other animals.

The **[l]** _____ is identified with the functions that allow us to think and remember. The cerebral cortex is deeply folded in order to increase the surface area of the covering. The cortex is divided into four main sections, or **[m]** _____. They are the *frontal*, *parietal*, *temporal*, and *occipital lobes*. The lobes are separated by deep groves called sulci. The cortex and its lobes have been divided into three major areas: the motor, sensory, and association areas.

The **[n]** _____ area of the brain is responsible for the control and direction of voluntary muscle movements.

Three areas are devoted to the **[o]** _____ area, that of touch, called the *somatosensory area*; that of sight, called the *visual area*; and that of hearing, called the *auditory area*. The **[p]** _____ area takes up most of the cortex and is devoted to mental processes like language, thinking, memory, and speech.

The two halves of the brain called **[q]** _____ are lateralized. The left hemisphere concentrates on verbal-based skills and controls the right side of the body. The right hemisphere deals with spatial understanding and pattern recognition and controls the left side of the body. This **[r]** _____ appears to vary greatly among individuals. The major difference that has been discovered is that the connecting fibers between the two hemispheres, called the *corpus callosum*, have different shapes in men and women.

The brain continually reorganizes itself by a process of [s] _____. The number of neurons grows throughout life, and the interconnections between cells become more complex. In studies with rats, brain cells have been produced in test tubes.

Evaluate

Test A

_____ 1.   central core

_____ 2.   medulla

_____ 3.   pons

_____ 4.   cerebellum

_____ 5.   reticular formation

a.   The part of the brain that joins the halves of the cerebellum, transmitting motor information to coordinate muscles and integrate movement between the right and left sides of the body.

b.   The part of the central core of the brain that controls many important body functions, such as breathing and heartbeat.

c.   The part of the brain that controls bodily balance.

d.   The "old brain," which controls such basic functions as eating and sleeping and is common to all vertebrates.

e.   A group of nerve cells in the brain that arouses the body to prepare it for appropriate action and screens out background stimuli.

Test B

_____ 1. electroencephalogram (EEG)

_____ 2. computerized axial tomography (CAT)

_____ 3. magnetic resonance imaging (MRI)

_____ 4. superconducting quantum interference device (SQUID)

_____ 5. positron emission tomography (PET)

a. Constructs an image of the brain structures.

b. Pinpoints changes in magnetic fields that occur when neurons are fired.

c. Provides a detailed, three-dimensional, computer-generated image of brain structures.

d. Records electrical activity in the brain.

e. Shows the biochemical activity within the brain at any given moment.

Rethink

7-1 How would you answer the argument that "psychologists should leave the study of neurons and synapses and the nervous system to biologists"?

7-2 Before sophisticated brain scanning techniques were developed, behavioral neuroscientists' understanding of the brain was largely based on the brains of people who had died. What limitations would this pose, and in what areas would you expect the most significant techniques were possible?

7-3 Suppose that abnormalities in an association area of the brain were linked through research to serious criminal behavior. Would you be in favor of mandatory testing of individuals and surgery to repair or remove those abnormalities? Why or why not?

7-4 Could personal differences in people's specialization of right and left hemispheres be related to occupational success? For example, might an architect who relies on spatial skills have a different pattern of hemispheric specialization than a writer?

Spotlight on Terminology and Language—ESL Pointers

The Brain

Page 71 "The brain is responsible for our **loftiest** thoughts—and our most primitive urges. It is the **overseer** of the intricate workings of the human body."

The **overseer** is the executor. To have **lofty** thoughts is to have great and superior thoughts. **Lofty** is often characterized by an elevation in character or speech.

Page 71 "The sheer quantity of nerve cells in the brain is enough to **daunt** even the most ambitious computer engineer."

Daunt refers to discouragement. The number of nerve cells in the brain is such a great number that it is **daunting** and intimidates many researchers.

Page 71 "However, it is not the number of cells that is the most astounding thing about the brain but its ability to allow the human intellect to **flourish** as it guides our behavior and thoughts."

Flourish means to thrive. Human intellect **flourishes** and increases.

Page 73 "Advances in our understanding of the brain are also paving the way for the development of new methods for **harnessing** the brain's neural signals."

Harnessing means to control and direct. What research would you like to see conducted to **harness** some of the brain's functions?

Page 74 "A portion of the brain known as the central **core** is quite similar to that found in all vertebrates (species with backbones)."

Core is the innermost or most important part.

Page 74 "The central core is sometimes referred to as the 'old brain' because its evolutionary **underpinnings** can be traced back some 500 million years to primitive structures found in nonhuman species."

Underpinnings are something serving as a support or foundation. The legs are the **underpinnings** of the body.

Page 74 " If we were to move up the spinal cord from the base of the skull to locate the structures of the central core of the brain, the first part we would come to would be the hindbrain, which contains the medulla, pons, and **cerebellum**."

The **cerebellum** is the brain structure responsible for coordination and regulation of complex voluntary muscular movement. The **cerebellum** is the brain region most involved in producing smooth, coordinated skeletal muscle activity. The **cerebellum** is involved in the workings of the intellect.

Page 75 "In fact, drinking too much alcohol seems to depress the activity of the cerebellum, leading to the unsteady gait and movement characteristic of drunkenness."

Gait is a particular way of walking, or running, or moving on foot. **Gait** controls the speed at which we walk and run.

Page 75 "Like an ever-**vigilant** guard, the reticular formation is made up of groups of nerve cells that can activate other parts of the brain immediately to produce general bodily arousal."

Vigilant is to be alert or watchful. Can you describe some situations in your life when you have felt the need to be **vigilant**?

Page 76 "Although tiny—about the size of a fingertip—the hypothalamus plays an **inordinately** important role.

Inordinately means exceeding in scope the ordinary, reasonable, or prescribed limits. The small size of the hypothalamus belies the importance of its function.

Page 76 "In an **eerie** view of the future, some science fiction writers have suggested that people someday will routinely have electrodes implanted in their brains."

An **eerie** view suggests a supernatural view that would be strange and mysterious.

Page 77 "Those unique features of the human brain—indeed, the very capabilities that allow you to come up with such a question in the first place—are **embodied** in the ability to think, evaluate, and make complex judgments."

To **embody** is to gather and organize—to incorporate several things—into an organized whole.

Page 77 "The principal location of these abilities, along with many others, is the **cerebral cortex**."

The **cerebral cortex** is the outer gray matter region of the cerebral hemispheres. The **cerebral cortex** accounts for the most sophisticated information processing in the brain.

Practice Tests

Test your knowledge of this set of modules by answering the following questions. These questions have been placed in three Practice Tests. The first two tests consist of questions that will test your recall of factual knowledge. The third test contains questions that are challenging and primarily test for conceptual knowledge and your ability to apply that knowledge. Check your answers and review the feedback using the Answer Key on the following pages of the *Study Guide*.

PRACTICE TEST 1:

1. The function of a neuron's dendrites is to:
    a. frighten potential cellular predators.
    b. make waves in the liquid that bathes the neurons.
    c. give personality or uniqueness to each neuron.
    d. receive incoming signals relayed from other neurons.

2. The specialized cells that allow the neurons to communicate with each other are called:
    a. glial cells.   c. somas.
    b. myelin sheaths.   d. dendrites and axons.

3. The _____ stores the neurotransmitters and is located at the end of the axon.
    a. terminal button   c. synapse
    b. cell body   d. refractory period

4. A neurotransmitter affects particular neurons, but not others, depending on whether:
    a. the receiving neuron expects a message to arrive.
    b. a suitable receptor site exists on the receiving neuron.
    c. the nerve impulse acts according to the all-or-none law.
    d. the receiving neuron is in its resting state.

5. The neural process of reuptake involves:
    a. the production of fresh neurotransmitters.
    b. the release of different neurotransmitter types by message-sending neurons.
    c. chemical breakdown of neurotransmitters by the receiving cell.
    d. soaking up of surplus neurotransmitters by the terminal button.

6. The portion of the nervous system that is particularly important for reflexive behavior is the:
    a. brain.   c. sensory nervous system.
    b. spinal cord.   d. motor nervous system.

7. Reflexes:
    a. are learned from infancy.
    b. involve the peripheral nervous system.
    c. always involve both the peripheral and central nervous systems.
    d. do not involve the cerebral cortex at all.

8. The autonomic nervous system controls:
    a. habitual, automatic movements such as applying the brakes of an automobile.
    b. the functions of the spinal cord.
    c. the body's response to an emergency or crisis.
    d. most of the spinal reflexes.

9. Which of the following is **not** likely to happen during activation of the sympathetic division of the nervous system?
   a. increase in digestion
   b. increase in heart rate
   c. increase in sweating
   d. increase in pupil sizes

10. Researchers involved in the study of teen drug abuse know that although "pleasure centers" are found at many brain sites, the most likely place to find them is in:
    a. the association areas of the cerebral cortex.
    b. the limbic system.
    c. the medulla.
    d. the cerebellum.

11. A car accident would probably lead to fatal results for the driver who damaged his _____, the part of the brain that controls important bodily functions such as heartbeat and breathing.
    a. medulla
    b. cerebellum
    c. thalamus
    d. hypothalamus

12. _____ in the cerebral cortex enhance(s) the most sophisticated integration of neural information by providing for much greater surface area and complex interconnections among neurons.
    a. Convolutions
    b. Mapping
    c. Lateralization
    d. Hemispheric dominance

13. Andrew's recent stroke has left him unable to undertake purposeful, sequential behaviors. This condition is known as:
    a. dyslexia.
    b. aphasia.
    c. apraxia.
    d. paraplegia.

14. Sequential information processing is a characteristic of:
    a. the left cerebral hemisphere.
    b. the right cerebral hemisphere.
    c. the frontal lobes.
    d. the occipital lobes.

15. Which statement about the cerebral hemispheres does **not** apply to most right-handed people?
    a. The left hemisphere processes information sequentially.
    b. The right hemisphere processes information globally.
    c. The right hemisphere is associated with language and reasoning.
    d. Women display less hemispheric dominance than men, particularly with skills such as language.

_____ 16. neurotransmitter

_____ 17. excitatory message

_____ 18. inhibitory message

_____ 19. endorphins

_____ 20. GABA

a. A chemical secretion that makes it more likely that a receiving neuron will fire and an action potential will travel down its axons.

b. A class of chemical secretions that behave like pain-killing opiates.

c. A chemical messenger that inhibits behaviors like eating and aggression.

d. A chemical secretion that prevents a receiving neuron from firing.

e. A chemical that carries the message from one neuron to another when secreted as the result of a nerve impulse.

21. The part of the brain's central core that transmits messages from the sense organs to the cerebral cortex and from the cerebral cortex to the cerebellum and medulla is the

_____.

22. The major function of the _____ is to maintain homeostasis. It is located below the thalamus of the brain.

23. The _____ is a bundle of fibers that connects one-half of the brain to the other and is thicker in women than in men.

24. The major area of the brain that is responsible for voluntary movement of particular parts of the body is called the _____.

25. _____ is the area within the cortex corresponding to the sense of touch.

26. Describe the specific benefits of our knowledge of brain function and the effect of injury on the brain. What are the possible consequences of research in neurotransmitters, biofeedback, and even sex differences in the brain?

Practice Test 2:

1. A deficiency of acetylcholine is associated with:
    a. depression.
    b. Alzheimer's disease.
    c. Parkinson's disease.
    d. Huntington's chorea

2. Neurons share many structures and functions with other types of cells, but they also have a specialized ability to:
    a. be active yet to consume almost no cellular energy.
    b. regenerate themselves even if injured seriously.
    c. send messages to specific targets over long distances.
    d. live for a long time even after the official death of the body.

3. Scientists have discovered that once an action potential has been fired, the neuron cannot fire again until:
    a. the resting state has been restored.
    b. the rising phase of the action potential has reached its peak.
    c. the reuptake of neurotransmitters has been complexed.
    d. the direction of the nerve impulse within the axon has been reversed.

4. Neural impulses generally travel:
    a. electrically between and within each neuron.
    b. chemically between and within each neuron.
    c. electrically between neurons and chemically within each neuron.
    d. chemically between neurons and electrically within each neuron.

5. Muscle tremors and rigidity result from _____ in neural circuits.
    a. excessive ACh   c. excessive dopamine
    b. not enough ACh   d. not enough dopamine

6. The peripheral nervous system consists of:
    a. the spinal cord and brain.
    b. all neurons with myelin sheath.
    c. all neurons other than those in the spinal cord or brain.
    d. entirely efferent neurons.

7. Sympathetic division is to parasympathetic division as:
    a. fight is to flight.   c. arousing is to calming.
    b. central is to peripheral.   d. helpful is to hurtful.

8. The _____ records the brain's ongoing neural activities via electrodes attached externally to the skull.
    a. electroencephalogram (EEG)   c. computerized axial tomography (CAT) scan
    b. magnetic resonance imaging (MRI) d. positron emission tomography (PET) scan

9. The capacities to think and remember probably best distinguish humans from other animals. These qualities are most closely associated with the function of the:
    a. cerebral cortex.   c. cerebellum.
    b. medulla.   d. limbic system.

10. In your text, the diagram with parts of the "little man" on the surface of the motor cortex of a cerebral hemisphere shows that:
    a. body structures requiring fine motor movements are controlled by large amounts of neural tissue.
    b. major motor functions are controlled by the right hemisphere.
    c. large body parts on the diagram (e.g., fingers on a hand) receive little motor input.
    d. certain areas of the body are more responsive to touch, temperature, and other stimulation.

11. Which area of the brain has the largest portion of the cortex?
    a. motor area   c. sensory area
    b. somatosensory area   d. association area

12. Erik has a deep appreciation of music, art, and dance, and an understanding of spatial relationships that are more likely to be processed in the:
    a. right side of the brain.   c. occipital lobes.
    b. left side of the brain.   d. temporal lobe.

13. Mr. Argulla is having difficulty with pattern recognition tasks and spatial memory since his recent stroke. Damage to which of the following areas is most likely to have caused this difficulty?
    a. frontal lobe
    b. left hemisphere
    c. right hemisphere
    d. temporal lobe

14. In order to control internal biological states, doctors have used a system of biofeedback that works by:
    a. following the suggestions and strategies of a biologically trained facilitator or therapist.
    b. thinking positively about the biological responses to be modified.
    c. listening to a soothing audiocassette containing biorhythmic signals that alter biological responses in the brain.
    d. electronically monitoring biological responses so that adaptive tactics for changing those responses can be applied.

15. In multiple sclerosis, the _____ deteriorates, exposing parts of the _____. The result is a short circuit between the nervous system and muscle, which leads to difficulties with walking, vision, and with general muscle coordination.
    a. cell body; nucleus
    b. dendrite; terminal button
    c. terminal button; nucleus
    d. myelin sheath; axon

____ 16. synapse

____ 17. acetylcholine

____ 18. EEG

____ 19. reflex

a. An imagining technique that involves monitoring the brain's metabolic activity.

b. The gap between neurons across which chemical messages are communicated.

c. Automatic behavior is response to a specific stimulus.

d. A chemical secretion that transmits messages relating to skeletal muscles and may also be related to memory.

20. The gap between neurons is called the _____.

21. The division of the nervous system that is particularly important for "fight or flight" is the _____.

22. The most likely place to find a "pleasure center" in the brain is the _____.

23. The _____ controls important bodily functions such as heartbeat and breathing.

24. The _____ areas of the brain deal with thinking, language, and speech.

25. Several recent developments raise important questions for ethical consideration. What are the problems that arise when surgery separates the two hemispheres? What are the potential dangers of transplanting fetal tissue into the brain? Discuss these ethical and moral issues. Are there other issues?

PRACTICE TEST 3: Conceptual, Applied, and Challenging Questions

1. The purpose of reverse flow of some substances from the axon to the cell body is to:
   a. release neurotransmitters.
   b. clear metabolites from the cell.
   c. bring nourishment to the cell.
   d. regenerate an action potential after firing.

2. After neurotransmitters have sent their message to the receiving neuron, they are usually:
   a. deactivated by enzymes.
   b. reabsorbed by the terminal buttons.
   c. absorbed into the body and filtered through the kidneys.
   d. absorbed into the receiving neuron.

3. The word most closely associated with the function of the limbic system is:
   a. thinking.
   b. waking.
   c. emergency.
   d. emotion.

4. Which of the following may be the most critical structure for maintaining homeostasis, a steady internal state of the body?
   a. hippocampus
   b. cerebral cortex
   c. hypothalamus
   d. cerebellum

5. Damage to or lesions in which of the following brain structures would be most likely to cause dramatic changes in emotionality and behavior?
   a. pons
   b. medulla
   c. cerebellum
   d. limbic system

6. Which of the following is **true** of both the sensory and motor areas of the cortex?
   a. They both contain pleasure centers.
   b. More cortical tissue is devoted to the most important structures.
   c. Electrical stimulation produces involuntary movement.
   d. Destruction of any one area affects all of the senses.

7. Mr. Costello was a shrewd, energetic business executive who persistently carried out all of his plans of operation. After a head injury, he was no longer able to make plans or complete them. The dramatic changes in him after his accident suggest that which area of his cerebral cortex was injured?
   a. neuromuscular
   b. association
   c. sensory-somatosensory
   d. motor

8. Mr. McCarthy had a great deal of difficulty *understanding* the speech of others and producing coherent speech after his surgery. He suffered from:
   a. Wernicke's aphasia.
   b. Lou Gehrig's disease.
   c. Broca's aphasia.
   d. Phineas Gage's disease.

9. Left hemisphere is to _____ function as right hemisphere is to _____ function.
   a. sequential; successive
   b. sequential; global
   c. successive; sequential
   d. global; sequential

10. Wernicke's aphasia is to _____ as Broca's aphasia is to _____.
    a. spasticity, flaccidity
    b. motor cortex; sensory cortex
    c. overeating, irregular gait
    d. difficulty in comprehending words; searching for the correct word.

11. One primary difference in the organization of male and female brains is that:
    a. logical abilities are on the opposite sides in males and females.
    b. language abilities are more evenly divided between the two hemispheres in females.
    c. the right hemisphere is almost always dominant in females.
    d. spatial abilities are on the opposite sides in males and females.

12. A split-brain patient has had:
    a. a stroke.
    b. the nerves between the hemispheres cut.
    c. damage to one of the hemispheres.
    d. epilepsy.

13. Audry has just been diagnosed with a disease that causes her neurons to die of starvation because they are unable to get chemical substances necessary for cell function to flow up the axon toward the cell body. The diagnosis is most likely:
    a. Alzheimer's disease.
    b. Parkinson's disease.
    c. multiple sclerosis.
    d. amyotrophic lateral sclerosis.

14. In the middle of a sentence, Joseph becomes rigid and stares into space. After a few minutes, he shakes a little bit and then seems to return to the discussion. He explains that he has a common neural disorder related to a shortage of a neurotransmitter. His disorder is probably:
    a. Alzheimer's disease.
    b. Parkinson's disease.
    c. multiple sclerosis.
    d. amyotrophic lateral sclerosis.

15. The neurologist recorded the activity of a set of neurons. As the neurons in the set increased their activity, surrounding neurons seemed to slow down. What kind of messages were these neurons most likely sending?
    a. sensory
    b. motor
    c. inhibitory
    d. autonomic

____ 16. homeostasis

____ 17. eating

____ 18. terminal buttons

____ 19. myelin sheath

____ 20. reuptake

a. The limbic system regulates a variety of motivated behaviors such as _____.

b. Located at the end of the axon, their purpose is to store neurotransmitters before release.

c. Characterized by the functioning of an optimal range of physiological processes, it is the tendency of the body to maintain a balanced state.

d. Method of clearing the neurotransmitter from the synaptic cleft, transmitter returns to terminal buttons.

e. Specialized cells of fat and protein that wrap themselves around the axon.

21. The function of the neuron's _____ is to receive incoming signals relayed from other neurons.

22. The _____ is one of the major areas of the brain, the site of the higher mental processes, such as thought, language, memory, and speech.

23. The _____ hemisphere of the brain concentrates on tasks requiring verbal competence.

24. Music and emotional experiences are located in the _____ hemisphere.

25 Located in the occipital lobe, the _____ receives input of images from the eyes.

26. Discuss the role that the media might play in the research of certain brain research. Consider what well-known celebrities have done for the research of their particular illness (Michael J. Fox, Muhammad Ali, Janet Reno—Parkinson's disease; Christopher Reeves, spinal cord regeneration).

■ ANSWER KEY: MODULES 5, 6, AND 7

Module 5:	Module 6:	Module 7:	Evaluate
[a] biopsychologists	[a] central nervous system (CNS)	[a] (EEG)	Part A
[b] neurons	[b] spinal cord	[b] (CAT)	1. d
[c] Dendrites	[c] reflexes	[c] (MRI)	2. b
[d] axons	[d] Sensory (afferent)	[d] (SQUID)	3. a
[e] terminal buttons	[e] Motor (efferent)	[e] (PET)	4. c
[f] myelin sheath	[f] Interneurons	[f] central core	5. e
[g] resting state	[g] peripheral nervous system	[g] cerebellum	
[h] action potential	[h] somatic division	[h] reticular formation	Part B
[i] all-or-none	[i] autonomic division	[i] thalamus	1. d
[j] synapse	[j] sympathetic division	[j] hypothalamus	2. a
[k] neurotransmitters	[k] parasympathetic division	[k] limbic system	3. c
[l] excitatory messages	[l] evolutionary psychology	[l] cerebral cortex	4. b
[m] inhibitory messages	[m] behavioral genetics	[m] lobes	5. e
[n] reuptake	[n] endocrine system	[n] motor	
	[o] hormones	[o] sensory	
Evaluate	[p] pituitary	[p] association	
Part A Part B		[q] hemispheres	
1. a 1. c	Evaluate	[r] lateralization	
2. e 2. d	1. b	[s] neuroplasticity	
3. c 3 e	2. e		
4. b 4. a	3. c		
5. d 5. f	4. d		
6 .b	5. a		

Selected Rethink Answers

5-1 Experiments could be designed to measure variables that define perceptual, motor, and behavioral characteristics of humans and the effects that certain neurotransmitters have on these characteristics. One group could be given medication to increase the amount of certain neurotransmitters in one's brain and the effects could be recorded. Done on several different subjects, patterns could develop that helped us understand the purpose and the activity of different neurotransmitters. Another way to look at the same issue would be to observe people who have a deficit of a certain neurotransmitter and record their behaviors. In Parkinson's disease, a great deal of data has now been collected on the effects of the lack of the neurotransmitter dopamine.

6-2 Fight or Flight. Part of the sympathetic division that acts to prepare the body for action in the case of a stressful situation. It engages the organs' resources to respond to a threat: heart races, palms sweat, etc. Reactions occur at the physiological level.

7-1 In studying the brains of people who have died, we have only a limited opportunity to see the effects that parts of the brain have on certain behaviors. We can assume from the damage we observe about the cause of certain behaviors. This correlational study does not prove cause and effect. In studying subjects who are alive, through the use of EEG, CAT, MRI, and PET scans, we can actually looking at brain functions while the subject performs certain tasks. The assumption here is that different tasks produce effects on different areas of the brain.

7-3 If abnormalities in an association of the brain were linked to criminal behavior, it would only be correlational data. Experimental methods would be necessary to prove causation. There may be many factors in combination that cause criminal behavior. Research is not yet refined enough to make a direct cause-and-effect relationship. Even if a subject has the potential to be a criminal, we measure behavior, not the potential for criminal behavior. On the other hand, if a person knew this information about himself and chose to have the surgery, the issue may have to be studied from a different perspective. One question could be "Does an individual have the right to agree to surgery on his brain that will alter behavior?" I think because we already allow the use of medications to alter the behavior of individuals, surgical procedures would also be allowed.

Practice Test 1:

1. d   mod. 5 p. 54
a.   Incorrect. Cellular predators cannot be frightened.
b.   Incorrect. The only waving done in the body is with the hand.
c.   Incorrect. Each neuron has a unique number and distribution of dendrites, but this is not the purpose of the dendrites.
*d. Correct. Dendrites act as the receivers for the neuron.

2. d   mod. 5 p. 54
a.   Incorrect. Glial cells support neurons.
b.   Incorrect. The myelin sheath is the fatty substance that forms an insulating covering around axons.
c.   Incorrect. The soma is the cell body of the neuron.
*d. Correct. Dendrites receive stimulation and axons convey information to the next neuron.

3. a   mod. 5 p. 54
*a. Correct. This is the end of the axon branches.
b.   Incorrect. This part contains the nucleus and metabolic units of the neuron.
c.   Incorrect. The word "synapse" even means gap.
d.   Incorrect. A refractory period is the conclusion of an action potential during which the neuron cannot fire again.

4. b   mod. 5 p. 57
a.   Incorrect. Individual neurons do not exhibit the cognitive skill of "expectation."
*b. Correct. Neurotransmitters lock into specific sites receptive to that type of neurotransmitter.
c.   Incorrect. All nerve impulses act according to the all-or-nothing law, thus this information would be irrelevant to the receiving neuron.
d.   Incorrect. If the neuron has the receptor sites, it always is affected by the neurotransmitter, whether it is firing or not.

5. d   mod. 5 p. 58
a.   Incorrect. The need for new production is minimized by reuptake.
b.   Incorrect. This is not reuptake.
c.   Incorrect. Some neurotransmitters are metabolized by enzymes in the synaptic cleft; this material may return to the neuron in another manner other than reuptake.
*d. Correct. Reuptake is the reabsorption of unmetabolized neurotransmitters in the area of the synapse.

6. b   mod. 6 p. 63
a.   Incorrect. Actually, it could be said that the role of the brain is to override reflexes.
*b. Correct. Many messages that are processed reflexively simply pass through the spinal cord and are not sent to the brain.
c.   Incorrect. We do sense the stimuli that cause reflexes, but we can actually have them without our sensation of them.
d.   Incorrect. However, without a motor system, we would not have reflexes.

7. d   mod. 5 p. 63
a.   Incorrect. Reflexes are inborn and not learned.
b.   Incorrect. They involve the peripheral nervous system and often the central nervous system.
c.   Incorrect. Some reflexes may not involve the central nervous system.
*d. Correct. Fundamentally, reflexes are processed through the spinal cord or by lower parts of the brain.

8. c   mod. 5 p. 64
a.   Incorrect. These kinds of processes do involve the brain and the voluntary muscles.
b.   Incorrect. The autonomic nervous system is not responsible for spinal cord functions.
*c. Correct. Of these choices, this is the only one included in the activity controlled by the autonomic system.
d.   Incorrect. The spinal reflexes involve the somatic system and voluntary muscles.

9. a   mod. 5 p. 65
*a. Correct. The sympathetic division activates and energizes responses necessary for survival and quick responses, thus it shuts down the digestive processes.
b.   Incorrect. The sympathetic response increases heart rate in order to increase energy availability.
c.   Incorrect. The sympathetic response increases sweating in order to provide additional cooling.
d.   Incorrect. The sympathetic response increases pupil sizes, probably to increase the available detail about the visible world.

10. b   mod. 7 p. 76
a.   Incorrect. Memory is stored here.
*b. Correct. Most of the structures related to pleasure, especially the hypothalamus and the amygdala, are part of the limbic system.
c.   Incorrect. The medulla controls things like breathing.
d.   Incorrect. The cerebellum controls voluntary muscle movements.

11. a   mod. 7 p. 75
*a. Correct. This is the medulla's role.
b. Incorrect. The cerebellum helps control voluntary muscle and coordinate movement.
c. Incorrect. The thalamus is responsible for handling incoming and outgoing messages for the cortex.
d. Incorrect. The hypothalamus is responsible for regulating basic biological needs.

12. a   mod. 7 p. 77
*a. Correct. The convolutions increase the surface area of the cortex dramatically.
b. Incorrect. Mapping helps the neuroscientists but not the brain itself.
c. Incorrect. Lateralization arises because of the cerebrum being divided into two hemispheres.
d. Incorrect. Hemispheric dominance is not related to the amount of surface area of the cortex.

13. c   mod. 7 p. 80
a. Incorrect. "Lexia" is related to the root of lexicon and refers to words.
b. Incorrect. "Aphasia" refers to processing errors, like the inability to process language or the inability to produce speech.
*c. Correct. The root of "praxia" means practice or action.
d. Incorrect. "Paraplegia" refers to paralysis in two limbs.

14. a   mod. 7 p. 83
*a. Correct. Logic, sequential, and many language functions are controlled in the left hemisphere.
b. Incorrect. The right hemisphere has been associated more with spatial relations and emotional expression.
c. Incorrect. The frontal lobes are more responsible for planning and physical movement.
d. Incorrect. The occipital lobes are devoted to visual experience.

15. c   mod. 7 p. 83
a. Incorrect. This is true of most right-handed people.
b. Incorrect. This is true of most right-handed people.
*c. Correct. The left hemisphere is associated with language and reasoning.
d. Incorrect. This applies to both left- and right-handed people.

16. e   mod. 5 p. 57
17. a   mod. 5 p. 57
18. d   mod. 5 p. 57
19. b   mod. 5 p. 60
20. c   mod. 5 p. 60

21. thalamus   mod. 7 p. 76
22. hypothalamus   mod. 7 p. 76
23. corpus callosum   mod. 7 p. 75
24. cerebellum   mod. 7 p. 75
25. The somatosensory area   mod. 7 p. 78

26.
▪ Knowledge of the brain leads to improved medical and psychological therapies of the injured and of stroke sufferers.
▪ Knowledge about brain function should provide greater knowledge about behavior.
▪ An understanding of neurotransmitter function can be applied to many phenomena, such as pain, drug abuse, healing processes, and thinking processes.
▪ Knowledge of male and female differences will help us understand differences and similarities among individuals as well.

Practice Test 2:
1. b   mod. 7 p. 59
a. Incorrect. Usually a lack of serotonin and dopamine.
*b. Correct. Lack of acetylcholine is a contributing factor.
c. Incorrect. Parkinson's occurs when there is a lack of dopamine.
d. Incorrect. Huntington's disease has a genetic component.

2. c   mod. 5 p. 53
a. Incorrect. Like any other cell, activity requires energy.
b. Incorrect. Actually, they regenerate only in special circumstances.
*c. Correct. Many neurons have very long axons, and the axons are attached to specific target.
d. Incorrect. Neurons live no longer than any other cells.

3. a   mod. 5 p. 55
*a. Correct. During the absolute refractory period before returning to the resting state, the neuron cannot fire.
b. Incorrect. There is no "rising phase."
c. Incorrect. Reuptake occurs continuously and independently of the firing of the neuron.
d. Incorrect. The nerve impulse never reverses (though many neurons have feedback loops).

4.　d　mod. 5　p. 57
a.　Incorrect. A chemical process takes place between neurons.
b.　Incorrect. An electrical process carries the message within the neuron.
c.　Incorrect. The parts are reversed; try chemically between neurons and electrically within each neuron.
*d.　Correct. A neurotransmitter (chemical) passes between neurons; an electrical charge moves down neurons.

5.　d　mod. 5　p. 60
a.　Incorrect. The answer is insufficient dopamine.
b.　Incorrect. The answer is insufficient dopamine.
c.　Incorrect. The answer is insufficient dopamine.
*d.　Correct. The answer is insufficient dopamine, and these symptoms are linked to Parkinson's disease.

6.　c　mod. 5　p. 64
a.　Incorrect. This is the central nervous system.
b.　Incorrect. Neurons with myelin sheath can be found in both the central and peripheral nervous systems.
*c.　Correct. The peripheral system consists of the voluntary and involuntary control systems of the body.
d.　Incorrect. It also includes efferent neurons.

7.　c　mod. 5　p. 65
a.　Incorrect. Fight and flight are the options available whenever the sympathetic system is activated.
b.　Incorrect. Both sympathetic and parasympathetic divisions are part of the peripheral system.
*c.　Correct. The sympathetic division arouses and the parasympathetic division calms.
d.　Incorrect. Both divisions are necessary to survival (thus helpful?).

8.　a　mod. 7　p. 72
*a.　Correct. EEG stands for electroencephalogram, or electrical recording of the brain.
b.　Incorrect. MRI scans use the magnetic fields of the object being scanned.
c.　Incorrect. CAT scans use computers and x-ray images.
d.　Incorrect. PET scans utilize recordings of the metabolism of isotopes of a special glucose.

9.　a　mod. 7　p. 77
*a.　Correct. The cortex is rich in axons and dendrites that are very close together, thus supporting rapid processing of large amounts of information.
b.　Incorrect. The medulla controls unconscious functions like breathing and blood circulation.
c.　Incorrect. The cerebellum helps smooth and coordinate muscle movement.
d.　Incorrect. The limbic system includes a number of structures related to emotion, motivation, memory, pain, and pleasure.

10.　a　mod. 7　p. 79
*a.　Correct. The parts of the "little man" are represented in proportion to the amount of surface area devoted to the feature controlled by that area.
b.　Incorrect. Motor functions are controlled by both hemispheres.
c.　Incorrect. The opposite is true.
d.　Incorrect. This is true, but this alternative is referring to the sensory cortex, not the motor cortex.

11.　d　mod. 7　p. 80
a.　Incorrect. Compared to the association areas, the motor area is quite small.
b.　Incorrect. Compared to the association areas, the somatosensory area is quite small.
c.　Incorrect. Compared to the association areas, the sensory areas are quite small.
*d.　Correct. All of the areas not specifically associated with an identified function, like sensation, motor activity, or language, are called association areas.

12.　a　mod. 7　p. 83
*a.　Correct. The right side of the brain is often associated with more global processing and emotional or expressive information.
b.　Incorrect. The left side of the brain is more often associated with linear and logical processing.
c.　Incorrect. The occipital lobes are necessary for the visual information about art and dance, but their role is more specialized to visual processing.
d.　Incorrect. The temporal lobes are primarily responsible for hearing, and they may contribute well to understanding dance and music, but less well to processing other forms of art.

13. c   mod. 7 p. 83
a. Incorrect. The frontal lobe is responsible for higher-order thought and planning, among other activities.
b. Incorrect. The left side of the brain is more often associated with linear and logical processing.
*c. Correct. The right side of the brain is often associated with more global processing, emotional or expressive information, and pattern recognition and spatial memory.
d. Incorrect. The temporal lobes are primarily responsible for hearing.

14. d   mod. 5 p. 86
a. Incorrect. In order to begin, one must attend to the directions of the person attaching the machine, but that is the only suggestion required.
b. Incorrect. This may be part of the process, but it is not the technique.
c. Incorrect. This may be feedback, but it is not biofeedback.
*d. Correct. The technique does involve focusing on electronic signals and attention to changes in them.

15. d   mod. 5 p. 54
a. Incorrect. The myelin sheath deteriorates, and the axon is then exposed to stimulation from other axons.
b. Incorrect. The myelin sheath deteriorates, and the axon is then exposed to stimulation from other axons.
c. Incorrect. The myelin sheath deteriorates, and the axon is then exposed to stimulation from other axons.
*d. Correct. The myelin sheath breaks down and loses its insulating capacity, allowing the short circuits to occur.

16. b   mod. 5 p. 57
17. d   mod. 5 p. 59
18. a   mod. 5 p. 73
19. c   mod. 5 p. 63

20. synapse   mod. 5 p. 57
21. sympathetic-division   mod. 5 p. 65
22. limbic system   mod. 7 p. 76
23. medulla   mod. 7 p. 75
24. Association   mod. 7 p. 80

25.
■ Split-brain research may actually create the phenomena observed, yet many people wish to use it to substantiate strong differences between left- and right-brain dominant individuals. Also, this research depends on this operation.

■ The danger of transplanting tissue is not that it will create some monster, but that tissue needed may come from sources that raise moral questions, like fetuses.
■ You should identify moral and ethical reasons both for and against this research and related procedures.

Practice Test 3:
1. c   mod. 5 p. 58
a. Incorrect. Neurotransmitters are released at the synapse as a result of an action potential.
b. Incorrect. This is the work of other structures in the cell body.
*c. Correct. Some nourishment is brought to the cell body through the process of reverse flow.
d. Incorrect. The action potential is regenerated in the refractory period by the sodium pump.

2. b   mod. 5 p. 58
a. Incorrect. Deactivation by enzymes in the receiving cell happens to all neurotransmitters.
*b. Correct. Most are reabsorbed in the process called reuptake, some are broken down by enzymes in the area surrounding the synapse.
c. Incorrect. Some, but not most, are processed out of the body this way.
d. Incorrect. None are absorbed by the receiving neuron.

3. d   mod. 7 p. 76
a. Incorrect. Thinking is associated with the frontal lobes.
b. Incorrect. Waking is associated with the pons and the reticular formation.
c. Incorrect. Emergencies are associated with the sympathetic nervous system.
*d. Correct. The limbic system is associated with emotions as well as pain and pleasure, motivation, and memory.

4. c   mod. 7 p. 76
a. Incorrect. The hippocampus is associated with memory and motivation.
b. Incorrect. The cerebral cortex is associated with thinking.
*c. Correct. This describes the primary role of the hypothalamus.
d. Incorrect. The cerebellum is responsible for smoothing and coordinating voluntary muscle activity.

5. d   mod. 7 p. 76
a. Incorrect. Damage here might affect motor behavior but not emotion, and the individual would probably have difficulty waking up from the coma.
b. Incorrect. Damage here would affect breathing and circulation; however, emotional expression would be limited by the mobility of the heart-lung machine.
c. Incorrect. The cerebellum is responsible for smoothing and coordinating voluntary muscle activity.
*d. Correct. The limbic system is associated with emotions as well as pain and pleasure, motivation, and memory.

6. b   mod. 7 p. 78
a. Incorrect. Pleasure centers are in the limbic system.
*b. Correct. The amount of surface area correlates to the sensitivity or refinement of control of the associated function.
c. Incorrect. This is true only in the motor cortex.
d. Incorrect. Damage to the somatosensory area may affect all of the bodily sensation for the corresponding body area, but it will not affect the motor control.

7. b   mod. 7 p. 80
a. Incorrect. The neuromuscular area is not very close to the area affected.
*b. Correct. The areas affected must have been association areas because they are important for planning.
c. Incorrect. The damage described does not relate to damage to the somatosensory areas.
d. Incorrect. The damage described does not relate to damage to the motor areas.

8. a   mod. 7 p. 81
*a. Correct. Wernicke's aphasia is associated with the comprehension of speech.
b. Incorrect. Lou Gehrig's disease does affect speech, but it affects motor control, not the comprehension of speech.
c. Incorrect. Broca's aphasia results in difficulty producing speech, while the sufferer may be able to understand the speech of others perfectly well.
d. Incorrect. Phineas Gage did not have a disease; he had an accident that effectively gave him a frontal lobotomy.

9. b   mod. 7 p. 83
a. Incorrect. Successive functioning sounds a lot like sequential functioning.
*b. Correct. In broad terms, these two choices reflect the description of the styles of activity associated with the hemispheres.
c. Incorrect. Successive functioning sounds a lot like sequential functioning.
d. Incorrect. The choices are reversed.

10. d   mod. 7 p. 80
a. Incorrect. Probably not, although the terms have a technical ring to them.
b. Incorrect. Actually, Wernicke's area is closely aligned with the sensory cortex and Broca's area is closely aligned with the motor cortex.
c. Incorrect. Overeating would be associated with the hypothalamus and other limbic structures, while an irregular gait could be associated with motor cortex damage or damage to the cerebellum.
*d. Correct. These choices describe the correct aphasias. Both aphasias have an effect on the production of speech.

11. b   mod. 7 p. 83
a. Incorrect. Logic processing tends to occur in the left side of the brain for males and females.
*b. Correct. Language is more localized in males in the left hemisphere.
c. Incorrect. It may occasionally be dominant in left-handed people.
d. Incorrect. Spatial abilities tend to be processed in the right hemisphere for both males and females.

12. b   mod. 7 p. 84
a. Incorrect. The bundle of neural fibers called the corpus callosum has been severed in split-brain patients.
*b. Correct. The bundle of neural fibers called the corpus callosum has been severed in split-brain patients.
c. Incorrect. The bundle of neural fibers called the corpus callosum has been severed in split-brain patients, but not all patients had damage to a hemisphere.
d. Incorrect. The bundle of neural fibers called the corpus callosum has not been cut in all patients with epilepsy.

13. d   mod. 5 p. 58-59
a. Incorrect. Alzheimer's disease has been associated with a deficiency of acetylcholine.
b. Incorrect. Parkinson's disease has been associated with an underproduction of dopamine.
c. Incorrect. Multiple sclerosis involves the deterioration of the myelin sheath.
*d. Correct. Also known as Lou Gehrig's disease.

14. b   mod. 5 p. 58-59
a. Incorrect. Alzheimer's disease does not come and go.
*b. Correct. Parkinson's disease has been associated with a shortage of dopamine, and one of the symptoms is this on-and-off type of behavior.
c. Incorrect. Multiple sclerosis involves the deterioration of the myelin sheath.
d. Incorrect. Lou Gehrig's disease involves the failure of the reverse flow mechanism in the neurons.

15. c   mod. 5 p. 57
a. Incorrect. These kinds of messages do occur in sensory messages, but they do not define the sensory message.
b. Incorrect. These kinds of messages do occur in motor messages, but they do not define the motor message.
*c. Correct. This is what happens in inhibitory messages.
d. Incorrect. The autonomic system utilizes both inhibitory and excitatory messages.

16. c   mod. 7 p. 76
17. a   mod. 7 p. 76
18. b   mod. 5 p. 54
19. e   mod. 5 p. 54
20. d   mod. 5 p. 58

21. dendrites   mod. 5 p. 54
22. association   mod. 7 p. 80
23. left   mod. 7 p. 83
24. right   mod. 7 p. 83
25. visual area   mod. 7 p. 79

26.
- The media helps us identify and understand different illnesses of the brain. News articles, movies of the week, and talk shows all make us aware of illnesses and their effects on human lives and the lives of their families.
- While it is unfortunate that famous people feel exploited, celebrity illnesses make good press. People like to read about those they know and like to watch their progress.
- Also, celebrities can successfully raise money for a particular cause (because they have access that many of us don't to people with money and influence).
- This has always been a lucrative avenue for those looking for research funding.

Sensation and Perception

Overview

This set of modules focuses on the nature of the information our body takes in through its senses and the way we interpret the information. Both sensation and perception are explored. Sensation encompasses the processes by which our sense organs receive information from the environment. Perception is the interpretation, analysis, and integration of stimuli involving our sense organs.

Module 8 introduces the examination of the major senses, including vision, hearing, balance, smell, taste, touch, and pain. It follows with an explanation of sensation and perception by exploring the relationships between the characteristics of a physical stimulus and the kinds of sensory responses they produce. This section defines absolute threshold, difference threshold, and the occurrence of sensory adaptation.

Module 9 illuminates the structure of the eye and the role each part of the eye plays in the production of sight. The process by which the eye sends messages to the brain is explained. This is followed by a discussion of color vision and the trichromatic theory.

Module 10 examines the structure of the ear as the center of sound, motion, and balance. The individual structures of the eardrum are discussed. This discussion is followed by an explanation of the physical characteristics of sound, its frequency, and amplitude. This module also explores the functions of taste and smell; the skin senses that are responsible for touch, pressure, temperature, and pain; and concludes with a discussion on the techniques used most frequently to alleviate pain: medication, stimulation, relaxation techniques, surgery, and cognitive therapy.

Module 11 offers an explanation of our organization of the world. The principles that allow us to make sense of our environment include the gestalt laws of organization, feature analysis, top-down processing, and perceptual constancy. This is followed by a discussion on depth and motion perception. In conclusion, the module discusses visual illusions and the clues they provide about our understanding of perceptual mechanisms.

To further investigate the topics covered in this chapter, you can visit the related Web sites by visiting the following link: www.mhhe.com/feldmanup6-04links.

Prologue: Now Hear This!
Looking Ahead

Module 8: Sensing the World Around Us

Absolute Thresholds: Detecting What's Out There
Difference Thresholds: Noticing Distinctions Between Stimuli
Sensory Adaptation: Turning Down Our Responses

- *What is sensation, and how do psychologists study it?*
- *What is the relationship between a physical stimulus and the kinds of sensory responses that result from it?*

Sensing the World Around Us

A **[a]** _____ is the activity of the sense organ when it detects a stimulus. The difference between perception and sensation is that sensation involves the organism's first encounter with physical stimuli, and **[b]** _____ is the process of interpreting, analyzing, and integrating sensations.

We detect the world around us through our senses. A **[c]** _____ is any physical energy that can be detected by a sense organ. Stimuli vary in type and intensity.

Intensity refers to the physical strength of the stimulus. **[d]** _____ studies the relationship between the strength of a stimulus and the nature of the sensory response it creates.

[e] _____ refers to the smallest amount of energy, the smallest intensity, needed to detect a stimulus. The absolute threshold for sight is illustrated by a candle burning at 30 miles away on a dark night; for hearing, the ticking of a watch 20 feet away in a quiet room; for taste, 1 teaspoon of sugar in 2 gallons of water; for smell, one drop of perfume in three rooms; and for touch, a bee's wing falling 1 centimeter onto a cheek. *Noise* refers to the background stimulation for any of the senses.

The smallest noticeable difference between two stimuli is called the **[f]** _____, or the **[g]** _____. The amount of stimulus required for the just noticeable difference depends on the level of the initial stimulus. **[h]** _____ states that the just noticeable difference is a constant proportion for each sense. Weber's law is not very accurate at extreme high or low intensities.

After prolonged exposure to a sensory stimulus, the capacity of the sensory organ adjusts to the stimulus through a process called **[i]** _____. The sensory receptor cells are most responsive to changes in stimuli, because constant stimulation produces adaptation.

Evaluate

_____ 1. sensation

_____ 2. intensity

_____ 3. absolute threshold

_____ 4. noise

_____ 5. difference threshold

a. The strength of a stimulus.

b. The smallest detectable difference between two stimuli.

c. The process of responding to a stimulus.

d. The smallest amount of physical intensity by which a stimulus can be detected.

e. Background stimulation that interferes with the perception of other stimuli.

Rethink

8-1   Do you think it is possible to have sensation without perception? Is it possible to have perception without sensation?

8-2   Do you think sensory adaptation is essential for everyday psychological functioning?

Spotlight on Terminology and Language—ESL Pointers

Sensing the World Around Us

Page 93 "Clearly, you would experience the dinner very differently than would someone whose sensory **apparatus** was intact."

Apparatus is the set of materials or equipment designed for a particular use. What are some of the ways in which you use your hearing and taste senses?

Page 93 "Although perhaps you were taught, as I was, that there are just five senses—sight, sound, taste, smell, and touch—that **enumeration** is too modest."

To **enumerate** is to list. This list of the senses is simply not complete. Which senses would you add to the list?

Page 93 "In formal terms, **sensation** is the activation of the sense organs by a source of physical energy."

Sensation is our first awareness of some outside stimulus.

Page 93 "**Perception** is the sorting out, interpretation, analysis, and integration of stimuli carried out by the sense organs and brain."

Perception is your brain assembling thousands of individual sensations into the experience of a meaningful pattern or image.

Page 94 "An absolute threshold is the smallest **intensity** of a stimulus that must be present for it to be detected."

Intensity refers to magnitude. Absolute threshold refers to the smallest amount of a stimulus that must be present for it to be determined that it exists.

Page 94 "For instance, if our ears were slightly more **acute**, we would be able to hear the sound of air molecules in our ears knocking into the eardrum—a phenomenon that would surely prove distracting and might even prevent us from hearing sounds outside our bodies."

Acute means more discerning or more perceptive. **Acute** hearing is responsive to slight impressions or stimuli.

Page 95 "The reason you **acclimate** to the odor is sensory adaptation."

When an organism **acclimates** to something, it makes a physiological adjustment to environmental changes.

Page 96 "Adaptation to the context of one stimulus (the size of the envelope) **alters** responses to another stimulus (the weight of the envelope) (Coren & Ward, 1989)."

When you **alter** something, you make it different without changing it into something else.

Module 9:
Vision: Shedding Light on the Eye

Illuminating the Structure of the Eye
Color Vision and Color Blindness: The Seven-Million-Color Spectrum

- ***What basic processes underlie the sense of vision?***
- ***How do we see colors?***

Vision: Shedding Light on the Eye

The stimulus that produces vision is light. Light is the electromagnetic radiation that our visual apparatus is capable of detecting. The range of visible light is called the **[a]** _____.

Light enters the eye through the **[b]** _____, a transparent, protective window. It then passes through the **[c]** _____, the opening in the iris. The iris is the pigmented muscle that opens and closes the pupil depending on how much light is in the environment. The narrower the pupil is, the greater is the focal distance for the eye. After the pupil, the light passes through the *lens*, which then bends and focuses the light on the back of the eye by changing its thickness, a process called **[d]** _____. The light then strikes the **[e]** _____, a thin layer of nerve cells at the back of the eyeball. The retina is composed of light-sensitive cells called **[f]** _____, which are long and cylindrical, and **[g]** _____, which are shorter and conical in shape. The greatest concentration of cones is in the *fovea*, an area that is extremely sensitive. Cones are responsible for color vision, and rods are insensitive to color and play a role in *peripheral vision*, the ability to see objects to our side, and in night vision.

When a person goes into a dark room from a well-lit space, the person becomes, after a time, accustomed to the dark and experiences **[h]** _____, an adjustment by the eyes to low levels of light. The changes that make this adjustment are chemical changes in the rods and cones.

Rods contain **[i]** _____, a complex substance that changes chemically when struck by light. This chemical change sets off a reaction. The response is then transmitted to two other kinds of cells, first to the *bipolar cells* and then to *ganglion cells*. The ganglion cells organize and summarize the information and then convey it to the **[j]** _____. Where the optic nerve goes from the retina back through the eyeball, there are no rods or cones, which results in the blind spot.

The optic nerves from both eyes meet behind the eyes at the **[k]** _____, where each optic nerve splits. Nerve impulses from the right half of each eye go to the right side of the brain, and nerve impulses from the left half of each eye go to the left half of the brain. The disease called *glaucoma* is a restriction of the nerve impulses across the optic nerve. The visual message is processed from the beginning by ganglion cells, and continues to the visual cortex, where many neurons are highly specialized. Their roles are specialized to detect certain visual features, and the process is called **[l]** _____.

Evaluate

_____ 1. pupil

_____ 2. cornea

_____ 3. iris

_____ 4. lens

_____ 5. retina

a. The colored part of the eye.

b. The part of the eye that converts the electromagnetic energy of light into useful information for the brain.

c. A dark hole in the center of the eye's iris that changes size as the amount of incoming light changes.

d. A transparent, protective window into the eyeball.

e. The part of the eye located behind the pupil that bends rays of light to focus them on the retina.

Rethink

9-1   If the eye were constructed with a second lens that "unreversed" the image hitting the retina, do you think there would be changes in the way people perceive the world?

9-2   From an evolutionary standpoint, why might the eye have evolved so that the rods, which we rely on in low light, do not provide sharp images? Are there any advantages to this system?

Spotlight on Terminology and Language—ESL Pointers

Vision: Shedding Light on the Eye

Page 98 "The ray of light we are tracing as it is reflected off the tree in Figure 2 first travels through the cornea, a **transparent**, protective window."

When something is **transparent**, it has the property of transmitting light without appreciable scattering, which makes it possible to see through it.

Page 98 "After moving through the cornea, the light **traverses** the pupil."

The light moves across the pupil.

Page 98 "The **dimmer** the surroundings are, the more the pupil opens to allow more light to enter."

When you **dim** the lights, you reduce the light. You provide only a limited amount of light when you **dim** the lights.

Page 99 "The lens focuses light by changing its own thickness, a process called **accommodation**: It becomes flatter when viewing distant objects and rounder when looking at closer objects."

Accommodation is the change that occurs in existing experience or knowledge as a result of assimilating some new information.

Page 99 "Having traveled through the pupil and lens, our image of the tree finally reaches its ultimate destination in the eye—the **retina**."

The **retina** is a thin film lining the back of the eye. It consists of three layers, the third and deepest of which contains two kinds of photoreceptors, rods and cones, that change light waves into nerve impulses.

Page 99 "The rods play a key role in **peripheral** vision—seeing objects that are outside the main center of focus—and in night vision."

Peripheral vision is the outer part of the field of vision. Do you have good **peripheral** vision?

Page 101 "Psychologists David Hubel and Torsten Wiesel won the Nobel Prize for their discovery that many neurons in the cortex are **extraordinarily** specialized, being activated only by visual stimuli of a particular shape or pattern—a process known as feature detection."

Extraordinary means exceptional to a very conspicuous degree. Some students have **extraordinary** powers of deduction; they have skills beyond what is usual in a college student.

Page 101 "Other cells are activated only by moving, as opposed to **stationary**, stimuli (Huber & Wiesel, 1979, Patzwahl, Zanker, & Altenmuller, 1994)."

When something is **stationary**, it is in a fixed mode. It is unchanging in condition. A **stationary** bicycle is one that is motionless.

Page 102 "Different parts of the brain seem to process nerve impulses in several individual systems **simultaneously**."

When something exists or occurs at the same time, it is occurring **simultaneously**.

Page 103 "For most people with color-blindness, the world looks quite **dull**."

Dull suggests a lack of sharpness or intensity. Vision that is **dull** may lack brightness or vividness.

Module 10: Hearing and the Other Senses

Sensing Sound

Applying Psychology in the 21st Century:
New Technology for Hearing and Seeing

Smell and Taste
The Skin Senses: Touch, Pressure, Temperature, and Pain

Becoming an Informed Consumer of Psychology:
Managing Pain

- *What role does the ear play in the senses of sound, motion, and balance?*
- *How do smell and taste function?*
- *What are the skin senses, and how do they relate to the experience of pain?*

Hearing and the Other Senses

[a] _____ is the movement of air that results from the vibration of objects. The outer ear collects sounds and guides them to the internal portions of the ear. Sounds are funneled into the auditory canal toward the [b] _____ . Sound waves hit the eardrum, which in turn transmits its vibrations into the [c] _____ . The middle ear contains three small bones: the hammer, the anvil, and the stirrup. These three bones transmit the vibrations to the [d] _____ . The inner ear contains the organs for transmitting the sound waves into nerve impulses as well as the organs for balance and position. The [e] _____ is a coiled tube that contains the [f] _____ . The basilar membrane is covered with [g] _____ that vibrate. Sound may also enter the cochlea through the bones that surround the ear.

Sound is characterized by *frequency*, or the number of waves per second, and *pitch* is our experience of this number as high or low. *Intensity* may be thought of as the size of the waves—how strong it is. Intensity is measured in *decibels*. The [h] _____ is based on the fact that parts of the basilar membrane are sensitive to different pitches.

The **[i]** _____ suggests that the entire basilar membrane vibrates in response to any sound, and the nerves send signals that are more frequent for higher pitches and less frequent for lower pitches.

The inner ear is also responsible for the sense of balance. The disturbance of the sense of balance is called *vertigo*. The structures responsible for balance are the **[j]** _____, three tubes filled with fluid that move around in the tubes when the head moves. The fluid affects

[k] _____, small motion-sensitive crystals in the semicircular canals.

We are able to detect about 10,000 different smells, and women have a better sense of smell than do men. Some animals can communicate using odor. Odor is detected by molecules of a substance coming into contact with the *olfactory cells* in the nasal passages. Each olfactory cell

responds to a narrow band of odors. **[l]** _____ are chemicals that can produce a reaction in members of a species. These chemicals have a role in sexual activity and identification. Tastes, such as sweet, sour, salty, or bitter flavors, are detected by *taste buds* on the tongue. The experience of taste also includes the odor and appearance of food.

The **[m]** _____ include touch, pressure, temperature, and pain. Receptor cells for each of these senses are distributed all over the body, although each sense is distributed in varying concentrations. The major theory of pain is called the

[n] _____. This theory states that nerve receptors send messages to the brain areas related to pain, and whenever they are activated, a "gate" to the brain is opened and pain is experienced. The gate can be shut by overwhelming the nerve pathways with nonpainful messages. It can also be closed by the brain producing messages to reduce or eliminate the

experience of pain. **[o]** _____ may be explained by the first option, in which the needles shut off the messages going to the brain. Endorphins may also close the gate.

Evaluate

Test A

_____ 1. outer ear

_____ 2. auditory canal

_____ 3. eardrum

_____ 4. middle ear

_____ 5. oval window

a. The visible part of the ear that acts as a collector to bring sounds into the internal portions of the ear.

b. A tiny chamber containing three bones—the hammer, the anvil, and the stirrup—which transmit vibrations to the oval window.

c. The part of the ear that vibrates when sound waves hit it.

d. A thin membrane between the middle ear and the inner ear that transmits vibrations while increasing their strength.

e. A tubelike passage in the ear through which sound moves to the eardrum.

Test B

_____ 1. cochlea

_____ 2. basilar membrane

_____ 3. hair cells

_____ 4. frequency

_____ 5. pitch

a. The number of wave crests occurring each second in any particular sound.

b. A structure dividing the cochlea into an upper and a lower chamber.

c. A coiled tube filled with fluid that receives sound via the oval window or through bone conduction.

d. The characteristic that makes sound "high" or "low."

e. Tiny cells that, when bent by vibrations entering the cochlea, transmit neural messages to the brain.

10-1 Much research is being conducted on repairing faulty sensory organs through such devices as personal guidance systems, eyeglasses, and so forth. Do you think that researchers should attempt to improve normal sensory capabilities beyond their "natural" range (e.g., make human visual or audio capabilities more sensitive than normal)? What benefits might this bring? What problems might it cause?

10-2 Why might sensitivity to pheromones have evolved differently in humans than in other species? What cultural factors might have played a role?

Spotlight on Terminology and Language—ESL Pointers

Hearing and the Other Senses

Page 107 "This sense allows people to navigate their bodies through the world and keep themselves **upright** without falling."

Upright is vertically upward. You are **upright** when you are standing.

Page 108 "When sound enters the inner ear through the oval window, it moves into the **cochlea**, a coiled tube that looks something like a snail and is filled with fluid that can vibrate in response to sound."

The **cochlea** is a coiled, fluid-filled structure in the inner ear that contains the receptors for hearing. The function of the **cochlea** is to transform vibrations into nerve impulses (electrical signals) that are sent to the brain for processing into sound sensations.

Page 108 "Inside the cochlea is the **basilar membrane**, a structure that runs through the center of the cochlea, dividing it into an upper chamber and a lower chamber."

The **basilar membrane** is a membrane within the cochlea that contains the auditory receptors, or hair cells.

Page 112 "After an auditory message leaves the ear, it is **transmitted** to the auditory cortex of the brain through a complex series of neural interconnections."

To **transmit** is to send something or cause something to spread, from one person, thing, or place to another. Many diseases are transmitted by airborne droplets.

Page 112 "By working directly at the brain stem, the new device **bypasses** the auditory nerves and nerve endings that often degenerate soon after people lose their hearing (LeVay, 2000; McCreery, Yuen, & Bullara, 2000)."

To **bypass** means to reroute, to avoid a place by traveling around it.

Page 112 "The semicircular canals of the inner ear consist of three tubes containing fluid that **sloshes** through them when the head moves, signaling rotational or angular movement to the brain."

When something **sloshes**, it moves with a splashing motion.

Page 113 "Although many animals have **keener** abilities to detect odors than we do, the human sense of smell (olfaction) permits us to detect more than 10,000 separate smells."

The **keen** sense of smell allows some animals to sense very minor differences and distinctions in smell.

Page 113 "We also have a good memory for smells, and long-forgotten events and memories can be brought back with the mere **whiff** of an odor associated with a memory (Gillyatt, 1997; Schiffman et al., 2002; DiLorenzo & Youngentob, 2003)."

A **whiff** is a slight or brief odor, just a trace of a smell of something. When you get a **whiff** of disinfectant, what is your immediate reaction?

Module 11: Perceptual Organization: Constructing Our View of the World

The Gestalt Laws of Organization
Feature Analysis: Focusing on the Parts of the Whole
Top-Down and Bottom-Up Processing
Perceptual Constancy
Depth Perception: Translating 2-D to 3-D
Motion Perception: As the World Turns
Perceptual Illusions: The Deceptions of Perceptions

Exploring Diversity: Culture and Perception

Subliminal Perception

- *What principles underlie our organization of the visual world, allowing us to make sense of our environment?*
- *How are we able to perceive the world in three dimensions when our retinas are capable of sensing only two-dimensional images?*
- *What clues do visual illusions give us about our understanding of general perceptual mechanisms?*

Perceptual Organization: Constructing Our View of the World

Errors in perception occur because perception is an *interpretation* of sensory information. The distinction between *figure* and *ground* is crucial to perceptual organization. The tendency is to form an object in contrast to its ground, or background.

Through perception, we try to simplify complex stimuli in the environment. This tendency toward simplicity and organization into meaningful wholes follows basic principles called the

[a] _____. *Gestalt* refers to a "pattern." Basic patterns identified by the gestalt psychologists are (1) *closure*, groupings tend to be in complete or enclosed figures; (2) *proximity*, elements close together tend to be grouped together; (3) *similarity*, elements that are similar tend to be grouped together; and (4) *simplicity*, the tendency to organize patterns in a basic, straightforward manner.

The recent approach called **[b]** _____ suggests that we perceive first the individual components and then formulate an understanding of the overall picture. Specific neurons respond to highly specific components of stimuli, suggesting that each stimuli is composed of a series of component features. One theory has identified 36 fundamental components that form the basic components of complex objects. Treisman has proposed that perception requires a two-stage process: a _preattentive stage_ and then a _focused-attention stage._

Perception proceeds in two ways, through top-down or bottom-up processing. In

[c] _____, perception is controlled by higher-level knowledge, experience, expectations, and motivation. Top-down processing helps sort through ambiguous stimuli or missing elements. Context is critical for filling in missing information. Isolated stimuli illustrate how context is important for top-down processing. **[d]** _____ consists of recognizing and processing information about individual components. If we cannot recognize individual components, recognizing the complete picture would be very difficult.

One phenomena that contributes to our perception of the world is that of

[e] _____, the tendency for objects to be perceived as unvarying and consistent even as we see them from different views and distances. The rising moon is one example of how perceptual constancy works. The moon illusion is explained as resulting from the intervening cues of landscape and horizon, which give it context. When it rises, there are no context cues. Perceptual constancies occur with size, shape, and color.

The ability to view the world in three dimensions is called **[f]** _____. The two slightly different positions of the eyes create minute differences in the visual representation in the brain, a phenomenon called **[g]** _____. Discrepancy between the two images from the retinas gives clues to the distance of the object or the distance between two objects. The larger the disparity, the larger the distance. Other cues for visual depth perception can be seen with only one eye, so they are called **[h]** _____.

The Parthenon in Athens is built with an intentional illusion to give the building a greater appearance of straightness and stability. **[i]** _____ are physical stimuli that produce errors in perception. The _Poggendorf illusion_ and the _Müller-Lyer illusion_ are two of the more well-known illusions. Explanations of the **[j]** _____ focus on the apparatus of the eye and the interpretations made by the brain.

[k] _____ is the process of perceiving messages without our awareness of their being presented. Research has shown that the subliminal message does not lead to attitude or behavior change. Another controversial area is that of _extrasensory perception_ (_ESP_). Claims of ESP are difficult to substantiate.

Evaluate

_____ 1. gestalts

_____ 2. closure

_____ 3. proximity

_____ 4. similarity

_____ 5. simplicity

a. The tendency to group together those elements that are similar in appearance.

b. Bits and pieces organized into patterns and studied by psychologists.

c. The tendency to perceive a pattern in the most basic, straightforward, organized manner possible—the overriding gestalt principle.

d. The tendency to group together those elements that are close together.

e. The tendency to group according to enclosed or complete figures rather than open or incomplete ones.

Rethink

11-1   Can you think of examples of the combined use of top-down and bottom-up processing in everyday life? Is one type of processing superior to the other?

11-2   In what ways do painters represent three-dimensional scenes in two dimensions on a canvas? Do you think artists in non-Western cultures use the same or different principles to represent three-dimensionality? Why?

Spotlight on Terminology and Language—ESL Pointers

Perceptual Organization: Constructing Our View of the World

Page 121 "Now that an **alternative** interpretation has been pointed out, you will probably shift back and forth between the two interpretations."

When you have an **alternative** interpretation, you have a choice between two or more interpretations.

Page 123 "According to feature analysis, when we encounter a stimulus—such as a letter—the brain's perceptual processing system initially responds to its **component** parts."

A **component** part is often an element or a section of something bigger.

Page 125 "You were able to figure out the meaning of the sentence with the missing letters because of your prior reading experience, and because written English contains **redundancies**."

When something is **redundant**, it is exceeding what is necessary or normal. Lectures are often characterized by using more words than necessary. The speaker is **redundant**. A **redundant** message has parts that can be eliminated without the loss of essential information.

Page 125 "We would make no **headway** in our recognition of the sentence without being able to perceive the individual shapes that make up the letters."

If you are not able to make **headway**, you are not able to make progress toward achieving something. Students often find themselves unable to make **headway** with a project because the directions are not clear.

Page 126 "Perceptual constancy is a phenomenon in which physical objects are perceived as **unvarying** and consistent despite changes in their appearance or in the physical environment."

Unvarying means constant and unchanging.

Page 126 "When the moon is near the horizon, the perceptual cues of intervening **terrain** and objects such as trees on the horizon produce a misleading sense of distance."

Terrain refers to the way the ground or a piece of land is seen as related to its surface features—the physical features of a piece of land.

Page 126 "In addition to size constancy, other factors have been hypothesized to produce the moon **illusion**."

An **illusion** is something with deceptive appearance. In reference to perceptual constancy, an illusion is a misinterpretation of an experience of sensory perception.

Page 127 "The brain then integrates the two images into one **composite** view."

A **composite** view means a combined view.

Page 132 "**Subliminal** perception refers to the perception of messages about which we have no awareness."

Subliminal messages are brief auditory or visual messages that are presented below the absolute threshold, so that their chance of perception is less than 50 percent.

Practice Tests

Test your knowledge of this set of modules by answering these questions. These questions have been placed in three Practice Tests. The first two tests consist of questions that will test your recall of factual knowledge. The third test contains questions that are challenging and primarily test for conceptual knowledge and your ability to apply that knowledge. Check your answers and review the feedback using the Answer Key on the following pages of the *Study Guide*.

PRACTICE TEST 1

1. A focus of interest on the biological activity of the sense organ is typical in:
   a. sensory psychology.
   b. perceptual psychology.
   c. gestalt psychology.
   d. illusionary psychology.

2. Absolute threshold is defined by psychophysicists as the:
   a. minimum amount of change in stimulation that is detectable.
   b. range of stimulation to which each sensory channel is sensitive.
   c. maximum intensity that is detectable to the senses.
   d. minimum magnitude of stimulus that is detectable.

3. Returning from the dentist, Tamara could not stop using her tongue to locate the new cap on her tooth, but two months later she does not notice the cap at all. This change has occurred because of the principle of:
   a. the difference threshold.
   b. sexual experience.
   c. bottom-up perceptual processing.
   d. sensory adaptation.

4. Feature detection is best described as the process by which specialized neurons in the cortex:
   a. identify fine details in a larger pattern.
   b. see things clearly that are far away.
   c. discriminate one face from another.
   d. recognize particular shapes or patterns.

5. The contemporary view of color vision is that the _____ theory is true only for early stages of visual processing, but the _____ theory applies correctly to both early and later stages.
   a. trichromatic; gate-control
   b. trichromatic; opponent-process
   c. place; gate-control
   d. opponent-process; trichromatic

6. Three tiny bones make up the middle ear. Their function is to:
   a. add tension to the basilar membrane.
   b. prevent the otoliths from becoming mechanically displaced.
   c. amplify sound waves being relayed to the oval window.
   d. minimize the disorienting effects of vertigo.

7. Compared with high-frequency sound, low-frequency sound:
   a. has more peaks and valleys per second.
   b. generates an auditory sensation of low pitch.
   c. has a lower decibel value.
   d. is heard by pets such as cats or dogs but not by humans.

8. The theory that certain nerve receptors lead to specific areas of the brain that sense pain is the:
   a. endorphin.
   b. opiate.
   c. opponent process.
   d. gate control.

9. The gestalt laws of organization are best described as:
   a. patterns of perceiving determined by specific functions of neural receptors.
   b. principles that describe how people perceive.
   c. an explanation for how neural networks in the sensory system operate.
   d. explanations of how people determine the quality of a work of art.

10. The fact that several instruments all blend together to form a symphony orchestra demonstrates:
    a. a figure/ground relationship.
    b. the law of similarity.
    c. that the whole is more than the sum of its parts.
    d. the law of perceptual constancy.

11. Perception that is guided by higher-level knowledge, experience, expectations, and motivations is called:
    a. top-down processing.
    b. bottom-up processing.
    c. perceptual constancy.
    d. feature analysis.

12. Officer Fazio is a police officer whose racial prejudices seem to influence whether she perceives the people on her beat as workers or vagrants. This would best demonstrate:
    a. preattentive perceptual processing.
    b. bottom-up processing.
    c. gestalt perceptual organization.
    d. top-down perceptual processing.

13. Binocular disparity refers to the fact that:
    a. the world looks different with prescription glasses than without.
    b. objects appear closer when they are larger.
    c. the visual image on the retina of each eye is slightly different.
    d. objects progressing into the distance, such as railroad tracks, appear to converge.

14. In the early days of movies, frames depicting popcorn and other snacks were often set into the movie reel without the moviegoers' knowledge. The perception of messages about which the person is unaware is called:
    a. extrasensory perception.
    b. subliminal perception.
    c. cognition in the Ganzfeld.
    d. otolithic preprocessing.

15. The signals that allow us to perceive distance and depth with just one eye are called:
    a. the gestalt principle of figure/ground.
    b. binocular disparity.
    c. monocular cues.
    d. motion parallax.

_____ 16. perceptual constancy

_____ 17. depth perception

_____ 18. binocular disparity

_____ 19. motion parallax

_____ 20. relative size

a. The ability to view the world in three dimensions and to perceive distance.

b. The change in position of the image of an object on the retina as the head moves, providing a monocular cue to distance.

c. The phenomenon by which, if two objects are the same size, the one that makes a smaller image on the retina is perceived to be farther away.

d. The phenomenon by which physical objects are perceived as unvarying despite changes in their appearance or the physical environment.

e. The difference between the images that reach the retina of each eye; this disparity allows the brain to estimate distance.

21. The _____ gets larger as the available light diminishes.

22. _____ is the process that causes incoming images to be focused in the eye.

23. Cones are found primarily in the _____ of the retina.

24. A receptor called a _____ is used in peripheral vision.

25. The senses of taste and smell are alike in that they both depend on _____ as stimuli.

26. Consider what it would be like if our senses were not within their present limits. What visual problems might we face? What would we hear if our hearing had a different range? What if we were more sensitive to smell? What about the other senses?

PRACTICE TEST 2:

1. A dog's nose is more sensitive to smells than is a human's nose. It then would be expected that the absolute threshold for smell will be _____ amount of odorant for a dog than for a person.
   a. a much larger
   b. a moderately larger
   c. about the same
   d. a smaller

2. The function of the retina is to:
   a. turn the image of the object upside down.
   b. redistribute the light energy in the image.
   c. convert the light energy into neural impulses.
   d. control the size of the pupil.

3. As Mrs. Bowman got older, she became aware that night driving was becoming more difficult. Along with many of her elderly friends, she has discovered that the _____, visual receptors most useful for night vision, are no longer adapting quickly enough for driving.
   a. buds
   b. cones
   c. ossicles
   d. rods.

4. Dark adaptation refers to the fact that:
   a. our eyes are less sensitive to a dim stimulus when we look directly at it rather than slightly to the side of it.
   b. the color of objects changes at dusk as light intensity decreases.
   c. the eyes become many times more sensitive after being exposed to darkness.
   d. some people have great difficulty seeing things under low levels of illumination.

5. Afterimages can best be explained by the:
   a. opponent-process theory of color vision.
   b. trichromatic theory of color vision.
   c. place theory of color vision.
   d. receptive-field theory of color vision.

6. Luz often doesn't recognize her own voice on the telephone answering machine. She experiences her own voice differently from the way others hear it primarily because of:
   a. bone conduction.
   b. tympanic vibrations.
   c. low-frequency vibrations.
   d. gradual hearing loss associated with age.

7. Which statement about the taste buds is accurate?
   a. Each receptor is able to respond to many basic tastes and to send the information to the brain.
   b. More than 12 types of receptors for different basic flavors have been described.
   c. Taste receptors on the tongue, the sides and roof of the mouth, and the top part of the throat send complex information about taste to the brain, where it is interpreted.
   d. Receptors for the four basic flavors are located on different areas of the tongue.

8. Look at these letters: *kkk kkk kkk kkk*. You see four groups, each containing three k's, rather than a single row of 12 k's because of the gestalt principle known as:
   a. similarity.
   b. proximity.
   c. closure.
   d. constancy.

9. Which principle of perceptual organization is used when we group items together that look alike or have the same form?
   a. proximity
   b. similarity
   c. figure/ground
   d. closure

10. Making sense of a verbal message by first understanding each word and then piecing them together is:
    a. top-down processing.
    b. bottom-up processing.
    c. selective attention.
    d. perceptual constancy.

11. When we perceive the characteristics of external objects as remaining the same even though the retinal image has changed, _____ has been maintained.
    a. sensory adaptation
    b. bottom-up processing
    c. subliminal perception
    d. perceptual constancy

12. The brain estimates the distance to an object by comparing the different images it gets from the right and left retinas using:
   - a. the gestalt principle of figure/ground.
   - b. binocular disparity.
   - c. monocular cues.
   - d. motion parallax.

13. The Parthenon in Athens looks as if it:
   - a. is leaning backward from the viewer.
   - b. is completely upright with its columns formed of straight lines.
   - c. has bulges in the middle of the columns.
   - d. is ready to fall over.

14. Mrs. Raehn's class is able to read the messages on the board even though part of each word has been erased. This is the gestalt principle of:
   - a. figure/group.
   - b. closure.
   - c. proximity.
   - d. similarity.

_____ 15. linear perspective

_____ 16. visual illusion

_____ 17. decibel

_____ 18. otoliths

_____ 19. figure/ground

   - a. Figure refers to the object being perceived, whereas ground refers to the background or spaces within the object.

   - b. A structure dividing the cochlea into an upper and a lower chamber.

   - c. The phenomenon by which distant objects appear to be closer together than nearer objects, a monocular cue.

   - d. A physical stimulus that consistently produces errors in perception (often called an optical illusion).

   - e. A measure of sound loudness or intensity.

20. The _____ holds that certain nerve receptors lead to specific areas of the brain that sense pain.

21. Perception that is guided by high-level knowledge, experience, expectations, and motivations is called _____.

22. _____ perspective makes railroad tracks appear to come closer together as they move away from the observer.

23. _____ is the study of the relationship between the physical nature of stimuli and a person's sensory responses to them.

24. The organ that gives your eyes their identifying color is the _____.

25. What are the basic differences between the gestalt organizational principles and the feature analysis approach to perception? Does one or the other approach explain some phenomena better? Are there phenomena that would be difficult for one approach to explain?

PRACTICE TEST 3: Conceptual, Applied, and Challenging Questions

1. _____ is to pinprick as _____ is to sharp pain.
   a. Threshold; just noticeable difference
   b. Stimulus; sensation
   c. Difference threshold; context
   d. Sensory adaptation; short-duration stimulation

2. Which statement about the rods and the cones of the retina is accurate?
   a. The rods are concentrated in the fovea of the retina; the cones are in the periphery.
   b. The rods are the receptors for dim illumination; the cones are for high illumination levels.
   c. The rods are responsible for the first 0–10 minutes of the dark adaptation curve; the cones are responsible for the remaining 11–40 minutes.
   d. Cones are found in larger numbers on the retina than are rods.

3. According to the text, blindness is frequently caused by:
   a. an underproduction of rhodopsin.
   b. a restriction of impulses across the optic nerve.
   c. tunnel vision.
   d. an inability of the pupil to expand.

4. Suppose you could hear nothing but your own voice. Of the following, which might your physician suspect as the source of the problem?
   a. the cochlea.
   b. the basilar membrane.
   c. the auditory cortex.
   d. the middle ear.

5. On a piano keyboard, the keys for the lower-frequency sounds are on the left side; the keys for the higher-frequency sounds are on the right. If you first pressed a key on the left side of the keyboard and then a key on the right side, you might expect that:
   a. pitch would depend on how hard the keys were struck.
   b. the pitch would be lower for the first key that was played.
   c. the pitch would be lower for the second key that was played.
   d. the pitch would be identical for each.

6. Intensity is to _____ as frequency is to _____.
   a. resonance; loudness
   b. loudness; pitch
   c. acoustic nerve; auditory canal
   d. external ear; consonance

7. The number of wave crests that occur in a second when a tuning fork is struck is referred to as:
   a. pitch.
   b. intensity.
   c. decibel level.
   d. frequency.

8. Frequency is to _____ as loudness is to _____.
   a. cycles per second; decibels
   b. millimicrometers; loudness
   c. cycles per second; wavelength
   d. cochlea; auditory nerve

9. Arial's mother suffers from vertigo. Her symptoms include:
   a. a strange taste in the mouth, described as garlic and seaweed.
   b. persistently heard voices, typically shouting for help.
   c. dizziness or motion sickness.
   d. phantom skin sensations, such as insects crawling up the arm.

10. The figure-ground principle:
   a. was formulated by gestalt psychologists to describe how objects seem to pop out from the background against which they are seen.
   b. states that figures are obscured by their backgrounds.
   c. suggests that elements that are located near to each other tend to be seen as part of the same perceptual unit, in most cases.
   d. states that individuals with attractive figures are likely to be viewed with interest.

11. An interesting reversible figure/ground stimulus for perceptual demonstrations:
   a. has a predominant ground.
   b. has a predominant figure.
   c. always gives the same dramatic visual image, no matter how it is viewed.
   d. has a figure and a ground that can alternate when viewed in certain ways.

12. Children at the Country Day Care Center are asked to sort geometric puzzle pieces, such as circles, squares, and triangles. This activity illustrates the gestalt principle of:
   a. figure/group.   c. proximity.
   b. closure.   d. similarity.

13. As you look at a car, you can see only the last part of the make, reading "mobile." You determine that the car is probably an Oldsmobile. This illustrates:
   a. top-down processing.   c. selective attention.
   b. bottom-up processing. d. feature analysis.

14. Which of the following statements concerning depth perception is **true**?
   a. It is not always necessary to use two eyes to perceive depth.
   b. Distant objects appear smaller because of linear perspective.
   c. The greater the discrepancy between two retinal images, the more difficult it is to reconcile depth.
   d. If two objects are the same size, the one that projects the smaller image on the retina is closer.

15. Suppose that you happened upon two buffalo grazing in an open field and one looked substantially larger than the other. Now suppose that the image of the smaller buffalo began to expand. You would probably assume that it was:
   a. growing.   c. moving away from you.
   b. running toward you.   d. turning sideways.

16. _____ is most important in order for major-league baseball players to be able to hit the ball when it reaches the plate.
   a. Tracking   c. Anticipation
   b. Focusing   d. Eye coordination

17. Abigail is trying to learn Spanish so that she can travel to Mexico during spring break, so she purchases some tapes to play while she is asleep. The concept that supports the notion of being able to learn in this manner is called _____. According to the text, will her tapes work?
   a. selective attention; yes   c. subliminal perception; yes
   b. selective attention; no   d. subliminal perception; no

18. Which alternative is **not** an important factor that influences illusions?
    a. amount of formal education
    b. cultural experiences
    c. structural characteristics of the eye
    d. interpretive errors of the brain

19. The visual receptors most useful for night vision are called _____.

20. _____ is a buildup of pressure within the eye that may lead to blindness.

21. In the study of perception, patterns are referred to as "_____."

22. Filling in the gaps is known as _____.

23. Chemical molecules that promote communication among members of a species are called _____.

24. _____ is an organism's first encounter with a raw sensory stimulus.

■ ANSWER KEY: MODULES 8, 9, 10, AND 11

Module 8:	Module 9:	Module 10:	Module 11:
[a] sensation	[a] visual spectrum	[a] Sound	[a] gestalt laws of
[b] perception	[b] cornea	[b] eardrum	organization
[c] stimulus	[c] pupil	[c] middle ear	[b] feature analysis
[d] Psychophysics	[d] accommodation	[d] oval window	[c] top-down processing
[e] Absolute threshold	[e] retina	[e] cochlea	[d] Bottom-up processing
[f] difference threshold	[f] rods	[f] basilar membrane	[e] perceptual constancy
[g] just noticeable	[g] cones	[g] hair cells	[f] depth perception
difference	[h] dark adaptation	[h] place theory of	[g] binocular disparity
[h] Weber's law	[i] rhodopsin	hearing	[h] monocular cues
[i] adaptation	[j] optic nerve	[i] frequency theory of	[i] Visual illusions
	[k] optic chiasm	hearing	[j] Müller-Lyer illusion
Evaluate	[l] feature detection	[j] semicircular canals	[k] Subliminal perception
1. c		[k] otoliths	
2. a		[l] Pheromones	
3. d	Evaluate	[m] skin senses	Evaluate
4. e	1. c	[n] gate-control theory	1. b
5. b	2. d	of pain	2. e
	3. a	[o] Acupuncture	3. d
	4. e		4. a
	5. b		5. c
		Evaluate	
		Test A Test B	
		1. a 1. c	
		2. e 2. b	
		3. c 3. e	
		4. b 4. a	
		5. d 5. d	

Selected Rethink Answers

8-1   Sensory adaptation, an adjustment in sensory capacity following prolonged exposure to stimuli. Decline in sensitivity is caused by the inability of nerve receptors to constantly fire messages to the brain. Receptor cells are most responsive to changes in stimulation, and constant stimulation is not effective in producing a reaction. Adaptation to the context of one stimulus alters responses to another. If our senses were constantly bombarded by stimuli that was intense, we would have a constant high rate of stimulation.

10-1   Benefits of increased sensory capacity might allow us to see great distance. We may also be able to hear sounds from far away. Our sense of touch could cause us to have increased pain from cuts and burns. Science already has invented equipment that allows these things: "Sonic Ear" advertised to hear long distances, new surgery that improves eyesight, etc. These could be great scientific achievements, but to have our senses bombarded by increased stimuli doesn't seem to have overall advantages. How would we distinguish between necessary and unnecessary stimuli?

10-2   Sensitivity to pheromones may have developed differently for humans because as the culture has evolved, sending out messages that you were available for sexual activity could have been dangerous (sent to others who were not potential partners). Also, societies now set up rules for sexual activity and partnerships that are different from that in the animal world.

Practice Test 1:

1. a   mod. 8 p. 93
*a. Correct. Sensory psychology focuses on sensation.
b. Incorrect. Perceptual psychology focuses on sensation and perception
c. Incorrect. Gestalt psychology focuses primarily on perception.
d. Incorrect. Do not know of any such field.

2. d   mod. 8 p. 94
a. Incorrect. This defines a difference threshold.
b. Incorrect. This is referred to as the range of stimulation.
c. Incorrect. This would be some kind of maximum threshold.
*d. Correct. The absolute threshold is the smallest magnitude of a physical stimulus detectable by a sensory organ.

3. d   mod. 8 p. 95
a. Incorrect. The difference threshold would account for the initial detection of the new stimulus.
b. Incorrect. Sexual experience may alter his cognitive understanding of the ring, but not his sensory attention to it.
c. Incorrect. Actually, if this applies, it would be the top-down processing of ignoring the stimulus as described in answer d.
*d. Correct. This phenomenon is called sensory adaptation.

4. d   mod. 9 p. 101
a. Incorrect. This kind of recognition of details occurs in other processing areas.
b. Incorrect. The fovea is responsible for this capability.
c. Incorrect. The discrimination of faces occurs in the association areas of the brain.
*d. Correct. Feature detection is responsible for pattern recognition.

5. b   mod. 9 p. 103
a. Incorrect. Gate control relates to pain perception.
*b. Correct. Trichromatic accounts for the three different color spectrums to which the cones are responsive, whereas the opponent-process theory explains how four colors can be perceived with only three types of cones.
c. Incorrect. Place relates to hearing, and gate control to pain perception.
d. Incorrect. These are reversed.

6. c   mod. 10 p. 107
a. Incorrect. They are not connected to the basilar membrane.
b. Incorrect. Otoliths are found in the semicircular canal, not the middle ear.
*c. Correct. The bones transfer, focus, and amplify mechanical sound from the eardrum to the oval window.
d. Incorrect. Nothing can minimize these effects.

7. b   mod. 10 p. 112
a. Incorrect. This describes high-frequency, not low-frequency sound.
*b. Correct. Our perception of low frequency is low sound.
c. Incorrect. The decibel value applies to all sound, regardless of frequency.
d. Incorrect. Many pets can hear both higher and lower frequencies than their human attendants.

8. d   mod. 10 p. 117
a. Incorrect. Endorphins are neurotransmitters involved in reduction of the perception of pain.
b. Incorrect. Opiates are like endorphins and have similar effects on the neural pain messages.
c. Incorrect. Opponent processes are related to pain in the release of endorphins and the persistence of their effects after the pain stimulus has subsided.
*d. Correct. This is the name of the theory of pain.

9. b   mod. 11 p. 122
a. Incorrect. This refers to feature detection.
*b. Correct. The gestalt psychologists suggested that people organize their perceptions according to consistent principles of organization based on figure/ground relationships and simplicity.
c. Incorrect. Although some of these neural networks may work in this fashion, this is not the foundation of neural networks.
d. Incorrect. This shall remain a mystery for some time.

10. c   mod. 11 p. 122
a. Incorrect. In a figure/ground relationship, one instrument would stand out against the others.
b. Incorrect. The law of similarity applies to the similarity of items leading to their being grouped together.
*c. Correct. The fact that the orchestra creates a sound that is more complex than merely the sum of the sounds made by the individual instruments illustrates this concept.
d. Incorrect. Perceptual constancy applies to other phenomena altogether.

11. a   mod. 11 p. 125
*a. Correct. Top-down processing refers to processing that begins with a broad, general perspective and then completes details from this context.
b. Incorrect. Bottom-up processing builds the final picture from the details.
c. Incorrect. Perceptual constancy refers to our tendency to view an object as having a constant size, shape, color, or brightness even when we see it in different environments or from different points of view.
d. Incorrect. Feature analysis refers to detection of patterns in an array of neural activity.

12. d   mod. 11 p. 125
a. Incorrect. See answer d.
b. Incorrect. See answer d.
c. Incorrect. See answer d.
*d. Correct. But this applies more to social perception than sensation and perception.

13. c   mod. 11 p. 127
a. Incorrect. This describes bifocal disparity.
b. Incorrect. This is retinal size.
*c. Correct. Because the eyes are a small distance apart, the images on the eyes vary slightly, and the disparity can be used to determine distance and depth.
d. Incorrect. This is called linear perspective, and it is a monocular cue.

14. b   mod. 11 p. 132
a. Incorrect. ESP typically involves messages about which only the perceiver is aware.
*b. Correct. Perceiving messages below the threshold of awareness is called subliminal perception.
c. Incorrect. Sounds good, but what is it?
d. Incorrect. Being tiny crystals, otoliths do not process anything.

15. c   mod. 11 p. 127
a. Incorrect. The gestalt principle of figure/ground suggests that we see an object in the context of its background.
b. Incorrect. Binocular disparity works on the basis of the slight disparity between the two images of the retinas because they have slightly different points of view.
*c. Correct. Monocular cues, by definition, come from only one eye.
d. Incorrect. Motion parallax arises when distant objects appear to move less than close objects when the observer moves by them.

16. d   mod. 11   p. 126
17. a   mod. 11   p. 127
18. e   mod. 11   p. 127
19. b   mod. 11   p. 127
20. c   mod. 11   p. 127

21. pupil   mod. 9   p. 98
22. Accommodation   mod. 9   p. 99
23. fovea   mod. 9   p. 99
24. rod   mod. 9   p. 99
25. chemical molecules mod. 9   p. 113

26. The major points that should be included in your answer are:
- Discuss the importance of sensory selectivity—of sense organs being sensitive to limited ranges of physical stimuli.
- Although we would probably adjust to the differences, additional information might create duplications.
- Describe the things we would be able to hear, smell, taste, and feel if our sensory ranges were broader.
- Reflect on the possibility that our ability at sensory adaptation might have to increase.

Practice Test 2:
1. d   mod. 8 p. 94
*a. Incorrect. See answer d.
b. Incorrect. See answer d.
c. Incorrect. See answer d.
d. Correct. Actually, the organ is the nasal epithelium, and the more area it has, the fewer odorant molecules are required to detect an odor.

2. c   mod. 9 p. 99
a. Incorrect. The lens turns the image upside down.
b. Incorrect. The light energy in the image is not redistributed, but it is converted to neural messages.
*c. Correct. This is the role of the retina, and the rods and the cones of the retina initiate the process.
d. Incorrect. The size of the pupil is controlled by the muscles of the iris.

3. d   mod. 9 p. 99
a. Incorrect. Buds occur on branches of dendrites, axons, and trees, and in the tongue, but they are not the name of visual receptors.
b. Incorrect. Cones are more responsive to bright light.
c. Incorrect. Ossicles are another pronunciation of the word "icicles."
*d. Correct. Rods are capable of detecting small amounts of light.

4. c   mod. 9 p. 99
a. Incorrect. This is because of the low number of rods in the fovea, our typical focal point in the eye in normal light.
b. Incorrect. This results from the low levels of light, making the operation of the cones less effective.
*c. Correct. Sensitivity changes in low levels of illumination, and coming into bright light can be painful.
d. Incorrect. These people have what is known as night blindness caused by problems related to the rods or to processing information from rods.

5. a   mod. 9 p. 104
*a. Correct. The opponent color is activated to balance, or adapt, to the intensity of the initial color. When the initial color is removed, the opponent color is seen (the afterimage).
b. Incorrect. Trichromatic theory could not account for negative afterimages.
c. Incorrect. There is not a place theory of color vision, only one for hearing.
d. Incorrect. The receptive-field theory of color vision is yet to be developed.

6. a   mod. 10 p. 107
*a. Correct. The bone conducts sound differently from the air, and the only voice we hear through bone is our own, so no one else hears it through your bone.
b. Incorrect. Everyone hears through tympanic vibrations.
c. Incorrect. Bone conduction is the reason we hear our voices differently from how others hear them.
d. Incorrect. But your voice changes too.

7. d   mod. 10 p. 114
a. Incorrect. Most receptors respond to only one taste.
b. Incorrect. Only four types are known.
c. Incorrect. Taste receptors are only on the tongue.
*d. Correct. The four basic tastes are sweet, sour, bitter, and salty.

8. b   mod. 11 p. 122
a. Incorrect. They are similar, but they are not selected from a larger set of dissimilar objects.
*b. Correct. Objects that are close together tend to be grouped together.
c. Incorrect. Closure would lead to filling in the missing p's in the sequence.
d. Incorrect. Constancy refers to the fact that we view P and p as the same object.

9. b   mod. 11 p. 123
a. Incorrect. Proximity applies to objects that are close to each other.
*b. Correct. Similar objects do tend to be grouped together.
c. Incorrect. Figure/ground refers to the tendency to see objects in contrast to their background.
d. Incorrect. Closure refers to our tendency to fill in missing or hidden parts of an object.

10. b   mod. 11 p. 125
a. Incorrect. Top-down processing would begin by understanding the sentence and then finding the missing words.
*b. Correct. Bottom-up processing identifies each part and then builds the larger picture.
c. Incorrect. Selective attention refers to our ability to ignore irrelevant information or sensory inputs and concentrate on a selected set of data.
d. Incorrect. Constancy refers to a principle of perception that concerns the tendency to view an object as if it is unchanged even when viewed from different points of view.

11. d   mod. 11 p. 126
a. Incorrect. This refers to habituation to a sensory stimulus.
b. Incorrect. In bottom-up processing, each new view would generate a new image and identity.
c. Incorrect. Subliminal perception may occur at the limits of conscious perception, but it does not influence perceptual constancy.
*d. Correct. When an object is perceived as not changing even though its visual image changes, perceptual constancy is at work.

12. b   mod. 11 p. 127
a. Incorrect. The gestalt principle of figure/ground suggests that we see an object in the context of its background.
*b. Correct. Binocular disparity works on the basis of the slight disparity between the two images of the retinas becausse they have slightly different points of view.
c. Incorrect. Monocular cues, by definition, come from only one eye.
d. Incorrect. Motion parallax arises when distant objects appear to move less than close objects when the observer moves by them.

13. b   mod. 11 p. 129
a. Incorrect. See answer b.
*b. Correct. Unseen bulges in the middle of the columns make it look more perfectly square and taller.
c. Incorrect. See answer b.
d. Incorrect. See answer b.

14. b   mod. 11 p. 122
a. Incorrect. There is no gestalt principle of "figure/group."
*b. Correct. Closure involves completing an incomplete figure by filling in missing components.
c. Incorrect. Proximity involves grouping elements that are close together.
d. Incorrect. This activity involves grouping according to similar features.

15. c   mod. 11   p. 128
16. d   mod. 11   p. 129
17. e   mod. 10   p. 109
18. b   mod. 10   p. 113
19. a   mod. 11   p. 121

20. Gate-control of pain theory   mod. 11 p. 117
21. top-down processing   mod. 11 p. 125
22. Linear   mod. 11 p. 128
23. Psychophysics   mod. 8 p. 93
24. Iris   mod. 9 p. 98

25.
- The major point is perception of wholes versus perception of parts. Top-down processing and bottom-up processing may also be used to distinguish the two approaches.
- Phenomena such as perception of objects when parts are hidden from view and the reading of words without having to identify each letter are better explained by the gestalt approach. Identification of unusual objects by identifying and analyzing parts of the object is better accounted for by feature analysis.

Practice Test 3:
1. b   mod. 8 p. 93
a. Incorrect. Just noticeable difference is inappropriate here.
*b. Correct. The pinprick is the stimulus and the pain is the sensation.
c. Incorrect. The pinprick does not represent a difference threshold.
d. Incorrect. Quite a few pinpricks would be needed to develop a sensory adaptation, especially if the pain is short in duration.

2. b   mod. 9 p. 99
a. Incorrect. This is reversed.
*b. Correct. Rods need little light to be activated, cones require much more.
c. Incorrect. The amount of rhodopsin is the relevant factor in dark adaptation, not the rod and cone differences.
d. Incorrect. This is the opposite as well.

3. b   mod 11 p. 101
a. Incorrect. The impulses across the optic nerve become restricted.
*b. Correct. There can be several causes of this phenomena, including diabetes.
c. Incorrect. This is a consequence of glaucoma, caused by increasing pressure within the eye.
d. Incorrect. This problem is not very common.

4. d   mod. 9 p. 108
a. Incorrect. If you could hear your own voice, then you could be hearing through bone conduction, and the cochlea, basilar membrane, and auditory cortex would be functioning properly.
b. Incorrect. See answer a.
c. Incorrect. See answer a.
*d. Correct. Some blockage would have had to occur in the middle ear, because you would be hearing through bone conduction, and the cochlea, basilar membrane, and auditory cortex would be functioning properly.

5. b   mod. 10 p. 109
a. Incorrect. Pitch does not depend on how hard the keys are struck on a piano.
*b. Correct. The keys on the left side would have a lower frequency, and thus lower pitch, than the keys on the right side.
c. Incorrect. The keys on the left side would have a lower frequency, and thus lower pitch, than the keys on the right side.
d. Incorrect. Pitch is a function of frequency.

6. b   mod. 10 p. 109
a. Incorrect. Intensity may affect resonance, but frequency does not relate to loudness.
*b. Correct. The greater the intensity, the louder the sound, and the higher the frequency, the higher the pitch.
c. Incorrect. These do not have a match at all.
d. Incorrect. Intensity will affect all of the ear, although the external ear will be affected least, yet consonance will be unaffected by frequency.

7. d   mod. 10 p. 109
a. Incorrect. However, pitch is how we perceive the differences between different frequencies.
b. Incorrect. Intensity refers to loudness, or how tall the crests would be.
c. Incorrect. This is intensity, or how tall the crests would be.
*d. Correct. The count of the number of crests per second is the frequency of the sound.

8. a   mod. 10 p. 109
*a. Correct. Loudness is measured in decibels and frequency is measured in cycles per second.
b. Incorrect. See answer a.
c. Incorrect. See answer a.
d. Incorrect. See answer a.

9. c   mod. 10 p. 113
a. Incorrect. This symptom is associated with something eaten, not vertigo.
b. Incorrect. This symptom is more likely to be found in schizophrenia.
*c. Correct. Vertigo is a disorder or disruption of the sense of balance, and it results in motion sickness and dizziness.
d. Incorrect. This results from taking too many illegal drugs.

10. a   mod. 11 p. 121
*a. Correct. This principle is central to the gestalt approach.
b. Incorrect. Only in illusions.
c. Incorrect. This is the principle of proximity.
d. Incorrect. That is the physical attraction principle found in later chapters.

11. d   mod. 11 p. 121
a. Incorrect. The less predominant the ground, the easier it is to alternate figure and ground.
b. Incorrect. The less predominant the figure, the easier it is to alternate figure and ground.
c. Incorrect. Often the images are quite different, causing a dramatic effect.
*d. Correct. If they can alternate, then the reversibility is possible.

12. d   mod. 11 p. 122
a. Incorrect. There is no gestalt principle of "figure/group."
b. Incorrect. Closure involves completing an incomplete figure by filling in missing components.
c. Incorrect. Proximity involves grouping elements that are close together.
*d. Correct. This activity involves grouping according to similar features.

13. a   mod. 11 p. 125
*a. Correct. In top-down processing, incomplete information is completed by drawing on context and memory.
b. Incorrect. Bottom-up processing would require all parts of the image.
c. Incorrect. While selective attention may be involved (the car may have actually been a snowmobile), this example does not illustrate selective attention.
d. Incorrect. Feature analysis helped you detect the word "mobile," but it was not used in completing the word.

14. a   mod. 11 p. 127
*a. Correct. There are many monocular, or single-eye, cues for depth.
b. Incorrect. They appear smaller because of the physics involved.
c. Incorrect. Actually, the greater discrepancy makes the depth determination easier.
d. Incorrect. This is backward.

15. b   mod. 11 p. 127
a. Incorrect. Right, and it's about to explode.
*b. Correct. Right, so you better take cover—the image is getting larger on your retina.
c. Incorrect. No, it would have to be moving toward you.
d. Incorrect. It could have started out sideways; if it is then turning sideways, it would be getting smaller.

16. c   mod. 11 p. 128
a. Incorrect. The ball moves too quickly for the player to track the ball all the way to the plate.
b. Incorrect. Focusing is less of a problem than tracking, and if the player cannot track the ball, he certainly cannot focus on it.
*c. Correct. The player must anticipate the location of the ball when it reaches the plate, because it approaches too quickly to be tracked all the way, and he must begin his swing before the ball reaches the plate.
d. Incorrect. Eye coordination is critical, but he would not be a major-league player if he did not already have good coordination.

17. d   mod. 11 p. 132
a. Incorrect. Try subliminal perception, and no, it probably will not work.
b. Incorrect. Try subliminal perception, and no, it probably will not work.
c. Incorrect. It is called subliminal perception, but it probably will not work.
*d. Correct. However, there is little evidence supporting the use of subliminal tapes for complex learning.

18. a   mod. 11 p. 129
*a. Correct. Educational level has no impact on the perception of illusions.
b. Incorrect. Culture does appear to influence the perception of illusions, especially illusions involving objects or situations unfamiliar to members of the culture.
c. Incorrect. The structure of the eye is one of the factors influencing how illusions work.
d. Incorrect. Some illusions arise from incorrect interpretations at the level of the brain.

19. rods	mod. 9	p. 99
20. Glaucoma	mod. 9	p. 93
21. gestalts	mod. 11	p. 122
22. closure	mod. 11	p. 122
23. Pheromone	mod. 10	p. 112
24. Sensation	mod. 8	p. 93

States of Consciousness

12: Sleep and Dreams
13: Hypnosis and Meditation
14: Drug Use: The Highs and Lows of Consciousness

Overview

This set of modules focuses on the states of consciousness. Although some psychologists prefer to exclude studying the topic because of its reliance on "unscientific" introspections of experimental participants, contemporary psychologists support the view that several approaches permit the scientific study of consciousness. We can study brain wave patterns under conditions of consciousness ranging from sleep to waking to hypnotic trances. Also, understanding the chemistry of drugs such as marijuana and alcohol has provided insights into the way they provide pleasurable—as well as adverse—effects.

Another reason for the study of consciousness is the realization that people in many different cultures routinely seek ways to alter their states of consciousness. Consciousness may alter thinking. It may alter people's sense of time and perceptions about oneself or the world. This chapter considers several states of consciousness.

Module 12 focuses on what happens when we sleep. The REM stage of sleep is discussed, along with the manifest and latent content of dreams that occur during this sleep stage. The dreams-as-survival theory suggests that relevant information is reconsidered and reprocessed. Sleep disorders and their treatment concludes this module.

Modules 13 presents an explanation of both hypnosis, a heightened state of susceptibility, and the technique of meditation and its effects on consciousness.

Module 14 explains drug-induced states of consciousness. Stimulants arouse the nervous system, whereas depressants, alcohol, and barbiturates decrease arousal of the CNS. Narcotics such as morphine and heroin produce relaxation and reduce pain. Hallucinogens produce changes in perception. This module concludes with signals that indicate when drug use becomes abuse.

To further investigate the topics covered in this chapter, you can visit the related Web sites by visiting the following link: www.mhhe.com/feldmanup6-05links.

Prologue: A Deadly Binge
Looking Ahead

Module 12:
Sleep and Dreams

The Stages of Sleep
REM Sleep: The Paradox of Sleep
Why Do We Sleep, and How Much Sleep Is Necessary?

Applying Psychology in the 21st Century: Tired
Teens: Adolescents Struggle to Balance Sleep and School

The Function and Meaning of Dreaming
Sleep Disturbances: Slumbering Problems
Circadian Rhythms: Life Cycles
Daydreams: Dreams Without Sleep

Becoming an Informed Consumer of Psychology:
Sleeping Better

- *What are the different states of consciousness?*
- *What happens when we sleep, and what are the meaning and function of dreams?*
- *What are the major sleep disorders, and how can they be treated?*
- *How much do we daydream?*

Sleep and Dreams

[a] _____ is defined as our awareness of the sensations, thoughts, and feelings being experienced at any given moment. Consciousness can range from the perceptions during wakefulness to dreams. The variation in how we experience stimuli can be wide as well, and consciousness varies from active to passive states.

Much of our knowledge of sleep comes from the use of the [b] _____ to record brain activity throughout the cycles of sleep. The amplitude and frequency of the wavelike patterns formed by the EEG during sleep show regular and systematic patterns of sleep.

These patterns identify four stages of sleep. The first stage, called [c] _____, is the stage of transition to sleep, and the brain waves are rapid, low-voltage waves.

[d] _____ is characterized by slower, more regular waves and by occasional sharply pointed waves called spindles.

[e] _____ brain waves become slower with higher peaks and lower valleys. [f] _____ has even slower wave patterns. Stage 4 is experienced soon after falling to sleep, and throughout the night, sleep becomes lighter and is characterized by more dreams.

The period of sleep associated with most of our dreaming is identified by the rapid back-and-forth movement of the eyes called [g] _____. REM sleep, which occupies about 20 percent of the total sleep time, is paradoxical because the body is in a state of paralysis even as the eyes are moving rapidly.

People who are deprived of sleep over long periods—up to 200 hours in some experiments—do not experience any long-term effects.

[h] _____ are the daily rhythms of the body, including the sleep and waking cycle, as well as the cycles of sleepiness throughout the day. Other functions, like body temperature, also follow circadian rhythms. *Seasonal affective disorder* and premenstrual syndrome (PMS) are two examples of rhythmic changes that have cycles longer than 24 hours.

[i] _____ are unusually frightening dreams. They appear to occur frequently, perhaps about 24 times per year on average. Most dreams, however, involve daily, mundane events. According to Freud's [j] _____, dreams are guides into the unconscious. The true meaning of these wishes was disguised, and Freud used the label of [k] _____ because the meanings were too threatening. Freud called the storyline of the dream the [l] _____. Freud sought to uncover the latent content by interpreting the symbols of the dream. Many psychologists reject this theory of dreams, instead preferring to interpret the content in terms of its more obvious references to everyday concerns. Another theory of dreams is called the [m] _____. This theory suggests that dreams flush away unnecessary information accumulated throughout the day. Dreams then have little meaning. Another theory is the [n] _____, which suggests that dreams involve a reconsideration and reprocessing of critical information from the day. Dreams in this theory have meaning as they represent important concerns drawn from daily experiences. Currently, the most influential theory is the [o] _____, which claims that dreams are by-products of biological processes. These processes are random firings related to changes in neurotransmitter production. Because these activities activate memories that have importance, what begins randomly becomes meaningful.

Evaluate

Test A

_____ 1. stage 1 sleep

_____ 2. stage 2 sleep

_____ 3. stage 3 sleep

_____ 4. stage 4 sleep

_____ 5. rapid eye movement (REM) sleep

a. The deepest stage of sleep, during which we are least responsive to outside stimulation.

b. Sleep characterized by increased heart rate, blood pressure, and breathing rate; erections; and the experience of dreaming.

c. Characterized by sleep spindles.

d. The state of transition between wakefulness and sleep, characterized by relatively rapid, low-voltage brain waves.

e. A sleep characterized by slow brain waves, with greater peaks and valleys in the wave pattern.

Test B

_____ 6. latent content of dreams

_____ 7. manifest content of dreams

_____ 8. reverse learning theory

_____ 9. dreams-for-survival theory

_____ 10. activation-synthesis theory

a. According to Freud, the "disguised" meaning of dreams, hidden by more obvious subjects.

b. Hobson's view that dreams are a result of random electrical energy stimulation and memories lodged in various portions of the brain, which the brain then weaves into a logical storyline.

c. The view that dreams have no meaning in themselves, but instead function to rid us of unnecessary information that we have accumulated during the day.

d. The proposal that dreams permit information that is critical for our daily survival to be reconsidered and reprocessed during sleep.

e. According to Freud, the overt storyline of dreams.

12-1   How would studying the sleep patterns of nonhuman species potentially help us figure out which of the theories of dreaming provides the best account of the functions of dreaming?

12-2   Suppose that a new "miracle pill" is developed that will allow a person to function with only 1 hour of sleep per night. However, a night's sleep is so short that a person who takes the pill will never dream again. Knowing what you do about the functions of sleep and dreaming, what would be some advantages and drawbacks of such a pill from a personal standpoint? Would you take such a pill?

Spotlight on Terminology and Language—ESL Pointers

Sleep and Dreams

Page 141 "People with the **malady** have been known to hit others, smash windows, punch holes in walls—all while fast asleep."

   A **malady** is a problem. Would you say that people who suffer with the **malady** of REM sleep behavior disorder are suffering from a physical or psychological disorder or disease?

Page 141 "With the help of clonazepam, a drug that **suppresses** movement during dreams, his malady vanished, permitting him to sleep through the night undisturbed."

   To **suppress** means to prevent something from happening.

Page 141 "Much of our knowledge of what happens during sleep comes from the **electroencephalogram**, or EEG, a measurement of electrical activity in the brain."

   An EEG (**electroencephalogram**) is a recording of brain waves produced by an **electroencephalograph** machine.

Page 141 "When **probes** from an EEG machine are attached to the surface of a sleeping person's scalp and face, it becomes clear that the brain is active throughout the night."

   A **probe** is a tool, an instrument, used to test the behavior of electrical circuits.

Page 141 "People progress through five distinct stages of sleep during a night's rest—known as stage 1 through stage 4 and REM sleep—moving through the stages in **cycles** lasting about ninety minutes."

   A **cycle** is an interval of time during which a sequence or a recurring chain of events or phenomena is completed.

Page 141 "This is actually a stage of **transition** between wakefulness and sleep and lasts only a few minutes."

   A **transition** is movement from one state to another.

Page 143 "**Paradoxically**, while all this activity is occurring, the major muscles of the body appear to be paralyzed—except in rare cases such as Donald Dorff's."

   A **paradox** is something with seemingly contradictory qualities or phases. During REM sleep, it appears that the major muscles of the body are paralyzed, while this sleep period is characterized by increased heart rate, blood pressure, breathing rate, and eye movement.

Page 147 "However, because these wishes are threatening to the dreamer's conscious awareness, the actual wishes—called the **latent** content of dreams—are disguised."

   Latent content is something that is hidden but capable of becoming visible. A **latent** fingerprint at the scene of a crime would be one that is scarcely visible but could be developed for study.

Page 147 "The true subject and meaning of a dream, then, may have little to do with its **overt** story line, which Freud called the **manifest** content of dreams."

Overt means open to view. Something that is conducted **overtly** is done openly and without any attempt at concealment.

When something is **manifest,** it is clear and apparent; it is obvious. Information that is **manifest** would be clear to see or understand.

Module 13: Hypnosis and Meditation

Hypnosis: A Trance-Forming Experience?
Meditation: Regulating Our Own State of Consciousness

Exploring Diversity: Cross-Cultural Routes to Altered States of Consciousness

- *What is hypnosis, and are hypnotized people in a different state of consciousness?*
- *What are the effects of meditation?*

Hypnosis and Meditation

[a] _____ is a state of heightened susceptibility to the suggestions of others. When people are hypnotized, they will not perform antisocial behaviors, carry out self-destructive acts, or reveal hidden truths about themselves, yet they are capable of lying. Between 5 and 20 percent of the population cannot be hypnotized at all, and about 15 percent are highly susceptible. Ernest Hilgard has argued that hypnosis does represent a state of consciousness that is significantly different from other states. The increased suggestibility, greater ability to recall and construct images, increased memories from childhood, lack of initiative, and ability to accept suggestions that contradict reality suggest that hypnotic states are different from other states. Some researchers have established that some people do pretend to be hypnotized. Moreover, adults do not have a special ability to recall childhood events while hypnotized. Hypnotism has been used successfully for the following: (1) controlling pain, (2) ending tobacco addiction, (3) treating psychological disorders, (4) assisting in law enforcement, and (5) improving athletic performance.

[b] _____ is a learned technique for refocusing attention that brings about the altered state. Transcendental meditation (TM), which was brought to the United States by the Maharishi Mahesh Yogi, is perhaps the best-known form of meditation. TM uses a

[c] _____, a sound, word, or a syllable, that is said over and over. In other forms, the mediator focuses on a picture, flame, or body part. In all forms, the key is to concentrate intensely. Following meditation, people are relaxed, they may have new insights, and in the long term, they may have improved health. The [d] _____ that accompany meditation are similar to relaxation: heart rate declines, oxygen intake declines, and brain-wave patterns change. The simple procedures of sitting in a quiet room, breathing deeply and rhythmically, and repeating a word will achieve the same effects as trained meditation techniques.

The cross-cultural aspects of altered states of consciousness are examined in the Exploring Diversity section. The search for experiences beyond normal consciousness is found in many cultures, and it may reflect a universal need to alter moods and consciousness.

Evaluate

_____1. hypnosis

_____2. meditation

_____3. Mesmer

_____4. hypnotic state

_____5. mantra

a. A technique for refocusing attention, it brings about an altered state of consciousness.

b. A sound, word, or syllable repeated over and over.

c. He argued that a form of "animal magnetism" could influence people and cure illness.

d. An altered state of consciousness brought about by refocusing attention.

e. A trance-like state of heightened susceptibility to suggestions of others.

Rethink

13-1   Meditation produces several physical and psychological benefits. Does this suggest that we are physically and mentally burdened in our normal state of waking consciousness? Why?

13-2   Why do you think people in almost every culture use psychoactive drugs and search for altered states of consciousness?

Spotlight on Terminology and Language—ESL Pointers

Hypnosis and Meditation

Page 155 "People under hypnosis are in a **trancelike** state of heightened susceptibility to the suggestions of others."

A **trance** is a state of profound absorption, different from both sleeping states and waking states.

Page 155 "Despite their **compliance** when hypnotized, people do not lose all will of their own."

Compliance involves conforming to the statements of the hypnotherapy operator. **Compliance** is a disposition to follow suggestions.

Page 156 "The question of whether hypnosis is a state of consciousness that is **qualitatively** different from normal waking consciousness is controversial."

When something is **qualitatively** different, it is different in its essential character. This is not to be confused with *quantitative*, which involves measurements of quantity or amount.

Page 157 "For example, it may be employed to heighten relaxation, reduce anxiety, increase expectations of success, or modify **self-defeating** thoughts (Fromm & Nash, 1992; Zarren & Eimer, 2002)."

Self-defeating thoughts are negative suggestions you give to yourself.

Page 158 "The **fundamentals** include sitting in a quiet room with the eyes closed, breathing deeply and rhythmically and repeating a word or sound—such as the word one—over and over."

The **fundamentals** are the essential, basic steps for experiencing the meditative state.

Page 159 "Some scholars suggest that the **quest** to alter consciousness represents a basic human desire (Siegel, 1989)."

A **quest** is a search for something. What kinds of **quests** have you found yourself pursuing during your educational experience?

Module 14: Drug Use: The Highs and Lows of Consciousness

Stimulants: Drug Highs
Depressants: Drug Lows
Narcotics: Relieving Pain and Anxiety
Hallucinogens: Psychedelic Drugs

Becoming an Informed Consumer of Psychology:
Identifying Drug and Alcohol Problems

- *What are the major classifications of drugs, and what are their effects?*

Drug Use: The Highs and Lows of Consciousness

[a] _____ affect consciousness by influencing a person's emotions, perceptions, and behavior. Drug use among high school students has declined, as today about half of seniors have used an illegal drug in their lives. The most dangerous drugs are those that are addictive. [b] _____ produce psychological or biological dependence in the user, and the withdrawal of the drug leads to cravings for it.

Any drug that affects the central nervous system by increasing its activity and by increasing heart rate, blood pressure, and muscle tension is called a [c] _____. An example of this kind of drug is *caffeine*, which is found in coffee, soft drinks, and chocolate. Caffeine increases attentiveness and decreases reaction time. Too much caffeine leads to nervousness and insomnia. *Nicotine* is the stimulant found in tobacco products.

[d] _____ and its derivative, crack, are illegal stimulants. This drug produces feelings of well-being, confidence, and alertness when taken in small quantities. Cocaine blocks the reuptake of excess dopamine, which in turn produces pleasurable sensations. Cocaine abuse makes the abusers crave the drug and go on binges of use.

[e] _____ are a group of very strong stimulants that bring about a sense of energy and alertness, talkativeness, confidence, and a mood "high." The amphetamines Dexedrine and Benzedrine are commonly known as speed, and excessive amounts of these drugs can lead to overstimulation of the central nervous system, convulsions, and death.

Drugs that slow the central nervous system are called [f] _____. Feelings of *intoxication* come from taking them in small doses.

One of the most disturbing trends among college students is **[h]** _____.

[i] _____ are a form of depressant drug used to induce sleep and reduce stress. They are addictive and can be deadly when combined with alcohol. Quaalude is an illegal drug similar to barbiturates.

[j] _____ increase relaxation and relieve pain and anxiety. *Morphine* and *heroin* are two powerful narcotics. Morphine is used to reduce pain, but heroin is illegal. Heroin effects include an initial rush followed by a sense of well-being. When this feeling ends, the heroin user feels anxiety and the desire to use the drug again. With each use, more heroin is needed to have any effect. A successful treatment for heroin addiction is the use of *methadone*, a drug that satisfies the cravings but does not produce the high. Methadone is biologically addicting.

[k] _____ are drugs capable of producing hallucinations, or changes in the perceptual processes, the most common of these being marijuana. Marijuana has various effects on people, and there are clear risks associated with long-term heavy marijuana use.

Evaluate

____ 1. caffeine

____ 2. nicotine

____ 3. cocaine

____ 4. amphetamines

____ 5. alcohol

____ 6. intoxication

a. An addictive stimulant present in cigarettes.

b. Strong stimulants that cause a temporary feeling of confidence and alertness but may increase anxiety and appetite loss and, taken over a period of time, suspiciousness and a feeling of persecution.

c. An addictive stimulant that, when taken in small doses, initially creates feelings of confidence, alertness, and well-being, but eventually causes mental and physical deterioration.

d. The most common depressant, which in small doses causes release of tension and feelings of happiness, but in larger amounts can cause emotional and physical instability, memory impairment, and stupor.

e. An addictive stimulant found most abundantly in coffee, tea, soft drinks, and chocolate.

f. A state of drunkenness.

Rethink

14-1   Why have drug education campaigns largely been ineffective in stemming the use of illegal drugs? Should the use of certain now-illegal drugs be made legal? Would it be more effective to stress reduction of drug use rather than a complete prohibition of drug use?

14-2   People often use the word *addiction* loosely, speaking of an addiction to candy or a television show. Can you explain the difference between this type of addiction and a true physiological addiction? Is there a difference between this type of addiction and a psychological addiction?

Spotlight on Terminology and Language—ESL Pointers

Drug Use: The Highs and Lows of Consciousness

Page 161 "A large number of individuals have used more **potent**—and dangerous—psychoactive drugs than coffee and beer; for instance, surveys find that 41 percent of high school seniors have used an illegal drug in the last year."

Potent means powerful. **Potent** drugs are very chemically or medicinally effective.

Page 161 "**Addictive** drugs produce a biological or psychological dependence in the user, and withdrawal from them leads to a **craving** for the drug that, in some cases, may be nearly irresistible."

An **addiction** is a compulsive need for and use of a habit-forming substance, such as caffeine, nicotine, and alcohol.

A **craving** is an intense and urgent or abnormal desire or longing.

Page 161 "Furthermore, it takes longer to become addicted to some drugs than to others, even though the ultimate consequences of addiction may be equally **grave** (Wickelgren, 1988a; Thombs, 1999)."

When something is **grave**, it can cause or involve very bad consequences.

Page 162 "Finally, the sense of helplessness experienced by unemployed individuals trapped in lives of poverty may lead them to try drugs as a way of escaping from the **bleakness** of their lives."

Bleak is something grim and depressing. The situation was **bleak**; it was not hopeful or encouraging.

Page 163 "Caffeine can also bring about an improvement in mood, most likely by **mimicking** the effects of a natural brain chemical, adenosine."

To **mimic** is to simulate and produce the same feelings.

Page 164 "Smokers develop a **dependence** on nicotine, and those who suddenly stop smoking develop strong cravings for the drug."

When you develop a dependence, you rely on something. When this **dependence** is on drugs or caffeine, this may now constitute an addiction. Many workers have a **dependence** on caffeine to help make them alert in the mornings.

Page 164 "Cocaine is inhaled or '**snorted**' through the nose, smoked, or injected directly into the bloodstream."

Snorting is when you force the drug into your system by inhalation.

Page 164 "However, there is a **steep** price to be paid for the pleasurable effects of cocaine."

A **steep** price is an extremely or excessively high price. Do you have knowledge of students who may have experienced a **steep** price for their use of stimulants or hallucinogens?

Page 166 "If taken in too large a quantity, amphetamines overstimulate the central nervous system to such an extent that **convulsions** and death can occur."

Convulsions are abnormally violent and involuntary contractions of the muscles.

Page 167 "Two-thirds of lighter drinkers said that they had had their studying or sleep disturbed by drunk students, and around one-third had been insulted or **humiliated** by a drunk student."

When someone is **humiliated**, this is a destructive insult to his or her self-respect and dignity.

Page 171 "In addition, marijuana smoked during pregnancy may have lasting effects on children who are exposed **prenatally**, although the results are inconsistent."

When children are exposed to drugs **prenatally**, they are exposed before their birth. **Pre-** is a prefix that means before, or earlier than.

Page 172 "Perceptions of colors, sounds, and shapes are altered so much that even the most **mundane** experience—such as looking at the knots in a wooden table—can seem moving and exciting."

Mundane is commonplace, like the **mundane** concerns of day-to-day life. What are some of the **mundane** activities of your daily existence?

Page 172 "Furthermore, people occasionally experience **flashbacks**, in which they hallucinated long after they initially used the drug (Baruss, 2003)."

Flashbacks are when past incidents recur vividly in the mind. A high proportion of the military personnel serving in Iraq are expected to experience **flashbacks** of this experience.

Page 173 "You can also get help from national **hotlines**."

Hotlines are direct telephone lines in constant operational readiness to facilitate immediate communication. A **hotline** is usually a toll-free telephone service available to the public for a specific purpose. What are some reasons you think college students might need to use a **hotline**?

Test your knowledge of this set of modules by answering these questions. These questions have been placed in three Practice Tests. The first two tests consist of questions that will test your recall of factual knowledge. The third test contains questions that are challenging and primarily test for conceptual knowledge and your ability to apply that knowledge. Check your answers and review the feedback using the Answer Key on the following pages of the *Study Guide*.

PRACTICE TEST 1:

1. Consciousness is mainly:
   a. our awareness of nervous system activity.
   b. actions observable by others.
   c. the deeply hidden motives and urges that influence our behavior in subtle ways but of which, for the most part, we are unaware.
   d. our own subjective mental activity of which we are aware.

2. Which stage represents the transition from wakefulness to sleep?
   a. stage 1   c. stage 3
   b. stage 2   d. rapid eye movement (REM)

3. Which sleep stage is characterized by electrical signals with the slowest frequency, waveforms that are very regular, and a sleeper who is unresponsive to external stimuli?
   a. rapid eye movement (REM)   c. stage 3
   b. stage 2   d. stage 4

4. REM sleep is considered paradoxical because:
   a. brain activity is low but eye movement is high.
   b. brain activity is low but muscle activity is high.
   c. eye movement becomes rapid and brain activity is high.
   d. the brain is active but body muscles are paralyzed.

5. The increase in REM sleep during periods after a person has been deprived of it is called:
   a. paradoxical sleep.   c. latent dreaming.
   b. the rebound effect.   d. somnambulism.

6. Freud concluded that dreams are reflections of:
   a. day-to-day activities.
   b. conscious activity.
   c. unconscious wish fulfillment.
   d. our evolutionary heritage.

7. The average person daydreams about _____ percent of the time.
   a. 10   c. 30
   b. 20   d. 40

8. Insomnia is a condition in which a person:
   a. falls asleep uncontrollably.
   b. routinely sleeps more than 12 hours per night.
   c. has difficulty sleeping.
   d. exhibits abnormal brain-wave patterns during rapid eye movement (REM) sleep.

9. Caleb is having difficulty sleeping and breathing simultaneously. His problem is called:
   a. narcolepsy.
   b. sleep apnea.
   c. hypersomnia.
   d. insomnia.

10. Sudden infant death syndrome (SIDS) may be caused by:
    a. narcolepsy
    b. sleep apnea
    c. somnambulism
    d. insomnia

11. People who are easily hypnotized tend to:
    a. enroll in general psychology.
    b. be very aware of the outdoors.
    c. spend a lot of time daydreaming.
    d. be very good at biofeedback.

12. During transcendental meditation, a person repeats a/an _____ over and over again..
    a. mantra
    b. allegory
    c. banta
    d. analogy

13. A psychoactive drug:
    a. affects a person's behavior only if he or she is receptive to mind-expanding experiences.
    b. influences thoughts and perceptions and is usually physically addictive.
    c. affects a person's emotions, perceptions, and behavior.
    d. acts primarily on biological functions such as heart rate and intestinal mobility.

14. _____ is the most common central nervous system depressant.
    a. Penobarbital
    b. Alcohol
    c. Valium
    d. Quaalude

____ 15. rebound effect

____ 16. nightterrors

____ 17. daydreams

____ 18. insomnia

____ 19. sleep apnea

a. An inability to get to or stay asleep.

b. Fantasies people construct while awake.

c. Unusually frightening dreams accompanied by a strong physiological arousal.

d. A sleep disorder characterized by difficulty in breathing and sleeping simultaneously.

e. An increase in REM sleep after one has been deprived of it.

20. Henry has been deprived of REM sleep and experiences a _____, which means he spends more time in the REM stage when allowed to rest undisturbed.

21. There is wide _____ in the amount of sleep people need, some requiring seven or eight hours and others only three hours per night.

22. As far as we know, most people suffer no permanent consequences from temporary _____.

23. A biological rhythm with a period (from peak to peak) of about 24 hours is called _____.

24. Sleep periods characterized by eye movement, loss of muscle tone, and dreaming are called _____.

25. Discuss the competing theories of dreams. Are the theories actually incompatible? Which appears most convincing? Defend your answer.

PRACTICE TEST 2:

1. The deepest stages of sleep are generally experienced:
   a. during the first half of the sleep interval.
   b. during the second half of the sleep interval.
   c. during continuous periods averaging 2 hours each.
   d. while the sleeper dreams.

2. Within a single sleep cycle, as we progress through the stages of sleep toward deepest sleep, the EEG pattern gets:
   a. faster and more regular.   c. slower and lower in amplitude.
   b. faster and more irregular.   d. slower and more regular.

3. Irregular breathing, increased blood pressure, and increased respiration during sleep are characteristics of:
   a. stage 1 sleep.   c. rapid eye movement (REM).
   b. stage 2 sleep.   d. non-rapid eye movement (NREM).

4. The major muscles of the body act as if they are paralyzed during:
   a. stage 1 sleep.   c. stage 4 sleep.
   b. stage 3 sleep.   d. rapid eye movement (REM).

5. The viewpoint that dreams are the outcome of the random exercising of neural circuits in the brain is called the:
   a. unconscious wish fulfillment theory.   c. activation-synthesis theory.
   b. dreams-for-survival theory.   d. reverse learning theory.

6. Freud referred to the storyline of a dream as its:
   a. libidinal content.   c. manifest content.
   b. unconscious content.   d. latent content.

7. Which of the following does **not** describe a common characteristic of daydreams?
   a. fantastic and creative   c. a part of normal consciousness
   b. mundane, ordinary topics   d. a predomination of sexual imagery

8. People pass directly from a conscious, wakeful state to REM sleep if they suffer from:
   a. narcolepsy.   c. somnambulism.
   b. insomnia.   d. rapid eye movement (REM) showers.

9. The uncontrollable need to sleep for short periods that can happen at any time during the day is called:
   a. narcolepsy.   c. hypersomnia.
   b. sleep apnea.   d. insomnia.

10. _____ is the most common hallucinogen in use in the United States.
    a. PCP   c. Cocaine
    b. LSD   d. Marijuana

11. All of the following are typical suggestions for overcoming insomnia **except**:
    a. choose regular bedtimes.
    c. avoid drinks with caffeine.
    b. don't try to go to sleep.
    d. watch TV in bed.

12. _____ is the procedure, introduced in the United States by Maharishi Mahesh Yogi, in which a person focuses on a mantra to reach a different state of consciousness.
    a. Transactional analysis
    c. Exorcism
    b. Zen Buddhism
    d. Transcendental meditation

13. Dr. Dayallan hesitates to use methadone in drug therapy because:
    a. the patient is likely to become addicted to methadone.
    b. methadone eventually causes mental retardation in the patient.
    c. methadone patients are at risk of becoming alcoholics.
    d. methadone users find the marijuana high to be very appealing.

14. Caffeine, nicotine, cocaine, and amphetamines are considered:
    a. anesthetic agents.
    c. anti-anxiety drugs.
    b. central nervous system stimulants.
    d. hallucinogens.

15. The depressants Nembutal, Seconal, and Phenobarbital are forms of:
    a. opiates.
    c. hallucinogens.
    b. barbiturates.
    d. hypnotics.

_____ 16. sudden infant death syndrome (SIDS)

_____ 17. narcolepsy

_____ 18. marijuana

_____ 19. lysergic acid diethylamide (LSD)

a. An uncontrollable need to sleep for short periods during the day.

b. A disorder in which seemingly healthy infants die in their sleep.

c. A common hallucinogen, usually smoked.

d. One of the most powerful hallucinogens, affecting the operation of neurotransmitters in the brain and causing brain cell activity to be altered.

20. Despite compliance when hypnotized, people will not perform antisocial behaviors or _____.

21. People _____ be hypnotized against their will.

22. People who are readily hypnotized often spend an unusual amount of time _____.

23. Psychologists working with seriously ill patients may use hypnosis to control _____.

24. The legal status of information gathered from a person in a hypnotic state is _____ because hypnotic recollections are sometimes inaccurate.

25. Debates regarding the legalization of drugs, especially marijuana, seem to come and go. If that debate were to arise today, what should psychology contribute? What are your feelings about the issue? Should some drugs be legalized or given through prescription? Defend your answer.

PRACTICE TEST 3: Conceptual, Applied, and Challenging Questions

1. Sleep involves four different stages. What is the basis for differentiating these stages of sleep?
    a. They are defined according to the electrical properties recorded by an electroencephalogram (EEG) attached to the sleeper.
    b. They are defined by the amount of time elapsed from the onset of sleep.
    c. They are based on the mental experiences described when sleepers are awakened and asked what they are thinking.
    d. They are characterized by patterns of overt body movements recorded with a video camera that is positioned over the sleeper.

2. Your friend Sandro comes to you concerned about his health after having stayed up for 36 hours straight studying. The most valid thing you could tell him is that:
    a. if he is going to stay up for so long, he should see a doctor regularly.
    b. if he continues to stay up for so long, he will probably get sick.
    c. there will probably be severe long-term consequences.
    d. research has demonstrated that lack of sleep will affect his ability to study.

3. Sharon dreams that Drew climbs a stairway and meets her at the top. According to Freudian dream symbols described in the text, this would probably suggest:
    a. that Sharon would like to start a friendship with Drew.
    b. that Sharon is really afraid to talk to Drew, although she would like to start a friendship.
    c. that Drew and Sharon probably work together in a building where there are stairs.
    d. that Sharon is dreaming of sexual intercourse with Drew.

4. If you had a dream about carrying grapefruits down a long tunnel, Freud would interpret the grapefruit as a dream symbol suggesting a wish to:
    a. take a trip to the tropics.   c. caress a man's genitals.
    b. caress a woman's body.   d. return to the womb.

5. Suppose that a study were done to show that people who are in new surroundings and involved in major unfamiliar activities have more dreams per night than others whose lives have been stable through the same intervals of the study. This study aims to test:
    a. the unconscious wish fulfillment dream theory.
    b. the dreams-for-survival dream theory.
    c. the activation-synthesis dream theory.
    d. the reverse learning dream theory.

6. During the movie, Tanya fantasized about running away and making love to Harrison Ford. She was experiencing a:
    a. nervous breakdown.   c. diurnal emission.
    b. daydream.   d. mantra.

7. Stephanie suffers from frequent sleepwalking. The doctor has told her all but which of the following statements about sleepwalking?
    a. Sleepwalkers should not be awakened.
    b. Sleepwalking occurs in stage 4 sleep.
    c. Sleepwalkers are somewhat aware of their surroundings.
    d. Sleepwalking occurs most frequently in children.

8. In what way are meditation and hypnosis similar?
   a. They are both accompanied by changes in brain activity.
   b. They both result in a decrease in blood pressure.
   c. They are both based on Eastern religious practices.
   d. They both result in total relaxation.

9. Which of the following statements about addiction to drugs is **not** true?
   a. Addiction may be biologically based.
   b. Addictions are primarily caused by an inherited biological liability.
   c. All people, with few exceptions, have used one or more "addictive" drugs in their lifetime.
   d. Addictions may be psychological.

10. Valerie took a tablet someone gave her. She felt a rise in heart rate, a tremor in the hands, and a loss of appetite. She probably took a:
    a. megavitamin.
    b. stimulant.
    c. depressant.
    d. hallucinogen.

11. Which of the following is a hallucinogen?
    a. heroin
    b. cocaine
    c. marijuana
    d. morphine

12. Meghan dreams about wearing a man's leather jacket and parading around town. In Freud's view, the leather jacket and showing off are:
    a. latent content.
    b. manifest content.
    c. irrelevant to the meaning.
    d. day residues.

13. Meghan dreams about wearing a man's leather jacket and parading around town. If the leather jacket is seen as a sexual encounter and the parade as a form of exhibitionism, then in Freud's view, they would have provided insight into:
    a. latent content.
    b. manifest content.
    c. activation processes.
    d. day residues.

14. Betsy has just been hypnotized. Which of the following acts is she **least** likely to commit?
    a. Completely undress
    b. Flirt with her escort
    c. Recall a past life
    d. Stand on a chair and crow like a rooster

15. Which of the following are narcotic drugs?
    a. LSD and marijuana
    b. morphine and heroin
    c. barbiturates and alcohol
    d. amphetamines and cocaine

_____ 16. barbiturates

_____ 17. morphine

_____ 18. heroin

_____ 19. methadone

_____ 20. hallucinogen

a. A powerful narcotic, usually injected, that gives an initial rush of good feeling but leads eventually to anxiety and depression; extremely addictive.

b. Addictive depressants used to induce sleep and reduce stress, the abuse of which, especially when combined with alcohol, can be deadly.

c. A drug that is capable of producing changes in the perceptual process, or hallucinations.

d. A chemical used to detoxify heroin addicts.

e. Derived from the poppy flower, a powerful narcotic that reduces pain and induces sleep.

21. Psychoactive drugs work primarily by affecting the _____.

22. After 6 months of using drugs, Matt developed a _____ and needed to take more and more drugs to achieve the same effect.

23. Amphetamines, cocaine, caffeine, and nicotine are all examples of _____.

24. The effects of drugs are often the result of their influence on the brain's _____ levels.

25. Physical and _____ factors influence the way a particular individual reacts to the use of a drug.

26. Although some consider hypnosis a result of dissociative processes, others believe it is a function of normal sociocognitive processes. Describe the nature of hypnosis and then explain each theory.

■ Answer Key: Modules 12, 13, and 14

Module 12:	Evaluate	Module 13:	Module 14:
[a] Consciousness	Test A	[a] Hypnosis	[a] Psychoactive drugs
[b] electroencephalogram (EEG)	1. d	[b] Meditation	[b] Addictive drugs
[c] stage 1 sleep	2. c	[c] mantra	[c] stimulant
[d] Stage 2 sleep	3. e	[d] physiological	[d] Cocaine
[e] Stage 3 sleep	4. a	changes	[e] Amphetamines
[f] Stage 4 sleep	5. b		[f] depressants
[g] rapid eye movement (REM)			[g] Alcohol
sleep	Test B	Evaluate	[h] binge drinking
[h] Circadian rhythms	6. a	1. a	[i] Barbiturates
[i] Night terrors	7. e	2. d	[j] Narcotics
[j] unconscious wish fulfillment	8. c	3. c	[k] Hallucinogens
theory	9. d	4. e	
[k] latent content of dreams	10. b	5. b	Evaluate
[l] manifest content of dreams			1. e
[m] reverse learning theory			2. a
[n] dreams-for-survival theory			3. c
[o] activation-synthesis theory			4. b
			5. d
			6. f

Selected Rethink Answers

12-2   List: (1) Wish Fulfillment Theory (Freud)—states that our dreams are one-way; our unconscious gets messages to us that our conscious state can't realize.
(2) Reverse Learning Theory—dreams flush out unnecessary information.
(3) Dreams-for-Survival Theory—permit information needed for survival to be reconsidered and reprocessed; may help us to remember.
(4) Activation-Synthesis Theory—(Hobson) brain makes sense of chaotic memories, could also be reflection of unconscious wishes.

Because all theories suggest purposes that help organize information and help us reflect on information, it might be dangerous to eliminate dreaming altogether. For society, if many people made the choice and took the pill and theories held true about dreams providing time for the organization of information and dreams being an avenue to our unconscious, not dreaming could cause a real deficit in the way we function as a society.

13-2   Physical and Psychological Effects of Meditation—Studies show long-term meditation may improve health and longevity. Oxygen use decreases, heart and blood pressure decline.

Psychological Effects—although we feel relaxed when we meditate, it does not suggest that we are overburdened physically or psychologically, but it may suggest that there is a stronger mind-body connection than we previously realized. Meditation may allow us greater opportunities to relax and take time out from our day.

Practice Test 1:

1. d   mod. 12 p. 140
a.   Incorrect. We are not aware of the functioning of our nervous system.
b.   Incorrect. Our individual consciousness is not observable by others.
c.   Incorrect. These are unconscious forces.
*d. Correct. This is the definition of our personal conscious experience.

2. a   mod. 12 p. 141
*a. Correct. The transition to sleep occurs in stage 1.
b.   Incorrect. See answer a.
c.   Incorrect. See answer a.
d.   Incorrect. The occurrence of REM is associated with dreaming, while the transition to sleep normally occurs in stage 1.

119

3.   d   mod. 12 p. 142
a.   Incorrect. REM sleep has very irregular waveforms; this describes stage 4 sleep.
b.   Incorrect. Stage 2 is characterized by electrical signals that are faster than stages 3 or 4.
c.   Incorrect. Stage 3 is characterized by electrical signals that are faster than stage 4.
*d. Correct. This is an accurate description of stage 4 sleep.

4.   d   mod. 12 p. 143
a.   Incorrect. Both brain activity and eye movement are high.
b.   Incorrect. Brain activity is high, and muscle activity is low.
c.   Incorrect. True, but this is not why it is called paradoxical.
*d. Correct. The brain is active, but the body is completely inactive.

5.   b   mod. 12 p. 143
a.   Incorrect. Paradoxical sleep refers to the period of REM during which the brain is active and the body is paralyzed.
*b. Correct. After sleep deprivation, the sleeper recovers lost REM time by having extra REM sleep for several nights.
c.   Incorrect. Latent dreaming would be hidden dreaming, which is not associated with REM.
d.   Incorrect. Somnambulism occurs most often in stage 4 sleep, and it is not a result of sleep deprivation.

6.   c   mod. 12 p. 147
a.   Incorrect. They include daily activities, but this is not what interested Freud.
b.   Incorrect. They tend to reflect unconscious activity.
*c. Correct. Unconscious and repressed wishes often find their way into the content of dreams.
d.   Incorrect. Freud might accept this view, but he was interested in the content of current dreams.

7.   a   mod. 12 p. 152
*a. Correct. This includes during work, school, and any other activity.
b.   Incorrect. People daydream at work, at school, and during any other activity about 10 percent of the time.
c.   Incorrect. See answer b.
d.   Incorrect. You might want to reappraise what you do with your time. People, on average, daydream at work, at school, and during any other activity about 10 percent of the time.

8.   c   mod. 12 p. 153
a.   Incorrect. Falling asleep uncontrollably is called narcolepsy.
b.   Incorrect. This is an unusual amount of sleep for an adult, but infants and small children sleep this much.
*c. Correct. Insomnia simply refers to having difficulty falling asleep or returning to sleep once awakened during the night.
d.   Incorrect. This is not a condition associated with insomnia.

9.   b   mod. 12 p. 150
a.   Incorrect. The symptom of narcolepsy is falling into REM sleep uncontrollably.
*b. Correct. Associated with snoring, the gasping for breath often awakens the person suffering from sleep apnea.
c.   Incorrect. This refers to excessive sleep.
d.   Incorrect. Insomnia is difficulty falling asleep and staying asleep.

10. b   mod. 12 p. 150
a.   Incorrect. Narcolepsy has not been associated with sudden infant death syndrome.
*b. Correct. Sleep apnea is thought to be the cause of sudden infant death syndrome—in effect, the child forgets to breathe.
c.   Incorrect. Somnambulism refers to sleep walking.
d.   Incorrect. Insomnia involves difficulties falling asleep.

11. c   mod. 13 p. 155
a.   Incorrect. "You will encourage your friends to enroll in this class."
b.   Incorrect. Most of us are aware of the outdoors.
*c. Correct. Frequent daydreamers do appear to be more easily hypnotized than infrequent daydreamers.
d.   Incorrect. This correlation has not been studied.

12. a   mod. 13 p. 157
*a. Correct. The repeated word is called a mantra.
b.   Incorrect. See answer a.
c.   Incorrect. See answer a.
d.   Incorrect. See answer a.

13. c   mod. 13 p. 161
a.   Incorrect. The drug works without regard to the person's willingness to be affected.
b.   Incorrect. Not all psychoactive drugs are addictive.
*c. Correct. Psychoactive drugs affect all three.
d.   Incorrect. Psychoactive drugs affect emotions, perceptions, and behavior.

14. b   mod. 13 p. 165
a.   Incorrect. The barbiturate phenobarbital is not as common as other depressants.
*b. Correct. Alcohol is the most common depressant.
c.   Incorrect. Valium is an antianxiety drug that is commonly prescribed.
d.   Incorrect. This is a common depressant, but not the most common.

15. e   mod. 12 p. 144
16. c   mod. 12 p. 151
17. b   mod. 12 p. 152
18. a   mod. 12 p. 153
19. d   mod. 12 p. 150

20. rebound effect   mod. 12 p. 144
21. variety   mod. 12 p. 144
22. sleep deprivation   mod. 12 p. 144
23. circadian rhythm   mod. 12 p. 151
24. REM sleep   mod. 12 p. 143

25. The major positions that should be considered in your answer are the following:
■   The psychoanalytic view argues that the symbols of dreams reflect deep meanings, many of which are unfulfilled wishes or repressed conflicts.
■   The opposing views hold that dreaming is a natural process of cleaning excess material from the day, a survival mechanism, or a by-product of random electrical activity in the brain. These views may not necessarily be incompatible.

Practice Test 2:
1.   a   mod. 12 p. 142
*a. Correct. Later in the night's sleep cycle, sleep is less deep.
b.   Incorrect. See answer a.
c.   Incorrect. See answer a.
d.   Incorrect. Dreams occur at the least deep levels of sleep.

2.   d   mod. 12 p. 142
a.   Incorrect. It gets slower and more regular.
b.   Incorrect. See answer a.
c.   Incorrect. See answer a.
*d. Correct. The waveforms during the slowest phase are called delta waves.

3.   c   mod. 12 p. 143
a.   Incorrect. During stage 1, breathing becomes more regular, blood pressure drops, and respiration slows.
b.   Incorrect. During stage 2, breathing continues to become more regular, blood pressure continues to drop, and respiration continues to slow.
*c. Correct. And this happens while the voluntary muscles are inhibited to the point of paralysis.
d.   Incorrect. During non-REM sleep, breathing becomes more regular, blood pressure drops, and respiration slows.

4.   d   mod. 12 p. 143
a.   Incorrect. Paralysis occurs during REM sleep.
b.   Incorrect. See answer a.
c.   Incorrect. See answer a.
*d. Correct. Ironically, REM sleep is also characterized by irregular breathing, increased blood pressure, and increased respiration.

5.   c   mod. 12 p. 149
a.   Incorrect. This view sees dreams as a means for repressed desires to be expressed.
b.   Incorrect. This approach understands dreams as a means of making sense of the information gathered throughout the day.
*c. Correct. This view accepts the notion of random activity as the source for dreams.
d.   Incorrect. Reverse-learning implies undoing, or "cleaning," unnecessary information.

6.   c   mod. 12 p. 147
a.   Incorrect. Libidinal content would be sexual and may or may not be the obvious storyline of the dream.
b.   Incorrect. The unconscious content of dreams is most often the hidden, or latent, content.
*c. Correct. This is the term he used for the storyline of the dream.
d.   Incorrect. The latent content is the hidden content of the dream.

7.   d   mod. 12 p. 152
a.   Incorrect. Daydreams are often a source of creative inspiration for the dreamer.
b.   Incorrect. We often daydream about the most mundane things, like doing laundry or writing answer explanations.
c.   Incorrect. Daydreams are very much a part of our normal conscious experiences.
*d. Correct. Few daydreams are sexual in nature (surprised?).

8. a   mod. 12 p. 151
*a. Correct. A narcoleptic can fall asleep at any time, although stress does seem to contribute to the narcoleptic's symptoms.
b. Incorrect. Insomnia involves difficulty getting to sleep or staying asleep.
c. Incorrect. Somnambulism is also known as sleepwalking.
d. Incorrect. This concept is from some sci-fi movie, no doubt.

9. a   mod. 12 p. 151
*a. Correct. Narcolepsy is uncontrollable.
b. Incorrect. Sleep apnea will make one tired throughout the next day because of the frequent awakening through the night.
c. Incorrect. Hypersomnia is excessive sleep at night.
d. Incorrect. Insomnia involves difficulty getting to sleep or staying asleep.

10. d   mod. 13 p. 170
a. Incorrect. PCP is common, but not the most common.
b. Incorrect. LSD is common, but not the most common.
c. Incorrect. Cocaine is a stimulant, not a hallucinogen.
*d. Correct. Marijuana is by far the most commonly used hallucinogen.

11. d   mod. 12 p. 153
a. Incorrect. A regular bedtime makes for a habit of falling asleep.
b. Incorrect. Here we apply "reverse" psychology on ourselves.
c. Incorrect. Caffeine contributes to sleeplessness.
*d. Correct. The TV belongs in the living room, not the bedroom. TV is usually stimulating, not restful.

12. d   mod. 13 p. 157
a. Incorrect. Transactional analysis comes from Berne's *I'm O.K., You're O.K.*
b. Incorrect. Zen Buddhists practice meditation, though.
c. Incorrect. Not quite.
*d. Correct. The name for this process is transcendental meditation, and research has shown that the effects can also be achieved through practiced relaxation methods.

13. a   mod. 13 p. 170
*a. Correct. Methadone produces an addiction, but it does not have the psychoactive properties of heroin.
b. Incorrect. Methadone does not cause mental retardation.
c. Incorrect. Everyone is at risk, but methadone does not increase the risk.
d. Incorrect. Most drug users find the marijuana high to be appealing, but nothing about the methadone causes this.

14. b   mod. 13 p. 163
a. Incorrect. Because they stimulate the nervous system, they do not have an anesthetic effect.
*b. Correct. Each of these is considered a stimulant.
c. Incorrect. In some cases, even small doses of these drugs can cause anxiety.
d. Incorrect. With extreme doses, hallucinations are possible, but they do not occur in typical doses.

15. b   mod. 13 p. 169
a. Incorrect. An opiate is a narcotic.
*b. Correct. These are all classes of the depressant group known as barbiturates.
c. Incorrect. These drugs do not cause hallucinations under normal circumstances.
d. Incorrect. These drugs do not cause hypnosis.

16. b   mod. 12 p. 150
17. a   mod. 12 p. 151
18. c   mod. 13 p. 170
19. d   mod. 13 p. 172

20. self-destructive acts   mod. 13 p. 155
21. cannot   mod. 13 p. 155
23. daydreaming   mod. 13 p. 152
23. pain   mod. 13 p. 157
24. Unresolved   mod. 13 p. 157

25.
- Identify the drugs that have been involved in this issue; include marijuana, but also, some have argued that drug use should be completely legalized and viewed as a medical or psychological problem.
- State your view, identifying which drug(s) should be decriminalized and which should not. Many people suggest that the medical benefits of some drugs cannot be explored and used because of their status. Other reasons should be offered as well. For instance, the use of some drugs can be considered victimless, although the drug trade has many victims.
- If you believe that all drugs should remain illegal, then support your reasoning. Harm to society and to individuals is a common argument. Provide examples.

Practice Test 3:

1. a   mod. 12 p. 142
*a. Correct. The electrical properties are recorded as waveforms by the EEG, and thus are referred to as brain waves.
b. Incorrect. The time from sleep to stage is not a factor in defining the stages, and people go through several cycles of the stages each night.
c. Incorrect. Stage 4 and REM sleep have specific sleep events associated with them, but these are not used to define the stages.
d. Incorrect. With the exception of REM sleep, when the sleeper is quite still, the body movements are generally the same from one stage to another.

2. d   mod. 12 p. 145
a. Incorrect. There are no long-term effects from sleep deprivation.
b. Incorrect. He is unlikely to get sick, although he might make mistakes at work and be prone to accidents elsewhere.
c. Incorrect. There are no long-term consequences for staying awake 36 hours.
*d. Correct. If he is staying awake to study, then he might be jeopardizing his grade; it would be more effective to break the study into smaller parts and get some rest.

3. d   mod. 12 p. 148
a. Incorrect. Probably more than a friendship.
b. Incorrect. Nothing in the dream suggests any anxiety about talking to Jim.
c. Incorrect. This is a possible reading of the manifest content of the dream, but a Freudian approach would not differ from any other approach on this view.
*d. Correct. Climbing stairs is an act symbolic of sexual intercourse.

4. b   mod. 12 p. 148
a. Incorrect. This may be what it means, but it is a strange way of making the image clear, and besides, this is not what a Freudian would see.
*b. Correct. Grapefruits can generally be viewed as feminine bodies, but more specifically as breasts.
c. Incorrect. This is not a likely interpretation.
d. Incorrect. The trip down the tunnel may have a quality of a wish to return to the womb, but the grapefruits do not fit the image.

5. b   mod. 12 p. 149
a. Incorrect. Although the increase in anxiety would lead to additional wish-fulfillment types of dreams.
*b. Correct. The need to make sense of environmental, survival-oriented information makes this choice the better candidate.
c. Incorrect. The random activity would be just as random in either circumstance.
d. Incorrect. Would they not dream less because more of the information from the day was important and relevant?

6. b   mod. 12 p. 152
a. Incorrect. This is not a common fantasy during nervous breakdowns.
*b. Correct. Fantasies about escape are common in daydreams.
c. Incorrect. Because she was in class, and probably not asleep, a nighttime emission is unlikely.
d. Incorrect. A mantra is a word repeated during meditation.

7. a   mod. 12 p. 151
*a. Correct. Sleepwalkers can be awakened, but they will probably be confused and disoriented.
b. Incorrect. Sleepwalking most often occurs in stage 4 sleep.
c. Incorrect. If awakened, sleepwalkers can have a vague sense of where they are and what they were doing.
d. Incorrect. Sleepwalking is common throughout age groups.

8. a   mod. 13 p. 157
*a. Correct. The changes in brain activity can be recorded on an EEG.
b. Incorrect. They both may result in a decrease in blood pressure, but they may not.
c. Incorrect. Hypnosis is an invention of European origin.
d. Incorrect. "Total relaxation" is a bit overstated.

9. b   mod. 13 p. 161
a. Incorrect. Addiction may be either or both biologically and psychologically based.
*b. Correct. This may be true in cases of alcoholism, but other addictions arise from the nature of the body-drug interaction.
c. Incorrect. There is no foundation for this statement.
d. Incorrect. Addiction may be either or both biologically and psychologically based.

10. b   mod. 13 p. 163
a. Incorrect. However, that must be some vitamin!
*b. Correct. This is what stimulants do.
c. Incorrect. Depressants slow the heart rate.
d. Incorrect. Among other things, a hallucinogen could cause these symptoms (among many others), but not necessarily.

11. c   mod. 13 p. 170
a. Incorrect. Heroin is a narcotic.
b. Incorrect. Cocaine is a stimulant.
*c. Correct. Marijuana is a hallucinogen.
d. Incorrect. Morphine is a narcotic.

12. b   mod. 12 p. 148
a. Incorrect. The latent content would be what the jacket and showing off might symbolize.
*b. Correct. This is what she actually did in her dream.
c. Incorrect. The manifest content can be relevant to the meaning because it contains the symbols.
d. Incorrect. These would be day residues only if this is what she did the day before.

13. a   mod. 12 p. 148
*a. Correct. As symbols, they hold the keys to the repressed or latent content of the dream.
b. Incorrect. The wearing of the jacket and the parading were the manifest content.
c. Incorrect. Activation process is not relevant to the dream interpretation.
d. Incorrect. He would only need to ask Meghan about the daytime activities to make this determination.

14. a   mod. 13 p. 155
*a. Correct. Unless she is an exhibitionist, she would not undress.
b. Incorrect. With slightly lowered inhibitions, she could easily flirt.
c. Incorrect. She is likely to recall a past life, even if she does not have one.
d. Incorrect. Making people do stupid animal tricks is a common hypnotic activity.

15. b   mod 16 p. 165
a. Incorrect. These are hallucinogens.
*b. Correct. These are the two primary examples of narcotics given in the text.
c. Incorrect. These are depressants.
d. Incorrect. These are stimulants.

16. b   mod. 14 p. 165
17. e   mod. 14 p. 165
18. a   mod. 14 p. 165
19. d   mod. 14 p. 165
20. c   mod. 14 p. 165

21. consciousness   mod. 14 p. 161
22. tolerance   mod. 14 p. 169
23. stimulants   mod. 14 p. 165
24. neurotransmitter   mod. 14 p. 161
25. Psychological   mod. 14 p. 161

26. Hypnosis is a state of heightened susceptibility to the suggestions of others.
- Dissociative processes involve a split in consciousness in which one part of the brain operates independently of another.
- Sociocognitive processes regard hypnotic behavior as falling on a continuum of normal and social and cognitive processes. It is the result of an interaction between the personal abilities and beliefs of the subject and the social influence of the hypnotist.

Learning

Overview

This set of modules presents the approaches that psychologists use in the study of learning. To understand what learning is, you must distinguish between performance changes caused by maturation and changes brought about by experience. Similarly, you must distinguish short-term changes in behavior caused by factors other than learning, such as declines in performance resulting from fatigue or lack of effort, from performance changes resulting from actual learning. Some psychologists have approached learning by considering it as simply any change in behavior.

Module 15 examines classical conditioning, the type of learning that explains responses ranging from a dog salivating when it hears the can opener to the emotions we feel when our national anthem is played. Concepts such as extinction, stimulus generalization, and stimulus discrimination are defined and explained.

Module 16 focuses on operant conditioning, a form of learning in which a voluntary behavior is strengthened or weakened through reinforcement. Theories that consider how learning is a consequence of rewarding circumstances are examined. Examples of primary and secondary reinforcers, along with an explanation of positive and negative reinforcers and punishment, are presented. The major categories of reinforcement schedules, shaping, and the biological constraints on the ability of the organism to learn are discussed.

Module 17 presents the cognitive-social approaches to learning. Latent learning, cognitive maps, and the imitation of observed behavior are all discussed, with a focus on the impact a person's cultural background and unique pattern of abilities play in the learning process.

To further investigate the topics covered in this chapter, you can visit the related Web sites by visiting the following link: www.mhhe.com/feldmanup6-06links.

Prologue: A Friend Named Bo
Looking Ahead

Module 15:
Classical Conditioning

The Basics of Classical Conditioning
Applying Conditioning Principles to Human Behavior
Extinction
Generalization and Discrimination
Beyond Traditional Classical Conditioning: Challenging Basic Assumptions

- *What is learning?*
- *How do we learn to form associations between stimuli and responses?*

Classical Conditioning

[a] _____ is distinguished from *maturation* on the basis of whether the resulting change in behavior is a consequence of experience (learning) or of growth (maturation). Short-term changes in performance, the key measure of learning, can also result from fatigue, lack of effort, and other factors that are not reflections of learning. According to some people, learning can only be inferred indirectly.

Ivan Pavlov's studies concerning the physiology of the digestive processes led him to discover the basic principles of [b] _____, a process in which an organism learns to respond to a stimulus that did not bring about the response earlier. An original study involved Pavlov's training a dog to salivate when a tuning fork was sounded. In this process, the tuning fork's sound is considered the [c] _____ because it does not bring about the response of interest. The meat powder, which does cause salivation, is called the [d] _____. The salivation, when it occurs because of the presence of the meat powder (UCS), is called the [e] _____. The conditioning process requires repeated pairing of the UCS and the neutral stimulus. After training is complete, the neutral stimulus—now called the [f] _____—will now bring about the UCR, now called the [g] _____. Pavlov noted that the neutral stimulus had to precede the UCS by no more than several seconds for the conditioning to be the most effective.

One of the more famous applications of classical conditioning techniques to humans is the case of the 11-month-old infant, Albert. Albert was taught to fear a laboratory rat, to which he had shown no fear initially, by striking a bar behind him whenever he approached the rat.

The process of ending the association of the UCS and the CS is called **[h]** _____, which occurs when a previously learned response decreases and disappears. If the tuning fork is repeatedly sounded without the meat powder being presented, the dog will eventually stop salivating. Extinction is the basis for the treatment principle called **[i]** _____, which is used to treat phobias. Systematic desensitization requires the repeated presentation of the frightening stimulus (a CS) without the presentation of the occurrence of the negative consequences.

When a CR has been extinguished, and a period of time has passed without the presentation of the CS, a phenomenon called **[j]** _____ can occur. The CS is presented and the previously extinguished response recurs, although it is usually weaker than in the original training and can be extinguished again more easily.

[k] _____ takes place when a conditioned response occurs in the presence of a stimulus that is similar to the original conditioned stimulus. In the case of baby Albert, the fear response was generalized to white furry things, including a white-bearded Santa Claus mask. **[l]** _____ occurs when an organism learns to differentiate (discriminate) one stimulus from another and responds only to one stimulus and not the others.

When a conditioned stimulus has been established and is then repeatedly paired with another neutral stimulus until the conditioned response becomes conditioned to the new stimulus, then **[m]** _____ has occurred. Some investigators have used the concept of higher-order conditioning to explain how people develop and maintain prejudices against members of racial and ethnic groups.

Many of the fundamental assumptions of classical conditioning have been challenged. One challenge has been to question the length of the interval between the neutral stimulus and the unconditioned stimulus. Garcia found that nausea caused by radiation, a state that occurred hours after exposure, could be associated with water drunk that has unusual characteristics or with water drunk in a particular place. Garcia's findings that the association could be made with delays as long as 8 hours is a direct challenge to the idea that the pairing must be made within several seconds to be effective.

Evaluate

_____ 1. neutral stimulus

_____ 2. unconditioned stimulus
          (UCS)

_____ 3. unconditioned response
          (UCR)

_____ 4. conditioned stimulus
          (CS)

_____ 5. conditioned response
          (CR)

a. A stimulus that brings about a response without having been learned.

b. A stimulus that, before conditioning, has no effect on the desired response.

c. A once-neutral stimulus that has been paired with an unconditioned stimulus to bring about a response formerly caused only by the unconditioned stimulus.

d. A response that, after conditioning, follows a previously neutral stimulus (e.g., salivation at the sound of a tuning fork).

e. A response that is natural and needs no training (e.g., salivation at the smell of food).

Rethink

15-1 Can you think of ways that classical conditioning is used by politicians? Advertisers? Moviemakers? Do ethical issues arise from any of these uses?

15-2 Is it likely that Albert, Watson's experimental subject, went through life afraid of Santa Claus? Describe what probably happened to prevent this behavior.

Spotlight on Terminology and Language—ESL Pointers

Classical Conditioning

Page 179 "**Classical conditioning** is one of a number of different types of learning that psychologists have identified, but a general definition **encompasses** them all: Learning is a relatively permanent change in behavior that is brought about by experience."

Classical conditioning is also called Pavlovian conditioning. **Encompass** is to include.

Page 182 "In a now-**infamous** case study, psychologist John B. Watson and colleague Rosalie Rayner (1920) showed that classical conditioning was at the root of such fears by conditioning an 11-month-old infant named Albert to be afraid of rats."

Infamous means well-known, renowned. An **infamous** activity is generally perceived negatively, something that has an extremely bad reputation. This **infamous** research study would not be allowed to be replicated in psychology laboratories today because of the questionable ethics of this research.

Page 182 "We do know that Watson, the experimenter, has been **condemned** for using ethically questionable procedures and that such studies would never be conducted today."

You **condemn** something when you state that it's wrong, or unacceptable.

Page 184 "If two stimuli are sufficiently distinct from one another that one **evokes** a conditioned response but the other does not, we can say that stimulus discrimination has occurred."

To **evoke** is to elicit a response.

Page 184 "For example, according to Pavlov, the process of linking stimuli and responses occurs in a **mechanistic**, unthinking way."

When you explain behavior **mechanistically**, you're explaining it **mechanically**, explaining human behavior and other natural processes in terms of physical causes and processes.

Page 185 "The ease with which animals can be conditioned to avoid certain kinds of dangerous stimuli, such as **tainted** food, supports evolutionary theory."

Tainted food is contaminated food, polluted food. When you eat **tainted** food, you often get sick.

Page 185 "Consequently, organisms that ingest **unpalatable** foods (whether coyotes that eat a carcass laced with a drug or humans who suffer food poisoning after eating spoiled sushi in a restaurant) are likely to avoid similar foods in the future, making their survival more likely (Steinmetz, Kim & Thompson, 2003)."

When food is **unpalatable**, it is not good food. It does not taste good. Have you ever put something in your mouth that you had to spit out right away, because the taste was bad? This food was **unpalatable**.

Module 16: Operant Conditioning

Thorndike's Law of Effect
The Basics of Operant Conditioning
Positive Reinforcers, Negative Reinforcers, and Punishment
The Pros and Cons of Punishment: Why Reinforcement Beats Punishment
Schedules of Reinforcement: Timing Life's Rewards
Discrimination and Generalization in Operant Conditioning
Shaping: Reinforcing What Doesn't Come Naturally
Biological Constraints on Learning: You Can't Teach an Old Dog Just Any Trick

Becoming an Informed Consumer of Psychology:
Using Behavioral Analysis and Behavior Modification

- *What is the role of reward and punishment in learning?*
- *What are some practical methods fro bringing about change, both in ourselves and in others?*

Operant Conditioning

[a] _____ is learning in which the response is strengthened or weakened according to whether it has positive or negative consequences. The term "operant" suggests that the organism *operates* on the environment in a deliberate manner to gain a desired result.

Edward L. Thorndike found that a cat would learn to escape from a cage by performing specific actions in order to open a door that allows it access to food, a positive consequence of the behavior. Thorndike formulated the [b] _____, stating that responses with satisfying results would be repeated, and those with less satisfying results would be less likely to be repeated.

[c] _____ is the process by which a stimulus increases the probability that a preceding behavior will be repeated. Releasing the food by pecking is a reinforcement, and the food is called a [d] _____, which is any stimulus that increases the probability that a preceding behavior will be repeated. A [e] _____ satisfies a biological need without regard to prior experience. A [f] _____ is a stimulus that reinforces because of its association with a primary reinforcer.

Reinforcers are also distinguished as positive or negative. [g] _____ bring about an increase in the preceding response. [h] _____ lead to an increase in a desired response when they are *removed*.

Negative reinforcement requires that an individual take an action to remove an undesirable condition. Negative reinforcement is used in [i] _____, where an organism learns to escape from an aversive situation, and in [j] _____, where the organism learns to act to avoid the aversive situation. [k] _____ refers to the use of an aversive stimulus, by adding it to the environment, in order to *decrease* the probability that a behavior will be repeated. Punishment includes the removal of something positive, such as the loss of a privilege.

The frequency and timing of reinforcement depends on the use of [l] _____. With [m] _____, the behavior is reinforced every time it occurs. [n] _____ describes the technique of using reinforcement some of the time but not for every response. Partial reinforcement schedules maintain behavior longer than continuous reinforcement before extinction occurs.

A [o] _____ delivers a reinforcement after a certain number of responses. A [p] _____ delivers reinforcement on the basis of a varying number of responses. The number of responses often remains close to an average. The fixed- and variable-ratio schedules depend on a *number* of responses, and the fixed- and variable-interval schedules depend on an *amount of time*. [q] _____ deliver reinforcements to the first behavior occurring after a set interval, or period, of time. [r] _____ deliver reinforcement after a varying interval of time. Fixed intervals are like weekly paychecks; variable intervals are like pop quizzes.

Discrimination and generalization are achieved in operant conditioning through [s] _____. In stimulus control training, a behavior is reinforced only in the presence of specific stimuli. The specific stimulus is called a *discriminative stimulus*, one that signals the likelihood of a particular behavior being reinforced.

[t] _____ refers to a behavior that involves the repetition of elaborate rituals. Learning theory accounts for superstitious behavior as behavior that occurs before a reinforcement but is coincidental to the behavior that leads to the reinforcement.

When a complex behavior is desired, a trainer may shape the desired behavior by rewarding closer and closer approximations of the behavior. Many complex human and animal skills are acquired through [u] _____.

Sometimes learning is constrained by behaviors that are biologically innate, or inborn. Not all behaviors can be taught to all animals equally well because of these *biological constraints*. Pigs might root a disk around their cages, and raccoons might horde and then clean similar disks.

Evaluate

_____ 1.   operant conditioning

_____ 2.   primary reinforcer

_____ 3.   secondary reinforcer

_____ 4.   positive reinforcer

_____ 5.   negative reinforcer

_____ 6.   punishment

_____ 7.   aversive stimuli

a.   An unpleasant or painful stimulus that is added to the environment after a certain behavior occurs, decreasing the likelihood that the behavior will occur again.

b.   Unpleasant or painful stimuli.

c.   A reward that satisfies a biological need (e.g., hunger or thirst) and works naturally.

d.   A stimulus added to the environment that brings about an increase in the response that preceded it.

e.   A stimulus that becomes reinforcing by its association with a primary reinforcer (e.g., money, which allows us to obtain food, a primary reinforcer).

f.   A stimulus whose removal is reinforcing, leading to a greater probability that the response bringing about this removal will occur again.

g.   A voluntary response is strengthened or weakened, depending on its positive or negative consequences.

Rethink

16-1   How might operant conditioning be used to address serious personal concerns, such as smoking and unhealthy eating?

16-2   Using the scientific literature as a guide, what would you tell parents who wish to know if the routine use of physical punishment is a necessary and acceptable form of child-rearing?

Spotlight on Terminology and Language—ESL Pointers

Operant Conditioning

Page 187 "Operant conditioning is at work when we learn that **toiling** industriously can bring about a raise or that studying hard results in good grades."

Toiling is working hard.

Page 188 "Thorndike's early research served as the foundation for the work of one of the twentieth century's most **influential** psychologists, B. F. Skinner, who died in 1990."

Influential means significant, prominent. An influential person is often a leader. Who have been some of your **influential** mentors?

Page 188 "You may have heard of the Skinner box, a **chamber** with a highly controlled environment that was used to study operant conditioning processes with laboratory animals."

A **chamber** is an enclosed space designed for experimental purposes.

Page 189 "Reinforcement is the process by which a stimulus increases the **probability** that a preceding behavior will be repeated."

When the **probability** of an act is increased, this means that the circumstance is likely to occur again.

Page 190 "In contrast, when a teenager is told she is 'grounded' and will no longer be able to use the family car because of her poor grades, punishment is in the form of the removal of something pleasant."

When adolescents are **grounded**, their activities are confined to a limited area, often their home or their room.

Page 191 "For instance, a parent may not have a second chance to warn a child not to run into a busy street, and so punishing the first **incidence** of this behavior may prove to be wise."

An **incidence** is an occurrence of an action or situation.

Page 191 "Moreover, the use of punishment to **suppress** behavior, even temporarily, provides an opportunity to reinforce a person for **subsequently** behaving in a more desirable way."

Suppress is to stop behavior. **Subsequently** is following in time, coming later.

Page 191 "Several disadvantages make the routine use of punishment **questionable**."

When something is **questionable**, it is doubted and challenged.

Page 194 "Students' study habits often **exemplify** this reality."

Students' study habits are an **example** of this behavior.

Page 195 "There are many complex behaviors, ranging from auto repair to zoo management, that we would not expect to occur naturally as part of anyone's **spontaneous** behavior."

Spontaneous behavior is voluntary behavior. It is not premeditated or planned.

Page 195 "Shaping is the process of teaching a complex behavior by rewarding closer and closer **approximations** of the desired behavior."

An **approximation** is an inexact result coming closer in degree to the quality that is desired.

Page 196 "Instead, there are biological **constraints**, built-in limitations in the ability of animals to learn particular behaviors."

A **constraint** is something that restricts you from a given course of action. A biological **constraint** is a built-in restriction.

Page 198 "If the target behaviors are not **monitored**, there is no way of knowing whether the program has actually been successful."

To **monitor** something is to check systematically, usually to collect data. Do you see a purpose for public or governmental **monitoring** of any specific behaviors?

Module 17: Cognitive-Social Approaches to Learning

Latent Learning
Observational Learning: Learning Through Imitation

Exploring Diversity:
Does Culture Influence How We Learn?

Applying Psychology in the 21st Century:
Violence in Television and Video Games:
Does the Media's Message Matter?

- *What is the role of cognition and thought in learning?*

Cognitive-Social Approaches to Learning

The approach that views learning in terms of thought processes is called **[a]** _____.
This approach does not deny the importance of classical and operant conditioning. It includes the

consideration of unseen mental processes as well. **[b]** _____ is behavior
that is learned but not demonstrated until reinforcement is provided for demonstrating the
behavior. Latent learning occurs when rats are allowed to wander around a maze without any
reward at the end, but once they learn that a reinforcement is available, they will quickly find
their way through the maze even though they were been reinforced for doing so in the past. The

wandering around apparently leads them to develop a **[c]** _____ of the
maze. Humans apparently develop cognitive maps of their surroundings based on landmarks.

    Accounting for a large portion of learning in humans, **[d]** _____ is

learning that occurs by observing the behavior of another person, called the **[e]** _____.
The classic experiment involved children observing a model strike a Bobo doll, and then later
those who had seen the behavior were more prone to act aggressively. Four processes are
necessary for observational learning: (1) paying attention to critical features; (2) remembering the
behavior; (3) reproducing the action; and (4) being motivated to repeat the behavior. We also
observe the kinds of reinforcement that the model receives for the behavior. Observational
learning has been related to how violence on television affects aggression and violence in children.

The Exploring Diversity section examines *learning styles* and how cultural differences are reflected in these different ways of approaching materials. Learning styles are characterized by cultural background and individual abilities.

[f] _____ refers to the formalized use of basic principles of learning theory to change behavior by eliminating undesirable behaviors and encouraging desirable ones. Behavior modification can be used to train mentally retarded individuals, to help people lose weight or quit smoking, and to teach people to behave safely. The steps of a typical behavior program include (1) identifying goals and target behaviors; (2) designing a data recording system and recording preliminary data; (3) selecting a behavior change strategy; (4) implementing the program; (5) keeping careful records after the program has been implemented; and (6) evaluating and altering the ongoing program.

Evaluate

____ 1. continuous reinforcement schedule

____ 2. partial reinforcement schedule

____ 3. schedules of reinforcement

____ 4. stimulus control training

____ 5. model

____ 6. behavior modification

a. A formalized technique for promoting the frequency of desirable behaviors and decreasing the incidence of unwanted ones.

b. A person serving as an example to an observer; the observer may imitate that person's behavior.

c. Reinforcing of a behavior every time it occurs.

d. Reinforcing of a behavior some, but not all, of the time.

e. The frequency and timing of reinforcement following desired behavior.

f. Training in which an organism is reinforced in the presence of a certain specific stimulus, but not in its absence.

Rethink

17-1 What is the relationship between a model (in Bandura's sense) and a role model (as the term is used popularly)? Celebrities often complain that their actions should not be scrutinized closely because they do not want to be role models. How would you respond?

17-2 The relational style of learning sometimes conflicts with the traditional school environment. Could a school be created that takes advantage of the characteristics of the relational style? How? Are there types of learning for which the analytical style is clearly superior?

Spotlight on Terminology and Language—ESL Pointers

Cognitive-Social Approaches to Learning

Page 201 "In **latent** learning, a new behavior is learned but not demonstrated until some incentive is provided for displaying it (Tolman & Honzik, 1930)."

Latent is something present but not evident or active. A fingerprint that is difficult to see but that can be made visible for examination is a **latent** fingerprint.

Page 203 "To answer this question, psychologists have **proposed** another form of cognitive-social learning: observational learning."

When you **propose** something, you put forward a plan or a hypothesis for discussion.

Page 203 "In what is now considered a classic experiment, young children saw a film of an adult wildly hitting a five-foot-tall **inflatable** punching toy called a Bobo doll (Bandura, Ross, & Ross, 1963a, 1963b)."

Something **inflatable** is able to be blown up. Many **inflatable** Spiderman balloons, made of expandable material that could be filed with air, were sold following the successful *Spiderman* movie.

Page 203 "In one experiment, for example, children who were afraid of dogs were exposed to a model—**dubbed** the Fearless Peer—playing with a dog (Bandura, Grusec, & Menlove, 1967)."

The model was **dubbed**, or named, the Fearless Peer. The name, the Fearless Peer, was used as a descriptive nickname for the model.

Page 205 "Finally, a continuous diet of aggression may leave us **desensitized** to violence, and what previously would have **repelled** us now produces little emotional response."

When we are **desensitized**, we become insensitive. Researchers are concerned that observing too much violence on television will **desensitize** us to physical aggression.

When something repels us, it disgusts us. Something that **repels** people causes an aversion. Is there any activity that previously would have **repelled** you, but now you have become **desensitized** to?

Test your knowledge of this set of modules by answering these questions. These questions have been placed in three Practice Tests. The first two tests consist of questions that will test your recall of factual knowledge. The third test contains questions that are challenging and primarily test for conceptual knowledge and your ability to apply that knowledge. Check your answers and review the feedback using the Answer Key on the following pages of the *Study Guide*.

PRACTICE TEST 1:

1. Which of the following statements concerning the relationship between learning and performance is correct?
    a. Learning refers to cognitive gains, whereas performance refers to gains in motor skills.
    b. Performance refers to permanent changes, whereas learning refers to temporary changes.
    c. Performance is synonymous with learning.
    d. Performance is measurable, whereas learning must be inferred.

2. The changes in behavior brought about by learning:
    a. are hard to measure.   c. must be measured indirectly.
    b. are easily extinguished.   d. are generally maturational.

3. The _____ in Pavlov's experiment was the meat powder.
    a. unconditioned stimulus   c. unconditioned response
    b. conditioned stimulus   d. conditioned response.

4. Over time, when the conditioned stimulus is presented repeatedly without being paired with the unconditioned stimulus, the result will be:
    a. learning.   c. systematic desensitization.
    b. perception.   d. extinction.

5. Systematic desensitization is most closely associated with:
    a. operant conditioning.   c. spontaneous recovery.
    b. token economy.   d. extinction.

6. Mrs. Tobin is used to turning off the lights to quiet the class, a classically conditioned behavior. This behavior can be extinguished by:
    a. adding another conditioned stimulus to the pairing.
    b. no longer presenting the unconditioned stimulus after the conditioned response.
    c. using stimulus substitution.
    d. reintroducing the unconditioned stimulus.

7. Garcia's behavioral investigations of rats that were treated with doses of radiation illustrate that:
    a. rats obey slightly different principles of classical conditioning than do humans.
    b. some research findings involving classical conditioning do not appear to obey Pavlov's conditioning principles.
    c. classical conditioning is a very robust form of learning because it is not weakened even by large doses of medication.
    d. changes in classical conditioning are highly sensitive indicators of radiation effects.

8. The _____ states that we will continue to act in a manner that will lead to pleasing consequences.
   a. law of frequency
   b. principle of similarity
   c. law of effect
   d. principle of contiguity

9. The distinction between primary reinforcers and secondary reinforcers is that:
   a. primary reinforcers satisfy some biological need; secondary reinforcers are effective because of their association with primary reinforcers.
   b. organisms prefer primary reinforcers to secondary reinforcers.
   c. primary reinforcers are not effective with all organisms.
   d. primary reinforcers depend on the past conditioning of the organism; secondary reinforcers have a biological basis.

10. Ariel gives her dog a treat each time the dog comes when he is called. This stimulus that increases the likelihood that the preceding behavior will be repeated is called a/an:
    a. apunisher.
    b. reinforcer.
    c. response.
    d. operant.

11. Negative reinforcement:
    a. is a special form of punishment.
    b. is a phenomenon that results when reward is withheld.
    c. involves the decrease or removal of an aversive stimulus.
    d. occurs in both classical and instrumental conditioning.

12. Constance receives checks from home to help subsidize her college activities. She never knows when or how much she will receive. In the variable schedule of reinforcement, the response rate is:
    a. always high.
    b. always constant and low.
    c. easily extinguished.
    d. highly resistant to extinction.

13. Because the number of lottery tickets a person must purchase before reinforcement occurs in the form of a winning ticket is not certain, he or she is working on a:
    a. variable-ratio schedule.
    b. fixed-ratio schedule.
    c. variable-interval schedule.
    d. fixed-interval schedule.

14. Superstitious behavior is thought to arise because of:
    a. continuously reinforced patterns of behavior that have led to results related to the behavior.
    b. universal biological constraints that guide specific kinds of behavior.
    c. religious dogma.
    d. partial reinforcement of the connection of incidental events to a specific consequence.

15. Given the opportunity to explore a maze with no explicit reward available, rats will develop:
    a. a cognitive map of the maze.
    b. an aversion to the maze.
    c. an increased interest in the maze.
    d. a superstitious fear of the maze.

_____ 16. cognitive-social learning theory

a. The study of the thought processes that underlie learning.

_____ 17. latent learning

b. Learning that involves the imitation of a model.

_____ 18. observational learning

c. A new behavior is acquired but not readily demonstrated until reinforcement is provided.

_____ 19. classical conditioning

_____ 20. neutral stimulus

d. A stimulus that, before conditioning, does not naturally bring about the response of interest.

e. A type of learning in which a neutral stimulus comes to bring about a response after it is paired with a stimulus that naturally brings about that response.

21. _____ is the process of teaching a complex behavior by rewarding closer and closer approximations of the desired behavior.

22. A(n) _____ stimulus is one that brings about a response without having been learned.

23. A(n) _____ stimulus is a once-neutral stimulus that has been paired with an unconditioned stimulus to bring about a response formerly caused only by the unconditioned stimulus.

24. A(n) _____ response is natural and needs no training.

25. The use of physical punishment has become quite controversial. Most school systems now outlaw its use, and many parents try to find alternatives to it. Define the issues related to the use of punishment, and answer the question, "Is it wrong to use physical punishment to discipline children?" As you answer, consider whether there are circumstances that may require routine use, or whether it should be rare. Describe alternatives for use in normal disciplining of children.

PRACTICE TEST 2:

1. Cognitive psychologists define learning as:
   a. a change in behavior brought about by growth and maturity of the nervous system.
   b. a measurable change in behavior brought about by conditions such as drugs, sleep, and fatigue.
   c. a behavioral response that occurs each time a critical stimulus is presented.
   d. a relatively permanent change in behavior brought about by experience.

2. In classical conditioning, the stimulus that comes to elicit a response that it would not previously have elicited is called the:
   a. classical stimulus.   c. conditioned stimulus.
   b. unconditioned stimulus.   d. discriminative stimulus.

3. Before the conditioning trials in which Watson planned to condition fear of a rat in Baby Albert, the rat—which Albert was known not to fear—would have been considered:
   a. an unconditioned stimulus.   c. a discriminative stimulus.
   b. an adaptive stimulus.   d. a neutral stimulus.

4. Pablo is afraid of flying, and the therapist he sees is attempting to help him by using systematic desensitization. Overcoming his fear will be achieved by:
    a. no longer allowing the conditioned stimulus and the unconditioned stimulus to be paired in real-life situations.
    b. constructing a hierarchy of situations that produce fear and then gradually pairing less stressful situations with strategies to relax.
    c. identifying the situations that produce fear in order to modify or eliminate them.
    d. gaining exposure to the most fearful situations so that the unpleasant reactions can be extinguished quickly.

5. When Tashiene's mother no longer pays any attention to her temper tantrums about getting ready for school, or when the conditioned stimulus is presented repeatedly without being accompanied by the unconditioned stimulus, _____ occurs.
    a. escape conditioning   c. stimulus generalization
    b. extinction   d. negative reinforcement

6. Pavlov's assumption that stimuli and responses were linked in a mechanistic, unthinking way has been challenged by:
    a. cognitive learning theorists.   c. Edward Thorndike's law of effect.
    b. the animal trainers, the Brelands.   d. operant conditioning.

7. A reinforcement given for the first correct or desired response to occur after a set period is called:
    a. a fixed-ratio reinforcement schedule.
    b. a continuous reinforcement schedule.
    c. a fixed-interval reinforcement schedule.
    d. a variable-interval reinforcement schedule.

8. Which alternative below is **not** an example of operant conditioning?
    a. A cat pushes against a lever to open a door on its cage.
    b. A student drives within the speed limit to avoid getting another speeding ticket.
    c. A dog rolls over for a dog biscuit.
    d. A student's blood pressure increases when she anticipates speaking with her chemistry professor.

9. Which name below is **not** associated with classical conditioning or operant conditioning?
    a. Pavlov   c. Wertheimer
    b. Skinner   d. Thorndike

10. Typically, food is a _____, whereas money is a _____.
    a. discriminative stimulus; conditioned reinforcer
    b. need; motive
    c. primary reinforcer; secondary reinforcer
    d. drive reducer; natural reinforcer

11. Which of the following is most likely to be considered a primary reinforcer?
    a. money   c. good grades
    b. water   d. a hammer

12. In which of the following situations would the use of punishment be most effective in reducing the undesired behavior?
    a. An employee is demoted for misfiling a report.
    b. A child is spanked for hitting her sister.
    c. A teenager is denied the opportunity to attend the Friday dance for staying out late on Monday.
    d. A child is spanked for running into the street.

13. Car sales, where a salesperson is paid for the number of cars sold, is an example of a:
    a. fixed-interval schedule of reinforcement.
    b. variable-interval schedule of reinforcement.
    c. variable-ratio schedule of reinforcement.
    d. fixed-ratio schedule of reinforcement.

14. With a fixed-interval schedule, especially in the period just after reinforcement, response rates are:
    a. speeded up.   c. relatively unchanged.
    b. extinguished.   d. relatively low.

15. Rewarding each step toward a desired behavior _____ the new response pattern.
    a. inhibits   c. disrupts
    b. shapes   d. eliminates

____ 16. extinction

____ 17. systematic desensitization

____ 18. spontaneous recovery

____ 19. stimulus generalization

____ 20. stimulus discrimination

a. The weakening and eventual disappearance of a conditioned response.

b. The reappearance of a previously extinguished response after a period of time, during which the conditioned stimulus has been absent.

c. Response to a stimulus that is similar to but different from a conditioned stimulus; the more similar the two stimuli, the more likely generalization is to occur.

d. The process by which an organism learns to differentiate among stimuli, restricting its response to one in particular.

e. A form of therapy in which fears are minimized through gradual exposure to the source of fear.

21. Learning that involves the imitation of a model is called _____.

22. The study of the thought processes that underlie learning is _____.

23. _____ is learning in which a voluntary response is strengthened or weakened, depending on its favorable or unfavorable consequences.

24. _____ is the process by which a stimulus increases the probability that a preceding behavior will be repeated.

25. Three approaches to learning are described in the text. Classical and operant conditioning rely on external determinants of behavior, and cognitive learning depends in part on internal, mental activity. How can the differences between these three approaches be reconciled?

PRACTICE TEST 3: Conceptual, Applied, and Challenging Questions

1. Through conditioning, a dog learns to salivate at the sound of a bell because the bell signals that food is coming. In subsequent learning trials, a buzzer is sounded just before the bell. Soon the dog salivates at the sound of the buzzer. In this case, the bell acts as the:
   a. unconditioned stimulus.
   c. unconditioned response.
   b. conditioned stimulus.
   d. conditioned response.

2. Juanita uses a blender to prepare food for her daughter. Soon the baby knows that the sound of the blender signals that food is on the way. In this case, the food acts as:
   a. an unconditioned stimulus.
   c. an unconditioned response.
   b. a conditioned stimulus.
   d. a conditioned response.

3. In preparing to take his dog for a walk, Daniel puts on his running shoes. Soon the dog learns that the running shoes signal that she is going for a walk. In this case, the running shoes act as:
   a. an unconditioned stimulus.
   c. an unconditioned response.
   b. a conditioned stimulus.
   d. a conditioned response.

4. Rats are sometimes sickened by poisoned bait that resembles their favorite foods. Afterward, the rats avoid eating food that resembles the poisoned bait. The sickness caused by the poisoned bait is _____ in classical conditioning.
   a. an unconditioned response
   c. a conditioned response
   b. an unconditioned stimulus
   d. a conditioned stimulus

5. Kumar sees his grandfather coming up the driveway; his grandfather puts his arms out, and Joseph runs and gently hugs his grandfather. In this case, the grandfather's outstretched arms are:
   a. evidence of stimulus generalization.
   b. an operant response, likely to be repeated.
   c. a reinforcer for the boy's subsequent hug of his grandfather.
   d. an aversive response established via classical conditioning.

6. In order to stop smoking, "Big Joe" participates in aversive conditioning. Now he dislikes cigarettes and has also linked his dislike to the store where he used to buy them. This reaction illustrates:
   a. operant conditioning.
   c. higher-order conditioning.
   b. stimulus discrimination.
   d. systematic desensitization.

7. Katie is being taught colors and their names. When shown a red, pink, or yellow rose, the child correctly identifies the color of each flower. This is an example of:
   a. stimulus discrimination.
   c. spontaneous generalization.
   b. stimulus generalization.
   d. spontaneous recovery.

8. High schools have sometimes used dogs to search student lockers. Typically, the dogs are trained to sniff out a specific drug, such as cocaine, and to ignore all other drugs. The ability of the dogs to respond only to the specific drug they were trained to detect is an example of:
   a. stimulus discrimination.
   c. partial reinforcement.
   b. response generalization.
   d. spontaneous recovery.

9. Students generally study very hard before midterms and then slack off immediately afterward, which is characteristic of behavior reinforced on a:
   a. fixed-ratio schedule.
   c. fixed-interval schedule.
   b. variable-ratio schedule.
   d. variable-interval schedule.

10. A study in which children are given an opportunity to explore a complicated play area for a time and then are asked to locate a specific item in the room has been designed by professors at a local university. Researchers claim that children's speed and accuracy results from unseen mental processes that intervene in learning the area. Which of the following labels best describes the researchers?
    a. personality psychologists
    c. cognitive psychologists
    b. sensory psychologists
    d. biopsychologists

11. The existence of _____ supports the idea that learning may occur even though it is not yet evident in performance.
    a. partial reinforcement
    c. shaping
    b. classical conditioning
    d. latent learning

12. Kachtia's roommate is playing her stereo with the volume turned almost all the way up. In order to study, Kachtia puts on her own headphones and plays softer music to block out the loud music. Because the headphones result in the removal of the aggravating sound, the action would be called:
    a. punishment by application.
    c. negative reinforcement.
    b. positive reinforcement.
    d. punishment by removal.

13. Research studies that show a positive relationship between hours of viewed TV violence and viewers' personal aggressiveness show a methodological weakness in the sense that:
    a. only a few hundred persons serve as subjects in the study.
    b. the researchers interpret the results with bias favoring their own theoretical viewpoints.
    c. people lie habitually on surveys regarding their viewing habits.
    d. correlational data cannot prove that the TV viewing caused the violent behavior.

14. Steve tends to view information from the context of a broad perspective, usually taking an intuitive approach rather than a structured one in understanding information, and is also more task oriented. Based on this information, which of the following best describes Steve?
    a. He has a relational learning style.
    b. He tends to learn through classical conditioning.
    c. He will probably serve as a model in observational learning processes.
    d. He has a tendency toward implicit learning.

15. Which of the following options should Kent select **first** if he wants to improve his study skills?
    a. He should determine how effective his strategies have been so far.
    b. He should identify specific tests and class projects on which he can show improvement.
    c. He should implement the program of skill improvement.
    d. He should select a study skill to change.

_____ 16. fixed-ratio schedule

_____ 17. variable-ratio schedule

_____ 18. fixed-interval schedule

_____ 19. variable-interval schedule

_____ 20. continuous reinforcment schedule

_____ 21. discriminative stimulus

a. Reinforcement occurs after a varying number of responses rather than after a fixed number.

b. Reinforcing of a behavior every time it occurs.

c. Reinforcement is given at various times, usually causing a behavior to be maintained more consistently.

d. A stimulus to which an organism learns to respond as a part of stimulus control training.

e. Reinforcement is given at established time intervals.

f. Reinforcement is given only after a certain number of responses is made.

22. A _____ is any stimulus that increases the probability that a preceding behavior will occur again.

23. A _____ reinforcer is a stimulus added to the environment that brings about an increase in a preceding response.

24. _____ is a stimulus that decreases the probability that a previous behavior will occur again.

25. Using the theory of operant conditioning, illustrate the steps you might take in shaping a student's behavior to get him to stop leaving his seat, being disruptive, and acting out in class.

■ ANSWER KEY: MODULES 15, 16, AND 17

Module 15:	Module 16:	Evaluate
[a] Learning	[a] Operant conditioning	1. g
[b] classical conditioning	[b] law of effect	2. c
[c] neutral stimulus	[c] Reinforcement	3. e
[d] unconditioned stimulus (UCS)	[d] reinforcer	4. d
[e] unconditioned response (UCR)	[e] primary reinforcer	5. f
	[f] secondary reinforcer	6. a
[f] conditioned stimulus (CS)	[g] Positive reinforcers	7. b
[g] conditioned response (CR)	[h] Negative reinforcers	
[h] extinction	[i] escape conditioning	**Module 17:**
[i] systematic desensitization	[j] avoidance conditioning	[a] cognitive-social learning theory
[j] spontaneous recovery	[k] Punishment	[b] Latent learning
[k] Stimulus generalization	[l] schedules of reinforcement	[c] cognitive map
[l] Stimulus discrimination	[m] continuous reinforcement schedule	[d] observational learning
[m] higher-order conditioning	[n] Partial reinforcement schedule	[e] model
	[o] fixed-ratio schedule	[f] Behavior modification
Evaluate	[p] variable-ratio schedule	
1. b	[q] Fixed-interval schedules	Evaluate
2. a	[r] Variable-interval schedules	1. c
3. e	[s] stimulus control training	2. d
4. c	[t] Superstitious behavior	3. e
5. d	[u] shaping	4. f
		5. b
		6. a

Selected Rethink Answers

15-2   It is unlikely that Watson's subject went through life afraid of Santa Claus. After the experiment:
- the conditioned response was no longer reinforced.
- the subject probably had future experiences that involved white, furry objects that were not fearful.
- the longer the CR was present without the CS, the less likely would be the conditioning; this is called extinction.

16-1   The habits of smoking and unhealthy eating can be changed by operant conditioning that would require:
- first, identifying the specific behavior to be changed.
- next, a reward has to be identified that will reinforce the new behavior (not smoking, healthy eating).
- finally, reinforcement schedules must be designed to increase the probability that the new behavior will occur.

16-2   Superstitious behavior could be "cured" by helping the subject (cognitively) become aware that no connection exists between two events or by demonstration that there is no cause-and-effect pattern to the behavior. Unless the behavior interferes with a person's ability to function in a given situation, it may continue. It may even be beneficial to continue, because it gives the person a sense of confidence and may reduce the stress of the performance, therefore giving them the extra edge in a demanding situation.

Practice Test 1:

1. d   mod. 15 p. 179
   a. Incorrect. Learning refers to performance changes as well.
   b. Incorrect. Learning refers to permanent changes.
   c. Incorrect. Performance changes can result from fatigue.
   *d. Correct. Performance is the means of measuring learning.

2. c   mod. 15 p. 179
   a. Incorrect. If learning has occurred, there must be a way to measure it.
   b. Incorrect. Learning should result in relatively permanent change.
   *c. Correct. Because learning is an internal change, it must be observed indirectly through the changes in behavior.
   d. Incorrect. Learning differs from maturational changes.

3. a   mod. 15 p. 180
   *a. Correct. Meat powder caused salivation to occur without any training and thus is "unconditioned."
   b. Incorrect. The conditioned stimulus originally did not cause any salivation.
   c. Incorrect. The response was salivation.
   d. Incorrect. The response was salivation.

4. d   mod. 15 p. 183
   a. Incorrect. Learning has already occurred in this scenario.
   b. Incorrect. Perception is a mental event related to understanding sensory stimuli.
   c. Incorrect. Systematic desensitization is a specialized technique for eliminating a learned response.
   *d. Correct. When the CS is repeatedly presented without the UCS being paired with it, then the CS-CR connection becomes extinguished.

5. d   mod. 15 p. 183
   a. Incorrect. Operant conditioning does not engage in systematic desensitization.
   b. Incorrect. A token economy is a method that applies operant conditioning to discipline.
   c. Incorrect. Spontaneous recovery occurs after extinction and may occur after systematic desensitization has occurred.
   *d. Correct. Systematic desensitization is a means of achieving extinction of a CS-CR relationship.

6. b   mod. 15 p. 183
   a. Incorrect. This method is unlikely to extinguish the initial response.
   *b. Correct. This is the standard method of extinction.
   c. Incorrect. This refers to the process of acquiring a UCS-CS connection initially.
   d. Incorrect. This will actually strengthen the CS.

7. b   mod. 15 p. 184
   a. Incorrect. The principles of classical conditioning are meant to apply uniformly to all organisms with the capacity to learn.
   *b. Correct. Garcia found that animals could be conditioned in open trial and that the time between the UCS and the CS could be quite long.
   c. Incorrect. This is not the point of Garcia's research.
   d. Incorrect. The effects can be achieved by spinning the rats, so this claim is not true.

8. c   mod. 15 p. 187
   a. Incorrect. The law of frequency suggests that conditioning requires frequent pairings.
   b. Incorrect. This is the gestalt principle of perception, not a rule for classical or operant conditioning.
   *c. Correct. The law of effect says that if a behavior has pleasing consequences, it is more likely to be repeated.
   d. Incorrect. The principle of contiguity in classical conditioning suggests that the CS and the UCS should be close together in time and space.

9. a   mod. 16 p. 189
   *a. Correct. Primary reinforcers are items like food and water; secondary are like praise and money.
   b. Incorrect. Organisms may differ in their preferences, but not in any uniform manner.
   c. Incorrect. For organisms that respond to operant conditioning, secondary reinforcers have an effect.
   d. Incorrect. This statement is reversed.

10. b   mod. 16 p. 189
    a. Incorrect. Punishers decrease the likelihood of a response being repeated.
    *b. Correct. This defines reinforcers.
    c. Incorrect. A response is the behavior, not the consequence.
    d. Incorrect. An operant is a kind of response.

11. c   mod. 16 p. 190
a. Incorrect. It is a form of reinforcement, and it results in the increase of the desired behavior.
b. Incorrect. Rewards are not withheld in negative reinforcement; in fact, the removal of the aversive stimulus is considered to be a reward.
*c. Correct. The removal of the aversive stimulus is a pleasing consequence and will lead to the repetition of the behavior.
d. Incorrect. Only instrumental conditioning utilizes reinforcement.

12. d   mod. 16 p. 193
a. Incorrect. The rate depends on the schedule of reinforcement that has been chosen.
b. Incorrect. The rate depends on the schedule of reinforcement that has been chosen.
c. Incorrect. The response is actually difficult to extinguish.
*d. Correct. The variability and the partial nature of the reinforcement results in behaviors that are highly resistant to extinction.

13. a   mod. 16 p. 193
*a. Correct. The ratio of successful sales to attempts made varies from sale to sale.
b. Incorrect. This would mean that the frequency of making a sale would be fixed at every fourth or every fifth attempt (or some number).
c. Incorrect. A variable interval would mean that another sale would not take place until a set amount of time had passed.
d. Incorrect. A fixed interval would mean that a sale would take place on a time schedule, say every hour or every two hours.

14. d   mod. 16 p. 195
a. Incorrect. Superstitious behaviors are rarely reinforced.
b. Incorrect. This results in some other behaviors, not superstitious ones.
c. Incorrect. This probably arises for other reasons.
*d. Correct. The superstitious behavior of a major-league batter might arise because he once hit a home run after tapping the back of his foot with the bat and then touching his hat. Now he repeats this pattern every time he goes to bat.

15. a   mod. 16 p. 202
*a. Correct. Quicker learning in later trials with reinforcement present suggest that some form of map or learning had developed in the unrewarded exploration.
b. Incorrect. No aversion would occur unless the maze were filled with traps.
c. Incorrect. Rat interest cannot yet be judged regarding mazes.
d. Incorrect. Because rats are very superstitious, the maze would have little effect on their beliefs.

16. a   mod. 2 p. 201
17. c   mod. 2 p. 201
18. b   mod. 2 p. 201
19. e   mod. 1 p. 180
20. d   mod. 1 p. 180

21. Shaping   mod. 16 p. 195
22. unconditioned   mod. 15 p. 180
23. conditioned   mod. 15 p. 180
24. unconditioned   mod. 15 p. 180

25.
▪ Cite examples of the use of physical punishment. Describe alternatives for each use.
▪ Identify the conditions under which physical punishment may be necessary. These could include the need for swift and attention-getting action to prevent physical harm. Some parents use corporal punishment when children hit one another, and some do so to establish control when alternatives have failed.

Practice Test 2:
1. d   mod. 15 p. 179
a. Incorrect. This definition fits maturation better.
b. Incorrect. This definition applies to circumstantial changes.
c. Incorrect. This definition applies to reflex.
*d. Correct. This is the definition given in the text.

2. c   mod. 15 p. 180
a. Incorrect. No such term is used in learning theory.
b. Incorrect. The unconditioned stimulus elicits the unconditioned stimulus without any conditioning.
*c. Correct. The term applied to this stimulus is the conditioned stimulus.
d. Incorrect. This stimulus helps an organism in instrumental conditioning discriminate between times when a reinforcement would be given and times when a reinforcement is not available.

3. d mod. 15 p. 182
a. Incorrect. Because the rat did not create a fear response, it could not have been considered an unconditioned stimulus for this study.
b. Incorrect. This has another meaning in some other area of science.
c. Incorrect. The discriminative stimulus helps an organism in instrumental conditioning discriminate between times when a reinforcement would be given and when it is not available.
*d. Correct. Because it would not create the fear response, it would be considered neutral.

4. b mod. 15 p. 183
a. Incorrect. This situation sounds more like extinction or avoidance.
*b. Correct. This hierarchy allows the learner to extinguish the fear gradually.
c. Incorrect. This sounds like avoidance.
d. Incorrect. This reverses the graduated approach used in systematic desensitization.

5. b mod. 15 p. 183
a. Incorrect. This does not describe escape conditioning.
*b. Correct. The conditioned stimulus loses its value as a predictor of the unconditioned stimulus.
c. Incorrect. This does not describe stimulus generalization.
d. Incorrect. Negative reinforcement actually is intended to increase a desired behavior.

6. a mod. 16 p. 202
*a. Correct. The cognitive learning theorists have demonstrated that learning can occur as the transformation of mental processes, like the construction of a cognitive map that later guides behavior.
b. Incorrect. The Brelands primarily utilized operant conditioning and are concerned with other issues.
c. Incorrect. Thorndike's law of effect does not repudiate classical ideas so much as add to them.
d. Incorrect. Operant conditioning does not repudiate the ideas of classical conditioning, and in fact, is subject to the same challenges.

7. c mod. 16 p. 194
a. Incorrect. See answer c.
b. Incorrect. See answer c.
*c. Correct. The period of time (interval) is set (fixed).
d. Incorrect. See answer c.

8. d mod. 16 p. 189
a. Incorrect. The consequence of the behavior is escape.
b. Incorrect. The consequence of the behavior is the avoided speeding ticket.
c. Incorrect. The consequence of the behavior is the biscuit reward.
*d. Correct. The chemistry professor is a conditioned stimulus to which high blood pressure is the response.

9. c mod. 16 p. 180
a. Incorrect. Pavlov developed classical conditioning.
b. Incorrect. Skinner developed operant conditioning.
*c. Correct. Wertheimer was one of the gestalt psychologists.
d. Incorrect. Thorndike developed the law of effect, a cornerstone of operant conditioning.

10. c mod. 16 p. 189
a. Incorrect. Food is not considered to be a discriminative stimulus unless an organism has been trained to view it as such.
b. Incorrect. Food satisfies a need, but it may also be a motive (as is true with money).
*c. Correct. Because food satisfies a basic need, it is considered primary; because money must be conditioned to have any reinforcing value, it is a secondary reinforcer.
d. Incorrect. Food may be a drive reducer, but money is not a natural reinforcer.

11. b mod. 16 p. 189
a. Incorrect. Money requires conditioning to become a reinforcer.
*b. Correct. Water satisfies a basic need, thus it is a primary reinforcer.
c. Incorrect. Good grades require conditioning to become reinforcers.
d. Incorrect. To be a reinforcer, the hammer would require some, though not much, conditioning.

12. d mod. 16 p. 190
a. Incorrect. The employee would probably become angry for being punished for such a minor offense.
b. Incorrect. The physical spanking reinforces the idea that violence is a way to make others cooperate.
c. Incorrect. Punishment for a teenager can often become an opportunity for reinforcement through attention from friends.
*d. Correct. When self-endangerment occurs, quick and angerless punishment can make the child become attentive to the danger.

13. d   mod. 16 p. 193
a. Incorrect. The time interval for making each piece can change, but the rate is one payment for every three pieces.
b. Incorrect. Variable interval would suggest that the worker would not know when payment would come.
c. Incorrect. In this pattern, the payment would come after five, then three, then four, etc. pieces were made—not every three.
*d. Correct. This is a fixed-ratio schedule.

14. d   mod. 16 p. 194
a. Incorrect. They may speed up just before the interval has ended.
b. Incorrect. They do not become extinguished.
c. Incorrect. They slow down just after the reinforcement.
*d. Correct. The predictability of the interval leads the organism to pause just after the reinforcement.

15. b   mod. 16 p. 195
a. Incorrect. Reinforcement does not inhibit the desired behavior.
*b. Correct. Shaping is the technique of rewarding each successive behavior that gets closer to the desired behavior.
c. Incorrect. Reinforcement would not disrupt the targeted behavior.
d. Incorrect. Reinforcement would not eliminate the target behavior.

16. a   mod. 15 p. 183
17. e   mod. 15 p. 195
18. b   mod. 15 p. 183
19. c   mod. 15 p. 183
20. d   mod. 15 p. 184

21. observational learning   mod. 17 p. 203
22. cognitive-social learning   mod. 17 p. 201
23. Operant conditioning   mod. 16 p. 188
24. Reinforcement   mod. 16 p. 189

25.
- Describe each of the three approaches in such a way that they are clearly distinguished.
- Identify points of contradiction with each. In classical conditioning, the stimuli must precede the responses; in operant conditioning, the reinforcing stimuli comes after the response; in observational learning, the behavior does not need to be practiced. Mental processes are also involved in observational learning.
- Observational learning may actually be reconciled with the other two once mental processes and reinforcement of the model (rather than the learner) are allowed.

Practice Test 3:
1. a   mod. 15 p. 180
*a. Correct. The bell is being used just as the unconditioned stimulus was in the earlier training.
b. Incorrect. While the bell is a conditioned stimulus, for the purpose of the second training event, it is an unconditioned stimulus.
c. Incorrect. The bell is not a response.
d. Incorrect. The bell is not a response.

2. a   mod. 15 p. 180
*a. Correct. The food elicits a response that has not been conditioned.
b. Incorrect. The juicer is the unconditioned response.
c. Incorrect. Food is not a response.
d. Incorrect. Food is not a response.

3. b   mod. 15 p. 180
a. Incorrect. The food is the unconditioned stimulus.
*b. Correct. The child has become conditioned to the blender as the signal for food.
c. Incorrect. The blender is not a response.
d. Incorrect. The blender is not a response.

4. a   mod. 15 p. 180
*a. Correct. The sickness occurs without any training, and should thus be considered the "unconditioned" response.
b. Incorrect. Sickness is a response, not a stimulus in this scenario.
c. Incorrect. As a response to the poison, the sickness is unconditioned.
d. Incorrect. If the response of sickness were to the sight of the bait, then it would be "conditioned."

5. b   mod. 16 p. 187
a. Incorrect. Generalization would imply the dog barking at any little boy.
*b. Correct. The bark may have occurred freely, without association and without reinforcement, and would thus be "operant."
c. Incorrect. Typically, a reinforcer follows the reinforced behavior.
d. Incorrect. Barking may accompany aversive responses, but the pattern requires something to be avoided.

6. c   mod. 15 p. 183
a. Incorrect. This appears to be a classically conditioned dislike.
b. Incorrect. In stimulus discrimination, he would probably have only learned to dislike his favorite brand of cigarette.
*c. Correct. This is an example of higher-order conditioning, where the store had once been a signal for buying the cigarettes, it is now a signal for the dislike of the cigarette.
d. Incorrect. Systematic desensitization would have been used to eliminate a fear or other phobia, not a desired habit.

7. a   mod. 15 p. 183
*a. Correct. Of these choices, this best fits; the child learns to discriminate among different qualities of roses.
b. Incorrect. With generalization, the discrimination of colors would decline.
c. Incorrect. There is no such concept as spontaneous generalization.
d. Incorrect. Spontaneous recovery occurs after extinction has been followed by a period of rest.

8. a   mod. 15 p. 183
*a. Correct. This is very discrete training and requires that the dog not respond to similar odors.
b. Incorrect. If response generalization existed, this would not be it.
c. Incorrect. Partial reinforcement may have been used in the training, but the ability indicates stimulus generalization.
d. Incorrect. Spontaneous recovery requires extinction to occur.

9. c   mod. 16 p. 192
a. Incorrect. See answer c.
b. Incorrect. See answer c.
*c. Correct. The learner quickly identifies the apparent "wait time" that follows a reinforcement in a fixed-interval training schedule and thus does not respond for a period because no reinforcement will be forthcoming.
d. Incorrect. See answer c.

10. c   mod. 17 p. 202
a. Incorrect. A personality psychologist would be more interested in traits than learned maps.
b. Incorrect. A sensory psychologist would measure the sensory responses of the children.
*c. Correct. He was demonstrating how children form cognitive maps and then demonstrate their knowledge at a later point in time.
d. Incorrect. A biopsychologist might be interested in the underlying processes that account for the learning.

11. d   mod. 17 p. 203
a. Incorrect. Partial reinforcement supports the idea that not all performance needs to be reinforced.
b. Incorrect. Classical conditioning depends on performance for evidence of learning.
c. Incorrect. Shaping involves the gradual modification of behavior toward a desired form.
*d. Correct. While performance is a measure of learning, the possibility of unmeasured learning is not ruled out.

12. c   mod. 16 p. 190
a. Incorrect. Playing the music loud in the first place was a form of punishment.
b. Incorrect. Positive reinforcement refers to pleasant consequences for a target behavior (studying is the target behavior, not finding peace and quiet).
*c. Correct. "Negative" in this case is the removal of an unwanted stimulus in order to increase a desired behavior (studying).
d. Incorrect. She is being rewarded by removal, not punished.

13. d   mod. 17 p. 203
a. Incorrect. Some scientists make stronger claims with only 20 or 30 subjects.
b. Incorrect. This cannot be determined from this statement.
c. Incorrect. The study does not indicate how the viewing data was gathered.
*d. Correct. This is correct only if the researchers claim or imply a causal relationship.

14. a   mod. 17 p. 206
*a. Correct. This describes the qualities of the relational learning style.
b. Incorrect. Classical conditioning may help him learn, but the style described is the relational learning style.
c. Incorrect. However, he could serve as a model, but this stem does not answer the question.
d. Incorrect. The relational style does include explicit learning.

15. b   mod. 17 p. 203
a. Incorrect. Identifying which area to work on first should precede this step.
*b. Correct. Identifying objective goals is the first step in making a realistic attempt to improve learning.
c. Incorrect. This is a later step of the program.
d. Incorrect. After identifying which classes to work on, he could then identify a specific study skill.

16. f   mod. 16 p. 193
17. a   mod. 16 p. 193
18. e   mod. 16 p. 193
19. c   mod. 16 p. 193
20. b   mod. 16 p. 192
21. d   mod. 16 p. 195

22. reinforcer   mod. 16 p. 190
23. positive   mod. 16 p. 190
24. Punishment   mod. 16 p. 190

25.
- Establish what behaviors need to be changed.
- Use the concept of Skinner's "shaping" to reward successive approximations of the desired behavior.
- Decide what reward will be used to reinforce the change.
- Explain the type of reinforcement schedule that would be most effective.

Memory

Overview

This set of modules looks at the nature of memory and the ways in which information is stored and retrieved.

Module 18 demonstrates the several ways that information is encoded, stored, and then later retrieved. The three systems of memory are discussed. An examination of the different kinds of memory is presented.

Module 19 presents a discussion about the causes and difficulties in remembering. The tip-of-the-tongue phenomenon, flashbulb memories, eyewitness testimony, and the process of recalling information in terms of schemas are all explanations of how remembering is facilitated.

Module 20 examines several processes that account for memory failure, including decay, interference, and cue-dependent forgetting. Finally, a discussion of some of the major memory impairments such as Alzheimer's disease, amnesia, and Korsakoff's syndrome is presented and followed by some techniques for improving memory.

To further investigate the topics covered in this chapter, you can visit the related Web sites by visiting the following link: www.mhhe.com/feldmanup6-07links.

Prologue: The Wife Who Forgot She Had a Husband
Looking Ahead

Module 18: Encoding, Storage, and Retrieval of Memory

The Three Systems of Memory: Memory Storehouses
Contemporary Approaches to Memory: Working Memory, Memory Modules, and
    Associative Models of Memory

- *What is memory?*
- *Are there different kinds of memory?*

Encoding, Storage, and Retrieval of Memory

Three processes comprise memory. **[a]** _____ is the process of placing

information in a form that can be used by memory. **[b]** _____ is the process

of retaining information for later use. **[c]** _____ is the process of recovering

information from storage. By definition, then, **[d]** _____ is the sum of these
three processes. Forgetting is an important part of memory because it allows us to make
generalizations and abstractions from daily life.

The memory system is typically divided into three storage components or stages. The initial

storage system is that of **[e]** _____, where momentary storage of sensory

information occurs. **[f]** _____ includes information that has been given

some form of meaning, and it lasts for 15 to 25 seconds. **[g]** _____ is the
relatively permanent storage of memory. Although there are no locations in the brain of these
memory stages, they are considered abstract memory systems with different characteristics.

Sensory memories differ according to the kind of sensory information, and the sensory
memory is thought of as several types of sensory memories based on the source of the sensory

messages. Visual sensory memory is called **[h]** _____, and its source is the

visual sensory system; auditory sensory memory is called **[i]** _____, and its
source is the auditory sensory system. Sensory memory stores information for a very short time.
Iconic memory may last no more than a second, and echoic memory may last for three to four
seconds. The duration of iconic memory was established by George Sperling's classic experiment
in which subjects were unable to recall an entire array of letters but could, on a cue after the array
was shown for one-twentieth of a second, recall any part of the array. Unless the information
taken into the sensory memories is somehow transferred to another memory system, the sensory
memories are quickly lost.

Sensory memories are raw information without meaning. In order to be transferred to the long-term memory, these sensory memories must be given meaning and placed in short-term memory. One view of this process suggests that the short-term memory is composed of verbal representations that have a very short duration. George Miller has identified the capacity of short-term memory as seven plus or minus two **[j]** _____, or meaningful groups of stimuli that are stored as a unit in the short-term memory. They can be several letters or numbers or can be complicated patterns, like the patterns of pieces on a chessboard. However, to be placed in a chunk, the board must represent a real or possible game.

Memory can be held in short-term memory longer by **[k]** _____, the repetition of information already in the short-term memory. Rehearsal is also the beginning of transferring short-term memory into long-term memory. The kind of rehearsal influences the effectiveness of the transfer to long-term memory. **[l]** _____ occurs whenever the material is associated with other information through placement in a logical framework, connection with another memory, the formation of an image, or some other transformation. The strategies for organizing memories are called **[m]** _____. Mnemonics are formal techniques for organizing information so that recall is more likely.

[n] _____ comes from Baddeley's theory that short-term memory has three components: the _central executive_, the _visuospatial sketch pad_, and the _phonological loop_.

Two kinds of long-term memory have been identified: **[o]** _____ and **[p]** _____. Procedural memory includes the memory for skills and habits, like walking, riding a bicycle, and other physical activity. Declarative memory includes **[q]** _____, memories of specific events related to individual experiences, and **[r]** _____, those that consist of abstract knowledge and facts about the world. Psychologists use **[s]** _____ to suggest that semantic memories represent the associations between mental representations of various pieces of information. When we think about a particular thing, related ideas are activated because of the association. **[t]** _____ refers to the activation of one item, thereby making recall of related items easier. **[u]** _____ refers to intentional or conscious effort to recall memory, and **[v]** _____ refers to memories of which people are not consciously aware but nevertheless affect later performance and behavior.

An alternative to the three-stage view of memory is the **[w]** _____. This theory suggests that the difference in memories depends on the depth to which particular information is processed, that is, the degree to which information is analyzed and considered. The more attention information is given, the deeper it is stored and the less likely it is to be forgotten. Superficial aspects of information are given shallow processing, and when meaning is given, the processing is at its deepest level. This approach suggests that memory requires more active mental processing than does the three-stage approach.

Evaluate

_____ 1. storage   a. Locating and using information stored in memory.

_____ 2. retrieval   b. Relatively permanent memory.

_____ 3. sensory memory   c. Information recorded as a meaningless stimulus.

_____ 4. short-term memory   d. Working memory that lasts about 15 to 25 seconds.

_____ 5. long-term memory   e. The location where information is saved.

Rethink

18-1   It is a truism that "you never forget how to ride a bicycle." Why might this be so? Where is information about bicycle riding stored? What happens when a person has to retrieve that information after not using it for a long time?

18-2   Priming often occurs without conscious awareness. How might this effect be used by advertisers and others to promote their products? What ethical principles are involved? Can you think of a way to protect yourself from unethical advertisers?

Spotlight on Terminology and Language—ESL Pointers

Encoding, Storage, and Retrieval of Memory

Page 215 "**Encoding** refers to the process by which information initially is recorded in a form usable to memory."

To **encode** is to transfer information from one system into another. During the **encoding** stage, information is changed into usable form. In the brain, sensory information becomes impulses that the central nervous system reads and codes. On a computer, **encoding** occurs when keyboard entries are transformed into electronic symbols, which are then stored on a computer disk.

Page 215 "You can think of these processes as being **analogous** to a computer's keyboard (encoding), hard drive disk (storage), and software that accesses the information for display on the screen (retrieval)."

An **analogy** is a comparison between two situations. During the storage stage of memory, information is held in memory. This is the mind's version of a computer hard drive. During the retrieval stage, stored memories are recovered from storage, just as a saved computer program is called up by name and used again.

Page 215 "The ability to forget **inconsequential** details about experiences, people, and objects helps us avoid being burdened and distracted by trivial stores of meaningless data."

Inconsequential details are minor and insignificant details.

Page 215 "Furthermore, forgetting permits us to form general impressions and **recollections**."

Recollect is to recall, as when you have a memory.

Page 215 "For example, the reason our friends consistently look familiar to us is our ability to forget their clothing, facial blemishes, and other **transient** features that change from one occasion to the next."

Transient is something that lasts only a short time. When you daydream, you are often having **transient** thoughts.

Page 218 "Information is recorded by the person's sensory system as an exact **replica** of the stimulus."

A **replica** is a copy or a duplicate. Sensory memory can store a nearly exact replica of each stimulus to which it is exposed.

Page 218 "Furthermore, although the three-part model of memory **dominated** the field of memory research for several decades, recent studies have suggested several newer models, as we'll discuss later."

To **dominate** means to influence and control. The three systems of memory theory had a strong influence on the field of memory research.

Page 218 "Such stimuli are initially—and briefly—stored in sensory memory, the first **repository** of the information the world presents to us."

A **repository** is a storehouse, or a place in which something is deposited or stored. A book can be a **repository** of knowledge.

Page 218 "If the storage capabilities of sensory memory are so limited and information stored within sensory memory so **fleeting**, it would seem almost impossible to find evidence for its existence; new information would constantly be replacing older information, even before a person could report its presence."

Fleeting means passing quickly. **Fleeting** often refers to a momentary event.

Page 219 " It was possible, then, that the information had initially been accurately stored in sensory memory, but during the time it took to **verbalize** the first four or five letters the memory of the other letters faded."

Verbalize is to state in words.

Page 220 "Some theorists suggest that the information is first translated into **graphical** representation or images, and others **hypothesize** that the transfer occurs when the sensory stimuli are changed to words (Baddeley & Wilson, 1985)."

Graphical representations are pictorial or symbolic.

To **hypothesize** is to assume. A **hypothesis** is a proposition tentatively assumed in order to draw out its logical or empirical consequences and so test its agreement with facts that are known or may be determined. A condition of the most genuinely scientific **hypothesis** is that it be developed so that it can be either proved or disproved by comparison with observed facts.

Module 19: Recalling Long-Term Memories

Retrieval Cues
Levels of Processing
Flashbulb Memories
Constructive Processes in Memory: Rebuilding the Past
Memory in the Courtroom: The Eyewitness on Trial

Applying Psychology in the 21st Century:
(Mis)Remembering Tragic Events

Repressed Memories: Truth or Fiction?
Autobiographical Memory: Where Past Meets Present

Exploring Diversity: Are There Cross-Cultural Differences in Memory?

- *What causes difficulties and failures in remembering?*

Recalling Long-Term Memories

Retrieving information from long-term memory may be influenced by many factors. The

[a] _____, where one is certain of knowing something but cannot recall it, represents one difficulty. The simple number of items of information that has been stored may

influence recall. We sort through this quantity with the help of **[b]** _____.
These are stimuli that allow recall from long-term memory. *Recall* consists of a series of processes—a search through memory, retrieval of potentially relevant information, then a decision whether the information is accurate, and a continuation of these steps until the right information is found. In contrast, *recognition* involves determining whether a stimulus that has been presented is correct, such as the selection of the stimulus from a list or determining whether the stimulus has been seen before.

In particularly intense events, we may develop **[c]** _____. A specific, important, or surprising event creates memories so vivid that they appear as if a snapshot of the event. Research regarding flashbulb memories concerning President Kennedy's assassination has revealed common details, such as where the person was, who told the person, the person's own emotions, and some personal detail of the event. Harsh and Neisser asked students the day after the *Challenger* accident how they had heard about it, and then asked the same question three years later. One-third were wrong, a result suggesting that flashbulb memories may be inaccurate. Memories that are exceptional may be more easily retrieved than commonplace information.

Our memories reflect **[d]** _____, in which memories are influenced by the meaning we have attached to them. Guesses and inferences thus influence memory. Sir Frederic Bartlett first suggested that people remember in terms of **[e]** _____, which are general themes without specific details. Schemas were based on an understanding of the event, expectations, and the motivation of others. The process of *serial reproduction*, which requires people to pass information from one to another in a sequence, has shown the effect of schemas. The final story is much changed in comparison to the original version, and it reflects the expectations of those retelling the story. Apparently, prior knowledge and expectations influence how we initially store the information. How we understand peoples' motivation also influences memory. In the **[f]** _____, knowledge about a person's motivation leads to an elaboration of past events involving that person.

The imperfection of memory has led to research into the accuracy of eyewitness testimony. The mistaken identification of individuals can lead to imprisonment. When a weapon is involved, the weapon draws attention away from other details. In research involving staged crimes, witnesses vary significantly in their judgment of the height of the perpetrator, with judgments differing by as much as two feet. The wording of questions can influence testimony. Children are especially prone to unreliable recollections.

The case of George Franklin illustrates the impact recovered memories can have (he was found guilty on the basis of these memories alone). Although childhood recollections can be forgotten and then recovered, the evidence does suggest that much distortion can take place as well, even to the point of fabricating false memories from childhood.

[g] _____ are our collections of information about our lives. People tend to forget information about the past that is incongruent with the way they currently see themselves. Depressed people tend to recall sad events more readily than happy ones from their past. More recent information also appears to be more affected than earlier recollections.

Evaluate

_____ 1. recall

_____ 2. recognition

_____ 3. flashbulb memories

_____ 4. serial reproduction

_____ 5. soap opera effect

a. Drawing from memory a specific piece of information for a specific purpose.

b. The phenomena by which memory of a prior event involving a person is more reliable when we understand that person's motivations.

c. Memories of a specific event that are so clear they seem like "snapshots" of the event.

d. Acknowledging prior exposure to a given stimulus, rather than recalling the information from memory.

e. The passage of interpretive information from person to person, often resulting in inaccuracy through personal bias and misinterpretation.

Rethink

19-1 How do schemas help people process information during encoding, storage, and retrieval? In what ways are they helpful? Can they contribute to inaccurate autobiographical memories?

19-2 How might courtroom procedure be improved, based on what you've learned about memory errors and biases?

Spotlight on Terminology and Language—ESL Pointers

Recalling Long-Term Memories

Page 229 "This common occurrence—known as the **tip-of-the-tongue** phenomenon—exemplifies the difficulties that can occur in retrieving information stored in long-term memory (Schwartz, Travis, Castro & Smith, 2000; Schwartz, 2001, 2002)."

Something that is on the **tip of the tongue** is ready to be retrieved from your memory but cannot be brought forth at this time.

Page 229 "Although the issue is far from settled, many psychologists have suggested that the material that makes its way to long-term memory is relatively **permanent** (Tulving & Psotka, 1971)."

Permanent is something that is going to remain, something that continues and endures (as in the same state, status, or place) without fundamental or marked change. You think of something **permanent** as fixed. Can you describe some of your **permanent** memories?

Page 230 "For instance, if you are like the average college student, your vocabulary includes some 50,000 words, you know hundreds of mathematical 'facts,' and you are able to **conjure up** images—such as the way your childhood home looked—with no trouble at all."

To **conjure up** is to call up or evoke an image. You can **conjure up** many images.

Page 230 "For example, the smell of roasting turkey may **evoke** memories of Thanksgiving or family gatherings (Schab & Crowder, 1995)."

When you **evoke** a memory, you call it up. You are summoning or eliciting this material.

Page 231 "Because we do not pay close attention to much of the information to which we are exposed, typically only **scant** mental processing takes place, and we forget new material almost immediately."

Scant means very little. You are likely to pay **scant** attention to information that does not involve you.

Page 231 "At **shallow** levels, information is processed merely in terms of its physical and sensory aspects."

Shallow is having little depth, penetrating lightly.

Page 231 "Those letters are considered in the **context** of words, and specific **phonetic** sounds may be attached to the letters."

When you consider items in **context**, you are examining the whole picture. You are looking at the interrelated conditions in which something exists or occurs.

Phonetic sounds represent the sounds and other phenomena, such as stress and pitch, of speech.

Page 231 "Although the concept of depth of processing has proved difficult to test experimentally and the levels-of-processing theory has its critics (e.g., Baddeley, 1990), it is clear that there are considerable practical **implications** to the notion that the degree to which information is initially processed affects recall."

To be able to make an **implication** means you are able to infer from this theory.

Page 232 "As we have seen, although it is clear that we can have detailed recollections of significant and distinctive events, it is difficult to **gauge** the accuracy of such memories."

To **gauge** is to be able to measure the dimensions or extent of something. It is difficult to **gauge** the extent of suffering experienced by someone else.

Page 235 "In short, the memories of witnesses are far from **infallible**, and this is especially true when children are involved (Howe, 1999; Goodman et al., 2002; Schaaf et al., 2002)."

Infallible means fail-safe, without error. Memories of witnesses are far from perfect.

Module 20: Forgetting: When Memory Fails

Proactive and Retroactive Interference: The Before and After of Forgetting
The Biological Bases of Memory
Memory Dysfunctions: Afflictions of Forgetting

Becoming an Informed Consumer of Psychology:
Improving Your Memory

- *Why do we forget information?*
- *What are the biological bases of memory?*
- *What are the major memory impairments?*

Forgetting: When Memory Fails

Herman Ebbinghaus studied forgetting by learning a list of nonsense syllables and then timing how long it took him, at a later trial, to relearn the list. The most rapid forgetting occurs in the first 9 hours. Two views concerning the forgetting of information have been developed. One theory explains forgetting by **[a]** _____, or loss of information through nonuse.

When a memory is formed, a **[b]** _____, or **[c]** _____, occurs. An engram is an actual physical change in the brain. The decay theory assumes that memories become more decayed with time, but the evidence does not support this happening, although there is support for the existence of decay. The other theory proposes that

[d] _____ between bits of information leads to forgetting. In interference, information blocks or displaces other information, preventing recall. Most forgetting appears to be the result of interference.

There are two kinds of interference. One is called **[e]** _____ *interference* that occurs when previously learned information blocks the recall of newer information.

[f] _____ *interference* is when new information blocks the recall of old information. Most research suggests that information that has been blocked by interference can eventually be recalled if appropriate stimuli are used.

The biological bases of memory at the level of the neuron point to the underlying process of

[g] _____, or the change in the excitability of a neuron at the synapse. As these changes occur, the work of **[h]** _____, or transfer of short-term memories to long-term memories, takes place.

It was originally thought that memories were evenly distributed throughout the brain. However, the current view suggests that the areas of the brain that are responsible for processing information about the world also store that information.

[i] _____ *disease* includes severe memory problems as one of its many symptoms. Initially, the symptoms appear as simple forgetfulness, progressing to more profound loss of memory, even failure to recognize one's own name and the loss of language abilities. The protein beta amyloid, which is important for maintaining neural connections, has been implicated in the progress of the disease. **[j]** _____ is another memory problem. Amnesia is a loss of memory occurring without apparent loss of mental function.

[k] _____ is memory loss for memories that preceded a traumatic event.

[l] _____ is a loss of memories that follow a traumatic event. Long-term alcoholics who develop *Korsakoff's syndrome* also have amnesia. Korsakoff's syndrome is related to thiamine deficiency. A perfect memory, one with total recall, might actually be very discomforting. A case studied by Luria of a man with total recall reveals that the inability to forget becomes debilitating.

The Informed Consumer of Psychology section outlines several mnemonic techniques and how they can be applied to taking tests. They include the *keyword technique*, in which one pairs a word with a mental image, or in the case of learning a foreign language, the foreign word with a similar-sounding English word. The *method of loci* requires that one imagine items to be remembered as being placed in particular locations. Another phenomenon that affects memory is called **[m]** _____. Recall is best when it is attempted in conditions that are similar to the conditions under which the information was originally learned. The organization of text and lecture material may enhance memory of it. Practice and rehearsal also improve long-term recall. Rehearsal to the point of mastery is called *overlearning*. It should be noted that cramming for exams is ineffective; the better approach is to distribute practice over many sessions.

Evaluate

_____ 1.	Alzheimer's disease	a.	An illness associated with aging that includes severe memory loss and loss of language abilities.
_____ 2.	amnesia	b.	A memory impairment disease among alcoholics.
_____ 3.	retrograde amnesia	c.	Memory loss unaccompanied by other mental difficulties.
_____ 4.	anterograde amnesia		
_____ 5.	Korsakoff's syndrome	d.	Memory loss of the events following an injury.
		e.	Memory loss of occurrences before some event.

Rethink

20-1 Does the phenomenon of interference help explain the unreliability of autobiographical memory? Why?

20-2 How might findings on the biological mechanisms of memory aid in the treatment of memory disorders such as amnesia?

Spotlight on Terminology and Language—ESL Pointers

Forgetting: When Memory Fails

Page 239 "Using himself as the only participant in his study, Ebbinghaus memorized lists of three-letter nonsense syllables—**meaningless** sets of two **consonants** with a vowel in between, such as FIW and BOZ."

Meaningless means unimportant and insignificant. These three-letter syllables had no meaning.

A **consonant** is any letter of the alphabet except a vowel.

Page 239 "Despite his **primitive** methods, Ebbinghaus's study had an important influence on subsequent research, and his basic conclusions have been **upheld** (Wixted & Ebbesen, 1991)."

Primitive means very simple. The research design for this work was **primitive**. It did not involve relying on modern technology.

When a research conclusion is **upheld**, it is maintained. Further replications of this research find the same result.

Page 241 "Finally, forgetting may occur because of cue-dependent forgetting, forgetting that occurs when there are insufficient retrieval cues to **rekindle** information that is in memory (Tulving & Thompson, 1983)."

To kindle interest means to arouse interest, to stir up interest. To **rekindle** this interest means to arouse it again.

Page 241 "If, for example, you have difficulty on a French achievement test because of your more recent exposure to Spanish, retroactive interference is the **culprit**."

A **culprit** is a cause of a problem.

Page 244 "Usually, lost memories gradually reappear, although full **restoration** may take as long as several years."

Restoration means return.

Page 244 "A second type of amnesia is **exemplified** by people who remember nothing of their current activities."

Anterograde amnesia is **exemplified** or illustrated by people who have no recollection of their current activities.

Test your knowledge of the material in these modules by answering these questions. These questions have been placed in three Practice Tests. The first two tests consist of questions that will test your recall of factual knowledge. The third test contains questions that are challenging and primarily test for conceptual knowledge and your ability to apply that knowledge. Check your answers and review the feedback using the Answer Key on the following pages of the *Study Guide*.

PRACTICE TEST 1:

1. The process of identifying and using information stored in memory is referred to as:
   a. storage.
   b. retrieval.
   c. recording.
   d. learning.

2. The process of recording information in a form that can be recalled is:
   a. encoding.
   b. storage.
   c. decoding.
   d. retrieval.

3. _____ stores information for approximately 15 to 25 seconds.
   a. Sensory memory
   b. Short-term memory
   c. Iconic memory
   d. Long-term memory

4. Researchers have discovered that short-term memory can hold approximately:
   a. five items.
   b. seven items.
   c. ten items.
   d. eighteen items.

5. Teresa's knack for storytelling keeps her friends highly entertained as she recalls the events of her childhood. This recall about what we have done and the kinds of experiences we have had best illustrates:
   a. periodic memory.
   b. episodic memory.
   c. semantic memory.
   d. serial production memory.

6. Saying things over and over, or repeating a task on numerous occasions is known as rehearsal, which:
   a. facilitates neither short-term memory nor long-term memory.
   b. has no effect on short-term memory duration, yet it facilitates the transfer of material into long-term memory.
   c. helps prolong information in short-term memory but has no effect on the transfer of material into long-term memory.
   d. extends the duration of information in short-term memory and assists its transfer into long-term memory.

7. You would be unable to _____ if your episodic long-term memory were disabled.
   a. remember details of your own personal life
   b. recall simple facts such as the name of the U.S. president
   c. speak, although you could still comprehend language through listening
   d. maintain information in short-term memory via rehearsal

8. Information from long-term memory is easier to access with the aid of:
   a. a retrieval cue.
   c. interpolated material.
   b. distractors.
   d. a sensory code.

9. Constructive processes are associated with all of the following **except**:
   a. episodic memory.
   c. procedural memory.
   b. motivation.
   d. organization.

10. The tip-of-the-tongue phenomenon exemplifies difficulties in:
    a. encoding.
    c. storage.
    b. decoding.
    d. retrieval.

11. Ebbinghaus, after memorizing a series of nonsense syllables, discovered that forgetting was most dramatic _____ following learning.
    a. two days
    c. ten days
    b. an hour
    d. one day

12. Jonathan met a girl on the bus and repeatedly recited her phone number all the way home. This recitation:
    a. minimizes the effects of proactive interference.
    b. prevents trace decay from occurring.
    c. activates different brain areas than when the word sequence is spoken the first time.
    d. is a characteristic symptom of the disorder known as Korsakoff's syndrome; this symptom can, in most cases, be treated with drugs.

13. Which situation is characteristic of anterograde amnesia?
    a. A person has loss of memory for events before some critical event.
    b. A person receives a physical trauma to the head and has difficulty remembering things after the accident.
    c. A person forgets simple skills such as how to dial a telephone.
    d. A person begins to experience difficulties in remembering appointments and relevant dates such as birthdays.

14. Memories lost under retrograde amnesia sometimes are recovered later; this implies that the amnesia interfered with the process of:
    a. encoding.
    c. retrieval.
    b. storage.
    d. association.

15. The keyword technique is a memory aid that can be helpful in learning a foreign language. The first step is to identify:
    a. a word that has similar meaning in a familiar language and pair it with the foreign word to be learned.
    b. a word that has a similar sound in a familiar language to at least part of the foreign word and pair it with the foreign word to be learned.
    c. a word that suggests similar imagery in a familiar language and pair it with the foreign word to be learned.
    d. the first word to come to mind in a familiar language and pair it with the foreign word to be learned.

_____ 16. echoic memory

a. Memory for skills and habits.

_____ 17. episodic memories

b. Stored information relating to personal experiences.

_____ 18. semantic memories

c. Stored, organized facts about the world (e.g., mathematical and historical data).

_____ 19. declarative memory

d. The storage of information obtained from the sense of hearing.

_____ 20. procedural memory

e. Memory for facts and knowledge.

21. Recording information in a form usable to memory is _____.

22. _____ memory is the storage of visual information.

23. A stimulus such as a word, smell, or sound that aids recall of information located in long-term memory is a _____.

24. Rehearsing material beyond the point of mastery to improve long-term recall is _____.

25. _____ is a technique of recalling information by thinking about related information.

26. What role should psychologists play in helping the courts deal with repressed memories of abuse that have been recovered? Consider both the advantages and disadvantages of the answer you give.

PRACTICE TEST 2:

1. Information deteriorates most quickly from:
   a. explicit memory.
   b. short-term memory.
   c. sensory memory.
   d. episodic declarative memory.

2. Recording information in the memory system is referred to as:
   a. encoding.
   b. storage.
   c. decoding.
   d. retrieval.

3. Information in short-term memory is stored according to its:
   a. meaning.
   b. intensity.
   c. length.
   d. sense.

4. The process of grouping information into units for storage in short-term memory is called:
   a. similarity.
   b. priming.
   c. chunking.
   d. closure.

5. Knowledge about grammar, spelling, historical dates, and other knowledge about the world best illustrates:
   a. periodic memory.
   b. episodic memory.
   c. semantic memory.
   d. serial production memory.

6. _____ may be necessary while information is in the short-term stage, in order to enhance consolidation of long-term memory.
   a. Massed practice
   b. Elaborative rehearsal
   c. Interpolation
   d. Interference

7. According to the levels-of-processing model, what determines how well specific information is remembered?
   a. the stage attained
   b. the meaning of the information
   c. the quality of the information
   d. the depth of information processing

8. Finding the correct answer on a multiple-choice test depends on:
   a. serial search.
   b. recall.
   c. mnemonics.
   d. recognition.

9. Your memory of how to skate is probably based on:
   a. procedural memory.
   b. semantic memory.
   c. elaborative rehearsal.
   d. declarative memory.

10. The detailed, vivid account of what you were doing when you learned of the *Challenger* disaster represents a:
    a. cognitive map.
    b. schema.
    c. flashbulb memory.
    d. seizure.

11. Which explanation has **not** been offered to account for how we forget information that was learned?
    a. decay
    b. interference
    c. spontaneous inhibition
    d. inadequate processing during learning

12. All of the following have been associated with the biological basis of memory **except**:
    a. the hippocampus.
    b. sulci.
    c. neurotransmitters.
    d. long-term potentiation.

13. Which of the following syndromes is the **least** common?
    a. retrograde amnesia
    b. anterograde amnesia
    c. Alzheimer's disease
    d. Korsakoff's syndrome

14. The fundamental issue surrounding the controversy about repressed memories is whether the memories:
    a. are retrieved from long-term memory or from another type of memory.
    b. can be counteracted by therapy.
    c. have any noticeable effect on mental activities or behavior.
    d. are genuine recollections from the past.

15. Which alternative is **least** likely to help you do well on your next psychology quiz?
    a. Use a prioritized strategy by studying the material only the day before the quiz and avoiding any other subjects that might interfere.
    b. Overlearn the material.
    c. Take brief lecture notes that focus on major points and that emphasize organization.
    d. Ask yourself questions about the material as you study.

_____ 16. memory trace

_____ 17. proactive interference

_____ 18. retroactive interference

_____ 19. keyword technique

_____ 20. memory

a. The pairing of a foreign word with a common, similar-sounding English word to aid in remembering the new word.

b. A physical change in the brain corresponding to the memory of material.

c. New information interferes with the recall of information learned earlier.

d. The system used to store the results of learning.

e. Information stored in memory interferes with recall of material learned later.

21. The ability to retrieve and reproduce previously encountered material is called _____.

22. _____ is the ability to identify previously encountered material.

23. _____ is the loss of ability to remember events or experiences that occurred before some particular point in time.

24. Breaking information into meaningful units of information is called _____.

25. Much of our knowledge about memory comes from strictly laboratory studies. Consider how the lack of "real-life" memory studies may bias the kinds of results obtained about how memory works in our daily lives. Do you have any suggestions for how psychologists might study memory in daily life?

PRACTICE TEST 3: Conceptual, Applied, and Challenging Questions

1. While Nick was watching a movie, his young son talked excitedly about the new bike his friend was getting. Somewhat frustrated, the boy exclaimed, "You're not paying attention to me!" At this point, Nick diverted his attention to his son and recited the last few things the boy had said. Which memory system is responsible for this ability?
   a. episodic memory
   b. echoic memory
   c. iconic memory
   d. short-term memory

2. Sensory memory is the information that is:
   a. held until it is replaced by new information.
   b. an accurate representation of the stimulus.
   c. an incomplete representation of the stimulus.
   d. lost if it is not meaningful.

3. A story is likely to be transformed when it has been told over and over and:
   a. ambiguous details become regularized to fit the person's expectations.
   b. distinctive features of the story are dropped out.
   c. engrams that were located will become lost.
   d. the original story will become a "flashbulb," with excellent recall even after several serial reproductions.

4. Older computer monitor screens sometimes have a brief persistence of the old image when the image is changed. This persistence of the monitor image is analogous to:
    a. flashbulb memory.
    b. iconic memory.
    c. echoic memory.
    d. declarative memory.

5. Beth's basketball coach instructs her to practice a basic foul shot for about 30 minutes each day to improve her shot. After she does what the coach has suggested, she discovers that she can make a shot without any thought and with complete confidence. This is a demonstration of what kind of memory?
    a. working memory
    b. declarative memory
    c. autobiographical memory
    d. procedural memory

6. After 20 years of not having been on a bicycle, the cycle-shop manager will allow Daniel's son to test a cycle only if Daniel rides one beside him. Within 10 seconds, Daniel has adjusted to the bicycle and is even more confident than his son, who has just learned to ride. This is a demonstration of which kind of memory?
    a. working memory
    b. procedural memory
    c. recovered, repressed memories
    d. autobiographical memory

7. Who was responsible for the concept of schemas?
    a. Sigmund Freud
    b. Jean Piaget
    c. Frederic Bartlett
    d. Robert Feldman

8. "The strength of a memory relates directly to the kind of attention given to it when the information was experienced." This statement most supports directly:
    a. the three-stage model of memory.
    b. the mental imagery model of memory.
    c. the levels-of-processing model of memory.
    d. the cultural diversity model of memory.

9. You are asked to write your new address and phone number on the back of a check. Instead, you write your previous address and number. You are experiencing:
    a. retroactive interference.
    b. fugue.
    c. amnesia.
    d. proactive interference.

10. Lyle learns the word-processing program "Easy Word" on his personal computer. Then he learns a second program, "Perfect Word," at work. He now finds it difficult to remember some of the commands when he uses his word processor at home. This is an example of:
    a. work-induced interference.
    b. retroactive interference.
    c. proactive interference.
    d. spontaneous interference.

11. A server forgets a customer's order because 20 other orders have been completed during the intervening hour. The reduced recall of that customer's order reflects:
    a. Alzheimer's disease.
    b. decay.
    c. proactive interference.
    d. retroactive interference.

12. Alzheimer's disease is associated with deterioration of the:
    a. neurological connection between the spinal cord and muscles.
    b. connection between the hemispheres.
    c. manufacture of beta amyloid.
    d. basal ganglia and lower brain structures.

13. Which situation is most characteristic of retrograde amnesia?
   a. A person begins to experience difficulties in remembering appointments and relevant dates such as birthdays.
   b. A person receives a physical trauma to the head and has difficulty remembering things after the accident.
   c. A person forgets simple skills such as how to dial a telephone.
   d. A person has loss of memory for events before some critical event.

14. Samantha, the star of the soap opera *Days and Nights,* has found herself without any memory of her past life from a point in time only a few episodes ago. If her memory failure is real, which of the following types of memory loss best describes her condition?
   a. retrograde amnesia
   b. anterograde amnesia
   c. infantile amnesia
   d. Korsakoff's syndrome

____ 15. priming

____ 16. associative models

____ 17. encoding specificity

____ 18. overlearning

____ 19. engram

a. A physical change in the brain corresponding to the memory of material.

b. Memory of information is enhanced when recalled under the same conditions as when it was learned.

c. A technique of recalling information by having been exposed to related information at an earlier time.

d. Rehearsing material beyond the point of mastery to improve long-term recall.

e. A technique of recalling information by thinking about related information.

20. _____ is the technique of recalling information by having been exposed to related information at an earlier time.

21. Scientists refer to changes in sensitivity at the neuron's synapse as _____.

22. One can create long-term memories by a process known as _____.

23. _____ are recollections of the facts about our own lives.

24. To increase the chance that information will be remembered, a person adds meaning to the information to be remembered, which is called _____.

25. List the factors that can reduce the accuracy of eyewitness testimony and describe how the misinformation effect works in memory dislocation.

■ ANSWER KEY: MODULES 18, 19, AND 20

Module 18:		Module 19:	Module 20:
[a] Encoding	[n] Working memory	[a] tip-of-the-tongue	[a] decay
[b] Storage	[o] declarative memory	phenomenon	[b] memory trace
[c] Retrieval	[p] procedural memory	[b] retrieval cues	[c] engram
[d] memory	[q] episodic memories	[c] flashbulb memories	[d] interference
[e] sensory memory	[r] semantic memories	[d] constructive processes	[e] proactive
[f] Short-term memory	[s] associative models	[e] schemas	[f] Retroactive
[g] Long-term memory	[t] Priming	[f] soap opera effect	[g] long-term potentiation
[h] iconic memory	[u] Explicit memory	[g] Autobiographical	[h] consolidation
[i] echoic memory	[v] implicit memory	memories	[i] Alzheimer's
[j] chunks	[w] levels-of-processing		[j] Amnesia
[k] rehearsal	theory		[k] Retrograde amnesia
[l] Elaborative rehearsal			[l] Anterograde amnesia
[m] mnemonics	Evaluate	Evaluate	[m] encoding specificity
	1. e	1. a	
	2. a	2. d	
	3. c	3. c	Evaluate
	4. d	4. e	1. a
	5. b	5. b	2. c
			3. e
			4. d
			5. b

Selected Rethink Answers

18-1 Memories for motor skills are extremely long-lasting; they may be encoded and stored as kinesthetic (muscular) instructions.

19-2 Autobiographical memories are our recollections of circumstances and episodes from our lives. Interference means that old memories often interfere with the ability to retrieve new information, or new memories interfere with the ability to retrieve old memories. Memories of our past are distorted. We may forget troubled childhoods. Remember passing grades, not failing grades.

Practice Test 1:

1. b   mod. 18 p. 215
a. Incorrect. Storage refers to the retention of the encoded memory.
*b. Correct. Retrieval is the recovery of stored, encoded information so that it can be used.
c. Incorrect. Recording is the work of committing information to a record, like taking notes, etc.
d. Incorrect. See Chapter 6.

2. a   mod. 18 p. 215
*a. Correct. Encoding places the information in a manageable form.
b. Incorrect. Storage refers to the retention of the encoded memory.
c. Incorrect. Decoding must mean the removal of the code into which something has been encoded.
d. Incorrect. Retrieval is the recovery of stored, encoded information.

3. b   mod. 18 p. 218
a. Incorrect. Sensory memory has a life of less than a second.
*b. Correct. Unless material is rehearsed, information is quickly lost from the short-term memory.
c. Incorrect. Iconic memory refers to visual sensory memory and has a duration of less than a quarter of a second.
d. Incorrect. The duration of long-term memory is indefinite.

4. b   mod. 18 p. 220
a. Incorrect. It can hold up to nine items, but the average would be seven.
*b. Correct. Psychologists accept the view that we can hold about seven, plus or minus two items in short-term memory.
c. Incorrect. See answer b.
d. Incorrect. See answer b.

5. b   mod. 18 p. 222
a. Incorrect. No such memory concept.
*b. Correct. Memory of life events, or episodes, is one of the types of long-term memory.
c. Incorrect. Semantic memory is memory for declarative knowledge like words and definitions.
d. Incorrect. No concept like this has been used in contemporary psychology.

6. d   mod. 18 p. 221
a. Incorrect. Rehearsal facilitates all memory.
b. Incorrect. It does help short-term memory items persist in short-term memory.
c. Incorrect. It does aid in the transfer of memory to long-term storage.
*d. Correct. It helps both short-term duration and long-term consolidation.

7. a   mod. 18 p. 223
*a. Correct. Episodic memory is the storage of stories and details about life—that is, episodes.
b. Incorrect. Facts like these are considered semantic.
c. Incorrect. Episodic memory has little to do with speaking.
d. Incorrect. This would not affect short-term memory.

8. a   mod. 19 p. 229
*a. Correct. Retrieval cues are aspects—connections, similarities, etc.—of information that help us recall, or retrieve, the information.
b. Incorrect. Distractors are the stems of multiple-choice questions that are designed to confuse the test-taker.
c. Incorrect. This is not the answer.
d. Incorrect. The sensory code is relevant to short-term memory and our ability to manipulate that memory.

9. d   mod. 19 p. 232
a. Incorrect. See answer d.
b. Incorrect. See answer d.
c. Incorrect. See answer d.
*d. Correct. In terms of memory phenomena, construction processes apply to episodic memory, motivation, and procedural memory.

10. d   mod. 19 p. 230
a. Incorrect. Difficulties in encoding may make it impossible to retrieve any information.
b. Incorrect. Decoding is not a memory phenomenon.
c. Incorrect. A difficulty with storage would appear in the inability to form new memories.
*d. Correct. We may know that we know something, but not be able to retrieve it.

11. b   mod. 20 p. 239
a. Incorrect. After two days, the memory loss had settled down.
*b. Correct. Within an hour, a significant portion of the list had been forgotten.
c. Incorrect. Only a supermemory could remember the list 10 days later.
d. Incorrect. The most dramatic loss occurred within the first hour.

12. c   mod. 20 p. 242
a. Incorrect. May actually magnify if an error is repeated.
b. Incorrect. Trace decay may not occur anyway.
*c. Correct. Different brain areas are at work as the rehearsal begins to influence consolidation.
d. Incorrect. This is not a symptom of this disease.

13. b   mod. 20 p. 244
a. Incorrect. This is retrograde amnesia, covers all the period prior to the trauma.
*b. Correct. This is common for head-injury patients, who lose the time following the accident.
c. Incorrect. This is an apraxia.
d. Incorrect. This is another kind of memory difficulty.

14. c   mod. 20 p. 243
a. Incorrect. Had they been encoded wrong, they could not be recovered.
b. Incorrect. Had they not been stored, they could never be recovered.
*c. Correct. Because they had not been destroyed, they could still be retrieved.
d. Incorrect. Association is not one of the traditional memory processes.

15. b   mod. 20 p. 244
a. Incorrect. The keyword technique suggests that a similar-sounding word would help in memory.
*b. Correct. In this description, a similar-sounding word is used.
c. Incorrect. One would already need to know the word to make similar imagery.
d. Incorrect. This is a free-association technique.

16. d   mod. 18 p. 219
17. b   mod. 18 p. 225
18. c   mod. 18 p. 224
19. e   mod. 18 p. 224
20. a   mod. 18 p. 224

21. encoding   mod. 18 p. 215
22. Iconic   mod. 18 p. 219
23. retrieval cue   mod. 19 p. 229
24. overlearning   mod. 20 p. 246
25. Associative model mod. 18 p. 225

26.

- State the evidence supporting the existence of repressed memories and describe the problems that can arise from mistaken, recovered memories.
- One might argue that psychologists interfere with and compound the problem further by encouraging clients to "recover " memories that they may not have actually had, something like the demand characteristic in research. Consider whether there are ways to reduce false memories.

Practice Test 2:

1. c   mod. 18 p. 218
a. Incorrect. This is a form of long-term memory.
b. Incorrect. Short-term memory can last about 15 to 25 seconds
*c. Correct. Sensory memory lasts for less than a second.
d. Incorrect. This is a form of long-term memory.

2. b   mod. 18 p. 215
a. Incorrect. Encoding involves getting the information in a form that can be stored.
*b. Correct. Storage refers to the process of retaining the information for later use.
c. Incorrect. Memory has no decoding process.
d. Incorrect. Retrieval refers to the recovery of memory from storage.

3. a   mod. 18 p. 220
*a. Correct. With meaning, the items in short-term memory have greater duration.
b. Incorrect. Memory does not have an intensity except in the emotional sense.
c. Incorrect. Memories cannot be measured in terms of length, although their duration can.
d. Incorrect. Some visual memory will be coded verbally for easier manipulation.

4. c   mod. 18 p. 220
a. Incorrect. Similarity is the gestalt organizational principle.
b. Incorrect. Priming refers to a cognitive theory suggesting that memories, thoughts, and other cognitive material can be primed.
*c. Correct. The technical term is chunking, and it refers to grouping information together in any way that can be recalled.
d. Incorrect. Closure is a gestalt principle of perceptual organization.

5. c   mod. 18 p. 224
a. Incorrect. There is no form of memory known as periodic memory.
b. Incorrect. Episodic memory refers to the personal memories of experiences and life events.
*c. Correct. This is a definition of the form of declarative memory known as semantic memory.
d. Incorrect. None of the researchers have suggested a process called interpolation (yet).

6. b   mod. 18 p. 221
a. Incorrect. Massed practice is not an effective approach to enhancing long-term memory consolidation.
*b. Correct. Elaborative rehearsal strengthens the memory by providing a rich array of retrieval cues.
c. Incorrect. None of the researchers have suggested a process called interpolation (yet).
d. Incorrect. Interference will actually make consolidation more difficult.

7. d   mod. 19 p. 230
a. Incorrect. The stage of memory?
b. Incorrect. The meaning can be important and significant but still be forgotten.
c. Incorrect. Memories do not have qualities in a sense relevant to the levels-of-processing approach.
*d. Correct. The depth of processing is determined by the extent of elaboration and the kinds of information to which the new information was associated.

8. d   mod. 19 p. 230
a. Incorrect. This is a form of guessing, like your selecting this answer.
b. Incorrect. Recall refers to the free recall of information without any specific cues.
c. Incorrect. Mnemonics refers to the techniques or memory aids that can be used to improve memory.
*d. Correct. Because the answer is among the four items presented as alternatives, the test-taker only needs to recognize the right answer.

9. a   mod. 19 p. 224
*a. Correct. Procedural memories are skill-based memories, like riding a bicycle or skating.
b. Incorrect. A semantic memory is memory of words, definitions, procedures, grammatical rules, and similarly abstract information.
c. Incorrect. This is a kind of rehearsal that involves making many connections and relationships for an item being remembered.
d. Incorrect. Declarative memory combines episodic and semantic memory.

10. c mod. 19 p. 231
a. Incorrect. A cognitive map is a more mundane memory item created while wandering about.
b. Incorrect. A schema is an organizational unit that gives structure or organization to a set of information.
*c. Correct. Significant events are often remembered in great detail and apparent specificity, as if a photograph were taken of the event (thus flashbulb memory).
d. Incorrect. A seizure is a traumatic experience and probably would not have this kind of memory associated with it.

11. d mod. 20 p. 240
a. Incorrect. Decay theory says that we lose memories because they fade away.
b. Incorrect. Interference accounts for memory by the displacement of one memory by another.
c. Incorrect. This is not a theory of forgetting.
*d. Correct. We may not have lost the memory, but with inadequate cues, we cannot recall it.

12. b mod. 20 p. 243
a. Incorrect. The hippocampus is thought to play a role in the consolidation of short-term memories into long-term memories.
*b. Correct. The sulci have yet to be implicated in memory.
c. Incorrect. Neurotransmitters support the memory consolidation process.
d. Incorrect. Changes at the synapse that are relatively permanent are called long-term potentiation.

13. a mod. 20 p. 244
*a. Correct. The loss of all memories before an accident is uncommon, although it is the most popularized form of amnesia.
b. Incorrect. See answer a,
c. Incorrect. See answer a.
d. Incorrect. See answer a.

14. d mod. 19 p. 236
a. Incorrect. True only if "other type" refers to fabrication.
b. Incorrect. Usually they are recovered in therapy, not treated.
c. Incorrect. They do have a noticeable effect, but this is not an identifying feature.
*d. Correct. The problem faced by all is the ability to verify the genuineness of the memories.

15. a mod. 20 p. 246
*a. Correct. This is called massed practice, and it is not very effective.
b. Incorrect. Overlearning is an effective form of study.
c. Incorrect. Organization helps memory by providing a meaningful scheme for the information.
d. Incorrect. This helps elaborate the material—putting it in your own words.

16. b mod. 20 p. 240
17. e mod. 20 p. 240
18. c mod. 20 p. 240
19. a mod. 20 p. 245
20. d mod. 18 p. 215

21. recall   mod. 18 p. 230
22. Recognition   mod. 19 p. 230
23. Retrograde amnesia   mod. 20 p. 244
24. Chunking   mod. 18 p. 220

25.
- Give several examples of laboratory research. The advantages include control over the experiment and the ability to document that prior memories do not influence the outcome.
- Identify experiences that are best examined in an everyday context. Much case study and archival research is based on reports that are made when an event occurs or on reports from several points of view and are thus a form of everyday memory research. Other examples should be given.
- As stated in the text, both of these techniques are needed to understand memory fully.

Practice Test 3:
1. d mod. 18 p. 218
a. Incorrect. Episodic memory would mean that the items had been committed to long-term memory.
b. Incorrect. This is the sensory memory for hearing, and it only lasts about a second.
c. Incorrect. This is the sensory memory for vision, and it only lasts about a quarter of a second.
*d. Correct. Short-term memory would account for most of this ability of recollection. Some, however, think this is a special skill developed by husbands who watch football too much.

2. b   mod. 18 p. 218
a. Incorrect. This is difficult to judge because our sensory receptors are always active.
*b. Correct. The sensory information in the sensory memory has not been processed any further than the sensory register, thus it represents the information as it was taken in.
c. Incorrect. The sensory information in the sensory memory has not been processed any further than the sensory register, thus it represents the information as it was taken in; it is therefore as complete as the sensory system makes it.
d. Incorrect. The information will be lost if it is not processed, but some information can be processed and be meaningless.

3. a   mod. 19 p. 232
*a. Correct. This constructive may help give the memory its narrative quality.
b. Incorrect. We tend not to lose the distinctive features.
c. Incorrect. Engrams are not sheep.
d. Incorrect. Ambiguous details are not a hallmark of flashbulb memories.

4. b   mod. 18 p. 219
a. Incorrect. A flashbulb memory implies a photo-like recollection.
*b. Correct. The visual echo or afterimage of the screen is much like the sensory activation in iconic memory.
c. Incorrect. The parallel here would be the persisting buzz of a tube radio for the brief moment after it is turned off.
d. Incorrect. Declarative memory is very long term and does not appear to fade in this manner.

5. d   mod. 18 p. 224
a. Incorrect. Working memory applies to memories that soon become insignificant, like what we ate for lunch yesterday or where we parked our car yesterday (although where we parked it today is very important).
b. Incorrect. Declarative does not account for physical skills like this.
c. Incorrect. This contributes to our personal experiences and episodic memory.
*d. Correct. The basketball shot is a procedural skill and thus would be stored in procedural memory.

6. b   mod. 18 p. 224
a. Incorrect. Working memory is significant for only a few days.
*b. Correct. Procedural memory is just this kind of skill-based memory.
c. Incorrect. Only if he had been in a serious bicycle accident could the possibility of a repressed memory play a role.
d. Incorrect. This may be an important moment in the lives of Daniel and his son, but it is the procedural memory that contributes to Daniel's ability to recall this old skill.

7. c   mod. 19 p. 233
a. Incorrect. Freud did not introduce this idea.
b. Incorrect. Piaget used it, but it was introduced by someone else.
*c. Correct. This was Bartlett's contribution.
d. Incorrect. This is the author of the textbook.

8. c   mod. 19 p. 230
a. Incorrect. If attention means rehearsal, then this would be true.
b. Incorrect. There is no mental imagery model of memory.
*c. Correct. "Attention" would have an effect on how the memory was elaborated (thus given depth).
d. Incorrect. There is no specific cultural diversity model of memory.

9. d   mod. 20 p. 241
a. Incorrect. Try the opposite, where the first list influences the later list.
b. Incorrect. This is a dissociative state similar to amnesia.
c. Incorrect. This is a type of memory failure.
*d. Correct. In proactive interference, an earlier list interferes with a later list.

10. b   mod. 20 p. 241
a. Incorrect. This is not a recognized form of interference.
*b. Correct. In retroactive interference, a later list interferes with an earlier list.
c. Incorrect. In proactive interference, an earlier list interferes with a later list.
d. Incorrect. This is not a recognized form of interference.

11. d   mod. 20 p. 241
a.   Incorrect. Alzheimer's disease would affect all of the transactions.
b.   Incorrect. Decay is not thought to be a significant factor, especially if the waiter would have remembered if the other transactions had not intervened.
c.   Incorrect. Proactive means the previous interfere with the current.
*d. Correct. Retroactive means the intervening events interfere with recall of the earlier event.

12. c   mod. 20 p. 244
a.   Incorrect. Try: the manufacture of beta amyloid.
b.   Incorrect. Try: the manufacture of beta amyloid.
*c. Correct. Platelets form and constrict brain tissue, causing it to die.
d.   Incorrect. Try: the manufacture of beta amyloid.

13. d   mod. 20 p. 244
a.   Incorrect. This sounds like Alzheimer's disease.
b.   Incorrect. This is anterograde amnesia.
c.   Incorrect. This sounds like advanced Alzheimer's disease or stroke victim.
*d. Correct. Memories are lost from before the accident.

14. a   mod. 20 p. 244
*a. Correct. Retrograde amnesia is marked by the loss of ability to recall events from before an accident or trauma.
b.   Incorrect. Anterograde amnesia involves the loss of memory from the point of an accident or trauma forward.
c.   Incorrect. This is a loss of memory from early childhood, usually before the development of language skills.
d.   Incorrect. This is a memory loss syndrome that results from severe, long-term abuse of alcohol.

15. c   mod. 18 p. 231
16. e   mod. 18 p. 225
17. b   mod. 20 p. 245
18. d   mod. 20 p. 229
19. a   mod. 19 p. 226

20. priming   mod. 18 p. 226
21. long-term potentiation   mod. 20 p. 242
22. Consolidation   mod. 20 p. 242
23. autobiographical memory   mod. 20 p. 236
24. elaborative rehearsal   mod. 18 p. 221

25. source confusion
▪   personal schema of the eyewitness
▪   power of the misinformation effect
▪   evidence related to the false memory syndrome
▪   relevant aspects of the encoding specificity theory

Thinking, Language, and Intelligence

Overview

This set of modules focuses on cognitive psychology, the branch of psychology that studies higher mental processes, including thinking, language, memory, problem solving, knowing, reasoning, judging, and decision making. This unit concentrates on three broad topics: thinking and reasoning, problem solving, and creativity and language.

Module 21 offers a definition of thinking, the manipulation of mental representations of information. Mental images and concepts of categorization, along with syllogistic reasoning and the use of algorithms, are discussed.

Module 22 offers examples of how people use language. The production of language and the reinforcement and conditioning of language development are presented. How the innate language acquisition device guides the development of language is explained. A discussion on how language is developed and acquired is also presented.

Module 23 considers intelligence in its many varieties. Intelligence represents a focal point for psychologists' intent on understanding how people adapt to their environment. It also is a key aspect in how individuals differ from one another. This section deals with the various conceptions of intelligence that have been offered by psychologists and the efforts made to develop standardized tests to measure it. Fluid and crystallized intelligence, information-processing approaches, and practical intelligence are discussed. Intelligence tests such as the Standford-Binet, the Wechsler Adult Intelligence Test, and achievement and other aptitude tests are explained. This chapter also discusses both the retarded and the gifted, two groups who display extremes in individual differences. Both their challenges and the programs developed to meet these challenges are presented. This module finally considers how and to what degree intelligence is influenced by heredity and by the environment and whether traditional intelligence tests are biased toward the dominant cultural groups in society.

To further investigate the topics covered in this chapter, you can visit the related Web sites by visiting the following link: www.mhhe.com/feldmanup6-08links.

Prologue: Eureka!
Looking Ahead

Module 21: Thinking

Becoming an Informed Consumer of Psychology:
Thinking Critically and Creatively

- *What is thinking?*
- *What processes underlie reasoning and decision making?*
- *How do people approach and solve problems?*
- *What are the major obstacles to problem solving?*

Thinking

The branch of psychology that studies problem solving and other aspects of thinking is called

[a] _____ . The term [b] _____ brings together the
higher mental processes of humans, including understanding the world, processing information,
making judgments and decisions, and describing knowledge.

[c] _____ is the manipulation of mental representations—words,
images, sounds, or data in any other modality—of information. Thinking transforms the
representation in order to achieve some goal or solve some problem. The visual, auditory, and

tactile representations of objects are called [d] _____ , and these are a key
component of thought. The time required to scan mental images can be measured. Brain scans
taken while people are forming and manipulating mental images are being used to study the

production and use of them. [e] _____ are categorizations of objects,
events, or people that share common properties. Because we have concepts, we are able to
classify newly encountered material on the basis of our past experiences. Ambiguous concepts

are usually represented by [f] _____ , which are typical, highly
representative examples of concepts. Concepts provide an efficient way of understanding events
and objects as they occur in the complex world.

Problem solving typically involves three major steps: preparation, production of solutions,
and evaluation of solutions. Problems are distinguished as either well-defined or ill-defined.

In a **[g]** _____, the problem and the information needed to solve it are clearly understood. The appropriate solution is thus easily identified. In an

[h] _____, both the problem and what information is needed may be unclear.

There are three categories of problem. **[i]** _____ like jigsaw puzzles require the recombination or reorganization of a group of elements in order to solve the problem.

With **[j]** _____, the problem solver must identify a relationship between elements and then construct a new relationship among them. A common example is number sequence problems, where a test taker may be asked to supply the next number in the sequence.

The third kind of problem is **[k]** _____. Transformation problems have a desired goal and require a series of steps or changes to take place in order to reach the goal. The Tower of Hanoi problem described in the text (Figure 8–3) is a transformation problem. Once the kind of problem is understood, it is easier to determine how to represent and organize the problem.

The creation of solutions may proceed at the simplest level as trial and error, but this approach may be inadequate for problems that have many possible configurations. The use of heuristics aids in the simplification of problems. The heuristic of **[l]** _____ proceeds by testing the difference between the current status and the desired outcome, and with each test, it tries to reduce the difference.

The use of **[m]** _____ takes a slightly different approach to problem solving, requiring a reorganization of the entire problem in order to achieve a solution. The reorganization of existing elements requires prior experience with the elements.

The final step of problem solving is to evaluate the adequacy of a solution. If the solution is not clear, criteria to judge the solution must be made clear.

In the progress toward a solution, several obstacles can be met. **[n]** _____ refers to the tendency to think of an object according to its given function or typical use.

Functional fixedness is an example of a broader phenomenon called **[o]** _____, the tendency for old patterns of solutions to persist.

[p] _____ is usually defined as the combining of responses or ideas in novel ways. **[q]** _____ refers to the ability to generate unusual yet appropriate responses to problems. **[r]** _____ produces responses that are based primarily on knowledge or logic. *Cognitive complexity* is the use of elaborate, intricate, and complex stimuli and thinking patterns. Humor can increase creative output as well. Apparently, intelligence is not related to creativity, perhaps because the tests for intelligence evaluate convergent thinking rather than divergent thinking.

Evaluate

Part A

_____ 1. syllogism

_____ 2. algorithm

_____ 3. heuristic

_____ 4. representativeness heuristic

_____ 5. availability heuristic

a. A rule in which people and things are judged by the degree to which they represent a certain category.

b. A set of rules that, if followed, guarantee a solution, although the reason they work may not be understood by the person using them.

c. A rule for judging the probability that an event will occur by the ease with which it can be recalled from memory.

d. A rule of thumb that may bring about a solution to a problem but is not guaranteed to do so.

e. A major technique for studying deductive reasoning, in which a series of two assumptions are used to derive a conclusion.

Part B

_____ 1. arrangement problems

_____ 2. problems of inducing structure

_____ 3. transformation problems

_____ 4. means-ends analysis

_____ 5. subgoals

a. Problems to be solved using a series of methods to change an initial state into a goal state.

b. A commonly used heuristic to divide a problem into intermediate steps and to solve each one of them.

c. Problems requiring the identification of existing relationships among elements presented so as to construct a new relationship among them.

d. Problems requiring the rearrangement of a group of elements in order to satisfy a certain criterion.

e. Repeated testing to determine and reduce the distance between the desired outcome and what currently exists in problem solving.

Rethink

21-1   How might the availability heuristic contribute to prejudices based on race, age, and gender? Can awareness of this heuristic prevent this from happening?

21-2   Are divergent thinking and convergent thinking mutually exclusive or complementary? Why? Are there situations in which one way of thinking is clearly superior? Can the two ways of thinking be combined? How?

Spotlight on Terminology and Language—ESL Pointers

Thinking

Page 251 "Although a clear sense of what specifically occurs when we think remains **elusive**, our understanding of the nature of the fundamental elements involved in thinking is growing."

It is difficult to understand and define, or identify, what is specifically happening when we think. The thinking process is hard to pin down; it is **elusive**. **Elusive** is when something is evasive; it tends to evade your grasp. Academic material can be considered **elusive** when it is not easily comprehended.

Page 251 "Some have **heralded** the production of mental images as a way to improve various skills."

When you **herald** the importance of mental images in learning and memory, you are proclaiming the value and importance of this memory technique. When you **herald** something, you signal or convey news. You make an announcement. The text has **heralded** the production of mental images as an effective way to enhance skills. Would you be willing to try the techniques of mental rehearsal to help you improve in one of your physical skills areas, perhaps in perfecting your swimming strokes?

Page 253 "For example, we can **surmise** that someone tapping a handheld screen is probably using some kind of computer or PDA, even if we have never encountered that specific brand before."

When you **surmise**, you deduce or infer without certain knowledge. Rather, you make infer or guess that something is the case on the basis of only limited evidence or intuition.

Page 256 "**Winnowing** out nonessential information is often a critical step in the preparation stage of problem solving." **Winnowing** is removing, or getting rid of, something undesirable or unwanted.

Module 22: Language

Grammar: Language's Language
Language Development: Developing a Way with Words
Understanding Language Acquisition: Identifying the Roots of Language

Applying Psychology in the 21st Century:
Music on the Mind

The Influence of Language on Thinking: Do Eskimos Have More Words for Snow Than Texans Do?
Do Animals Use Language?

Exploring Diversity: Teaching with Linguistic Variety: Bilingual Education

- *How do people use language?*
- *How does language develop?*

Language

[a] _____ is the systematic, meaningful arrangement of symbols. It is important for cognition and for communication with others. The basic structure of language is

[b] _____, the framework of rules that determine how thoughts are expressed.

The three components of grammar are (1) [c] _____, the smallest units of

sound, called [d] _____, that affect the meaning of speech and how words are

formed; (2) [e] _____, the rules that govern how words and phrases are

combined to form sentences; and (3) [f] _____, the rules governing meaning of words and sentences.

Language develops through set stages. At first, children [g] _____, producing speech-like but meaningless sounds. Babbling gradually sounds like actual speech, and by one year old, sounds that are not part of the language disappear. After the first year, children

produce short, two-word combinations followed by short sentences. [h] _____ refers to the short sentences that contain a critical message but sound as if written as a telegram, with noncritical words left out. As children begin to learn speech rules, they will apply them

without flexibility, a phenomenon known as [i]_____, where an "ed" might be applied to every past-tense construction. By the age of 5, most children have acquired the rules of language.

The **[j]** _____ to language acquisition suggests that the reinforcement and conditioning principles are responsible for language development. Praise for saying a word like "mama" reinforces the word and increases the likelihood of its being repeated. Shaping then makes child language become more adultlike. This approach has difficulty explaining the acquisition of language rules, because children are also reinforced when their language is incorrect. An alternative proposed by Noam Chomsky suggests that innate mechanisms are responsible for the acquisition of language. All human languages have a similar underlying structure he calls

[k] _____, and a neural system in the brain, the **[l]** _____, is responsible for the development of language.

Psychologists are also concerned whether the structure of language influences the structure of thought or whether thought influences language. The **[m]** _____ _hypothesis_ suggests that language shapes thought, determining how people of a particular culture perceive and understand the world. In an alternative view, language may reflect the different ways we have of thinking about the world, essentially that thought produces language.

Children who enter school as non-native English speakers face several hardships. The debate over whether to take a bilingual approach or whether all instruction should be in English is a major controversy. Evidence suggests that bilingual children have cognitive advantages, being more flexible, more aware of the rules of language, and having higher scores on verbal and nonverbal intelligence tests. Bilingual students raise questions of the advantage of

[n] _____, in which a person is a member of two cultures. Some have argued that society should promote an **[o]** _____, in which members of minority cultures are encouraged to learn both cultures.

Evaluate

_____ 1. grammar

_____ 2. phonology

_____ 3. phonemes

_____ 4. syntax

_____ 5. semantics

a. The framework of rules that determine how our thoughts can be expressed.

b. Rules governing the meaning of words and sentences.

c. The rules governing how words form sentences.

d. The study of how we use those sounds to produce meaning by forming them into words.

e. The smallest units of sound used to form words.

Rethink

22-1 Why is overgeneralization seen as an argument against a strict learning-theory approach to explaining language acquisition?

22-2 Do people with two languages, one at home and one at school, automatically have two cultures? Why might people who speak two languages experience cognitive advantages over those who speak only one?

Spotlight on Terminology and Language—ESL Pointers

Language

Page 266 "Semantic rules allow us to use words to convey the subtlest **nuances**."

A **nuance** is a tiny variation, just a shade of difference. You see a **nuance** as a very subtle distinction.

Page 267 "Anyone who spends even a little time with children will notice the enormous **strides** that they make in language development throughout childhood."

Stride is developmental advancement or progress. Children **stride** forward in their development of language skills.

Page 267 "Psychologists have offered two major explanations, one based on learning theory and the other based on **innate** processes."

Innate belongs to the essential nature of something. When a capability is **innate** in humans or other living organisms, these characteristics exist from birth.

Page 268 "To support the learning-theory approach, research shows that the more parents speak to their young children, the more **proficient** the children become in language use."

Proficient is skilled. The more parents speak to their young children, the more capable and competent the children become in language use.

Page 268 "Pointing to such problems with learning-theory approaches to language acquisition, linguist Noam Chomsky (1968, 1978, 1991) provided a **groundbreaking** alternative."

This **groundbreaking** theory was a new theory, a revolutionary theory. Your future research contributions may provide **groundbreaking** tools to treat mental and physical disease.

Page 270 "To **reconcile** such data, some theorists suggest the brain's **hardwired** language-acquisition device that Chomsky and geneticists **posit** provides the hardware for our acquisition of language, whereas the exposure to language in our environment that learning theorists observe allows us to develop the appropriate software."

When data is **reconciled**, we look at the conflicting ideas or interpretations, and work to make these apparently conflicting interpretations consistent or compatible.

If something is **hardwired**, this is affected by means of logic circuitry that is permanent.

To **posit** is to speculate, to hypothesize.

Page 271 "Many animals communicate with one another in **rudimentary** forms."

Rudimentary is basic. You would learn **rudiments**, or fundamental skills, during your early school years.

Page 272 "Proponents of bilingualism believe that students must **develop a sound footing** in basic subject areas and that, initially at least, teaching those subjects in their native language is the only way to provide them with that **foundation**."

To **develop a sound footing** is to have a strong base, or groundwork to build upon.

Foundation is the basis on which something stands or is supported.

Page 273 "Although the controversial issue has strong political **undercurrents**, evidence shows that the ability to speak two languages provides significant cognitive benefits over speaking only one language."

An **undercurrent** is an underlying feeling, often at odds with what is evident superficially.

Module 23: Intelligence

Theories of Intelligence: Are There Different Kinds of Intelligence?

Practical Intelligence and Emotional Intelligence: Toward a More Intelligent View of Intelligence

Assessing Intelligence

> **Applying Psychology in the 21st Century:**
> When a High IQ Keeps You from Getting a Job:
> Are You Too Smart for the Job You Want?

Variations in Intellectual Ability

Individual Differences in Intelligence: Hereditary and Environmental Determinants

> **Exploring Diversity:** The Relative Influence of Genetics and Environment: Nature, Nurture, and IQ

- *What are the different definitions and conceptions of intelligence?*
- *What are the major approaches to measuring intelligence, and what do intelligence tests measure?*
- *How can the extremes of intelligence be characterized?*
- *Are traditional IQ tests culturally biased?*
- *To what degree is intelligence influenced by the environment, and to what degree by heredity?*

Intelligence

[a] _____ has been defined by psychologists as the capacity to understand the world, think rationally, and use resources effectively.

Alfred Binet developed the first formal [b] _____ to identify the "dullest" students in the Parisian school system. His test was able to distinguish the "bright" from the "dull" and eventually made distinctions between age groups. The tests helped assign children a [c] _____, the average age of children who achieved the same score. In order to compare individuals with different *chronological ages*, the [d] _____ score was determined by dividing the mental age by the chronological age and multiplying by a factor of 100. Thus an IQ score is determined by the level at which a person performs on the test in relation to others of the same age.

188

The SAT is an **[e]** _____ meant to determine the level of achievement of an individual, that is, what the person has actually learned. An **[f]** _____ measures and predicts an individual's ability in a particular area. There is quite a bit of overlap among the IQ, achievement, and aptitude tests.

Psychological tests must have **[g]** _____, that is, they must measure something consistently from time to time. The question of whether a test measures the characteristic it is supposed to measure is called **[h]** _____. If a test is reliable, that does not mean it is valid. However, if a test is unreliable, it cannot be valid. A reliable test will produce similar outcomes in similar conditions. All types of tests in psychology, including intelligence tests, assessments of psychological disorders, and the measurement of attitudes, must meet tests of validity and reliability. **[i]** _____ are the standards of test performance that allow comparison of the scores of one test-taker to others who have taken it. This standard for a test is determined by calculating the average score for a particular group of people for whom the test is designed to be given. Then, the extent to which each person's score differs from the others can be calculated. The selection of the subjects who will be used to establish a norm for a test are critical.

In the two dominant tests, the score is considered to be a reflection of the person's intelligence. It remains unclear whether intelligence is a single factor or a combination of factors. The single-factor view suggests that there is a general factor for mental ability called

[j] _____.

In an alternate formulation, Howard Gardner has proposed the existence of eight multiple intelligences: (1) musical intelligence; (2) bodily-kinesthetic intelligence; (3) logical-mathematical intelligence; (4) linguistic intelligence; (5) spatial intelligence; (6) interpersonal intelligence; (7) intrapersonal intelligence; and (8) naturalist intelligence. Gardner suggests that these separate intelligences do not operate in isolation. Results from Gardner's work include the acceptance of more than one answer as correct on a test.

The information-processing approach to intelligence views intelligence as the ability to process information. Effective problem solvers have traditionally been those who also score high on intelligence tests.

More than 7 million people in the United States are classified as mentally retarded, and the populations that comprise the mentally retarded and the exceptionally gifted require special attention in order to reach their potential.

[k] _____ is defined by the American Association on Mental Deficiency (1992) as when there is "significantly subaverage general intellectual functioning existing concurrently with deficits in adaptive behavior and manifested during the developmental period." This definition includes mild to severe retardation. _Mild retardation_ includes individuals whose IQ scores fall in the 55 to 69 range. This comprises about 90 percent of the people with mental retardation. _Moderate retardation_, with scores ranging from 40 to 54; _severe retardation_, with scores from 25 to 39; and _profound retardation_, with scores below 25, present difficulties that become more pronounced the lower the IQ score.

The moderately retarded require some supervision during their entire lives, and the severe and profound groups require institutionalization. One-third of the people classified as retarded suffer from biological causes of retardation, mostly from **[l]** _____, a genetic disorder caused by an extra chromosome. **[m]** _____ occurs in cases when there is no biological cause but instead may be linked with a family history of retardation. This may be caused by environmental factors like severe poverty, malnutrition, and possibly a genetic factor that cannot be determined. In 1975, Congress passed a law (Public Law 94–142) that entitles individuals who are mentally retarded to a full education and to education and training in the

[n] _____. This law leads to a process of returning individuals to regular classrooms, called **[o]** _____. The view is that by placing individuals in typical environments, they interact with individuals who are not retarded and benefit from the interaction.

The **[p]** _____ comprise about 2 to 4 percent of the population. This group is generally identified as those individuals with IQ scores higher than 130. Contrary to the stereotype, these individuals are usually outgoing, well-adjusted, popular people who do most things better than the average person. Lewis Terman conducted a well-known longitudinal study following 1,500 gifted children (with IQs above 140). They have an impressive record of accomplishments, although being gifted does not guarantee success.

In the determination of the causes of individual differences, cultural differences in the framing of questions on a test can play an important role. On **[q]** _____, some culture and ethnic groups score lower than others, as with African-Americans, who tend to score 15 points lower than whites. One view suggests that the tests are biased toward Western individualism and against African communalism. Because of the possibility of bias and discrimination, some jurisdictions have banned the use of traditional intelligence tests.

Attempts to develop a **[r]** _____ test that does not discriminate have led in some cases to even greater disparities in scores. The controversy based on ethnic and minority differences in intelligence tests reflects a greater concern of whether intelligence is predominantly a result of genetics or environment.

Evaluate

Part A

____ 1. severe retardation

____ 2. profound retardation

____ 3. Down syndrome

____ 4. familial retardation

____ 5. intellectually gifted

a. Characterized by an IQ between 25 and 39 and difficulty in functioning independently.

b. Mental retardation in which there is a history of retardation in a family but no evidence of biological causes.

c. Characterized by higher-than-average intelligence, with IQ scores above 130.

d. A common cause of mental retardation, brought about by the presence of an extra chromosome.

e. Characterized by an IQ below 25 and an inability to function independently.

Part B

____ 1. mental age

____ 2. chronological age

____ 3. fluid intelligence

____ 4. crystallized intelligence

____ 5. practical intelligence

a. Intelligence related to overall success in living, rather than to intellectual and academic performance.

b. A person's physical age.

c. The store of specific information, skills, and strategies people have acquired through experience.

d. The typical intelligence level found for people at a given chronological age.

e. The ability to deal with new problems and encounters.

f. A measure of intelligence that takes into account an individual's mental and chronological ages.

Part C

_____ 1. intelligence tests

_____ 2. Stanford-Binet Test

_____ 3. Wechsler Adult Intelligence Scale-III (WAIS-III)

_____ 4. Wechsler Intelligence Scale for Children-III (WISC-III)

a. A test of intelligence consisting of verbal and nonverbal performance sections, providing a relatively precise picture of a person's specific abilities.

b. A test of intelligence that includes a series of items varying in nature according to the age of the person being tested.

c. A battery of measures to determine a person's level of intelligence.

d. An intelligence test for children consisting of verbal and nonverbal performance sections, providing a relatively precise picture of a child's specific abilities.

Rethink

23-1   Job interviews are really a kind of test. In what ways does a job interview resemble an aptitude test? An achievement test? Do you think job interviews can be shown to have validity? Reliability?

23-2   Why do you think negative stereotypes persist of gifted individuals and people with mental retardation, even in the face of contrary evidence? How can these stereotypes be changed?

Spotlight on Terminology and Language—ESL Pointers

Intelligence

Page 275 "Some might say that the inability of the Trukese to explain in Western terms how their sailing technique works is a sign of **primitive** or even unintelligent behavior."

Primitive behavior relates to an early or original state and is often marked by simplicity or an unsophisticated manner.

Page 279 "Some psychologists broaden the concept of practical intelligence even further beyond the intellectual **realm** and consider intelligence involving emotions."

Realm is the defined area of interest. Some psychologists are suggesting that practical intelligence is a robust characteristic.

Page 281 "If performance on certain tasks or test items improved with **chronological** or physical age, performance could be used to distinguish more intelligent people from less intelligent ones within a particular age group."

When something is arranged **chronologically**, it is arranged in order of time of occurrence. **Chrono-** or **chron-** is a prefix relating to time.

Page 281 "On the basis of this principle, Binet devised the first **formal** intelligence test, which was designed to identify the "dullest" students in the Paris school system in order to provide them with remedial aid."

Formal here relates to the official and prescribed nature of the design of this intelligence test.

Page 281 "By using mental age alone, for instance, we might assume that a 20-year-old responding at a 18-year-old's level would be as bright as a 5-year-old answering at a 3-year-old's level, when actually the 5-year-old would be displaying a much greater **relative** degree of slowness."

Relative means dependent on or interconnected with something else for significance or intelligibility. The text example expresses why mental age is **relative** to chronological age.

Page 282 "**Remnants** of Binet's original intelligence test are still with us, although the test has been revised in significant ways."

Remnants are pieces. Some of the components of Binet's test remain in use today.

Page 282 "An examiner begins by finding a mental age level at which a person is able to answer all the questions correctly, and then moves on to **successively** more difficult problems."

Successively is to follow in order or sequence.

Page 283 "However, **sacrifices** are made in group testing that in some cases may **outweigh the benefits**.

If you have **outweighed the benefits**, you have sacrificed too much.

Sacrifices are things that you forfeit for another thing thought to be of greater value. Students frequently **sacrifice** sleep and social activities to study and earn high grades.

Page 283 "Finally, in some cases, it is simply impossible to **employ** group tests, particularly with young children or people with unusually low IQs (Aiken, 1996)."

To **employ** group tests is to use them.

Page 288 "Test validity and reliability are **prerequisites** for accurate assessment of intelligence—as well as for any other measurement task carried out by psychologists."

A **prerequisite** is something that is required as a prior condition. To take many courses in college, you first must take a **prerequisite**, a course that teaches you the skills you must have to enter the next course.

Page 288 "**Norms** are standards of test performance that permit the comparison of one person's score on a test to the scores of others who have taken the same test."

Norms are standards that allow you to compare one item to another.

Page 288 "The basic **scheme** for developing norms is for test designers to calculate the average score achieved by a particular group of people for whom the test has been designed."

A **scheme** is a system, an orderly plan of action.

Test your knowledge of the material in this set of modules by answering these questions. These questions have been placed in three Practice Tests. The first two tests consist of questions that will test your recall of factual knowledge. The third test contains questions that are challenging and primarily test for conceptual knowledge and your ability to apply that knowledge. Check your answers and review the feedback using the Answer Key on the following pages of the *Study Guide*.

PRACTICE TEST 1:

1. Manipulation of mental images is best shown by subjects' abilities to:
   a. use mental images to represent abstract ideas.
   b. anticipate the exit of a toy train from a tunnel.
   c. understand the subtle meanings of sentences.
   d. rotate mentally one image to compare it with another.

2. A concept is defined as:
   a. an idea or thought about a new procedure or product.
   b. a group of attitudes that define an object, event, or person.
   c. a categorization of people, objects, or events that share certain properties.
   d. one of many facts that collectively define the subject matter for a specific area of knowledge (such as psychology).

3. In the military, applying the honor code of conduct to a particular situation in the field requires:
   a. inductive reasoning.   c. transductive reasoning.
   b. linguistic reasoning.   d. deductive reasoning.

4. On Alfred Binet's IQ test, suppose that an 8-year-old child can solve the problems that an average 10-year-old can solve. Her chronological age would be:
   a. 8.   c. 12.
   b. 10.   d. impossible to judge from these data.

5. All but which of the following are major steps in problem solving?
   a. evaluation of solutions generated
   b. preparation for the creation of solutions
   c. documentation of all solutions
   d. production of solutions

6. Andrew said, "I retook that last test three times, and my score was incredibly different each time." The test he described was:
   a. invalid.   c. culturally biased.
   b. unreliable.   d. subscaled

7. The most frequently used heuristic technique for solving problems is:
   a. the availability heuristic.   c. the representativeness heuristic.
   b. categorical processing.   d. means-ends analysis.

8. Which of the following is **not** associated with defining and understanding a problem?
   a. discarding inessential information   c. dividing the problem into parts
   b. simplifying essential information   d. clarifying the solution

9. Insight is a:
   a. sudden awareness of the relationships among various elements in a problem that previously appeared to be independent of one another.
   b. sudden awareness of the solution to a problem with which one has had no prior involvement or experience.
   c. sudden awareness of a particular algorithm that can be used to solve a problem.
   d. spontaneous procedure for generating a variety of possible solutions to a problem.

10. Which approach do cognitive psychologists use to understand intelligence?
    a. structure-of-intellect
    b. deviation IQ
    c. aptitude-testing
    d. information-processing

11. Logic and knowledge are exemplified by _____ thinking.
    a. creative
    b. convergent
    c. divergent
    d. imaginal

12. Mary Ellen was able to think of 50 distinct uses for a plastic spoon in a 5-minute thinking interval; therefore, she:
    a. has an especially strong mental set.
    b. has superior intelligence.
    c. is especially prone to functional fixedness.
    d. is particularly good at divergent thinking.

13. The syntax of a language is the framework of rules that determine:
    a. the meaning of words and phrases.
    b. how words and phrases are combined to form sentences.
    c. the sounds of letters, phrases, and words.
    d. how thoughts can be translated into words.

14. Children sometimes use telegraphic speech. This refers to:
    a. speech that is very rapid.
    b. seemingly nonessential words omitted from phrases and sentences.
    c. the tonal quality of speech is limited.
    d. speech that may speed up, slow down, or contain pauses.

15. The Regents family is anxious to have little conversations with the newest member of their family, Emily. She will acquire most of the basic rules of grammar by:
    a. 2 years of age.
    b. 3 years of age.
    c. 4 years of age.
    d. 5 years of age.

_____ 16. mental set

_____ 17. confirmation bias

_____ 18. creativity

_____ 19. divergent thinking

_____ 20. convergent thinking

a. The tendency for patterns of problem solving to persist.

b. A type of thinking that produces responses based on knowledge and logic.

c. The ability to generate unusual but appropriate responses to problems or questions.

d. Favoring an initial hypothesis and disregarding contradictory information suggesting alternative solutions.

e. The combining of responses or ideas in novel ways.

21. _____ is characterized by an IQ of between 55 and 69 and the ability to function independently.

22. Frederick's mental age is the same as his chronological age. His IQ score is _____.

23. The WAIS III and the WISC-III intelligence tests are different from the Standford Binet because they include both a verbal score and a _____ score.

24. Congress passed Public Law 94-172 to provide that people with mental retardation must be educated and trained in the _____ environment.

25. The Terman Study has followed 1,500 _____ for more than 60 years.

26. Identify a major challenge that you anticipate facing in the next several years. It can involve choosing a career, getting married, selecting a major, choosing a graduate school, or one of many others. Describe the problem or challenge briefly, then describe how you would apply the problem-solving steps presented in the text to the problem to generate solutions that you might try.

PRACTICE TEST 2:

1. Cognitive psychologists study all of the following **except**:
    a. how the sensory system takes in information.
    b. how people understand the world.
    c. how people process information.
    d. how people make judgments.

2. Prototypes of concepts are:
    a. new concepts to describe newly emerging phenomena.
    b. new concepts that emerge within a language spontaneously and then are retained or discarded.
    c. representative examples of concepts.
    d. concepts from other languages that are incorporated into a native language if they appear useful.

3. The first IQ test was devised for the purpose of:
    a. diagnosing brain damage.
    b. identifying slow learners for remedial teaching.
    c. screening applicants for medical school.
    d. selecting candidates for a school for the intellectually gifted.

4. Thomas relied on _____ by failing to solve a problem because he misapplied a category or set of categories.
    a. an availability heuristic
    b. a mental set
    c. functional fixedness
    d. a representativeness heuristic

5. Problems fall into one of three categories. Which of the following is **not** one of them?
    a. arrangement
    b. affability
    c. structure
    d. transformation

6. Identifying existing relationships among elements and constructing a new relationship is an example of:
   - a. an inducing-structure problem.
   - b. an organization problem.
   - c. an arrangement problem.
   - d. a transformation problem.

7. Problems that are solved by changing an initial state into a goal state are called:
   - a. transformation problems.
   - b. problems of inducing structure.
   - c. insight problems.
   - d. arrangement problems.

8. Patricia tells her roommate sardonically, "As a student, I measure success one midterm at a time." Her statement implies that her strategy for achieving a college degree is through:
   - a. means-ends analysis.
   - b. achieving subgoals.
   - c. trial and error.
   - d. application of algorithms.

9. Insight:
   - a. is an unexplained discovery of a solution without prior experience with any elements of the problem.
   - b. results from a methodical trial-and-error process.
   - c. is a sudden realization of relationships among seemingly independent elements.
   - d. is a solution that is independent of trial-and-error and experience.

10. Functional fixedness and mental set show that:
    - a. the person's first hunches about the problem are typically correct.
    - b. one's initial perceptions about the problem can impede the solution.
    - c. convergent thinking is needed when the problem is well defined.
    - d. the person who poses the problem is the one who solves it best.

11. A creative thinker often demonstrates which of the following characteristic?
    - a. convergent thought
    - b. divergent thought
    - c. high intelligence
    - d. recurrent thought

12. IQ scores falling below _____ fit the criterion for mental retardation.
    - a. 80
    - b. 70
    - c. 60
    - d. 50

13. Keenan has reached the age where babbling is a big part of his day. It is **not** true that babbling:
    - a. occurs from 3 to 6 months of age.
    - b. includes words such as "dada" and "mama."
    - c. is speechlike.
    - d. produces sounds found in all languages.

14. The fact that "mama" and "dada" are among the first words spoken in the English language:
    - a. is unusual because these words do not contain the first sounds a child can make.
    - b. suggests that they are responses the child is born with.
    - c. is not surprising because these words are easy to pronounce, and the sound capabilities of the young child are limited.
    - d. demonstrates that the sounds heard most frequently are the sounds spoken first.

15. According to Noam Chomsky, the brain contains a neural system designed for understanding and learning language called the:
    - a. linguistic relativity system.
    - b. language-acquisition device.
    - c. limbic system.
    - d. phonological linguistic device.

____ 16. David Wechsler

____ 17. Spearman

____ 18. Howard Gardner

____ 19. Binet

____ 20. Daniel Goleman

____ 21. Robert Sternberg

a. Suggested there were eight factors of intelligence called primary mental abilities.

b. First designed IQ tests with verbal and performance scales.

c. Emotional intelligence underlies the accurate assessment, evaluation, and expression of emotions.

d. Assumed there was a general factor for mental ability, the g-factor.

e. Devised the first formal intelligence test.

f. Triarchic theory of intelligence: componential, experiential, and contextual.

22. Producing many answers to the same question is called _____.

23. The notion that language determines our thought and feelings is called _____.

24. When you mentally manipulate information, it is called _____.

25. That there is a certain window of opportunity in which humans learn language is called the _____ of development.

26. Research shows that chimps can learn the meaning of _____.

27. Some consider language to be the capability that uniquely distinguishes us as human. Weigh the arguments for the language skills of specially trained chimpanzees and develop your position on this issue. Is language unique to humans? If so, how would you characterize the communication skills of chimpanzees? If not, what capability does distinguish us from other animals?

PRACTICE TEST 3: Conceptual, Applied, and Challenging Questions

1. Which alternative does **not** fit within the text's definition of cognition?
    a. the higher mental processes of humans
    b. how people know and understand the world
    c. how people communicate their knowledge and understanding to others
    d. how people's eyes and ears process the information they receive

2. Concepts are similar to perceptual processes in that:
    a. concepts, like visual illusions, can produce errors in interpretation.
    b. concepts allow us to simplify and manage our world.
    c. concepts are to language what figure-ground relationships are to perception.
    d. some concepts and perceptual processes are innate.

3. You have had several troublesome, time-consuming, expensive, and emotionally trying experiences with telemarketers. Then you find out that your roommate for next term is a telemarketer. You are convinced, even without meeting your future roommate, that you should not be paired with this person. You have used the _____ heuristic to arrive at your conclusion.
    a. means-ends
    b. representativeness
    c. availability
    d. personality

4. Thinking of a George Foreman Grill in conventional terms may handicap your efforts to solve a problem when a possible solution involves using the grill for a novel use. This phenomenon is called:
    a. functional fixedness.
    b. insight.
    c. awareness.
    d. preparation.

5. The slight difference in meaning between the sentences "The mouse ate the cheese" and "The cheese was eaten by the mouse" is determined by the rules of:
    a. grammar.
    b. phonology.
    c. syntax.
    d. semantics.

6. Which of the following is the first refinement in the infant's learning of language?
    a. production of short words that begin with a consonant
    b. disappearance of sounds that are not in the native language
    c. emergence of sounds that resemble words
    d. production of two-word combinations

7. Generalizing from information presented in the text, which of the following two-word combinations is **least** likely to be spoken by a 2-year-old?
    a. Daddy up.
    b. Mommy cookie.
    c. I'm big.
    d. More, more.

8. Rabia exhibits a speech pattern characterized by short sentences, with many noncritical words missing. Which of the following is **not** true?
    a. Rabia is between 2 and 3 years old.
    b. Rabia is exhibiting telegraphic speech.
    c. Rabia is building complexity of speech.
    d. Rabia is using overgeneralization.

9. Dr. Slocum, a cognitive psychologist, has argued that the language of the child depends on exposure to the language of the parents. She would say that language is acquired through:
    a. classical conditioning.
    b. shaping.
    c. universal grammar.
    d. biological unfolding.

10. Raphael and Alix were told that their youngsters have very high IQs and:
    a. are gifted in every academic subject.
    b. will have adjustment problems later in life.
    c. should not be mainstreamed.
    d. should show better social adjustment in school than others.

11. The Navaho have many names for the bluish aquamarine color of turquoise. Based on how other, similar facts have been understood, this too could be used to support:
    a. the theory that language determines thought.
    b. the theory that thought determines language.
    c. the existence of the language acquisition device.
    d. development of the nativistic position.

199

12. The notion that language shapes the way that people of a particular culture perceive and think about the world is called the:
    - a. semantic-reasoning theory.
    - b. cultural-language law.
    - c. prototypical hypothesis.
    - d. linguistic-relativity hypothesis.

13. Charise participates in a study in which she is asked to imagine a giraffe. After indicating that she has constructed the entire image, she is then asked to focus on the giraffe's tail. What should the experimenter be doing as she completes this task?
    - a. observing her reaction
    - b. timing each step
    - c. recording her respiration
    - d. getting the next subject ready

14. In a study concerned with concept formation and categorization, you are asked to think about a table. Which of the following would be considered a prototype if you were to have imagined it?
    - a. your grandmother's dining room table
    - b. a four-legged, rectangular table
    - c. the coffee table in the student lounge
    - d. a round, pedestal-style oak table

_____ 15. insight

_____ 16. cognitive psychology

_____ 17. prototypes

_____ 18. linguistic relativity

_____ 19. creativity

a. Typical, highly representative examples of a concept.

b. Sudden awareness of the relationships among various elements that had previously appeared to be independent of one another.

c. The branch of psychology that specializes in the study of cognition.

d. "Language determines thought."

e. Associated truth, divergent thinking, and playful thinking.

20. Dr. Finelli insisted that Megan, a student with special needs, be integrated into regular classroom activities. This is called _____.

21. A main shortcoming of the Stanford-Binet IQ test is the focus on _____.

22. Most school systems administer group intelligence tests because the primary advantage is the _____ of administration.

23. The _____ is the phenomenon that demonstrates that the number of correct answers for the average person have risen significantly in the past several generations.

24. In Terman's longitudinal study of the gifted, he found that at 40 years of age, the _____ reported more life satisfaction than the _____.

25. Discuss the controversy regarding bilingual education.

■ ANSWER KEY: MODULES 21, 22, AND 23

Module 21:	Module 22:	Module 23:	Evaluate
[a] cognitive psychology	[a] Language	[a] Intelligence	Part A
[b] cognition	[b] grammar	[b] intelligence tests	1. a
[c] Thinking	[c] phonology	[c] mental age	2. e
[d] mental images	[d] phonemes	[d] intelligence quotient	3. d
[e] Concepts	[e] syntax	[e] achievement test	4. b
[f] prototypes	[f] semantics	[f] aptitude test	5. c
[g] well-defined problem	[g] babble	[g] reliability	
[h] ill-defined problem	[h] Telegraphic speech	[h] validity	Part B
[i] Arrangement problems	[i] overgeneralization	[i] Norms	1. c
[j] problems of inducing	[j] learning-theory approach	[j] g, or g-factor	2. b
structure	[k] universal grammar	[k] Mental retardation	3. a
[k] transformation	[l] language-acquisition device	[l] Down syndrome	4. d
problems	[m] linguistic-relativity	[m] Familial retardation	
[l] means-ends analysis	[n] biculturalism	[n] least restrictive	Part C
[m] insight	[o] alternation model	environment	1. d
[n] Functional fixedness		[o] mainstreaming	2. b
[o] mental set	Evaluate	[p] intellectually gifted	3. e
[p] Creativity	1. a	[q] standardized intelligence	4. c
[q] Divergent thinking	2. d	test	5. a
[r] Convergent thinking	3. e	[r] culture-fair	
	4. c		
Evaluate	5. b		
Part A Part B			
1. e 1. d			
2. b 2. c			
3. d 3. a			
4. a 4. e			
5. c 5. b			

Selected Rethink Answers

21-1   Define what is meant by the term *availability heuristic*. Knowing that we act on thoughts that we believe represent certain groups, negative thoughts about any race, age, or gender could lead to our developing a prejudice about that group. The media draws tragic events to our attention on a daily basis. If we believe these events to be true, we develop availability heuristics and use this information to guide future decision making (i.e., "People froze while hiking, so I shouldn't hike anymore."). Awareness can prevent this by allowing us to assess what the real risks in a situation are and not rely on heuristics.

21-2   They are complimentary. Divergent thinking generates a variety of creative solutions on how to solve a problem, which can then be offered as choices. Convergent thinking takes choices and, with knowledge and logic, selects the best solution.

23-1   Aptitude is defined as the measure of an individual's ability in a particular area. Achievement is a measure of what a person has learned. Job interviews are designed to address both of these areas. Applicants who are hired because of these interview criteria and then are capable on the job would confirm the validity of the interview methods; the interviews assess what they're intended to. If this arrangement worked repeatedly with job applicants, it would be considered a reliable hiring practice.

Practice Test 1:

1. d   mod. 21 p. 251
a. Incorrect. This is difficult to document.
b. Incorrect. This probably relates to spatial-temporal skills.
c. Incorrect. This has to do with language skills.
*d. Correct. Mental rotation and comparison is one technique used to study how people manipulate mental images.

2. c   mod. 21 p. 252
a. Incorrect. Concepts include more than new procedures and products.
b. Incorrect. The term "attitudes" is too restrictive, and this is a definition of a stereotype.
*c. Correct. Concepts are used to categorize thought.
d. Incorrect. Concepts can include natural objects as well as scientific knowledge.

3. d   mod. 21 p. 253
a. Incorrect. Inductive reasoning works from a series of examples to generate a conclusion.
b. Incorrect. Not sure what this is.
c. Incorrect. The term "transductive" has been applied to reasoning during the preoperational period of childhood.
*d. Correct. Deriving a solution or conclusion from a set of laws or principles describes deductive reasoning.

4. a   mod. 23 p. 282
*a. Correct. The chronological age is the age in years.
b. Incorrect. See answer a.
c. Incorrect. See answer a.
d. Incorrect. See answer a.

5. c   mod. 21 p. 254
a. Incorrect. This is an important step.
b. Incorrect. Good preparation is an important step in effective problem solving.
*c. Correct. To reach a solution, it is not necessary to document all possible solutions.
d. Incorrect. To solve a problem, one must produce at least one solution.

6. b   mod. 23 p. 286
a. Incorrect. The test may have tested what it sought to test but generated different results on each taking.
*b. Correct. Typically, if a test produces different results for the same subject in different administrations, the test reliability is low.
c. Incorrect. Culturally biased tests do not account for variability in the score for the same subject.
d. Incorrect. Many tests have subscales, but this would not cause unreliability.

7. d   mod. 21 p. 257
a. Incorrect. The text names means-ends analysis as the most common.
b. Incorrect. See answer a.
c. Incorrect. See answer a.
d. Correct. Consider how often we turn to the desired outcome and let it shape how we approach the problem.

8. d   mod. 21 p. 257
a. Incorrect. Removing the inessential may help make the definition of the problem clearer.
b. Incorrect. Making the information simpler, even putting it in a graphic form like a chart, helps make the problem easier to understand.
c. Incorrect. Often dividing the problem into parts helps define the whole problem more clearly.
*d. Correct. Clarifying the solution applies more the later stages of solving the problem.

9. a   mod. 21 p. 258
*a. Correct. This is the definition of insight, where one becomes aware of a new or different arrangement of elements.
b. Incorrect. Insight does not suggest that an individual has no experience of a problem.
c. Incorrect. While one might discover an algorithm for a problem through insight, it is not a necessary aspect of insight.
d. Incorrect. This refers more to brainstorming than insight.

10. d   mod. 23 p. 277
a. Incorrect. "Structure-of-intellect" is associated with another approach.
b. Incorrect. The deviation IQ is a formula introduced to adjust the conventional way of calculating IQ scores to fit any age.
c. Incorrect. Aptitude testing is used by school counselors and personnel counselors to guide job selection and placement.
*d. Correct. Cognitive psychologists use the information-processing approach because it addresses how people store, recall, and utilize information.

11. b   mod. 21 p. 262
a.   Incorrect. Creativity draws on knowledge and experience, but not necessarily so.
*b. Correct. Convergent thinking is defined as thinking exemplified by the use of logical reasoning and knowledge.
c.   Incorrect. Divergent thinking often defies logic and is not dependent on a knowledge base.
d.   Incorrect. The use of the imagination does not exemplify logical processes and is perhaps the least dependent knowledge.

12. d   mod. 21 p. 262
a.   Incorrect. If the mental set is strong, it is not having any impeding effect.
b.   Incorrect. Because intelligence and creativity have not been correlated, this is not necessarily true.
c.   Incorrect. Exactly the opposite.
*d. Correct. Divergent thinking involves recognizing alternatives and optional uses.

13. b   mod. 22 p. 265
a.   Incorrect. Semantics determines the meaning of words and phrases.
*b. Correct. Syntax refers to the meaningful structuring of sentences.
c.   Incorrect. Phonology governs the production of sounds.
d.   Incorrect. Somewhat broader than syntax, grammar governs the translation of thoughts into language.

14. b   mod. 22 p. 267
a.   Incorrect. Speed and rate of speech are not factors in telegraphic speech.
*b. Correct. Like sending a telegraph, some words may be omitted, but the message is still clear.
c.   Incorrect. The sound of speech is not relevant to telegraphic speech.
d.   Incorrect. Speed and rate of speech are not factors in telegraphic speech.

15. d   mod. 21 p. 266
a.   Incorrect. At 2 years, children are just beginning to utilize speech and build vocabularies.
b.   Incorrect. At 3 years, vocabulary and grammatical rules are still being acquired.
c.   Incorrect. At 4 years, vocabulary and grammatical rules are still being acquired.
*d. Correct. By 5 years, most children can produce grammatically correct speech.

16. a   mod. 21 p. 260
17. d   mod. 21 p. 261
18. e   mod. 21 p. 261
19. c   mod. 21 p. 262
20. b   mod. 21 p. 262

21. mild retardation   mod. 27 p. 289
22. 100   mod. 26 p. 281
23. performance   mod. 26 p. 284
24. least restrictive   mod. 27 p. 290
25. high IQ subjects   mod. 27 p. 290

26.
- Describe your problem or challenge. It would be best to identify both the positive and the negative aspects of the challenge. What is gained and what is given up.
- Define the problem in terms of the steps that must be taken to achieve the solution.
- State several possible solution strategies as they apply to your problem.
- State how you will know when you have effectively solved the problem. Remember, if the problem is long-term, selecting one solution strategy may preclude using another.

Practice Test 2:
1.   a   mod. 21 p. 251
*a. Correct. Perceptual psychologists focus on how the sensory system takes in information.
b.   Incorrect. Our understanding of the world is a focal point of study for cognitive psychologists.
c.   Incorrect. How we process information is a focal point of study for cognitive psychologists.
d.   Incorrect. Decision making is a focal point of study for cognitive psychologists.

2.   c   mod. 21 p. 252
a.   Incorrect. While "prototype" may refer to a new or first type, it also refers to the template or standard.
b.   Incorrect. Prototypes are neither spontaneous nor discarded quickly.
*c. Correct. In this sense, the prototype is the template or standard for a concept.
d.   Incorrect. The concept described here is known as "cognate" or "loan words."

3.   b   mod. 23 p. 281
a.   Incorrect. No IQ test has been devised for diagnosing brain damage.
*b. Correct. Binet was trying to develop a means of placing slower children in special classes.
c.   Incorrect. This probably would not work anyway.
d.   Incorrect. This is a common use today, but the original use was to identify slow learners.

4.   d   mod. 21 p. 253
a.   Incorrect. In the availability heuristic, one applies the most available category to the situation.
b.   Incorrect. A mental set is a set of expectations and inferences drawn from memory that may cause reasoning errors, but not in this manner.
c.   Incorrect. Functional fixedness refers specifically to applying objects to a problem in the manner of their typical or common function, thus being fixated on a particular approach.
*d.   Correct. The representative heuristic selects a category that may represent the situation but can be erroneously applied (or misapplied).

5.   b   mod. 21 p. 254
a.   Incorrect. Problems of arrangement may include puzzles and similar problems.
*b.   Correct. No such type of problem!
c.   Incorrect. A problem of inducing structure involves finding relationships among existing elements.
d.   Incorrect. Transformation problems involve changing from one state to another (the goal state).

6.   a   mod. 21 p. 254
*a.   Correct. True, this describes a problem of inducing structure.
b.   Incorrect. This is not one of the three types of problems, and thus the definition does not apply.
c.   Incorrect. An arrangement problem is more like a jigsaw puzzle, where elements may be rearranged.
d.   Incorrect. A transformation problem involves moving from one state to another (goal state).

7.   a   mod. 21 p. 254
*a.   Correct. Changing from one state to another is a transformation.
b.   Incorrect. This refers to another kind of problem.
c.   Incorrect. Insight is a means of solving a problem, not a type of problem (unless someone is without any insight).
d.   Incorrect. This refers to another kind of problem.

8.   b   mod. 21 p. 254
a.   Incorrect. A means-ends approach might be more like "I know the steps I need to take, and I am taking them."
*b.   Correct. Each step is a subgoal.
c.   Incorrect. Trial and error might be more like "I think I'll try this major next semester."
d.   Incorrect. Algorithmic approach might be more like "I need three course from this group, two from that, etc."

9.   c   mod. 21 p. 258
a.   Incorrect. Insight may be difficult to explain or articulate, and it may occur without prior experience, but these are not the defining elements of insight.
b.   Incorrect. Insight does not result from trial-and-error processes.
*c.   Correct. This sudden realization of relationship or recognition of patterns is key to insight.
d.   Incorrect. Insight may be founded on trial-and-error and experience, although the restructuring that occurs during insight may be independent, it may also be a result of experience or creative reorganization.

10.   b   mod. 21 p. 268
a.   Incorrect. These hunches may actually make it hard to see alternatives.
*b.   Correct. Initial perceptions may include more conventional ways of using the elements of the problem and tools at hand to solve it.
c.   Incorrect. While true, it does not apply to these two concepts.
d.   Incorrect. Not really sure what this means.

11.   b   mod. 21 p. 262
a.   Incorrect. Convergent thinking involves logical reasoning and knowledge in the process of thinking.
*b.   Correct. Divergent thinking is the only consistently identified characteristic of creative thinking.
c.   Incorrect. Many creative thinkers are highly intelligent, but this is not a necessary characteristic.
d.   Incorrect. Recurrent thought does not characterize creativity.

12.   b   mod. 23 p. 289
a.   Incorrect. See answer b.
*b.   Correct. Any score below 70 is considered to indicate mental retardation.
c.   Incorrect. Any score below 70 is considered to indicate mental retardation, and the answer is incorrect because all scores below 60 are considered, but other scores belong as well.
d.   Incorrect. See answer b.

13. b   mod. 22 p. 266
a. Incorrect. Babbling occurs from 3 to 6 months.
*b. Correct. "Dada" and "Mama" are early words formed of babbling sounds.
c. Incorrect. Babbling had many speech-like patterns.
d. Incorrect. Babbling does produce all the sounds that humans make.

14. c   mod. 22 p. 266
a. Incorrect. Actually, it is usual because they are among the first sounds made.
b. Incorrect. We know of no words that are innate.
*c. Correct. These are easy and composed of sounds commonly heard in the babbling phase.
d. Incorrect. Babies can even make sounds they have never heard before, especially if the parents' language does not include the sound.

15. b   mod. 22 p. 267
a. Incorrect. There is no linguistic relativity system; instead, it is the linguistic relativity hypothesis, a theory about how language and thought interrelate.
*b. Correct. This is the term used by Noam Chomsky to refer to this neural wiring.
c. Incorrect. The limbic system is the organization of several parts of the brain that is generally devoted to pleasure, emotion, motivation, and memory.
d. Incorrect. Sounds good, but this is not the term used, and it does not refer to any actual concept.

16. b   mod. 23 p. 283
17. d   mod. 23 p. 276
18. a   mod. 23 p. 277
19. e   mod. 23 p. 281
20. c   mod. 23 p. 279
21. f   mod. 23 p. 279

22. divergent thinking   mod. 21 p. 262
23. linguistic relativity   mod. 22 p. 270
24. thinking   mod. 21 p. 251
25. critical period   mod. 22 p. 266
26. Symbols   mod. 22 p. 271

27.
- Chimpanzees acquire an ability to speak that is comparable to a 2-year-old child.
- The physical ability in humans to produce language has the greatest production capability.
- You may be familiar with research in dolphin and whale communication or work with other animals. Examples could be used to support your answer.
- What is meant by "unique" must be defined to complete this answer. Human language is unique, but other animals do communicate.

Practice Test 3:
1. d   mod. 21 p. 251
a. Incorrect. This is one of the components of the text's definition.
b. Incorrect. Cognition refers to the processes involved in how people come to know their world.
c. Incorrect. Cognition includes language and the interpretation of language.
*d. Correct. This statement describes the processes of sensation and perception; while not part of cognition, they are companion processes.

2. b   mod. 21 p. 252
a. Incorrect. Concepts may result from errors in some way, but they do not produce errors.
*b. Correct. Like perception, concepts help make the world understandable by simplifying and organizing it.
c. Incorrect. Even if this is true, it does not address the similarity between concepts and perception.
d. Incorrect. We know of no innate concepts.

3. b   mod. 21 p. 253
a. Incorrect. The means-ends does not apply here.
*b. Correct. Because your roommate is a member of the category of telemarketers, the representative heuristic suggests that somehow he might be representative of that group of people.
c. Incorrect. The availability heuristic would suggest that you utilized only currently available or the most prominent information about telemarketers and ignored other more important information that is easily recalled from memory. While true, you had no other information about your roommate.
d. Incorrect. There is no such heuristic.

4. a   mod. 21 p. 260
*a. Correct. Functional fixedness forces us to focus on the grill's traditional function, ignoring that it could be used as a weight or a clamp, or even an electrical conductor.
b. Incorrect. Insight is the restructuring of given elements.
c. Incorrect. Awareness seems to be restricted in this case.
d. Incorrect. Overpreparation may lead to functional fixedness by encouraging the habitual use of an object, but it is not the name of the phenomena.

5.   d   mod. 22 p. 266
a.   Incorrect. Grammar governs how a thought becomes language in a general sense, and a more precise possibility is given in the options.
b.   Incorrect. Phonology governs the production of sounds.
c.   Incorrect. Syntax refers to the structure of sentences and not their meaning.
*d. Correct. Semantics governs the use of words and sentences to make specific meanings and would govern how the same words can be rearranged to make different meanings.

6.   b   mod. 22 p. 266
a.   Incorrect. This occurs shortly after the first major development of dropping sounds that the native language does not contain.
*b. Correct. The first thing that happens occurs when babbling sounds that are not in the native language disappear.
c.   Incorrect. This can happen at any time but becomes consistent after dropping sounds that the native language does not contain.
d.   Incorrect. This occurs after several other milestones.

7.   c   mod. 22 p. 266
a.   Incorrect. This two-word phrase has a telegraphic quality common to the language of 2-year-olds.
b.   Incorrect. This two-word phrase has a telegraphic quality common to the language of 2-year-olds.
*c. Correct. Contractions will not occur until later.
d.   Incorrect. Here is a holophrase meaning "I want you to get me more food now." It is repeated for emphasis.

8.   d   mod. 22 p. 267
a.   Incorrect. This commonly occurs in this age range.
b.   Incorrect. This is a description of telegraphic speech.
c.   Incorrect. The complexity of speech is built slowly, first by combining critical words and succeeding in communicating and then by building on this foundation.
*d. Correct. Overgeneralization involves the use of a grammatically correct construction in more than the correct situation, like making the past tense by adding "-ed" to everything, producing the term "goed."

9.   b   mod. 22 p. 266
a.   Incorrect. Classical conditioning would be insufficient to account for language, as the language response must be, in effect, combined with new stimuli (and thus the language would need to be a preexisting response).
*b. Correct. As babbling may suggest, the language of the infant does progress through a process of successive approximations (shaping).
c.   Incorrect. A universal grammar would not require exposure to the language of the parents.
d.   Incorrect. Biological unfolding suggests an innate, rather than learned, process.

10. d   mod. 27 p. 290
a.   Incorrect. They may be gifted in only one subject, and they may not show academic achievement in any subject.
b.   Incorrect. They are typically well-adjusted.
c.   Incorrect. They are almost always in the mainstream setting.
*d. Correct. Intellectually gifted students have fewer social problems and adjustment problems than their peers.

11. a   mod. 22 p. 270
*a. Correct. By having many names for turquoise, the Navaho may be able to make more refined distinctions about turquoise (thus think about it differently).
b.   Incorrect. This is a reverse statement of the linguistic-relativity hypothesis and is the general view of how grammar works.
c.   Incorrect. The language-acquisition device does not address how having many words for an object would influence how we think.
d.   Incorrect. While the Navaho are considered Native Americans, this example does not support the nativist position.

12. d   mod. 22 p. 270
a.   Incorrect. If this theory existed, this might be a good definition of it.
b.   Incorrect. No such law has ever been stated.
c.   Incorrect. No such hypothesis has been named.
*d. Correct. The linguistic-relativity hypothesis states that language determines thought.

13. b   mod. 21 p. 261
a.   Incorrect. Reactions might be possible items to observe, but little about cognition could be gained from them in this study.
*b.   Correct. Timing the process actually provides evidence of how different images can be formed and how people may produce images.
c.   Incorrect. After some study, the experimenter would probably find that respiration does not change much while imagining giraffes.
d.   Incorrect. Someone has been the subject of too many experiments!

14   a   mod. 21 p. 252
*a.   Correct. This example would probably come to mind more readily than the other options.
b.   Incorrect. This is not a specific example but is instead a definition of one type of table.
c.   Incorrect. This specific table would be less familiar to you, but could serve as a prototype for someone else.
d.   Incorrect. This is not a specific example but is instead a definition of one type of table.

15. b   mod. 21 p. 258
16. c   mod. 22 p. 250
17. a   mod. 21 p. 253
18. d   mod. 22 p. 270
19. e   mod. 21 p. 261

20. mainstreaming   mod. 23 p. 289
21. performance   mod. 23 p. 284
22. ease   mod. 23 p. 283
23. Flynn effect   mod. 23 p. 291
24. gifted; nongifted   mod. 23 p. 290

25. Positive:
- Attempts to teach immigrants subject material in their own language and slowly adding English instruction.
- Respecting their cultural differences by acknowledging their language illustrates value for their cultural heritage.
- Supporters quote research that states that maintaining a native language will not interfere with learning English.
- Bilingual children score higher on intelligence and achievement tests.

Negative:
- Those not in favor say bilingual children will be left behind in school and in the workplace.

Motivation and Emotion

Overview

This set of modules focuses on the major conceptions of motivation, discussing how the different motives and needs people experience jointly affect behavior. The theories of motivation draw on basic instincts, drives, levels of arousal, expectations, and self-realization as possible sources of motives.

Module 24 explores the factors that direct and energize behavior. Homeostasis, along with arousal, incentive, and cognitive approaches are defined and discussed. Maslow's hierarchy is offered as an explanation of five basic needs and the motivation a person needs to fulfill these needs.

Module 25 offers a discussion of the factors that underlie hunger. Thirst and hunger are two motives that have a physiological basis. Social factors that play a role in the regulation of hunger are explored, along with factors related to obesity. Needs relating to achievement, affiliation, and power motivation are also presented here.

Module 26 offers a definition of emotions and illustrates how they have both a physiological and a cognitive component. Three major theories of emotion—the James-Lange Theory, the Cannon-Bard Theory, and the Schachter-Singer Theory—are presented, with recent approaches that are based on biological aspects discussed as well. The module concludes with a presentation on nonverbal behavior.

To further investigate the topics covered in this chapter, you can visit the related Web sites by visiting the following link: www.mhhe.com/feldmanup6-10links.

Prologue: Armed with Bravery
Looking Ahead

Module 24:
Explaining
Motivation

Instinct Approaches: Born to Be Motivated
Drive-Reduction Approaches: Satisfying Our Needs
Arousal Approaches: Beyond Drive Reduction
Incentive Approaches: Motivation's Pull
Cognitive Approaches: The Thoughts Behind Motivation
Maslow's Hierarchy: Ordering Motivational Needs
Applying the Different Approaches to Motivation

- ***How does motivation direct and energize behavior?***

Explaining Motivation

The factors that direct and energize behavior comprise the major focus of the study of

[a] _____. **[b]** _____ are the desired goals that underlie
behavior. Psychologists who study motivation seek to understand why people do the things they
do. The study of emotions includes the internal experience at any given moment.

There are several approaches to understanding motivation. An early approach focused on

[c] _____ as inborn, biologically determined patterns of behavior. Proponents
of this view argue that there exist preprogrammed patterns of behavior.

[d] _____ *approaches to motivation* focus on behavior as an attempt to

remedy the shortage of some basic biological requirement. In this view, a **[e]** _____
is a motivational tension, or arousal, that energizes a behavior to fulfill a need.

[f] _____ meet biological requirements, while **[g]** _____ have no obvious
biological basis. Primary drives are resolved by reducing the need that underlies it. Primary drives

are also governed by a basic motivational phenomena of **[h]** _____, the goal of
maintaining optimal biological functioning. Drive-reduction theories have difficulty explaining
behavior that is not directed at reducing a drive but may be directed instead at maintaining or
increasing arousal. Also, behavior appears to be motivated occasionally by curiosity as well.

The theory that explains motivation as being directed toward maintaining or increasing

excitement is the **[i]** _____ *approach to motivation*. If the levels of stimulation
are too low, arousal theory says that we will try to increase the levels.

In motivational terms, the reward is the **[j]** _____. **[k]** _____
approaches to motivation explain why behavior may be motivated by external stimuli.

[l] _____ _approaches to motivation_ focus on our thoughts, expectations, and understanding of the world. For instance, **[m]** _____ combines our expectations of reaching a goal with the value we place on it to account for the degree of motivation. **[n]** _____ refers to the value an activity has in the enjoyment of participating in it, and **[o]** _____ refers to behavior that is done for a tangible reward. We work harder for a task that has intrinsic motivation. Also, as tangible rewards become available, intrinsic motivation declines and extrinsic motivation increases.

Evaluate

_____ 1. motives

_____ 2. emotions

_____ 3. instinct

_____ 4. drive

_____ 5. primary drives

a. An inborn pattern of behavior that is biologically determined.

b. Desired goals that prompt behavior.

c. The internal feelings experienced at any given moment.

d. Biological needs such as hunger, thirst, fatigue, and sex.

e. A tension or arousal that energizes behavior in order to fulfill a need.

Rethink

24-1 Which approaches to motivation are most commonly used in the workplace? How might each approach be used to design employment policies that can sustain or increase motivation?

24-2 A writer who works all day composing copy for an advertising firm has a hard time keeping her mind on her work and continually watches the clock. After work she turns to a collection of stories she is creating and writes long into the night, completely forgetful of the clock. What ideas from your reading on motivation help to explain this phenomenon?

Spotlight on Terminology and Language—ESL Pointers

Explaining Motivation

Page 301 "His treatment was **grueling**."

When something is **grueling**, it is demanding and exhausting.

Page 302 "As a result of these **shortcomings**, newer explanations have replaced conceptions of motivation based on instincts."

Shortcomings are deficiencies or flaws. What were some of the **shortcomings** of the early explanations defining motivation?

Page 302 "We usually try to satisfy a primary drive by reducing the need **underlying** it."

Underlying means lying under or beneath. To satisfy the primary drive, we would identify the need.

Page 302 "Using feedback loops, **homeostasis** brings deviations in body functioning back to an optimal state, similar to the way a thermostat and a furnace work in a home heating system to maintain a steady temperature."

Homeostasis is the steady state of physiological equilibrium. It is the ability of a cell or an organism to maintain internal equilibrium by adjusting internal processes.

Page 303 "People vary widely in the **optimal** level of arousal they seek out, with some people looking for especially high levels of arousal."

Optimal is the most desirable or favorable.

Page 303 "**Incentive** approaches to motivation suggest that motivation stems from the desire to obtain valued external goals, or incentives."

An **incentive** is something that stimulates. Can both the fear of punishment and the expectation of reward be an **incentive**? What **incentives** do you find are the most effective in motivating you to set time aside for studying?

Page 303 "Although the theory explains why we may **succumb** to an incentive (such as a mouthwatering dessert) even though we lack internal cues (such as hunger), it does not provide a complete explanation of **motivation**, because organisms sometimes seek to fulfill needs even when incentives are not apparent."

When a person **succumbs**, he yields to an overwhelming desire or overpowering force.

Motivation is an inner state that energizes people toward fulfillment of a goal. This would be the psychological process that arouses, directs, and maintains behavior toward a goal.

Page 305 "**Intrinsic motivation** causes us to participate in an activity for our own enjoyment rather than for any concrete, **tangible** reward that it will bring us."

Intrinsic motivation is the inner drive that motivates people in the absence of external reward or punishment. What are some of your activities that are **intrinsically motivated**?

A **tangible** reward is something able to be perceived as materially existent. When you receive money for your efforts, you receive a **tangible** reward.

Page 305 "In contrast, **extrinsic motivation** causes us to do something for money, a grade, or some other concrete, tangible reward."

Extrinsic motivation is the desire to engage in an activity for money, recognition, or other tangible benefits. Describe some examples of how your educational institution motivates you both intrinsically and **extrinsically**.

Page 305 "**Self-actualization** is a state of self-fulfillment in which people realize their highest potentials, each in his or her own unique way."

In Maslow's theory, **self-actualization** is the individual's predisposition to try to fulfill his or her **potential**. **Potential** is the inherent ability or capacity for growth or development.

Page 306 "The important thing is that people **feel at ease** with themselves and satisfied that they are using their talents to the fullest."

When people **feel at ease** with themselves, they are comfortable.

Page 306 "In a sense, achieving self-actualization reduces the striving and **yearning** for greater fulfillment that mark most people's lives and instead provides a sense of satisfaction with the current state of affairs (Jones & Crandall, 1991; Hamel, Leclerc & Lefrancois, 2003; Piechowski, 2003)."

When you **yearn** for something, you experience a strong desire. You want something very badly. Are there goals you **yearn** for?

Page 306 "Actually, many of the approaches are **complementary**, rather than **contradictory**."

Complement means something that completes or brings to perfection, such as the several theories of motivation are **complementary**, and provide a more complete analysis and understanding of motivation. Be cautious not to confuse this with "compliment," which means an expression of courtesy or praise, such as the professor paid the entire class a compliment on the quality of the grades they had earned on the exam.

When you **contradict** something, you express or assert the opposite of a statement. A **contradiction** is an inconsistency or discrepancy.

Module 25: Human Needs and Motivation: Eat, Drink, and Be Daring

The Motivation Behind Hunger and Eating
Eating Disorders

Becoming an Informed Consumer of Psychology: Dieting and Losing Weight Successfully

Sexual Motivation: The Facts of Life

Exploring Diversity: Female Circumcision: A Celebration of Culture or Genital Mutilation?

The Need for Achievement: Striving for Success
The Need for Affiliation: Striving for Friendship
The Need for Power: Striving for Impact on Others

- *What biological and social factors underlie hunger?*
- *What are the varieties of sexual behavior?*
- *How are needs relating to achievement, affiliation, and power motivation exhibited?*

Human Needs and Motivation: Eat, Drink, and Be Daring

One-third of Americans are considered more than 20 percent overweight and thus suffering from

[a] _____. Most nonhumans will regulate their intake of food even when it is abundant. Hunger is apparently complex, consisting of several mechanisms that signal changes in the body. One is the level of the sugar glucose in the blood. The higher the level of glucose, the

less hunger is experienced. The **[b]** _____ monitors the blood chemistry. A rat

with a damaged **[c]** _____ will starve to death, and one with a damaged

[d] _____ will experience extreme overeating.

One theory suggests that the body maintains a **[e]** _____. This set point controls whether the hypothalamus calls for more or less food intake. Differences in people's

metabolism may also account for being overweight. **[f]** _____ is the rate at which energy is produced and expended. People with high metabolic rates can eat as much food as they want and not gain weight. People with low metabolism eat little and still gain weight. As an alternative to the set-point explanation, the **[g]** _____ proposes a combination of genetic and environmental factors.

[h] _____ is a disease that afflicts primarily young females. Sufferers refuse to eat and may actually starve themselves to death. **[i]** _____ is a condition in which individuals binge on large quantities of food and then purge with vomiting or laxatives. People suffering from bulimia are treated by being taught to eat foods they enjoy and to control their eating. Anorexia is treated by reinforcing weight gain, that is, giving privileges for success.

Sexual behavior is influenced by expectations, attitudes, beliefs, and the state of medical and biological knowledge. Defining what is normal can be approached by determining the deviation for an average or typical behavior, although many behaviors are statistically unusual but not abnormal. Another approach is to compare behavior against a standard or ideal form. However, the selection of a standard is difficult because it must be universally acceptable.

[j] _____ is sexual self-stimulation, and its practice is quite common. Males masturbate more often than females, with males beginning in their early teens, although females start later and reach a maximum frequency later. Negative attitudes about masturbation continue, although it is perfectly healthy and harmless.

[k] _____ refers to sexual behavior between men and women. It includes all aspects of sexual contact—kissing, caressing, sex play, and intercourse. Premarital sex continues to be viewed through a **[l]** _____, as something acceptable for males but unacceptable for females. The double standard appears to be changing to an attitude of

[m] _____, meaning that premarital intercourse is permissible if affection exists between the two persons.

With the increase in marital intercourse, there has also been an increase in

[n] _____, or sexual activity between a married person and someone other than the spouse. Extramarital sex remains something that is consistently disapproved of.

Humans are not born with an innate attraction to the opposite sex. **[o]** _____ are individuals sexually attracted to members of the same sex, whereas **[p]** _____ are sexually attracted to both sexes. At least 20 to 25 percent of males and about 15 percent of females have had an adulthood homosexual experience, and between 5 and 10 percent of both males and females are exclusively homosexual. Although people view homosexuality and heterosexuality as distinct orientations, Kinsey places the two orientations on a scale from exclusively heterosexual behavior to exclusively homosexual behavior.

The **[q]** _____ is a learned characteristic involving the sustained striving for and attainment of a level of excellence. People with high needs for achievement seek out opportunities to compete and succeed. People with low needs for achievement are motivated by the desire to avoid failure.

The **[r]** _____ is used to test achievement motivation. It requires that the person look at a series of ambiguous pictures and then write a story that tells what is going on and what will happen next.

The **[s]** _____ refers to the needs we have of establishing and maintaining relationships with others. People who have high affiliation needs tend to be more concerned with relationships and to be with their friends more. The **[t]** _____ is a tendency to seek impact, control, or influence over others. People with a strong need for power tend to seek office more often than people with a weak need for power. Men tend to display their need for power through aggression, drinking, sexual exploitation, and competitive sports, whereas women who have a high need for power are more restrained.

Evaluate

Part A

_____ 1. expectancy-value theory

_____ 2. self-actualization

_____ 3. need for achievement

_____ 4. need for affiliation

_____ 5. need for power

a. A tendency to want to seek impact, control, or influence over others in order to be seen as a powerful individual.

b. A need to establish and maintain relationships with other people.

c. A stable, learned characteristic, in which satisfaction comes from striving for and achieving a level of excellence.

d. A state of self-fulfillment in which people realize their highest potential.

e. A view that people are motivated by expectations that certain behaviors will accomplish a goal and their understanding of the importance of the goal.

Part B

_____ 1. heterosexuality

_____ 2. extramarital sex

_____ 3. homosexuality

_____ 4. bisexuality

a. A sexual attraction to a member of one's own sex.

b. Sexual behavior between a man and a woman.

c. Sexual activity between a married person and someone who is not his or her spouse.

d. A sexual attraction to members of both sexes.

216

Rethink

25-1 How do societal expectations, expressed by television shows and commercials, contribute to both obesity and excessive concern about weight loss? How could television contribute to better eating habits and attitudes toward weight? Should it be required to do so?

25-2 Can hiring managers use traits such as need for achievement, need for power, and need for affiliation to select workers for jobs? What other criteria, both motivational and personal, would have to be considered when making such a selection?

Spotlight on Terminology and Language—ESL Pointers

Human Needs and Motivation: Eat, Drink, and Be Daring

Page 309 "We begin with hunger, the primary drive that has received the most attention from researchers, and then turn to secondary drives—those uniquely human endeavors, based on learned needs and past experience, that help explain why people strive to achieve, to **affiliate** with others, and to seek power over others."

Affiliate means to associate with. Have you noticed that you choose to **affiliate** with particular people?

Page 310 "It's not just a matter of an empty stomach causing hunger pangs and a full one **alleviating** those pangs."

To **alleviate** is to relieve. We may work to **alleviate** mental suffering through the use of psychotherapy.

Page 311 "The brain's **hypothalamus** monitors glucose levels."

The **hypothalamus** tracks glucose levels.

Page 311 "They refuse food when it is offered, and unless they are **force-fed**, they eventually die."

To **force-feed** is to compel someone to take in nourishment. Sometimes people become so weak or ill that they must be made to take in nutrition intravenously, or to swallow food, against their will.

Page 311 "Suddenly your host announces with great **fanfare** that he will be serving his "house specialty" dessert, bananas flambé, and that he has spent the better part of the afternoon preparing it."

When your host makes an announcement with great **fanfare**, he is making a showy and dramatic announcement. In this case, he is marking the arrival of the dessert that he worked so hard to prepare for this event.

Page 311 "Some of us head toward the refrigerator after a difficult day, seeking **solace** in a pint of Heath Bar Crunch ice cream."

We seek **solace** when we want a source of comfort. Do you have any private "comfort food" that provides **solace**?

Page 313 "What are the causes of **anorexia nervosa** and **bulimia**?"

Anorexia is the prolonged loss of appetite. **Anorexia nervosa** is the pathological loss of appetite typically accompanied by emaciation and wasting away of bodily tissues or organs. **Anorexia nervosa** is marked by aversion to food and severe nutritional deficiency.

Bulimia is an eating disorder characterized by excessive episodic, uncontrolled eating. This food intake is often followed by self-induced vomiting or diarrhea.

Page 314 "In light of the difficulty of losing weight, psychologists Janet Polivy and C. Peter Herman suggest—**paradoxically**—that the best approach may be to avoid dieting in the first place."

A **paradox** is a seemingly contradictory statement that may nevertheless be true.

Page 315 "Few of us choose to lead our lives as **hermits**."

A **hermit** is a person who chooses to live alone and to have little contact with other people.

Module 26: Understanding Emotional Experiences

The Functions of Emotions
Determining the Range of Emotions: Labeling Our Feelings
The Roots of Emotions

Applying Psychology in the 21st Century: The Appearance of Deception: Can Nonverbal Behavior Be Used to Reveal Terrorists?

- *What are emotions, and how do we experience them?*
- *What are the functions of emotions?*
- *What are the explanations of emotions?*

Understanding Emotional Experiences

Although difficult to define, [a] _____ are understood to be the feelings that have both physiological and cognitive aspects and that influence behavior. Physical changes occur whenever we experience an emotion, and we identify these changes as emotions.

Several important functions of emotions have been identified:

- *Preparing us for action.* Emotions prepare effective responses to a variety of situations.
- *Shaping our future behavior.* Emotions promote learning that will influence making appropriate responses in the future by leading to the repetition of responses that lead to satisfying emotional feelings.
- *Helping us to regulate social interactions.* Emotions also help regulate interactions with others.

Psychologists have been attempting to identify the most important fundamental emotions. Many have suggested that emotions should be understood through their component parts. There may be cultural differences as well, although these differences may reflect different linguistic categories for the emotions.

We have many ways to describe the experiences of emotion that we have. The physiological reactions that accompany fear are associated with the activation of the autonomic nervous system. They include (1) an increase in breathing rate; (2) an increase in heart rate; (3) a widening of the pupils; (4) a cessation of the functions of the digestive system; and (5) a contraction of the muscles below the surface of the skin.

Although these changes occur without awareness, the emotional experience of fear can be felt intensely. Whether these physiological responses are the cause of the experience or the result of the experience of emotion remains unclear.

The **[b]** _____ *theory of emotion* states that emotions are the perceived physiological reactions that occur in the internal organs. They called this *visceral experience*.

The **[c]** _____ *theory of emotion* rejects the view that physiological arousal alone leads to the perception of emotion. In this theory, the emotion-producing stimuli is first perceived, then the thalamus activates the viscera, and simultaneously a message is sent to the cortex.

The **[d]** _____ *theory of emotion* emphasizes that the emotion experienced depends on the environment and on comparing ourselves with others.

For each of the three major theories, there is some contradictory evidence. Emotions are a complex phenomena that no single theory can yet explain adequately.

Evaluate

_____ 1. James-Lange theory of emotion

_____ 2. Cannon-Bard theory of emotion

_____ 3. Schachter-Singer theory of emotion

_____ 4. emotions

a. Emotions are experienced by comparing our feelings with the feelings of others

b. The belief that emotions are determined jointly by a nonspecific kind of physiological arousal and its interpretation, based on environmental cues.

c. The belief that emotional experience is a reaction to bodily events occurring as a result of an external situation.

d. Feelings that generally have both physiological and cognitive elements and that influence behavior.

Rethink

26-1 Many people enjoy watching movies, sporting events, and music performances in crowded theaters and arenas more than they like watching them at home alone. Which theory of emotions may help explain this? How?

26-2 If researchers learned how to control emotional responses so that targeted emotions could be caused or prevented, what ethical concerns might arise? Under what circumstances, if any, should such techniques be used?

Spotlight on Terminology and Language—ESL Pointers

Understanding Emotional Experiences

Page 323 "Although everyone has an idea of what an emotion is, formally defining the concept has proved to be an **elusive** task."

An **elusive** task is something that's hard to get a hold of; it is often not able to be defined.

Page 326 "The James-Lange theory has some serious **drawbacks**, however."

A **drawback** is a disadvantage, or an objectionable feature.

Page 327 "Although some types of physiological changes are associated with specific emotional experiences, it is difficult to imagine how each of the **myriad** emotions that people are capable of experiencing could be the result of a unique visceral change."

Myriad is countless, innumerable.

Page 327 "Instead, the theory assumes that both physiological arousal and the emotional experience are produced simultaneously by the same nerve stimulus, which Cannon and Bard suggested **emanates** from the thalamus in the brain."

Emanate is originate, to come from.

Page 331 "For one thing, emotions are not a simple phenomenon but are **intertwined** closely with motivation, cognition, neuroscience, and a host of related branches of psychology."

Intertwined is tangled, knotted. More than one factor must be examined when emotions are evaluated.

Page 331 "In short, emotions are such complex phenomena, encompassing both biological and cognitive aspects, that no single theory has been able to explain fully all the **facets** of emotional experience."

Facets are the features, the components of emotional experience.

Practice Tests

Test your knowledge of the modules by answering these questions. These questions have been placed in three Practice Tests. The first two tests are composed of questions that will test your recall of factual knowledge. The third test contains questions that are challenging and primarily test for conceptual knowledge and your ability to apply that knowledge. Check your answers and review the feedback using the Answer Key in the following pages of the *Study Guide*.

PRACTICE TEST 1:

1. A newborn baby's behavior is based on primary drives, motives that:
   a. people rate as being most important to them.
   b. seem to motivate an organism the most.
   c. are least likely to be satisfied before self-actualization can occur.
   d. have a biological basis and are universal.

2. _____ activate behavior and orient it toward achieving goals.
   a. Instincts   c. Emotions
   b. Motives   d. Homeostatic energizers

3. _____ is the process by which an organism tries to maintain an optimal level of internal biological functioning.
   a. Primary drive equilibrium   c. Drive reduction
   b. Homeostasis   d. Opponent-process theory

4. The definition of a motivation behind behavior in which no obvious biological need is being fulfilled is:
   a. a primary drive.   c. a secondary drive.
   b. an achievement.   d. an instinct.

5. The desirable qualities of the external stimulus are the focus of:
   a. the incentive motivational approach.
   b. the drive-reduction motivational approach.
   c. the instinctive motivational approach.
   d. the cognitive motivational approach.

6. The incentive theory of motivation focuses on:
   a. instincts.
   b. the characteristics of external stimuli.
   c. drive reduction.
   d. the rewarding quality of various behaviors that are motivated by arousal.

7. The expectancy-value theory states that the two types of cognitions that control motivation are:
   a. drive reductions and positive incentives.
   b. rewards and punishments.
   c. intrinsic motivation and extrinsic motivation.
   d. hopes and disappointments.

8. The erotic character of a stimulus is determined for the most part by:
   a. genetic history.
   b. whether it depicts nudity.
   c. society.
   d. hereditary factors.

9. Kiana has experienced a major weight loss and has begun refusing to eat. She denies that she has an eating problem and does not recognize that she suffers from:
   a. hyperphagia.
   b. bulimia.
   c. rolfing.
   d. anorexia nervosa.

10. Which of the following is thought to be primarily involved in the physiological regulation of eating behavior?
    a. cortex
    b. amygdala
    c. hypothalamus
    d. hippocampus

11. Which of the following statements about masturbation is **true**?
    a. All of society views masturbation as a healthy, normal activity.
    b. Most people surveyed have masturbated at least once.
    c. Males and females begin masturbation at puberty.
    d. Psychologists view people who masturbate as poorly adjusted.

12. Tanisha and her brother have different rules, established by their parents and based on society's customs around the issue of premarital sex. This double standard in Western society means:
    a. twice as many men have premarital sex as women.
    b. premarital sex is discouraged for both men and women.
    c. even people who are marrying for a second time should refrain from sex before their remarriage.
    d. premarital sex is discouraged for women but not for men.

13. Which theory postulates that emotions are identified by observing the environment and comparing ourselves with others?
    a. Schachter-Singer theory
    b. Cannon-Bard theory
    c. James-Lange theory
    d. Ekman's theory

14. William James and Walter Lange suggested that major emotions correlate with particular "gut reactions" of internal organs. They called this internal response:
    a. a physiological pattern.
    b. a psychological experience.
    c. an autonomic response.
    d. a visceral experience.

15. The facial-affect program is:
    a. developed during early childhood.
    b. unique to American culture.
    c. a technological breakthrough.
    d. the activation of nerve impulses.

_____ 16. drive-reduction theory

_____ 17. arousal approach to motivation

_____ 18. homeostasis

_____ 19. incentive approach to motivation

_____ 20. cognitive approaches to motivation

a. Motivation by focusing on an individual's thoughts, expectations, and understanding of the world.

b. The theory that claims that drives are produced to obtain our basic biological requirements.

c. The belief that we try to maintain certain levels of stimulation and activity, changing them as necessary.

d. The theory explaining motivation in terms of external stimuli.

e. The process by which an organism tries to maintain an internal biological balance.

21. The internal motivational state that is created by a physiological need is called a

_____.

22. The _____ model views motivated behavior as directed toward the reduction of a physiological need.

23. _____ is the body's mechanism for maintaining an optimum, balanced range of physiological processes.

24. Theories that stress the active processing of information are _____ of motivation.

25. Describe each of the main theories of motivation and attempt to explain a single behavior from the point of view of each theory.

PRACTICE TEST 2:

1. The main function of motivation is to:
   a. create tension.
   b. provide feeling.
   c. promote learning of survival behaviors.
   d. provide direction to behavior.

2. The best example of a drive that is common to both humans and animals is:
   a. power.
   b. hunger.
   c. cognition.
   d. achievement.

3. The compensatory activity of the autonomic nervous system, which returns the body to normal levels of functioning after a trauma, is called:
   a. homeostasis.
   b. biorhythmicity.
   c. biofeedback.
   d. transference.

4. Gender differences are determined by:
   a. societal forces.
   b. cultural forces.
   c. biological sex forces.
   d. biological and environmental forces.

5. Some psychologists feel that the incentive theory of motivation is strengthened when combined with complementary concepts drawn from:
   a. instinct theory.
   b. drive-reduction theory.
   c. arousal theory.
   d. cognitive theory.

6. Our hopes that a behavior will cause us to reach a certain goal and our understanding that the goal will be meaningful or important to us are combined in:
   a. the expectancy-value theory of motivation.
   b. the drive-reduction theory of motivation.
   c. Maslow's hierarchy of motivation.
   d. arousal theory of motivation.

7. At what point in life does the human male secrete the greatest amount of androgen?
   a. just after birth
   b. just after puberty
   c. upon entering young adulthood
   d. upon entering middle adulthood

8. In Maslow's hierarchal pyramid of motivation, self-actualizers:
   a. are notably self-sufficient at all levels: growing their own food, finding their own friends, creating their own artwork, etc.
   b. depend on others but are inwardly focused.
   c. have achieved their major goals in life.
   d. encourage others to do their best while remaining modest themselves.

9. At which of the following ages does the amount of fat cells in the body usually stop declining?
   a. 24 years of age
   b. 20 years of age
   c. 12 years of age
   d. 2 years of age

10. An eating disorder usually affecting attractive, successful females between the ages of 12 and 40 who refuse to eat and sometimes literally starve themselves to death is called:
   a. metabolic malfunction.
   b. bulimia.
   c. anorexia nervosa.
   d. obesity.

11. Which of the following is **not** true of the need for achievement?
   a. Individuals with a high need for achievement choose situations in which they are likely to succeed easily.
   b. It is a learned motive.
   c. Satisfaction is obtained by striving for and attaining a level of excellence.
   d. High need for achievement is related to economic and occupational success.

12. Women, as opposed to men, tend to channel their need for power through:
   a. socially responsible ways.
   b. questionable means.
   c. quietly aggressive ways.
   d. uncharted, high-risk opportunities.

13. Which of the following trends was most pronounced between the mid-1960s and mid-1980s in America?
   a. An increased percentage of females engaged in premarital sex.
   b. An increased percentage of males engaged in extramarital sex.
   c. A decreased percentage of males engaged in premarital sex.
   d. A decreased percentage of females engaged in extramarital sex.

14. There is convincing evidence that the way in which basic emotions are displayed and interpreted is:
   a. culture-specific.
   b. universal.
   c. gender-specific.
   d. learned.

15. The reflex that makes our facial expressions of emotions occur automatically when triggered is called:
    a. the facial-feedback hypothesis.
    c. the display rules.
    b. the James-Lange theory.
    d. the facial-affect program.

____ 16. hypothalamus

____ 17. lateral hypothalamus

____ 18. ventromedial hypothalamus

____ 19. metabolism

____ 20. weight set point

a. The part of the brain that, when damaged, results in an organism's starving to death.

b. The particular level of weight that the body strives to maintain.

c. The part of the brain that, when injured, results in extreme overeating.

d. The structure in the brain that is primarily responsible for regulating food intake.

e. The rate at which energy is produced and expended by the body.

21. The view that basic needs must be met before an individual can move on to higher levels of satisfaction is illustrated by _____.

22. Kendra has been within 5 pounds of the weight she was in high school. This weight range maintained over time is referred to as the _____.

23. Louise is on the phone or having friends over during most of her waking hours. This behavior describes _____, the need to be with others and avoid being alone.

24. According to your text, Eleanor Roosevelt, Abraham Lincoln, and Albert Einstein all fulfilled the highest levels of motivational needs, Maslow's level of _____.

25. The _____ is the tiny brain structure primarily responsible for food intake.

26. Under what conditions might a polygraph test be considered fair? Outline the possible ethical and scientific concerns that arise from the use of a polygraph in support of your answer. In contrast, discuss the same concerns regarding the use of honesty, or integrity tests, by employers who attempt to discover the likelihood that job applicants would steal.

PRACTICE TEST 3: Conceptual, Applied, and Challenging Questions

1. Some college catalogs boast that their school offers generous financial aid packages, roommate selection, and smaller classes. These catalogs emphasize the concept of:
   a. opponent-process motivation.
   c. drive-reduction motivation.
   b. arousal motivation.
   d. extrinsic motivation.

2. Two friends, Damon, the thin one, and Jarrod, the obese one, had lunch just before boarding their plane. When flight attendants serve lunch, what will the two brothers be expected to do, according to the external-cue theory?
   a. Neither will eat the lunch on the plane.
   b. The obese man will eat a second lunch, while the thin man may skip it.
   c. The thin man will eat a second lunch, but the obese man will skip it.
   d. Both men will eat a second lunch.

3. Which factor appears to play the **least** significant role in hunger for the American public?
   a. blood chemistry
   b. stomach contractions
   c. number and size of fat cells
   d. weight set point

4. Abby developed a cycle of binge eating, during which she consumed enormous quantities of high-calorie foods and then induced vomiting afterward. Dr. Slocum told Abby that she could do permanent damage to her health if she continued the behavior and that if she continued she could become:
   a. ischemic.
   b. depressed.
   c. volumetric.
   d. bulimic.

5. Tanya finished her college degree with honors and received a variety of excellent job offers. Instead, she decided to enter graduate school to acquire more advanced skills and get even better job offers. Tanya is demonstrating her:
   a. need for affiliation.
   b. need for achievement.
   c. fear of failure.
   d. need for power.

6. Emotions play an important role in all of the following **except**:
   a. making life interesting.
   b. helping us regulate social interaction.
   c. informing us of internal bodily needs.
   d. preparing us for action in response to the external environment.

7. Rudy, who devotes her efforts to maintaining her standing on the Dean's List, is highly motivated in her need for:
   a. affiliation.
   b. cognition.
   c. power.
   d. achievement.

8. The notion that the same nerve impulse triggers simultaneously the physiological arousal and the emotional experience is a hallmark of:
   a. the Cannon-Bard theory of emotion.
   b. the facial-affect theory of emotion.
   c. the Schachter-Singer theory of emotion.
   d. the James-Lange theory of emotion.

9. A polygraph is an electronic device that detects lying by measuring:
   a. brain waves.
   b. brain waves and sweating.
   c. breathing patterns and sweating.
   d. breathing patterns and brain waves.

10. Jan, a Korean-American, has become good friends with Eugene, an African-American. On some occasions, Jan has difficulty determining the emotion that Eugene is expressing, and vice versa. Which of the following is most likely to account for their difficulty in interpreting each other's emotions?
    a. the facial-feedback hypothesis
    b. the facial-affect program
    c. the two-factor theory of emotions
    d. display rules

11. Which of the following is **not** one of the six basic categories of nonverbal emotion identified by Ekman?
    a. happiness
    b. love
    c. anger
    d. surprise

12. Which of the following is most typical of an individual who is high in the need for power?
    a. Tina, who is aggressive and flamboyant
    b. Daniel, who has joined the local chapter of a political party
    c. Barbara, who shows concern for others and is highly nurturing
    d. Mary, who enjoys competitive sports

13. Which of the following is most typical of an individual who is high in the need for affiliation?
    a. Marie, who appears sensitive to others and prefers to spend all her free time with friends
    b. Nicolas, who joins a local political group
    c. Therese, who enjoys team sports and likes to attend parties
    d. Michael, who is aggressive and controlling whenever he is in groups

14. If a theory claims that all emotions are universally determined by evolutionary forces, which of the following would be necessary to account for differences that arise from culture to culture?
    a. the facial-feedback hypothesis
    b. the facial-affect program
    c. the two-factor theory of emotions
    d. display rules

15. Carlos is quite excited about keeping his new car cleaned and serviced, and he does it without being asked. His father then begins a system of rewarding his efforts with an additional allowance. According to the cognitive approach to motivation, what is the most likely response that Carlos will have?
    a. His tendency to clean his car will be increased.
    b. He will probably be less eager to clean his car.
    c. He will be even more enthusiastic, but he will not clean his car any more frequently.
    d. He will be unwilling to clean his car at all.

_____ 16. secondary drives

_____ 17. intrinsic motivation

_____ 18. extrinsic motivation

_____ 19. incentive

_____ 20. obesity

a. Anticipated rewards in motivation.

b. Participating in an activity for a tangible reward.

c. Participating in an activity for its own enjoyment, not for a reward.

d. Having weight that is more than 20 percent above the average weight for a person of a given height.

e. Drives in which no biological need is fulfilled.

21. In order to increase your _____, the rate at which food is converted to energy, you need to increase exercise.

22. Parents who are demanding and overcontrolling may increase the likelihood that their daughters will develop _____.

23. Jason has the tendency to seek impact, control, and influence over his friends and the people he works with. This is called the _____.

24. There are cross-cultural differences in the _____, the guidelines that govern the appropriateness of nonverbal emotion.

25. Preparing us for action, shaping future behavior, and helping us act more effectively with others are all functions of _____.

26. Explain how parents can attempt to minimize the negative affects of a culture that demands an unreasonable focus on thinness for its youth, especially females.

■ ANSWER KEY: MODULES 24, 25, AND 26

Module 24:	Module 25:	Evaluate	Module 26:
[a] motivation	[a] obesity	Part A	[a] emotions
[b] Motives	[b] hypothalamus	1. e	[b] James-Lange
[c] instincts	[c] lateral hypothalamus	2. d	[c] Cannon-Bard
[d] Drive-reduction	[d] ventromedial	3. c	[d] Schachter-Singer
[e] drive	hypothalamus	4. b	
[f] Primary drives	[e] weight set point	5. a	Evaluate
[g] secondary drives	[f] Metabolism		1. c
[h] homeostasis	[g] settling point	Part B	2. b
[i] arousal	[h] Anorexia nervosa	1. b	3. a
[j] incentive	[i] Bulimia	2. c	4. d
[k] Incentive	[j] Masturbation	3. a	
[l] Cognitive	[k] Heterosexuality	4. d	
[m] expectancy value	[l] double standard		
[n] Intrinsic motivation	[m] permissiveness with		
[o] extrinsic motivation	affection		
	[n] extramarital sex		
Evaluate	[o] Homosexuals		
1. b	[p] bisexuals		
2. c	[q] need for achievement		
3. a	[r] Thematic Apperception		
4. e	Test (TAT)		
5. d	[s] need for affiliation		
	[t] need for power		

Selected Rethink Answers

24-1   The arousal approach might be seen in the workplace by employees who seek either a very high or a very low level of stimulation and activity. Individuals may self-select into jobs that meet this need. Employees should look for "goodness of fit" in employee–job matching. The incentive approach, the desire to obtain valued external goals, would encourage employers to find out what they can provide for employees to work toward. In the cognitive approach, employers should encourage the development of intrinsic motivation by rewarding employees for the job they do.

26-1   Schachter-Singer Theory: Attending group events allows an individual to identify his or her own emotions by experiencing, observing, and comparing these emotions with the emotional experience of others.

Practice Test 1:

1. d   mod. 24 p. 302
a. Incorrect. Because we may satisfy our primary drives without much difficulty, they may not hold much importance when compared with other types of drives.
b. Incorrect. Other types of drives may motivate an organism more.
c. Incorrect. They must be satisfied for self-actualization to occur.
*d. Correct. By definition, primary drives are those that have a biological basis.

2. b   mod. 24 p. 301
a. Incorrect. True, but "motives" is a more comprehensive choice.
*b. Correct. This defines "motives."
c. Incorrect. This is also true, but "motives" is a more comprehensive choice.
d. Incorrect. These are currently unknown to earthling science.

3. b   mod. 24 p. 302
a. Incorrect. There is no concept such as "primary drive equilibrium."
*b. Correct. "Homeostasis" is the term used to describe a biological balance or equilibrium.
c. Incorrect. But drive reduction might be used to achieve a state of homeostasis.
d. Incorrect. Opponent-process theory is one of the theories that depends on the tendency toward homeostasis to account for many phenomena.

4. c   mod. 24 p. 302
a. Incorrect. A primary drive has a clear biological need that it satisfies.
b. Incorrect. An achievement may or may not have a biological drive.
*c. Correct. By definition, secondary drives are not based on biological needs.
d. Incorrect. An instinct is a species-specific behavior governed by genetics and is thus biological.

5. a   mod. 24 p. 303
*a. Correct. External stimuli provide for "incentives" to act in a certain way.
b. Incorrect. The drive-reduction model focuses on internal stimuli.
c. Incorrect. Desirableness would be irrelevant to instincts.
d. Incorrect. Although important for this theory, external stimuli would not be the focus.

6. b   mod. 24 p. 303
a. Incorrect. Instinct theory, not incentive theory, focuses on instincts.
*b. Correct. The characteristics of external stimuli provide the incentive, or promise of reinforcement, that governs incentive theory.
c. Incorrect. Drive reduction is a core concept of drive theory.
d. Incorrect. This refers to arousal theory.

7. c   mod. 24 p. 305
a. Incorrect. These two factors are taken from two other approaches to motivation.
b. Incorrect. Both of these are typically extrinsic.
*c. Correct. Actually, motivations can only be one or the other of these two types.
d. Incorrect. These would have more to do with expectancy-value motivation.

8. .c   mod. 24 p. 311
a. Incorrect. Genetic history does not determine erotic qualities of a stimulus.
b. Incorrect. A stimulus can be quite erotic without nudity.
*c. Correct. The erotic nature of a stimulus does appear to be socially determined.
d. Incorrect. Hereditary factors do not determine the character of erotic stimuli.

9. d   mod. 25 p. 312
a. Incorrect. Hyperphagia would not account for the refusal to admit to the eating problem.
b. Incorrect. Unlike the anorexic, the bulimic eats, and then regurgitates the meal.
c. Incorrect. This is a deep massage technique.
*d. Correct. Someone suffering from anorexia refuses to eat and claims that she is overweight.

10. c   mod. 25 p. 311
a. Incorrect. The cortex plays a role, but it is not central.
b. Incorrect. In the limbic system but not correct.
*c. Correct. The hypothalamus monitors blood sugar and other body chemistry to regulate eating behavior.
d. Incorrect. In the limbic system but not correct.

11. b   mod. 25 p. 315
a. Incorrect. The views on masturbation in our society are quite mixed.
*b. Correct. And most of that number have done it more than once.
c. Incorrect. Masturbation can begin much earlier, and some begin much later than puberty.
d. Incorrect. Masturbation is a normal, healthy activity.

12. d   mod. 25 p. 316
a. Incorrect. However, does this mean that there are a large number of unmarried women or just a few very busy women?
b. Incorrect. This would be a single standard.
c. Incorrect. This would be a single standard.
*d. Correct. A double standard means that one group is held to one standard, and another group is held to another standard.

13. a   mod. 26 p. 328
*a. Correct. Schachter and Singer proposed a theory of emotions that includes the cognitive element of interpretation of surroundings.
b. Incorrect. Cannon and Bard were critical of the James-Lange theory and proposed that exciting information went to the thalamus and then to the cortex and the physiological systems simultaneously.
c. Incorrect. The James-Lange theory is based on the perception of visceral changes.
d. Incorrect. Ekman's theory states that nonverbal responses to emotion-evoking stories seems to be universal.

14. d   mod. 25 p. 326
a. Incorrect. See answer d.
b. Incorrect. See answer d.
c. Incorrect. See answer d.
*d. Correct. Visceral refers to the internal organs.

15. d   mod. 26 p. 324
a. Incorrect. It may be innate.
b. Incorrect. It is found in every culture.
c. Incorrect. It is not a computer program.
*d. Correct. The "program" refers to the neural pathways involved in expressing an emotion.

16. b   mod. 24 p. 302
17. c   mod. 24 p. 303
18. e   mod. 24 p. 302
19. d   mod. 24 p. 303
20. a   mod. 24 p. 305

21. drive   mod. 24 p. 302
22. drive-reduction   mod. 24 p. 302
23. Homeostasis   mod. 24 p. 302
24. cognitive theories mod. 24 p. 305

25.
▪ Describe each of the main theories: instinct, drive reduction, arousal, incentive, opponent process, cognitive, and need theories.
▪ Select an activity—it could be anything from watching television to playing a sport—and describe the behavior involved from the point of view of the motivation theories (no more than one sentence each).
▪ Remember, some behaviors, like those satisfying basic needs, are easier to describe from the points of view of some theories, whereas others are easier to describe from other theories.

Practice Test 2:
1. d   mod. 24 p. 301
a. Incorrect. It may be focused on alleviating tension.
b. Incorrect. Feelings come from other aspects of behavior, although feelings and motivation may both be processed at least in part in the limbic system.
c. Incorrect. Many survival behaviors do not have to be learned, and many motivations are not survival oriented.
*d. Correct. Motivation guides and energizes behavior.

2. b   mod. 26 p. 310
a. Incorrect. Some animals and some humans may not be interested in power.
*b. Correct. Hunger appears to be a rather universal drive among humans, animals, and insects.
c. Incorrect. Cognition is not considered a drive.
d. Incorrect. Achievement is a particularly human drive.

3. a   mod. 24 p. 302
*a. Correct. This is the activity of the parasympathetic system.
b. Incorrect. This new term may soon find its way into scientology.
c. Incorrect. Biofeedback requires intentional activity to control body processes.
d. Incorrect. This is a technical, psychoanalytic term that is not relevant to homeostasis.

4. d   mod. 26 p. 317
a. Incorrect. Societal forces determine only some of the gender differences.
b. Incorrect. Cultural forces determine only some of the gender differences.
c. Incorrect. Biological sex forces determine only a few of the gender differences.
*d. Correct. Gender differences result from both biological and environmental pressures.

5. b   mod. 24 p. 303
a. Incorrect. Instinct theory focuses on innate drives and thus would not complement incentive theory.
*b. Correct. Incentives account for external factors, whereas drive reduction would account for internal factors.
c. Incorrect. Arousal theory says that we actually seek ways to increase stimulation (in contrast to drive reduction).
d. Incorrect. Cognitive theory suggests that motivation is a product of people's thoughts, expectations, and goals.

6. a   mod. 24 p. 305
*a. Correct. Expectancy-value motivation is one of the cognitive approaches, and thus it includes our understanding.
b. Incorrect. Drive reduction is not goal-oriented in this way and may occur without our awareness.
c. Incorrect. Maslow's approach does not necessarily involve goals and awareness of goals.
d. Incorrect. Arousal theory says that we seek ways to increase stimulation.

7. b   mod. 26 p. 315
a. Incorrect. The greatest amount of androgen is secreted just after puberty.
*b. Correct. Just after puberty, many changes occur in males, and androgens play an important role in these changes.
c. Incorrect. See answer a.
d. Incorrect. See answer a.

8. c   mod. 24 p. 305
a. Incorrect. This is a gross overstatement of the idea of self-actualization.
b. Incorrect. Everyone is dependent on others for some aspect of living.
*c. Correct. Self-actualizers are striving toward goals and seeking to express their potential.
d. Incorrect. Self-actualizers are often not as concerned with the successes of others.

9. d   mod. 25 p. 312
a. Incorrect. The number of fat cells is fixed by the age of about 2.
b. Incorrect. See answer a.
c. Incorrect. See answer a.
*d. Correct. By 2, the number of fat cells stops declining.

10. c   mod. 25 p. 313
a. Incorrect. Try anorexia nervosa.
b. Incorrect. Bulimia is a similar disorder, but it involves binging and purging behavior to maintain or lose weight.
*c. Correct. Sufferers of this disorder often will not eat or will develop the disorder known as bulimia and then binge and purge.
d. Incorrect. But these females appear to have an extreme fear of obesity and will perceive themselves as obese even when they are dramatically underweight.

11. a   mod. 25 p. 321
*a. Correct. They are more likely to choose situations that are moderately challenging, not easy.
b. Incorrect. It is learned, or acquired.
c. Incorrect. Individuals with a high need for achievement do find satisfaction from attainment.
d. Incorrect. This is true as well.

12. a   mod. 25 p. 321
*a. Correct. Women tend to find power through socially acceptable ways more often than do men.
b. Incorrect. The means are rarely questionable and do tend to be socially acceptable.
c. Incorrect. The quality of aggression is not necessarily a matter of power.
d. Incorrect. This is much more likely with men than women.

13. a   mod. 25 p. 316
*a. Correct. Of all the trends, the change in the frequency of female premarital sexual activity was the most significant.
b. Incorrect. This number was small in comparison to the changes in female rates.
c. Incorrect. Males did not decrease their rate of premarital sexual activity; instead, it increased slightly.
d. Incorrect. Females did not decrease their rate of premarital sexual activity; instead, it increased dramatically.

14. b   mod. 26 p. 323
a. Incorrect. The evidence suggests universal patterns.
*b. Correct. The basic emotions are expressed and interpreted similarly across all cultures that have been studied.
c. Incorrect. See answer a.
d. Incorrect. See answer a.

15. d   mod. 26 p. 326
a. Incorrect. Close, but this hypothesis says that if we make the expression of an emotion, the feedback will cause us to experience the emotion.
b. Incorrect. James and Lange thought it was our perception of the bodily changes that was the emotion.
c. Incorrect. Display rules govern the variations of expression from one culture to another.
*d. Correct. This view suggests that we are programmed to express the basic emotions in the same manner from one group to another.

16. d   mod. 25 p. 311
17. a   mod. 25 p. 311
18. c   mod. 25 p. 311
19. e   mod. 25 p. 311
20. b   mod. 25 p. 311

21. Maslow's hierarchy   mod. 24 p. 306
22. weight set point   mod. 25 p. 311
23. Affiliation   mod. 25 p. 321
24. self-actualization   mod. 24 p. 305
25. Hypothalamus   mod. 25 p. 311

26.
- State the conditions for which you consider polygraph use to be appropriate. Give an example from your own experience, if you have one.
- Indicate the rationale that makes its use fair or appropriate. Are the rights of the test-taker protected? Would incrimination lead to damage to the individual?
- Is it fair to use a technique that has established scientific validity in specific areas in applications that go beyond the established validity?
- Integrity tests have now replaced the polygraph, and the issues now include concern for prejudging someone as "likely to steal." Like the polygraph, these honesty tests are considered of questionable validity.

Practice Test 3:
1. d   mod. 24 p. 305
a. Incorrect. No opponent processes are indicated here.
b. Incorrect. Arousal motivation suggests that we would seek an exciting college, not necessarily a high-quality one.
c. Incorrect. However, the money may eventually lead to a reduction drive.
*d. Correct. The extrinsic rewards are quite evident.

2. b   mod. 25 p. 311
a. Incorrect. See answer b.
*b. Correct. Because food is an external cue, the obese man is more likely to experience "hunger" as a result of the food, even though he already had lunch.
c. Incorrect. The thin man is probably not so easily influenced by the external cue of another meal.
d. Incorrect. Only if the thin man is one of those people who can eat all the time and gain no excess weight.

3. b   mod. 25 p. 312
a. Incorrect. See answer b.
*b. Correct. Blood chemistry, number and size of fat cells, and weight set point are more important factors than stomach contractions.
c. Incorrect. See answer b.
d. Incorrect. See answer b.

4. d   mod. 25 p. 313
a. Incorrect. Interesting word, though.
b. Incorrect. Depression is not the cause.
c. Incorrect. Any type of measurement having to do with volume.
*d. Correct. The disorder is known as bulimia.

5. b   mod. 25 p. 320
a. Incorrect. A need for affiliation could be at work here, if she thought she would be isolated from friends once she began work.
*b. Correct. This sounds most like a need for achievement.
c. Incorrect. A fear of failure could be operative here, if she is avoiding beginning her career for fear of failure.
d. Incorrect. Power can be achieved without education.

6. c   mod. 24 p. 311
a. Incorrect. Life would probably be interesting without emotions, but far less so.
b. Incorrect. Emotion plays a major role in regulating social interaction.
*c. Correct. We are informed of our bodily needs through other mechanisms, mainly those related to motivation.
d. Incorrect. Emotions are crucial for our preparation for actions, especially emergencies.

7. d   mod. 25 p. 320
a. Incorrect. A need for affiliation would explain joining a sorority.
b. Incorrect. The need for cognition might better explain a desire to know and solve problems.
c. Incorrect. A need for power would account for a student running for student government offices.
*d. Correct. If the effort is aimed at retaining the recognition of the Dean's List, then this describes a need for achievement.

8. a   mod. 26 p. 327
*a. Correct. Their position differed from that of James and Lange, who thought our perception of the bodily changes was the emotion.
b. Incorrect. This suggests that the facial changes result in emotional feelings.
c. Incorrect. Schachter and Singer thought that the emotion resulted from the interpretation of the perception of a bodily change.
d. Incorrect. James and Lange thought our perception of the bodily changes was the emotion.

9. c   mod. 26 p. 330
a. Incorrect. See answer c.
b. Incorrect. See answer c.
*c. Correct. The polygraph measures breathing rate, heart rate, blood pressure, and sweating but not brain waves.
d. Incorrect. See answer c.

10. d   mod. 26 p. 323
a. Incorrect. The facial-feedback hypothesis suggests that information is linked to our self-perception of the emotion.
b. Incorrect. The facial-affect program is the pattern of neural responses that govern any given emotional expression.
c. Incorrect. The two-factor theory addresses how we utilize environmental information in evaluating our own emotional states.
*d. Correct. Display rules may affect how easily Eugene and Jan interpret each other's emotions and expressions, since they do have cultural elements.

11. b   mod. 26 p. 330
a. Incorrect. See answer b.
*b. Correct. The six emotions are happiness, anger, sadness, surprise, disgust, and fear.
c. Incorrect. See answer b.
d. Incorrect. See answer b.

12. c   mod. 25 p. 321
a. Incorrect. Being aggressive and flamboyant is not a typical approach for women who are high in the need for power.
b. Incorrect. Belonging to a political party is not a sign of a need for power.
*c. Correct. Women tend to display their need for power through socially acceptable methods, like concern for others and nurturing behavior.
d. Incorrect. Competitive sports are not themselves related to individual need for power.

13. a   mod. 25 p. 321
*a. Correct. Sensitivity to others and desires to spend time with friends reflect a need for affiliation.
b. Incorrect. Membership in a political group is not sufficient to indicate a need for affiliation.
c. Incorrect. Partying and sports are not signs of high need for affiliation.
d. Incorrect. Aggressive behavior does not signal a need for affiliation.

14. d   mod. 26 p. 323
a. Incorrect. Facial-feedback would be a support for the hereditary aspect of emotions.
b. Incorrect. A facial-affect program could be argued as part of the evolutionary aspect of emotions.
c. Incorrect. The two-factor theory of emotions would help account for how individuals differ in their interpretations, but not for the differences between cultures.
*d. Correct. Display rules are culturally defined, so they would be the means of accounting for cultural differences.

15. b   mod. 24 p. 305
a. Incorrect. See answer b.
*b. Correct. The shift from intrinsic to extrinsic rewards can undermine the behavior.
c. Incorrect. See answer b.
d. Incorrect. The shift from intrinsic to extrinsic rewards can undermine the behavior, but it will not necessarily destroy it.

16. e   mod. 24 p. 302
17. c   mod. 24 p. 305
18. b   mod. 24 p. 305
19. a   mod. 24 p. 303
20. d   mod. 25 p. 309

21. metabolism   mod. 25 p. 311
22. anorexia   mod. 25 p. 312
23. need for power   mod. 25 p. 321
24. display rules   mod. 26 p. 325
25. Emotions   mod. 26 p. 324

26.
- Discuss the biological and sociocultural viewpoints about weight control. Suggest behavioral alternatives.
- Allow children to select food and only eat until thy are full, not until they clean their plate. Don't use food as a reward, escape, or for consolaxtion.
- Increase opportunities for exercise.
- Encourage individuals to focus on what they can do, not how they look.

Development

Overview

The fundamental issue for developmental psychology is the interaction between nature and nurture in human development. Development from conception to birth illustrates the nature-nurture interaction.

Module 27 discusses various topics of study within the field of developmental psychology, with an emphasis on the nature-nurture issue. This is followed by a discussion of research methods. Cross-sectional research compares people of different ages with one another, and longitudinal research traces the behavior of one or more individuals as they become older. Finally, sequential research combines the two methods. Next the module explains the nature of human development before birth. Genetic abnormalities and environmental influences that affect prenatal development are listed.

Module 28 offers an explanation of the reflexes and sensory abilities of newborns. Both the physical development and the social development of newborns are discussed in detail and include the concepts of attachment, peer social interactions, child-rearing, and Erikson's psychosocial developmental stages.

Module 29 examines development during adolescence. The module on adolescence covers the physical, emotional, and cognitive changes that occur during the transition to adulthood.

Module 30 focuses on adulthood. These years are marked by the formation of a family, the establishment and success (or failure) in work, and the gradual progress toward old age. Finally, the module shows how old age does not conform to our myths about it. Many elderly people are still quite capable of leading active and happy lives. An examination of the physical, intellectual, and social changes that occur at this time of life shows both improvements and declines in various types of functioning.

To further investigate the topics covered in this chapter, you can visit the related Web sites by visiting the following link: www.mhhe.com/feldmanup6-12links.

Prologue: The One-Pound Wonder
Looking Ahead

Module 27: Nature, Nurture, and Prenatal Development

Determining the Relative Influence of Nature and Nurture
Conducting Developmental Research
Prenatal Development: From Conception to Birth

Applying Psychology in the 21st Century:
Cloning, Gene Therapy, and the Coming Medical Revolution

- *How do psychologists study the degree to which development is an interaction of hereditary and environmental factors?*
- *What is the nature of development before birth?*
- *What factors affect a child during the mother's pregnancy?*

Nature, Nurture, and Prenatal Development

[a] _____ is the branch of psychology focused on explaining the similarities and differences among people that result from the growth and change of individuals throughout life.

Developmental psychologists are interested in a fundamental question of distinguishing the causes of behavior that are *environmental* from the causes that result from *heredity*. This question is identified as the [b] _____. However, both nature and nurture are involved, and it is not a question of nature or nurture. Some theories focus on learning and the role of the environment, and other theories focus on the role of growth and [c] _____, or the development of biologically predetermined patterns, in causing developmental change. Environment plays a role in enabling individuals to reach the potential allowed by their genetic background. Developmental psychologists take an [d] _____ position, arguing that behavior and development are determined by genetic and environmental influences.

One approach used by developmental psychologists is the study of [e] _____. Different behaviors displayed by identical twins must have some environmental component. Many studies seek to find identical twins who were separated at birth by adoption. Nontwin siblings who are raised apart also make contributions to these kinds of studies. The opposite approach takes people of different genetic backgrounds and examines their development and behavior in similar environments.

236

Development begins at the point of **[f]** _____ when the male's sperm penetrates the female's egg. The fertilized egg is at this point called a **[g]** _____. It contains 23 pairs of **[h]** _____, one-half from the father and the other half from the mother. Each chromosome contains thousands of **[i]** _____, the individual units that carry genetic information. Genes are responsible for the development of the systems of the body, heart, circulatory, brain, lungs, and so on. At four weeks, the zygote becomes a structure called the **[j]** _____. It has a rudimentary heart, brain, intestinal tract, and other organs. By the eighth week, the embryo has arms and legs. Beginning at the eighth week, the embryo faces a **[k]** _____ of development—a period during which specific growth must occur if the individual is to develop normally. Eyes and ears must form, and environmental influences can have significant effects. At the ninth week, the individual is called a **[l]** _____. At 16 to 28 weeks, the movement of the fetus can be felt by the mother. At the 24th week, the fetus has the characteristics of a newborn, although it cannot survive outside the mother if born prematurely. At 28 weeks, the fetus will weigh about three pounds, can survive if born prematurely, and is at the **[m]** _____.

Evaluate

Part A

_____ 1.　environment

_____ 2.　heredity

_____ 3.　genetic makeup

_____ 4.　maturation

_____ 5.　interactionist

a.　The unfolding of biologically predetermined behavior patterns.

b.　Influences on behavior that occur in the world around us—in family, friends, school, nutrition, and others.

c.　Biological factors that transmit hereditary information.

d.　Influences on behavior that are transmitted biologically from parents to a child.

e.　Combination of genetic predisposition and environmental influences determines the course of development.

Part B

_____ 1. conception

_____ 2. zygote

_____ 3. chromosomes

_____ 4. genes

_____ 5. embryo

_____ 6. fetus

a. A zygote that has a heart, a brain, and other organs.

b. The one-celled product of fertilization.

c. A developing child, from nine weeks after conception until birth.

d. Structures that contain basic hereditary information.

e. The parts of a chromosome through which genetic information is transmitted.

f. The process by which an egg cell is fertilized by a sperm.

Rethink

27-1 When researchers find similarities in development between different cultures, what implications might such findings have for the nature-nurture issue?

27-2 Describe the policy you might create for notifying persons who have genetically based disorders that can be identified by genetic testing. Would your policy treat potentially fatal disorders differently from less serious ones? Would it make a distinction between treatable and nontreatable disorders?

Spotlight on Terminology and Language—ESL Pointers

Nature, Nurture, and Prenatal Development

Page 339 "This question **embodies** the nature-nurture issue."

   This question pretty much sums up the nature-nurture issue. The nature-nurture issue is **embodied**, or represented, by the question, "How can we distinguish between the environmental causes of behavior and the hereditary causes of behavior."

Page 339 "Although the question was first **posed** as a nature-versus-nurture issue, developmental psychologists today agree that both nature and nurture interact to produce specific developmental patterns and outcomes."

   The question was first **posed**, or presented, a bit differently.

Page 339 "Consequently, the question has **evolved** into, how and to what degree do environment and heredity both produce their effects?"

The question has **evolved** into, or advanced into, one that better reflects the awareness of the influence of the two factors.

Page 339 "However, the debate over the **comparative** influence of the two factors remains active, with different approaches and theories of development emphasizing the environment or heredity to a greater or lesser degree (de Waal, 1999; Pinker, 2002)."

Comparative is proportional.

Page 340 "Despite their differences over theory, developmental psychologists **concur** on some points."

Developmental psychologists **concur**, or agree, on some points.

Page 340 "They agree that genetic factors not only provide the potential for particular behaviors or traits to emerge, but also place limitations on the **emergence** of such behavior or traits."

Emergence is the appearance of, or coming out, of some traits.

Page 341 "Longitudinal research **traces** the behavior of one or more participants as the participants age."

Longitudinal research **traces**, or follows, the behavior of the research participants.

Page 342 "Unfortunately, longitudinal research requires an enormous **expenditure** of time (as the researcher waits for the participants to get older), and participants who begin a study at an early age may drop out, move away, or even die as the research continues."

Expenditure of time refers to the outlay of time that is necessary for longitudinal research.

Page 342 "A few years ago, when Elizabeth Carr's class was learning how an egg combines with sperm in the mother's body to create a child, she felt **compelled** to interrupt."

When you feel **compelled**, you feel forced to do something, or obligated to do this.

Page 342 "Because her mother's **landmark** pregnancy was documented in great detail by a film crew, Elizabeth has seen pictures of the egg and sperm that united to become her, the **Petri dish** where she was conceived, the embryonic blob of cells that grew into the bubbly young woman who now plays field hockey and sings in the school chorus (Rosenthal, 1996, pp. A1, B8)."

Her mother's **landmark** pregnancy was a momentous, ground-breaking event for in vitro fertilization.

A **Petri dish** is a small, shallow dish of thin glass or plastic with a loose cover used especially for cultures in science research.

Page 342 "Each chromosome contains thousands of **genes**—smaller units through which genetic information is transmitted."

The **genes** transmit, or pass on, genetic information.

Page 342 "Composed of **sequences** of DNA (deoxyribonucleic acid) molecules, genes are the biological equivalent of 'software' that programs the future development of all parts of the body's hardware."

The **sequence** is the order, or the succession, of related genes.

Page 345 "For example, fetuses are particularly **susceptible** to environmental influences such as drugs during certain critical periods before birth."

Susceptible is vulnerable or at risk.

Page 346 "Such newborns, who may weigh as little as two pounds at birth, are in **grave** danger because they have immature organs; they have less than a 50-50 chance of survival."

These infants in **grave** danger are in serious danger.

Module 28: Infancy and Childhood

The Extraordinary Newborn
The Growing Child: Infancy through Middle Childhood

- *What are the major competencies of newborns?*
- *What are the milestones of physical and social development during childhood?*
- *How does cognitive development proceed during childhood?*

Infancy and Childhood

At birth, the newborn baby is called a **[a]** _____. The neonate looks strange because the journey through the birth canal squeezes and shapes the skull. The neonate is covered

with **[b]** _____, a white, greasy material that protects the skin before birth, and

soft hair called **[c]** _____. The neonate is born with several **[d]** _____, unlearned, involuntary responses. Most are necessary for survival and maturation. The

[e] _____ fans out the toes when the edge of the foot is touched. These reflexes are lost within a few months and replaced by more complex behaviors.

In the first year of life, children triple their birth weight, and their height increases by 50 percent. From 3 to 13 years of age, the child adds an average of 5 pounds and 3 inches per year. The proportion of body and body parts changes throughout the time period as well. In addition to physical and perceptual growth, infants grow socially as well.

[f] _____ refers to the positive emotional bond between a child and a particular individual. Harry Harlow demonstrated the importance of attachment by showing that baby monkeys preferred a terrycloth "mother" to a wire "mother," even though the wire version provided food and the terrycloth one did not. Infants play an active role in the development of the bond. Recently, the father's role in children's development has been researched. Fathers spend less time caring for their children, but the attachments can be just as strong.

[g] _____ with peers are crucial for a preschooler's social development. Play increases social competence, provides a perspective on the thoughts and feelings of others, and helps teach children self-control.

Diana Baumrind has proposed three main categories of child-rearing patterns:

[h] _____ are rigid and punitive and expect unquestioning obedience.

[i] _____ are lax and inconsistent although warm. **[j]** _____ set limits and are firm, but as their children get older, they reason and explain things to them.

Children of authoritarian parents tend to be unsociable, unfriendly, and withdrawn. Children of permissive parents are immature, moody, and dependent with low self-esteem. Children of authoritative parents are likable, self-reliant, independent, and cooperative.

Children are born with [k] _____, or basic, innate dispositions. The temperament can elicit a certain child-rearing style. The child-rearing styles may be applicable to American culture, where independence is highly valued. For instance, Japanese parents encourage dependence to promote values of community and cooperation.

Erik Erikson has proposed an eight-stage theory of social development. Each stage of

[l] _____ involves a basic crisis or conflict. Although each crisis is resolved as we pass through the stages, the basic conflict remains throughout life.

[m] _____ refers to the developmental changes in a child's understanding of the world. Theories of cognitive development attempt to explain the intellectual changes that occur throughout life. Jean Piaget proposed that children passed through four distinct stages of cognitive development, and that these stages differed in both the quantity of information acquired and the quality of knowledge and understanding. Maturation and relevant experiences are needed for children to pass through the stages.

An alternative to Piaget's theory is [n] _____, which examines how people take in, use, and store information. According to the Russian developmental psychologist Lev Vygotsky, children's cognitive abilities increase when they are exposed to information that falls

into their [o] _____, which he describes as the level at which a child can almost, but not fully, comprehend or perform a task on his or her own. Parents, teachers, and peers provide supportive information that serves as [p] _____ for the child's development.

Evaluate

Part A

_____ 1. authoritarian parents

_____ 2. permissive parents

_____ 3. authoritative parents

_____ 4. temperament

_____ 5. psychosocial development

a. Parents who are lax, inconsistent, and undemanding, yet warm toward their children.

b. Development of individuals' interactions and understanding of one another and their knowledge and understanding of themselves as members of society.

c. Basic, innate disposition.

d. Parents who are rigid and punitive and who value unquestioning obedience from their children.

e. Parents who are firm, set clear limits, and reason with and explain things to their children.

241

_____ 1.   sensorimotor stage

_____ 2.   object permanence

_____ 3.   preoperational stage

_____ 4.   principle of conservation

_____ 5.   concrete operational stage

a.   Objects do not cease to exist when they are out of sight.

b.   Little competence in representing the environment.

c.   Characterized by language development.

d.   Characterized by logical thought.

e.   Quantity is unrelated to physical appearance.

Rethink

28-1   In what ways might the infant's major reflexes—the rooting, sucking, gagging, and Babinski reflexes—have had survival value, from an evolutionary perspective? What value might the infant's ability to mimic the facial expressions of adults have?

28-2   Do you think the widespread use of IQ testing in the United States contributes to parents' views that their children's academic success is largely a result of their children's innate intelligence? Why? Would it be possible (or desirable) to change this view?

Spotlight on Terminology and Language—ESL Pointers

Infancy and Childhood

Page 350 "They also show the **rudiments** of depth perception, as they react by raising their hands when an object appears to be moving rapidly toward the face (Gelman & Kit-Fong Au, 1996; Maurer et al., 1999)."

Infants show the **rudiments,** or the basics, of depth perception.

Page 350 "However, researchers have devised a number of **ingenious** methods, relying on the newborn's biological responses and innate reflexes, to test perceptual skills."

Their **ingenious** methods are clever and imaginative methods of perceptual assessment.

Page 351 "For instance, infants who see a **novel** stimulus typically pay close attention to it, and, as a consequence, their heart rates increase."

When the infant sees a **novel** stimulus, a fresh or unusual stimulus, the heart rate increases.

Page 351 "A change in the rate and **vigor** with which the babies suck helps researchers infer that babies can perceive variations in stimuli."

Vigor is strength or force.

Page 351 "At birth, babies prefer patterns with **contours** and edges over less distinct patterns, indicating that they can respond to the configuration of stimuli."

They prefer shapes and forms.

Page 352 "To the **chagrin** of the teachers in the day care center, not to speak of the children's parents, soon other children were following his lead, removing their own caps at will."

Chagrin is distress and annoyance.

Page 352 "Russell's mother, made aware of the **anarchy** at the day care center—and the other parents' distress over Russell's behavior—pleaded innocent."

Anarchy is lawlessness, rebellion. The children in the day care center were creating chaos with the constant removal of their caps.

Page 353 "As anyone who has seen an infant smiling at the sight of his or her mother can guess, at the same time that infants grow physically and **hone** their perceptual abilities, they also develop socially."

The infants are **honing** their perceptual abilities; they are practicing and improving these capabilities.

Page 353 "Lorenz focused on newborn **goslings**, which under normal circumstances instinctively follow their mother, the first moving object they perceive after birth."

A **gosling** is a young goose.

Page 354 " They spent most of their time clinging to the warm cloth 'monkey,' although they made occasional **forays** to the wire monkey to nurse."

A **foray** is a short trip to a place, usually for a specific purpose.

Page 356 "Fathers engage in more physical, **rough-and-tumble** sorts of activities, whereas mothers play more verbal and traditional games, such as peek-a-boo."

Rough-and-tumble is rowdy and somewhat unrestrained play-fighting.

Module 29:
Adolescence:
Becoming an Adult

Physical Development: The Changing Adolescent
Moral and Cognitive Development: Distinguishing Right from Wrong
Social Development: Finding Oneself in a Social World

Exploring Diversity: Rites of Passage:
Coming of Age around the World

- *What major physical, social, and cognitive transitions characterize
adolescence?*

Adolescence: Becoming an Adult

Development continues throughout life, from adolescence to adulthood and old age. The major
biological changes that begin with the attainment of physical and sexual maturity and the changes
in social, emotional, and cognitive function that lead to adulthood mark the period called

[a] _____ .

The dramatic physical changes of adolescence include a growth in height, the development of
breasts in females, the deepening of the male voice, the development of body hair, and intense
sexual feelings. The growth spurt begins around age 10 for girls and age 12 for boys. The
development of the sexual organs begins about a year later. There are wide individual variations,
however. Better nutrition and medical care in Western cultures is probably the cause of the

decreasing age of onset of **[b]** _____ . Early-maturing boys have an advantage
over later-maturing boys, doing better in athletics and being more popular, although they do have
more difficulties in school. Early-maturing girls are more popular and have higher self-concepts
than those who mature late, but the obvious changes in breasts can cause separation from peers
and ridicule. Late-maturers suffer because of the delay, with boys being ridiculed for their lack of
coordination and girls holding lower social status in junior high and high school.

Erikson's theory of psychosocial development (introduced in Chapter 12) identifies the

beginning of adolescence with his fifth stage, called the **[c]** _____ *stage*. During

this stage, individuals seek to discover their abilities, skills, and **[d]** _____ . If one
resolves this stage with confusion, then a stable identity will not be formed, and the individual
may become a social deviant or have trouble with close personal relationships later. The stage is
marked by a shift from dependence on adults for information and the turn toward the peer group
for support.

During college, the **[e]** _____ *stage* describes the basic conflict. This stage focuses on developing relationships with others. Middle adulthood finds people in the

[f] _____ *stage*. The contribution to family, community, work, and society comprise generativity; and feelings of triviality about one's activities indicate the difficulties of

the stage and lead to stagnation. The final stage is the **[g]** _____ *stage*, which is marked by a sense of accomplishment if a person has been successful in life or a sense of despair if one regrets what might have been.

Evaluate

____ 1. identity vs. role confusion stage

       a. A period from late adulthood until death during which we review life's accomplishments and failures.

____ 2. intimacy vs. isolation stage

       b. A period in middle adulthood during which we take stock of our contributions to family and society.

____ 3. generativity vs. stagnation stage

       c. A period during early adulthood that focuses on developing close relationships with others.

____ 4. ego integrity vs. despair stage

       d. A time in adolescence of testing to determine one's own unique qualities.

Rethink

29-1   In what ways do school cultures help or hurt teenage students who are going through adolescence? What school policies might benefit early-maturing girls and late-maturing boys? Explain how same-sex schools help, as some have argued.

29-2   Many cultures have "rites of passage" through which young people are officially recognized as adults. Do you think such rites can be beneficial? Does the United States have any such rites? Would setting up an official designation that one has achieved "adult" status have benefits?

Spotlight on Terminology and Language—ESL Pointers

Adolescence: Becoming an Adult

Page 367 "'I went to a National Honor Society **induction**.'"

An **induction** is an initiation experience.

Page 367 "It is a time of profound changes and, occasionally, **turmoil**."

Turmoil is a period of extreme confusion, agitation, or commotion.

Page 367 "At the same time, and **rivaling** these physiological changes, important social, emotional, and cognitive changes occur as adolescents strive for independence and move toward adulthood."

When something is **rivaled**, it is in competition with competing forces.

Page 367 "Furthermore, adolescents spend considerably less time with their parents, and more with their peers, than they did several **decades** ago."

A **decade** is a period of 10 years.

Page 369 "Adolescents, however, can reason on a higher **plane**, having typically reached Piaget's formal operational stage of cognitive development."

Reasoning on a higher **plane** refers to a higher level of consciousness or intellectual and moral development.

Page 371 "Compassion for individuals is a more **salient** factor in behavior for women than it is for men."

A **salient** factor is something that stands out conspicuously.

Page 371 "As we will see, this **quest** takes adolescents along several routes."

Adolescents are going on a **quest**, a journey, in search of many answers.

Page 372 "In sum, adolescence is not an end point but rather a **way station** on the path of psychosocial development (Whitbourne et al., 1992; McAdams et al., 1997)."

A **way station** is an intermediate stopping place.

Page 372 "Does puberty invariably **foreshadow** a stormy, rebellious period of adolescence?"

When an event **foreshadows** something, it warns of, or indicates, the next event.

Page 373 "One reason for the increase in **discord** during adolescence appears to be the **protracted** period in which children stay at home with their parents."

Discord is the increase in conflict and friction.

Protracted is the much longer and drawn-out period children are now staying at home.

Module 30: Adulthood

Physical Development: The Peak of Health
Social Development: Working at Life
Marriage, Children, and Divorce: Family Ties
The Later Years of Life of Life: Growing Old
Physical Changes in Late Adulthood: The Aging Body
Cognitive Changes: Thinking About—and During—Late Adulthood
The Social World of Late adulthood: Old But Not Alone

Becoming an Informed Consumer of Psychology:
Adjusting to Death

- *What are the principal kinds of physical, social, and intellectual changes that occur in early and middle adulthood, and what are their causes?*
- *How does the reality of late adulthood differ from the stereotypes about the period?*
- *How can we adjust to death?*

Adulthood

Early adulthood is generally considered to begin at about 20 years of age and to last until about 40 to 45 years, and middle adulthood lasts from 40 to 45 to about 65 years of age. These ages have been studied less than any other. Fewer significant physical changes occur, and the social changes are diverse.

The peak of physical health is reached in early adulthood, and quantitative changes begin at about 25 years as the body becomes less efficient and more prone to disease through time. The

major physical development is the female experience of **[a]** _____, the cessation of menstruation and the end of fertility. The loss of estrogen may lead to hot flashes, a condition that is successfully treated with artificial estrogen. Problems that were once blamed on menopause are now seen as resulting from the perceptions of coming old age and society's view of it. Although men remain fertile, the gradual decline of physical abilities has similar effects to menopause, causing the man to focus on the social expectations of youthfulness.

Daniel Levinson's model of adult development identifies six stages from beginning adulthood through the end of middle adulthood. At the beginning, the individual formulates a "dream" that guides career choices and the vision the person has of the future. At about 40 or 45, people enter

a period called the **[b]** _____, during which past accomplishments are assessed,

and, in some cases, the assessment leads to a **[c]** _____, in which the signs of

physical aging and a sense that the career will not progress combine to force a reevaluation of and

247

an effort to remedy their dissatisfaction. Most people go through the midlife transition without any difficulties. During their fifties, people become more accepting of others and their own lives. They realize that death is inevitable and seek to understand their accomplishments in terms of how they understand life. Since Levinson's research was based on males, the difference in roles and socialization has raised questions about whether women go through the same stages.

   [d] _____ study development and the aging process from the age of about 65. Gerontologists reexamine our understanding of aging, suggesting that the stereotype of aging is inaccurate. Napping, eating, walking, and conversing are the typical activities of both the elderly and college students. The obvious physical changes that appear in old age include thinning and graying hair, wrinkling and folding skin, and a loss of height. Vision and hearing become less sharp, smell and taste are less sensitive, reaction time slows, and oxygen intake and heart-pumping abilities decrease. Two types of theories have been offered to account for these changes.

One group includes the **[e]** _____ _theories of aging_, which suggest that there are preset time limits on the reproduction of human cells governed by genetics. The other group includes the **[f]** _____ _theories of aging_, which suggest that the body simply stops working efficiently. By-products of energy production accumulate, and cells make mistakes in their reproduction.

   The view that the elderly are forgetful and confused is no longer considered an accurate assessment. Tests show declines in **[g]** _____ in old age, but

[h] _____ actually increases. Fluid intelligence may be more sensitive to changes in the nervous system than crystallized intelligence.

   One assumption about the elderly is that they are more forgetful. Evidence suggests that forgetfulness is not inevitable. The decline in cognitive function associated with old age is called

[i] _____, but this is now viewed as a symptom caused by other factors, like

[j] _____, anxiety, depression, or even overmedication.

   Loneliness is a problem for only a small portion of the elderly, although social patterns do change in old age. Two theories account for how people approach old age. The

[k] _____ _theory of aging_ views aging as a gradual withdrawal from the world on physical, psychological, and social levels. Energy is lower and interaction lessens. This view sees aging as an automatic process. The **[l]** _____ _theory of aging_ suggests that the happiest people are ones who remain active and that people should attempt to maintain the activities and interests they develop during middle age. The nature of the activity is the most important factor, not the quantity.

   Death requires major adjustments, as the death of those near you causes changes in life and makes you consider the possibility of your own death. Elisabeth Kübler-Ross outlined five stages of the death process: (1) **[m]** _____, the person denies the fact that he or she is dying; (2) **[n]** _____, the person becomes angry at people who are healthy, angry at the medical profession for not being able to help, and angry at God; (3)

[o] _____, after anger, the person may try to postpone death through a bargain in exchange for extended life; (4) [p] _____, once bargaining fails, the person experiences depression, realizing that death is inevitable; and (5) [q] _____, which is signaled by the end of mourning one's own life, becoming unemotional and noncommunicative as if at peace with oneself.

Evaluate

Part A

_____ 1.   Erik Erikson

_____ 2.   Lawrence Kohlberg

_____ 3.   Jean Piaget

_____ 4.   Elisabeth Kübler-Ross

_____ 5.   Daniel Levinson

a.   Moral development.

b.   Death and dying.

c.   Psychosocial development.

d.   Cognitive development.

e.   Adult social development.

Part B

_____ 1.   genetic preprogramming theories of aging

_____ 2.   wear-and-tear theories of aging

_____ 3.   disengagement theory of aging

_____ 4.   activity theory of aging

a. Theories that suggest that the body's mechanical functions cease efficient activity and, in effect, wear out.

b. A theory that suggests that the elderly who age most successfully are those who maintain the interests and activities they had during middle age.

c. Theories that suggest a built-in time limit to the reproduction of human cells.

d. A theory that suggests that aging is a gradual withdrawal from the world on physical, psychological, and social levels.

30-1 Is the possibility that life might be extended for several decades a mixed blessing? What societal consequences might an extended life span bring about?

30-2 Does the finding that people in late adulthood require intellectual stimulation have implications for the societies in which older people live? In what way might stereotypes about older individuals contribute to their isolation and lack of intellectual stimulation?

Spotlight on Terminology and Language—ESL Pointers

Adulthood

Page 378 "These uncertainties make the routine use of HRT **controversial** (Kittell & Mansfield, 2000; National Heart, Lung, & Blood Institute, 2002; Rymer, Wilson, & Ballard, 2003)."

The routine use of hormone replacement therapy is **controversial**; there are many arguments both for and against it.

Page 378 "According to **anthropologist** Yewoubdar Beyene (1989), the more a society values old age, the less difficulty its women have during menopause."

An **anthropologist** is a person who studies people. **Anthropologists** study all human beings, cultures, and human development.

Page 378 "Whereas physical changes during adulthood reflect development of a **quantitative** nature, social developmental transitions are **qualitative** and more profound."

Quantitative relates to quantity. Something **quantitative** is measurable based on its amount, capacity, or magnitude.

When something is measured **qualitatively**, you're looking at it based on its distinguishing characteristics or its essential properties.

Page 378 "People **envision** life goals and make career choices."

Envision is to visualize and imagine.

Page 378 "A major developmental **thrust** of this period is coming to terms with one's circumstances (Whitbourne, 2000)."

The **thrust** of this period, the major developmental focus of this period, is coming to terms with your life circumstances.

Page 379 "People come to accept the fact that death is **inevitable**, and they try to understand their accomplishments in terms of the broader meaning of life."

Death is **inevitable**; it is unavoidable and inescapable.

Page 379 "In a typical fairy tale, a **dashing** young man and a beautiful young woman marry, have children, and live happily ever after."

Dashing is handsome, good-looking.

Page 379 "Even though divorce rates have been declining since they **peaked** in 1981, about half of all first marriages end in divorce."

When something **peaks**, it hits a high number. The divorce rate was much higher in 1981.

Test your knowledge of the modules by answering these questions. These questions have been placed in three Practice Tests. The first two tests consist of questions that will test your recall of factual knowledge. The third test contains questions that are challenging and primarily test for conceptual knowledge and your ability to apply that knowledge. Check your answers and review the feedback using the Answer Key in the following pages of the *Study Guide*.

PRACTICE TEST 1:

1. When theories stress the role of heredity in their explanations of change in individual development, the focus of their accounts would be on:
   a. maturation.
   b. nurture.
   c. environmental factors.
   d. social growth.

2. A study in which several different age groups are examined over different points in time is called:
   a. cross-sectional.
   b. maturational.
   c. longitudinal.
   d. cross-sequential.

3. Hereditary information is represented in thousands of _____, which are tiny segments of stringy material called _____.
   a. zygotes; embryos.
   b. chromosomes; zygotes.
   c. genes; neonates.
   d. genes; chromosomes.

4. In prenatal development, the age of viability is a developmental stage in which:
   a. the eyes and other sense organs are functional.
   b. the fetus can survive if born prematurely.
   c. development has advanced sufficiently so that the fetus is capable of learning from environmental cues.
   d. the sexual organs of the fetus are differentiated.

5. Which of the following is caused by genetic birth defects?
   a. phenylketonuria (PKU)
   b. AIDS
   c. diethylstilbestrol (DES)
   d. fetal alcohol syndrome

6. The infant's later temperament is known to be affected by the mother's:
   a. consumption of "junk foods" during pregnancy.
   b. sleep patterns during early fetal development.
   c. attitude about whether the baby is wanted or unwanted.
   d. emotional state during the late fetal period.

7. Which reflex helps the newborn infant position its mouth onto its mother's breast when it feeds?
   a. rooting reflex
   b. startle reflex
   c. gag reflex
   d. surprise reflex

8. What changes in perception do **not** take place in the first six months after birth in human infants?
    a. They develop discrimination of tastes and smells.
    b. They can recognize two- and three-dimensional objects.
    c. They can discriminate all sounds important for language production.
    d. They understand their native language.

9. In order to proceed from one of Piaget's stages of cognitive development to another, it is necessary for children to achieve a certain level of:
    a. perceptual and cognitive development.
    b. maturation and experience.
    c. memory capacity and physical development.
    d. social and cognitive development.

10. Which of the following is a possible reason for the steadily decreasing age at which adolescents reached puberty during the last century?
    a. Nutrition and medical care have increased.
    b. Cultural prohibitions about sexuality have weakened.
    c. Sexual promiscuity among children has increased.
    d. Puberty rituals have been abandoned in most Western societies.

11. If a person's behavior reflected the desire to please other members of society, he or she would be considered to be at Kohlberg's:
    a. preconventional level of moral reasoning.
    b. conventional level of moral reasoning.
    c. postconventional level of moral reasoning.
    d. nonconventional level of moral reasoning.

12. The most noteworthy feature of Erikson's theory of psychosocial development is that:
    a. both men and women are included in its descriptions of developmental changes.
    b. it accurately describes developmental changes that people in other cultures also experience.
    c. it has greatly increased understanding of infant development.
    d. it suggests that development is a lifelong process.

13. Several warning signs indicate that a teenager may attempt suicide. Which alternative is **not** one of them?
    a. loss of appetite or excessive eating
    b. withdrawal from friends or peers
    c. a preoccupation with death, the afterlife, or what would happen "if I died"
    d. an increase in praying, going to church, or other religious behavior

14. The primary cause of a midlife crisis tends to be:
    a. an awareness of the detrimental physical changes associated with aging.
    b. a series of disappointments and shortcomings in a person's children.
    c. a recognition that a person's reproductive capabilities are decreasing or will soon end.
    d. a failure to achieve desired career goals and objectives.

15. Which stage of development seems to show important differences between men and women according to adult development researcher Daniel Levinson?
    a. culmination   c. dream
    b. challenge   d. reality

16. Genetic preprogramming theories suggest which of the following about physical decline of aging?
   a. Women live four to ten years longer than men.
   b. The body, like a machine, eventually wears out.
   c. There is a built-in time limit to the ability of human cells to reproduce.
   d. Physical aging is a biological process in which all physical functions decline.

17. Fluid intelligence provides the capabilities for many adaptive and functional human behaviors. Which alternative correctly describes a person's fluid-intelligence capabilities?
   a. Fluid intelligence increases after birth until early adulthood.
   b. Fluid intelligence is high all through a person's lifetime.
   c. Fluid intelligence increases more slowly during late adulthood and old age.
   d. Fluid intelligence remains fairly constant until a person's death.

18. What natural condition, to date, is explained by neither the genetic preprogramming theory nor the wear-and-tear theory, according to developmental psychologists?
   a. circulatory system deterioration   c. women living longer than men
   b. confusion and forgetting   d. reduced visual acuity

19. A pattern of reduced social and physical activity as well as a shift toward the self rather than a focus on others characterizes the:
   a. deactivation theory of aging.   c. withdrawal theory of aging.
   b. activity theory of aging.   d. disengagement theory of aging.

Part A

____ 20. trust vs. mistrust stage

____ 21. autonomy vs. shame and doubt stage

____ 22. initiative vs. guilt stage

____ 23. industry vs. inferiority stage

a. The stage of psychosocial development where children can experience self-doubt if they are restricted and overprotected.

b. The first stage of psychosocial development, occurring from birth to 18 months of age.

c. The period during which children may develop positive social interactions with others or may feel inadequate and become less sociable.

d. The period during which children experience conflict between independence of action and the sometimes negative results of that action.

253

Part B

_____ 24. adolescence

_____ 25. identity

_____ 26. menopause

_____ 27. midlife transition

_____ 28. midlife crisis

a. The point at which women stop menstruating, generally at around 45 years of age.

b. The stage between childhood and adulthood.

c. The negative feelings that accompany the realization that we have not accomplished all that we had hoped.

d. The distinguishing character of the individual: who each of us is, what our roles are, and what we are capable of.

e. Beginning around age 40, a period during which we come to realize that life is finite.

29. Considering the discussion of the nature-nurture issue at the beginning of the chapter, what is your assessment of the role of child-rearing practices in the development of the person as a unique individual? Are certain styles more likely to help individuals reach their potential?

30. Describe the factors that contribute to problems between parents and teenagers and suggest ways that these may be overcome. Are the recent changes in childhood and adolescence that result in changes in the family to blame for some of these factors?

PRACTICE TEST 2:

1. The philosophical view that infants are born with a blank slate favors which of the following as a dominant influence on development?
   a. interactionism
   b. nature
   c. nurture
   d. dualism

2. Identical twins are especially interesting subjects for developmental studies because they:
   a. communicate via telepathy (i.e., direct mental transfer of ideas).
   b. have typically shared their lives together in their parents' home.
   c. have identical genetic makeup since they developed from one zygote.
   d. are highly cooperative in their dealings with psychologists.

3. What is the next stage the organism progresses through after the zygote has developed at conception?
   a. embryo
   b. neonate
   c. fetus
   d. fertilization

4. The unborn fetus has many of the features and characteristics of a newborn as early as:
   a. 8 weeks.
   b. 12 weeks.
   c. 16 weeks.
   d. 24 weeks.

5. A genetic defect that leads to a very short life because of a breakdown in strategic metabolic processes and occurs most frequently among Jews of Eastern European descent is called:
   a. Tay-Sachs disease.
   b. Down syndrome.
   c. meningitis.
   d. phenylketonuria (PKU).

6. The presence of an extra chromosome results in the developmental disorder called:
   a. Down syndrome.
   b. sickle-cell anemia.
   c. Tay-Sachs disease.
   d. phenylketonuria (PKU).

7. Rubella is also known as:
   a. Down syndrome.
   b. German measles.
   c. phenylketonuria (PKU).
   d. sickle-cell anemia.

8. A neonate is:
   a. a prenatal infant in its 30th to 38th week of development.
   b. a newborn infant.
   c. an infant born with deformities because of chromosomal abnormalities.
   d. a premature baby up to the time at which the normal due date passes.

9. A researcher compares visual abilities in four groups of infants of ages 1 month, 3 months, 5 months, and 7 months. This is an application of:
   a. the longitudinal research method.
   b. the critical period research method.
   c. the cross-sectional research method.
   d. the cross-sequential research method.

10. According to research by Diana Baumrind's categories of parental styles, _____ parents are those who are firm and set limits and goals, reasoning with their children and encouraging their independence.
   a. authoritarian
   b. permissive
   c. militaristic
   d. authoritative

11. In Erikson's developmental stage, college-age people typically contend with the conflicts found in the:
   a. intimacy vs. isolation stage.
   b. generativity vs. stagnation stage.
   c. ego integrity vs. despair stage.
   d. identity vs. role confusion stage.

12. Multiple research studies have demonstrated that the "storm and stress" of adolescence:
   a. is a myth for most teenagers.
   b. is lessened because teenagers remain under parental supervision for a longer timeframe than is the case in other societies.
   c. is reflected in the concerns of the industry vs. inferiority stage.
   d. characteristically applies to all teenagers.

13. A major developmental task for people age 40 to 50 years old who are experiencing the initial stages of middle adulthood is to:
   a. maintain harmonious relationships with their children.
   b. accept that the die has been cast and that they must come to terms with circumstances.
   c. carefully choose goals so that all major career advances can still be realized before old age.
   d. adjust to changes brought about by menopause and physical deterioration.

14. Professor Costello, a 46-year-old female, reviews her past actions and failed personal goals. She devoted her efforts to her academic career rather than to marriage or children, yet she now realizes that her colleagues regard her research as trivial and uninspired. She feels old and knows that she has accomplished little in her life. She is experiencing:
   a. menopause.
   b. delayed identity crisis.
   c. midlife transition.
   d. midlife crisis.

15. One way that the developmental stages of adult women differ from those of men is that:
    a. women have more difficulties developing a vision of what their future life will include.
    b. women's midlife crises are more likely to occur later in their lives.
    c. women's midlife crises are usually precipitated by their children leaving home, causing the "empty nest syndrome."
    d. women's developmental stages are more influenced by hormonal and physical changes.

16. The _____ theory of aging states that aging involves a gradual withdrawal from the world on multiple levels.
    a. wear-and-tear
    b. genetic preprogramming
    c. disengagement
    d. activity

17. Which type of intelligence actually increases with age?
    a. fluid intelligence
    b. verbal intelligence
    c. basic intelligence
    d. crystallized intelligence

18. The reaction of women to menopause is:
    a. better in cultures that value old age more than youth.
    b. universally negative because of its effects on female reproduction.
    c. positive if the woman is single but negative if she is married.
    d. positive for heterosexuals but negative for lesbians.

Part A

_____ 19. rooting reflex

_____ 20. sucking reflex

_____ 21. gag reflex

_____ 22. startle reflex

a. The reflex in response to a sudden noise where the infant flings its arms, arches its back, and spreads its fingers.

b. A neonate's tendency to turn its head toward things that touch its cheek.

c. A reflex that prompts an infant to suck at things that touch its lips.

d. An infant's reflex to clear its throat.

Part B

_____ 23. egocentrism

_____ 24. personal fables

_____ 25. sexual attraction

_____ 26. formal operations

_____ 27. caring

a. Piaget's stage of cognitive development where the individual is able to think abstractly and see things from another point of view.

b. A state of self-absorption in which the world is viewed from one's own point of view.

c. Gilligan's theory of morality suggests that women display a morality of more _____.

d. An adolescent's view that what happens to him or her is unique, exceptional, and shared by no one else.

e. Begins early in adolescence as sexual organs mature.

28. Define Vygotsky's cognitive theory and explain how his Zone of Proximal Development (ZPD), with the assistance of scaffolding, promotes better learning.

29. Apply the disengagement and activity theories of aging to the question of mandatory retirement. Should there be a mandatory retirement age, and what are the exceptions and who shall judge?

PRACTICE TEST 3: Conceptual, Applied, and Challenging Questions

1. One-tenth of the African-American population in the United States has the possibility of passing on _____, which leaves the newborn with a variety of health problems and very short life expectancy.
   a. hypertension
   b. sickle-cell anemia
   c. phenylketonuria
   d. Tay-Sachs disease

2. Which statement about the sensory and perceptual capabilities of infants is **not** true?
   a. At 4 days of age, they can distinguish between closely related sounds such as "ba" and "pa."
   b. At 60 days of age, they can recognize their mother's voice.
   c. After 6 months of age, they are capable of discriminating virtually any difference in sounds that is relevant to the production of language.
   d. They prefer sweetened liquids to unsweetened liquids.

3. Attachment between the baby and its mother and father are different in that:
   a. mothers spend more time directly nurturing their children, whereas fathers spend more time playing with them.
   b. mothers spend more time playing with their children, whereas fathers spend more time nurturing them.
   c. mothers generally are identified as primary caregivers, so the attachment is stronger.
   d. fathers spend more time doing things with their children than mothers.

4. A father's typical attachment to his children:
   a. is superior to the mother's attachment in most situations.
   b. is aloof and detached.
   c. is generous with affection, especially during verbal interaction.
   d. is qualitatively different, but comparable to the mother's attachment.

5. Play in young children has many consequences. Which alternative is **not** one of them?
   a. They become more competent in their social interactions with other children.
   b. They learn to take the perspective of other people and to infer others' thoughts and feelings.
   c. They learn to control emotional displays and facial expressions in situations where this is appropriate.
   d. They become more independent of other children from ages 2 to 6.

6. Dr. Liefeld, a developmental psychologist, is evaluating a young child's cognitive development. Dr. Liefeld shows the child two separate arrangements of red disks. Eight disks are laid in a straight line in one arrangement. Another eight disks are arranged in a random "scatter" pattern in the other. The psychologist asks, "Is the amount of disks in each arrangement the same?" Dr. Liefeld is testing the child's understanding of:
   a. spatial reversibility.   c. spatial inertia.
   b. conservation.   d. reorganization.

7. Jess and Kelly were playing with two balls of clay. Kelly was molding a cake and Jess was making a bowl. Jess then suggested they get new balls of clay so they could make something different. Kelly informed her that no new clay was necessary; the clay could be remolded to make different objects. What principle was Kelly teaching to Jess?
   a. the principle of conservation   c. the principle of egocentric thought
   b. the principle of reversibility   d. the principle of logic

8. The last time Shareen used her personal computer, she observed that several files were not copied onto the floppy disk as she had expected. She carefully checked her sequence of operations and considered the characteristics of the software. After evaluating alternative explanations for what had happened, she correctly deduced why the files were not copied. Shareen is in Piaget's:
   a. concrete operational stage of cognitive development.
   b. preoperational stage of cognitive development.
   c. sensorimotor stage of cognitive development.
   d. formal operational stage of cognitive development.

9. Piaget found that _____ is mastered early in the _____ for most children.
   a. reversibility; sensorimotor stage   c. object permanence; formal operational stage
   b. conservation; concrete operational stage   d. abstraction; preoperational stage

10. Jason thinks, "If I hit my brother, I will get sent to my room." In which level of moral development is this child functioning?
    a. amorality   c. conventional morality
    b. preconventional morality   d. postconventional morality

11. Mary Margaret leads a group that has as its focus rape prevention and assistance in recovery from rape. The group represents moral development consistent with Gilligan's notion of:
    a. morality of nonviolence.   c. goodness as self-sacrifice.
    b. orientation toward individual survival. d. preconventional morality.

12. Which factor does not contribute to the stresses experienced by adolescents outside the home that may cause stress at home?
    a. the number of school changes made
    b. volatile relationships with friends and other peers
    c. frequent arguments about money with family members
    d. holding a part-time job while maintaining studies

13. Divorce produces many changes in the emerging single-parent family. Which alternative is **not** one of them?
    a. Time is always at a premium.
    b. The painful experience of divorce may hinder the building of close relationships throughout life.
    c. Children in a single-parent family develop interpersonal skills, so they are less likely to divorce.
    d. High levels of parental conflict before the divorce may produce increased anxiety and aggressive behavior in the children.

14. When a child's mother and father work, the mother is generally still viewed as holding the main child-rearing responsibility. Yet, there are also great benefits to working. In what way do the benefits outweigh the disadvantages?
    a. Women who work feel a greater sense of mastery and pride, and generally have higher self-esteem.
    b. Women who work play a greater role in the decisions that affect the lives of their families.
    c. Women who work enjoy more responsibility than those who don't work, yet allow their husbands valuable time alone with their children.
    d. Women who work have better-developed social lives.

15. Dr. Perini is an authority on Egyptian mummies and has been retired for 13 years. He was recently asked to speak at a monthly faculty luncheon. If he gives one of his "canned" presentations on mummies to the faculty, he will be drawing heavily from his:
    a. crystallized intelligence.   c. fluid intelligence.
    b. common sense.   d. practical intelligence.

16. Marcus is satisfied with his teaching position, is quite comfortable with his single lifestyle, and has begun to expand his reflections on the subject he has taught and researched to consider its broader implications for society. He hopes to write a book that appeals to a wider audience than the typical academic book. Which of the following best describes Marcus's situation?
    a. disengagement theory of aging   c. generativity vs. stagnation
    b. concrete operations   d. conventional morality

17. Marta has reached a point where she says, "If I can only live to see my Ginny graduate from college, I will devote the rest of my time to the church." Marta is expressing which of the following?
    a. Kübler-Ross's stage of bargaining
    b. the wear-and-tear theory of aging
    c. Erikson's stage of ego integrity vs. despair
    d. Kübler-Ross's stage of acceptance

18. Why do so many rites of passage seemed to be focused on males?
    a. Societies need to know when children have become adults.
    b. Menarche serves to demarcate female achievement of adulthood.
    c. It is important for males to be able to stand up to ridicule and face pain.
    d. The rituals are devised and administered by men.

Part A

____ 19. phenylketonuria (PKU)

____ 20. sickle-cell anemia

____ 21. Tay-Sachs disease

____ 22. Down syndrome

____ 23. rubella

____ 24. fetal alcohol syndrome

a. A disease of the blood that affects about 10 percent of America's African-American population.

b. German measles.

c. A disorder caused by the presence of an extra chromosome, resulting in mental retardation.

d. An inherited disease that prevents its victims from being able to produce an enzyme that resists certain poisons, resulting in profound mental retardation.

e. A genetic defect preventing the body from breaking down fat and typically causing death by the age of 4.

f. An ailment producing mental and physical retardation in a baby as a result of the mother's behavior.

Part B

____ 25. forgetfulness

____ 26. crystallized intelligence

____ 27. fluid intelligence

____ 28 senility

____ 29. life review

a. An examination and evaluation of one's life.

b. A broad, imprecise term typically applied to older persons with progressive deterioration of mental abilities.

c. Intelligence such as reasoning, memory, and information processing.

d. Not the issue in old age that it was once believed to be.

e. Intelligence based on information, skills, and problem solving.

30. One of the main points of the chapter is that developmental psychologists are interested in finding ways that the individual potential can be maximized. Children can be stimulated through contact with parents, through play, and while at day care, and they can be encouraged to explore by having the appropriate attachments. What would the world of a perfectly "enriched" child look like? Is it possible to overstimulate children?

31. What does the author of the text suggest are some reasons for the high rates of suicide in adolescence? What are some of the signs that may suggest to friends and family that a teen is contemplating taking his or her own life?

■ ANSWER KEY: MODULES 27, 28, 29, AND 30

Module 27:
[a] Developmental psychology
[b] nature-nurture issue
[c] maturation
[d] interactionist
[e] identical twins
[f] conception
[g] zygote
[h] chromosomes
[i] genes
[j] embryo
[k] critical period
[l] fetus
[m] age of viability

Evaluate

Part A	Part B
1. b	2. b
2. d	3. d
3. c	4. e
4. a	5. a
5. e	6. c

Module 28:
[a] neonate
[b] vernix
[c] lanugo
[d] reflexes
[e] Babinski reflex
[f] Attachment
[g] Friendships
[h] authoritarian parents
[i] Permissive parents
[j] Authoritative parents
[k] temperaments
[l] psychosocial development
[m] Cognitive development
[n] information processing
[o] zone of proximal development, or ZPD,
[p] scaffolding

Evaluate

Part A	Part B
1. d	1. b
2. a	2. a
3. e	3. c
4. c	4. e
5. b	5. d

Module 29:
[a] adolescence
[b] puberty
[c] identity vs. role confusion
[d] identity
[e] intimacy vs. isolation
[f] generativity vs. stagnation
[g] ego integrity vs. despair

Evaluate
1. d
2. c
3. b
4. a

Module 30:
[a] menopause
[b] midlife transition
[c] midlife crisis
[d] Gerontologists
[e] genetic preprogramming
[f] wear-and-tear
[g] fluid intelligence
[h] crystallized intelligence
[i] senility
[j] Alzheimer's disease
[k] disengagement
[l] activity
[m] denial
[n] anger
[o] bargaining
[p] depression
[q] acceptance

Evaluate

Part A	Part B
1. c	1. c
2. a	2. a
3. d	3. d
4. e	4. b
5. b	

Selected Rethink Answers

27-1   When similarities are discovered in development between very different cultures, there is a tendency to see the similarities as a result of the genetic makeup, but researchers would probably take an *interactionist* approach, which considers both nature and nurture when viewing these similarities.

29-2   Rights of passage are beneficial because they allow us to be publicly acknowledged for different stages in maturity. It helps adolescents to both expect and accept certain responsibilities that go with the age. In the United States, getting a driver's license, graduating from high school, moving out of parents' homes, and the right to vote are a few rites of passage. In the United States, turning 18 years of age does give people adult status and holds them legally responsible for their actions.

30-2   When older people retire, they often lack the cognitive activity and intellectual stimulation that is provided by raising children and participating in the work environment. Older people who move into less stimulating environments or who live alone lack the environmental energy previously supplied by their lifestyle. Lifestyle choices are often made because of the stereotypes that might include the elderly as needing a calmer environment where many life decisions are made *for* them and the misguided thinking that all older people's physical and cognitive abilities naturally decrease as part of aging.

Practice Test 1:

1. a   mod. 27 p. 339
*a. Correct. Maturation involves, to a large extent, the unfolding of genetic code.
b. Incorrect. Nurture refers to the element of environmental influence, not heredity.
c. Incorrect. Environmental factors are not hereditary.
d. Incorrect. Social growth would reveal environmental, nurturing types of factors and some hereditary factors.

2. d   mod. 27 p. 341
a. Incorrect. A cross-sectional study examines several groups at one given point in time.
b. Incorrect. There is no type of study called "maturational."
c. Incorrect. A longitudinal study follows a single group through a given span of time, taking measurements at points along the way.
*d. Correct. The cross-sequential study combines longitudinal and cross-sectional approaches by studying different groups in a longitudinal fashion, often allowing for a shorter timeframe to complete the study.

3. d   mod. 27 p. 343
a. Incorrect. Zygotes and embryos refer to different stages of the fetus.
b. Incorrect. Zygotes are fetuses, not genes.
c. Incorrect. Neonates are newborn, not chromosomes.
*d. Correct. Each of our 46 chromosomes is composed of thousands of genes.

4. b   mod. 27 p. 345
a. Incorrect. Many sense organs are functional long before the fetus reaches a level of physical maturity that would allow it to survive if born.
*b. Correct. This age continues to be earlier and earlier as medical technology evolves.
c. Incorrect. Viability and learning are independent of each other in that viability depends on the ability of the fetus to function physically independent of the mother, and this may be highly reflexive.
d. Incorrect. Sexual organs are differentiated long before viability.

5. a   mod. 27 p. 346
*a. Correct. This disease is inherited and causes mental retardation through the accumulation of toxins.
b. Incorrect. AIDS results from HIV infection.
c. Incorrect. This is a hormone that was prescribed in the 1960s and has resulted in abnormalities in the cervix and vagina in the daughters of women who took the hormone.
d. Incorrect. This syndrome occurs in children who are exposed to high levels of alcohol as fetuses.

6. d   mod. 27 p. 347
a. Incorrect. Junk food might affect some other aspect of development, but this link has not been established.
b. Incorrect. This link has not been established.
c. Incorrect. This is more likely to affect the marriage and the child's later behavior.
*d. Correct. Research suggests that this is true, possibly because the chemicals in the mother's system enter and influence the child's temperament.

7. a   mod. 28 p. 349
*a. Correct. Whenever the baby's cheek is stroked, it will turn its head in the direction of the stroked cheek.
b. Incorrect. The startle reflex is a pattern of actions related to being startled in which the baby flings out its arms, spreads its fingers, and arches its back.
c. Incorrect. This reflex helps the baby clear its throat.
d. Incorrect. The startle reflex would probably be considered a "surprise" reflex, but there is not a reflex officially named this.

8. d   mod. 28 p. 350
a. Incorrect. Taste and smell discriminations occur throughout the six months.
b. Incorrect. From birth, infants refine their ability to distinguish different shapes and objects.
c. Incorrect. As early as four days after birth, infants can distinguish sounds like *ba* and *pa*.
*d. Correct. Within the first six months, infants do not develop an understanding of their native language.

9. b   mod. 28 p.360
a. Incorrect. Only the first stage of Piaget's developmental scheme utilizes perceptual development.
*b. Correct. The child must develop a level of maturation and experience appropriate to the stage he or she is currently completing before moving on to the next stage; in fact, experience and maturation are the forces that create the concerns of the next stage.
c. Incorrect. Memory organization, not capacity, plays a role in Piaget's scheme, and physical growth is only a minor element in the earliest stage.
d. Incorrect. The social development that is associated with the cognitive development is not one of the necessary elements of cognitive development, rather a by-product of it.

10. a   mod. 29 p. 369
*a. Correct. Nutrition and medical care are the commonly assumed causes of this change.
b. Incorrect. Cultural prohibition about sexuality would have nothing to do with this physical change.
c. Incorrect. Sexual promiscuity would have little to do with this physical change.
d. Incorrect. The timing of a puberty ritual does not affect the timing of puberty.

11. b   mod. 29 p. 370
a. Incorrect. In the preconventional stage, people are more likely to be motivated by rewards and avoidance of punishment.
*b. Correct. The conventional stage is marked by a desire to get along socially.
c. Incorrect. Individuals in the postconventional stage are not likely to be concerned with how others think about them.
d. Incorrect. Kohlberg did not define a nonconventional stage.

12. d   mod. 29 p. 371
a. Incorrect. Many of the other theories are inclusive of both males and females.
b. Incorrect. Cross-cultural studies have not supported or rejected a universal application of Erikson's views.
c. Incorrect. Erikson does not place any special emphasis on understanding infant development in comparison to the rest of the life span.
*d. Correct. Erikson has been a leader in placing emphasis on the entire life span.

13. d   mod. 29 p. 375
a. Incorrect. Changes in regular habits are important signals that something is wrong.
b. Incorrect. Suicide often follows a withdrawal from friends and peers.
c. Incorrect. A common and persistent theme among those contemplating suicide is the nature of death and the afterlife.
*d. Correct. People contemplating suicide do not increase their attendance at church or amount of prayer (these may actually be signs of hope and contrary to suicidal thoughts).

14. d   mod. 30 p. 378
a. Incorrect. The detrimental changes are only beginning to occur, and this does not seem to be a major issue during a midlife crisis.
b. Incorrect. These disappointments can occur at any time and are not necessarily associated with midlife crises.
c. Incorrect. For males, the reproductive capability does not end.
*d. Correct. More often than other reasons, the midlife crisis is a result of a recognition of failure to meet many personal goals.

15. c   mod. 30 p. 380
a. Incorrect. Culmination is not a relevant aspect of Levinson's theory.
b. Incorrect. Challenge is not a relevant aspect of Levinson's theory.
*c. Correct. Women have more difficulty than men in forming a clear dream, and they experience a conflict between family and career goals.
d. Incorrect. Everyone has difficulty with reality.

16. c   mod. 30 p. 381
a. Incorrect. The genetic preprogramming approach would suggest that this results from genetic programming, but this is not what they would say about the decline.
b. Incorrect. This is the point of view of the wear-and-tear theorists.
*c. Correct. The preprogramming theories suggest that cells can only reproduce a certain number of times, and then they begin to decline.
d. Incorrect. This view is held by many, and not exclusive to the genetic preprogramming theories.

17.	a	mod. 30 p. 382
*a.	Correct. Fluid intelligence and its adaptive power are most needed during the earlier part of life.
b.	Incorrect. Fluid intelligence does begin a decline after middle adulthood.
c.	Incorrect. Fluid intelligence actually declines slowly during these periods.
d.	Incorrect. Fluid intelligence increases early and declines later.

18.	c	mod. 30 p. 381
a.	Incorrect. Both can explain this.
b.	Incorrect. This could be explained by the wear-and-tear theories.
*c.	Correct. If women live longer than men, there would have to be some genetic coding at the level of the cells that accounts for it, or they would have to have less wear-and-tear, both of which are not plausible views.
d.	Incorrect. Reduced visual acuity is easily explained by the wear-and-tear approaches.

19.	d	mod. 30 p. 384
a.	Incorrect. Deactivation theory sounds good, but its actual name is "disengagement."
b.	Incorrect. Activity theory sounds good, but its actual name is "disengagement."
c.	Incorrect. Withdrawal theory sounds good, but its actual name is "disengagement."
*d.	Correct. This defines the disengagement theory of aging.

20.	b	mod. 28 p. 359
21.	a	mod. 28 p. 359
22.	d	mod. 28 p. 359
23.	c	mod. 28 p. 359

24.	b	mod. 29 p. 367
25.	d	mod. 29 p. 372
26.	a	mod. 30 p. 378
27.	e	mod. 30 p. 378
28.	c	mod. 30 p. 378

29.
▪	Identify the relative importance of nature and nurture for your views. Do you see them as equal or is one stronger than the other?
▪	Each of the styles may imply a view of the nature-nurture debate. The authoritarian style, for instance, may see children as naturally unruly and in need of strict discipline to come under control. The permissive parent may expect the child to find his or her own potential, such that exploration is natural.

▪	The view that sees nature and nurture as interacting would suggest that the parenting style is the place that an inherited potential can be realized, so child-rearing practices are crucial.

30.
•	Note that the text considers the notion of excessive stress to be unsupported.
•	Describe specific instances where parents and adolescents have conflicts (e.g., rules, self-determination, school performance), and describe the nature of the disagreements. Identify things either parents or children can do to solve the problem. Are some of the problems an effort to assert a sense of self and identity?
•	Home life has changed significantly, and many adolescents are growing up in single-parent homes.

Practice Test 2:
1.	c	mod. 27 p. 340
a.	Incorrect. Interactionism admits to genetic (not a blank slate) influences.
b.	Incorrect. The "nature" element is that of heredity, suggesting that some aspects of development are influenced by one's disposition.
*c.	Correct. Nurture implies the forces of the environment, including the caregiving and socializing influences, so nurture would be the dominant influence for someone with such a view.
d.	Incorrect. Dualism refers to the philosophical perspective of the duality of the mind and body, not the duality of nature and nurture.

2.	c	mod. 27 p. 341
a.	Incorrect. Only those born of alien parents.
b.	Incorrect. Nontwin siblings have shared their lives just as much.
*c.	Correct. Having identical genes makes the difference.
d.	Incorrect. Most subjects are highly cooperative in their dealings with psychologists.

3.	a	mod. 27 p. 343
*a.	Correct. The next stage is an embryo, which is followed by the stage known as a fetus.
b.	Incorrect. A neonate is a newborn, and an embryo would not survive birth.
c.	Incorrect. A fetus is the stage that follows embryo, which follows zygote.
d.	Incorrect. Fertilization precedes the zygote phase.

4.   d   mod. 27 p. 345
a.   Incorrect. At eight weeks, only arms, legs, and face are discernible.
b.   Incorrect. At this stage, the face does not have any characteristics of later life to it, and eyes do not open, among many other differences.
c.   Incorrect. At this stage, the fetus can move noticeably, the face has characteristics it will have later, and major organs begin to function.
*d. Correct. At 24 weeks, most of the characteristics that will be seen in the newborn are present: eyes will open and close, it can cry, grasp, and look in directions.

5.   a   mod. 27 p. 346
*a. Correct. Children with Tay-Sachs disease are unable to break down fat, and they die by the age of 4.
b.   Incorrect. Down syndrome can occur in any child, but it is more frequent with children of older parents.
c.   Incorrect. Meningitis is not a genetic disease.
d.   Incorrect. Phenylketonuria, or PKU, is a genetic disease that can afflict anyone, and it does not result in early death; rather, it results in retardation if not treated properly.

6.   a   mod. 27 p. 346
*a. Correct. Down syndrome children have an extra chromosome, which results in mental retardation and unusual physical features.
b.   Incorrect. Sickle-cell anemia is a recessive trait common among people of African descent.
c.   Incorrect. Children with Tay-Sachs disease are unable to break down fat, and they die by the age of 4.
d.   Incorrect. Phenylketonuria, or PKU, is a genetic disease that results in retardation if not treated properly.

7.   b   mod. 27 p. 346
a.   Incorrect. Down syndrome children have an extra chromosome, which results in mental retardation and unusual physical features.
*b. Correct. This disease can cause serious malformation and prenatal death.
c.   Incorrect. Phenylketonuria, or PKU, is a genetic disease that results in retardation if not treated properly.
d.   Incorrect. Sickle-cell anemia is a recessive trait common among people of African descent.

8.   b   mod. 28 p. 349
a.   Incorrect. A neonate is a newborn.
*b. Correct. This is the official term used to refer to newborns in their first week.
c.   Incorrect. A neonate is any newborn.
d.   Incorrect. A neonate is a newborn, and can be early, late, or on time.

9.   c   mod. 27 p. 341
a.   Incorrect. Longitudinal method follows one group through many years.
b.   Incorrect. However, the length of funding for the project would probably define the critical period.
*c. Correct. The researcher is comparing different age groups at the same time to compare the different abilities shown by each group.
d.   Incorrect. This combines longitudinal and cross-sectional, following several groups for an extended period.

10. d   mod. 28 p. 357
a.   Incorrect. However, children of authoritarian parents are also quite well behaved.
b.   Incorrect. Children of permissive parents tend to be unpleasant and demanding of attention.
c.   Incorrect. This is not one of the presumed types, but militaristic parents would get this behavior from their children as well.
*d. Correct. According to this view, children of authoritative parents are well behaved.

11. a   mod. 29 p. 372
*a. Correct. In college, the stage of intimacy vs. isolation begins as the individual begins to experience self-defined roles and independence.
b.   Incorrect. See answer a.
c.   Incorrect. See answer a.
d.   Incorrect. See answer a.

12. a   mod. 29 p. 373
*a. Correct. Highly troubled adolescence is fairly rare.
b.   Incorrect. This would probably increase the storm and stress if it occurred very much at all.
c.   Incorrect. This stage is before adolescence, so it should not have much to do with storm and stress.
d.   Incorrect. Applies to only a few; see answer a.

13. b   mod. 30 p. 378
a.   Incorrect. Most people maintain harmonious relationships with their children.
*b. Correct. It is the prospect that personal goals and dreams may not be completely fulfilled and that there is now less chance for achieving them.
c.   Incorrect. All major career advances may no longer be possible.
d.   Incorrect. Menopause and physical deterioration may be yet to come, and not all females experience problems with menopause, and certainly physical deterioration is not evident in every 40 to 50 year old.

14. d   mod. 30 p. 378
a.   Incorrect. No evidence of menopause here.
b.   Incorrect. The term for this is "midlife crisis," in which one examines one's identity.
c.   Incorrect. This is too traumatic to be considered a mere transition.
*d. Correct. Unlike the milder form of transition, this sounds like a crisis.

15. a   mod. 30 p. 376
*a. Correct. In addition, the conflict between family and career appears to influence the difficulties of developing a clear dream.
b.   Incorrect. Timing does not appear to differ significantly for those who experience this crisis.
c.   Incorrect. The empty nest can precipitate a crisis, but many women view it quite positively.
d.   Incorrect. Menopause does not necessarily precipitate a crisis any more than does the physical change experienced by men.

16. c   mod. 30 p. 384
a.   Incorrect. The wear-and-tear theories suggest that the body wears out.
b.   Incorrect. The genetic preprogramming theories suggests that the body is programmed to slow and die.
*c. Correct. The disengagement theory says that people age because they consciously withdraw.
d.   Incorrect. The activity theory of aging suggests that people who remain active have a more successful old age.

17. d   mod. 30 p. 383
a.   Incorrect. Fluid intelligence declines with age.
b.   Incorrect. Verbal intelligence may increase as crystallized intelligence increases.
c.   Incorrect. Basic intelligence is not defined adequately to suggest that it exists, much less changes with age.
*d. Correct. As described, crystallized intelligence increases as the experiences and memories become more important aspects of intelligent behavior in later adulthood.

18. a   mod. 30 p. 378
*a. Correct. In cultures that value old age, a menopausal woman has reached "old age."
b.   Incorrect. It varies from culture to culture.
c.   Incorrect. There is little or no evidence to support this claim.
d.   Incorrect. There is no difference between the way lesbians and heterosexuals handle menopause.

19. b   mod. 28 p. 350
20. c   mod. 28 p. 350
21. d   mod. 28 p. 350
22. a   mod. 28 p. 350

23. b   mod. 29 p. 373
24. d   mod. 29 p. 373
25. e   mod. 29 p. 369
26. a   mod. 29 p. 369
27. c   mod. 29 p. 371

28.
▪ Vygotsky theorized that the culture in which one is raised has an important influence on our cognitive development.
▪ Cognitive developmental occurs as a consequence of social interactions with others to jointly solve problems.
▪ ZPD is the level at which children can almost learn, but not quite, on their own.
▪ Scaffolding occurs when parents, teachers, and skilled peers assist by presenting information that is both new and within the ZPD.

29.
• First, describe each of these two theories and offer an example of how they differ.
• The activity theory suggests that a successful retirement would require a level of activity that would allow continuity.
• Retirement serves as an important marker of age in the disengagement theory.
• Describe the benefits (such as making room for people entering the job market) or costs (loss of expertise) of mandatory retirement in order to support your answer.

Practice Test 3:

1. b   mod. 27 p. 346
a. Incorrect. While hypertension has some genetic disposition, it is not identifiable enough to be said to be directly transmitted, and it does not cause a short life expectancy.
*b. Correct. This disease results from recessive genes (passed on by both parents), and the red blood cells have a deformed, sickle shape.
c. Incorrect. Children with Tay-Sachs disease are unable to break down fat, and they die by the age of 4, but they are usually of Jewish descent.
d. Incorrect. Phenylketonuria, or PKU, is a genetic disease that can afflict anyone, and it does not result in early death; rather, it results in retardation if not treated properly.

2. b   mod. 28 p. 352
a. Incorrect. And the infant's production of speech sounds and recognition of sounds continues to grow rapidly.
*b. Correct. Infants can recognize their mother's voice as early as three days.
c. Incorrect. This too is true.
d. Incorrect. The sweet tooth must be built in.

3. a   mod. 28 p. 357
*a. Correct. The style of interaction between mother and child differs from that of father and child.
b. Incorrect. This is reversed.
c. Incorrect. The attachment is not stronger or weaker, but of a different style.
d. Incorrect. Fathers probably spend less time with their children, but this is not universally true.

4. d   mod. 28 p. 356
a. Incorrect. Few would describe the difference as one of superiority.
b. Incorrect. Rather than aloof and detached, fathers are often quite physical and in close contact with their children.
c. Incorrect. While affectionate, fathers do not express this as verbally as do mothers.
*d. Correct. Due to the differences in how fathers and mothers interact with their children, the best description is that the attachment differs in quality.

5. d   mod. 28 p. 356
a. Incorrect. See answer d.
b. Incorrect. See answer d.
c. Incorrect. See answer d.
*d. Correct. Play may actually increase mutual dependence and support. Play builds social competence, encourages taking the perspective of others, and requires emotional control.

6. b   mod. 28 p. 361
a. Incorrect. Reversibility would refer to the ability to reverse an operation.
*b. Correct. This test describes an effort to determine the ability of the child to conserve a number even if the objects are arranged differently.
c. Incorrect. A developmental psychologist would not test for spatial inertia.
d. Incorrect. Reorganization is not one of the principles that could be tested by a developmental psychologist.

7. b   mod. 28 p. 361
a. Incorrect. The principle of conservation would be applied to whether a lump of clay was more if it was long or short and fat—even if it was the same ball of clay.
*b. Correct. As simple as it sounds, Jess is learning that he can reverse his bowl back into a ball of clay.
c. Incorrect. If egocentric thought were at work, Jess might simply decide that the cake Kelly made was a pot of soup for his bowl.
d. Incorrect. Logic will come much later.

8. d   mod. 28 p. 362
a. Incorrect. See answer d.
b. Incorrect. See answer d.
c. Incorrect. See answer d.
*d. Correct. This sequential and systematic problem-solving approach is most common of someone in the formal operations stage.

9. b   mod. 28 p. 361
a. Incorrect. Reversibility is mastered in the concrete operations stage, not the sensorimotor stage.
*b. Correct. Conservation is one of the major accomplishments of the stage.
c. Incorrect. Object permanence occurs in the sensorimotor stage.
d. Incorrect. Abstraction occurs in the formal stage.

10. b   mod. 29 p. 370
a. Incorrect. Amorality has been used to describe the period before when cognitive processes are much involved in behavior, but it does not describe the phase illustrated in the question.
*b. Correct. The preconventional level of morality is driven by rewards and punishments.
c. Incorrect. The conventional level of morality is marked by efforts to please others and becoming a good member of society.
d. Incorrect. People in the postconventional level of morality make judgments according to moral principles that are seen as broader than society.

11. a   mod. 29 p. 370
*a. Correct. Rape prevention and mutual assistance is not only the survival of an earlier stage, but the principle that views violence as immoral.
b. Incorrect. Prevention may be focused on survival, but mutual assistance focuses on higher concerns.
c. Incorrect. Rape awareness does not specifically call on self-sacrifice.
d. Incorrect. This is not one of Gilligan's stages, and preconventional morality would understand rape through the punishment it deserves.

12. c   mod. 29 p. 373
a. Incorrect. The number of school changes does affect stress in the home.
b. Incorrect. Volatile relationships with peers do increase stress at home.
*c. Correct. Arguments about money with family members is not a stress outside the home.
d. Incorrect. Holding part-time jobs causes stress and may lead to stress at home.

13. c   mod. 30 p. 379
a. Incorrect. Since the parent must work as well as care for children and maintain the household, time is always at a premium.
b. Incorrect. This is one of the effects of divorce on children, a later fear of repeating the same "mistakes" of the parents.
*c. Correct. All children develop interpersonal skills, and these skills do not seem to prevent divorce.
d. Incorrect. The stress before divorce can often be as bad as the stress of divorce.

14. a   mod. 30 p. 379
*a. Correct. Working does provide a basis for building self-esteem that is easier to identify than the sense of worth gained from doing the job of mothering.
b. Incorrect. This is not always true.
c. Incorrect. The amount of time spent by husbands with children does not increase as the time the wife spends working outside the home increases.
d. Incorrect. There is no evidence for this, and given the amount of time required for household work, one wonders where the social life would fit.

15. a   mod. 30 p. 383
*a. Correct. Crystallized intelligence depends on memory and experience.
b. Incorrect. Common sense would not have us all informed about Egyptian mummies.
c. Incorrect. Fluid intelligence is used earlier in life to help people adapt to new challenges.
d. Incorrect. Practical intelligence refers to a type of intelligence that helps one survive and thrive in domains like work and social life.

16. c   mod. 29 p. 372
a. Incorrect. The disengagement theory of aging would predict that Marcus would withdraw from society.
b. Incorrect. Concrete operations occurs at the ages of 6 to 11.
*c. Correct. Marcus is considering becoming productive in a broad sense of making a contribution to society, rather than stagnating in his comfortable position.
d. Incorrect. Conventional morality would be the level of morality focused on getting along with the social group, not necessarily contributing to it.

17. a   mod. 30 p. 385
*a. Correct. She is bargaining with death.
b. Incorrect. The wear-and-tear theory of aging does not address the rationalizations we make in order to finish life.
c. Incorrect. This bargain does not sound like ego integrity.
d. Incorrect. Allison has not yet accepted her impending death.

18. b   mod. 29 p. 378
a. Incorrect. While this may be true, it would apply to males and females.
*b. Correct. Since menarche makes the female passage easy to identify, a rite is necessary to make the male passage as clear.
c. Incorrect. Not all rites of passage involve ridicule and pain.
d. Incorrect. This may be true, but it would then suggest that females would undergo similar rites more often.

19. d   mod. 27 p. 346
20. a   mod. 27 p. 346
21. e   mod. 27 p. 346
22. c   mod. 27 p. 346
23. b   mod. 27 p. 347
24. f   mod. 27 p. 337

25. d mod. 30 p. 384
26. e mod. 30 p. 383
27. c mod. 30 p. 383
28. b mod. 30 p. 384
29. a mod. 30 p. 385

30.
- Describe the factors that you consider important for early exposure. Can a child's later learning be enhanced through early exposure to academic skills like spelling and math? Or should the focus be on processes like imagination and creative work?
- What criteria would you use to identify overstimulation? Keep in mind that the child must feel safe and have a secure attachment in order to explore the environment freely.

31. Factors that put adolescents at risk are:
- Depression
- Unhappiness
- Extreme fatigue
- Profound hopelessness

Warning signs are when teens exhibit:
- Loss of appetite
- Self-destructive behavior
- Signs of depression
- Preoccupation with death
- Putting affairs in order
- Explicit announcement of thoughts of suicide

Personality

Overview

This set of modules introduces both the approaches to the understanding of personality along with methods psychologists use to assess individual personality characteristics.

Module 31 defines personality as the sum of the enduring characteristics that differentiate individuals and provide the stability in a person's behavior across situations and time. First, the psychoanalytic approach to personality is discussed. Psychoanalysis understands personality in terms of how a person manages the unconscious that seeks to dominate behavior. Freud's psychoanalytic theory suggests that personality develops in stages. Defense mechanisms are unconscious strategies that reduce anxieties. The theories of Jung, Adler, and Horney conclude this module.

Module 32 investigates four major alternatives to the psychoanalytic approach: trait approaches, learning approaches, biological approaches, and humanistic approaches. The substantial differences in these theories focus on the various aspects of personality and the overall complexity of personality

Module 33 illustrates several ways that personality can be assessed. Psychological tests that demonstrate both reliability and validity and also have standardized norms are studied. The most frequently given assessments include the MMPI, the Rorschach test, and the TAT.

To further investigate the topics covered in this chapter, you can visit the related Web sites by visiting the following link: www.mhhe.com/feldmanup6-14links.

Prologue: The Dapper Don
Looking Ahead

Module 31:
Psychodynamic
Approaches to Personality

Freud's Psychoanalytic Theory
The Neo-Freudian Psychoanalysts

- ***How do psychologists define and use the concept of personality?***
- ***What do the theories of Freud and his successors tell us about the structure and development of personality?***

Psychodynamic Approaches to Personality

The field of psychology known as **[a]** _____ studies the characteristics that make a person unique and attempts to explain what makes a person act the same in different situations and through time.

[b] _____ are concerned with understanding the hidden forces that govern people's behavior and remain outside of awareness. These forces have their roots in childhood experiences. This theory, called **[c]** _____, was developed by Sigmund Freud. Slips of the tongue are examples of how thoughts and emotions are held in the

[d] _____, the part of the personality that remains beyond the person's awareness. Slips reflect these hidden concerns. The unconscious also contains *instinctual drives*, which include infantile wishes, desires, demands, and needs that remain hidden because of the conflicts they can cause. Freud described conscious experience as the top of an iceberg, suggesting that the larger part of our personality was unconscious. In order to understand personality, these unconscious elements must be illuminated. The contents of the unconscious are disguised, thus requiring that slips of the tongue, fantasies, and dreams be interpreted in order to understand how unconscious processes direct behavior.

Freud described a general model of the personality that contains three interacting structures.

The **[e]** _____ is the raw, unorganized, inherited part of the personality aimed at reducing the tension caused by basic drives of hunger, sex, aggression, and irrational impulses.

The drives are powered by **[f]** _____, or "psychic energy," and the id operates

according to the **[g]** _____, or the desire for immediate gratification of all needs.

Reality limits the expression of these id impulses. The **[h]** _____ is responsible for constraining the id. It serves as a buffer between reality and the pleasure-seeking demands of the

id. The ego operates on the **[i]** _____, in which restraint is based on the safety of the individual and an effort to integrate into society. The ego is the seat of the higher cognitive functions.

The **[j]** _____ represents the rights and wrongs of society as represented by the parents and is composed of two parts. The **[k]** _____ prevents us from behaving immorally and the **[l]** _____ motivates us to do the morally correct thing. Both the superego and the id make unrealistic demands. The ego must compromise between the moral-perfectionist demands of the superego and the pleasure-seeking gratification sought by the id.

Freud proposed a theory of development that accounted for how the adult personality comes into existence. Difficulties and experiences from a childhood stage may predict adult behaviors, and each stage focuses on a biological function. The first period of development is the **[m]** _____ **stage,** during which the baby's mouth is the focus of pleasure. This suggested to Freud that the mouth is the primary site of sexual pleasure. **[n]** _____ means that an adult shows personality characteristics that are related to that stage. At about 12 to 18 months until the age of 3, the child is in the **[o]** _____ **stage.** The major source of pleasure moves to the anal region, and the child derives pleasure from the retention and expulsion of feces. If toilet training is particularly demanding, fixation can occur. Fixation can lead to unusual rigidity and orderliness or the extreme opposite of disorder or sloppiness.

At the age of 3, the **[p]** _____ **stage** begins and the source of pleasure moves to the genitals. In the end, girls identify with their mothers and repress these feelings. The next period is called the **[q]** _____ **period,** beginning around 5 or 6 and lasting to puberty. Sexual concerns become latent. The final period, the **[r]** _____ **stage,** begins at puberty. Mature adult sexuality emerges during this period.

Anxiety, an intense, negative emotional experience, arises as a signal of danger to the ego. Although anxiety may arise from realistic fears, the *neurotic anxiety* arises because of the irrational impulses from the id that threaten to break into consciousness. The ego has developed unconscious strategies to control the impulses called **[s]** _____. *Regression* involves using behavior from earlier stages of development to deal with the anxiety. *Displacement* is the process of redirecting the unwanted feeling onto a less threatening person. *Rationalization* occurs when reality is distorted by justifying events with explanations that protect our self-esteem. *Denial* occurs when a person simply refuses to acknowledge the existence of an anxiety-producing piece of information. *Projection* involves protecting oneself by attributing unwanted impulses and feelings to someone else. *Sublimation* is the diversion of unwanted impulses to socially acceptable behaviors. According to Freud, these mechanisms are used to some degree by everyone, although some people devote a large amount of energy to dealing with unacceptable impulses to the extent that daily life becomes hampered. He identified this tendency as *neurosis.*

Evaluate

_____ 1. unconscious

_____ 2. instinctual drives

_____ 3. id

_____ 4. libido

_____ 5. fixation

a. Behavior reflecting an earlier stage of development.

b. Infantile wishes, desires, demands, and needs hidden from conscious awareness.

c. A person is unaware of this determinant of behavior.

d. The raw, unorganized, inherited part of personality created by biological drives and irrational impulses.

e. The sexual energy underlying biological urges.

Rethink

31-1 Can you think of ways in which Freud's theories of unconscious motivations are commonly used in popular culture? How accurately do you think such popular uses of Freudian theories reflect Freud's ideas?

31-2 What are some examples of archetypes in addition to those mentioned in this chapter? In what ways are archetypes similar to and different from stereotypes?

Spotlight on Terminology and Language—ESL Pointers

Psychodynamic Approaches to Personality

Page 393 "As he walked toward her, he **mulled** over a line he had heard in an old movie the night before: 'I don't believe we've been properly introduced yet.'"

He **mulled** over; he thought about and gave consideration to using this line as an opening statement.

Page 393 "Psychodynamic approaches to personality are **founded** on the idea that personality is motivated by inner forces and conflicts about which people have little awareness or control."

This idea is the **foundation**, or basis, for the psychodynamic approach to personality;

Page 393 "Like the unseen mass of a floating iceberg, the memories, knowledge, beliefs, and feelings in the unconscious far **surpass** in quantity the information about which we are aware."

To **surpass** is to exceed. This theory proposes we have much more information in the unconscious than just the information about which we are aware.

Page 393 "The unconscious provides a '**safe haven**' for our recollections of threatening events."

A **safe haven** is a place of safety.

Page 394 "The **id** operates according to the **pleasure principle**, in which the goal is the immediate reduction of tension and the maximization of satisfaction."

The **id** is Freud's first division of the mind. The goal of the **id** is to pursue pleasure and satisfy the biological drives.

The goals of someone operating according to the **pleasure principle** would be the satisfaction of drives and avoidance of pain, without concern for moral restrictions or society's regulations. According to Freud, this is the operating principle of the id.

Page 394 "The **ego** strives to balance the desires of the id and the realities of the objective, outside world."

The **ego** is Freud's second division of the mind. The **ego** develops from the id during infancy. The goal of the **ego** is to find safe and socially acceptable ways of satisfying the desires of the id and to negotiate between the wants of the id and the prohibitions of the superego.

Page 394 "The **superego**, the final personality structure to develop, represents the rights and wrongs of society as taught and modeled by a person's parents, teachers, and other significant individuals."

The goal of the **superego** is to apply the moral values and standards of one's parents or caregivers and society in satisfying one's wishes.

Module 32: Other Major Approaches to Personality: In Search of Human Uniqueness

Trait Approaches: Placing Labels on Personality

> **Applying Psychology in the 21st Century:**
> The A-Team: What Personality Does It Take to Travel into Space

Learning Approaches: We Are What We've Learned
Biological and Evolutionary Approaches: Are We Born with Personality?
Humanistic Approaches: The Uniqueness of You
Comparing Approaches to Personality

- *What are the major aspects of trait, learning, biological and evolutionary, and humanistic approaches to personality?*

Other Major Approaches to Personality: In Search of Human Uniqueness

A number of theories take a different approach than that of psychoanalysis. These include

[a] _____, which assumes that individuals respond to different situations in a fairly consistent manner. **[b]** _____ are the enduring dimensions of personality characteristics along which people differ. Trait theories assume that all people have certain traits, and the degree to which a trait applies to a specific person varies.

Gordon Allport identified 18,000 separate terms that could be used to describe personality, which he then reduced to 4,500 descriptors. In order to make sense of this number, he defined three basic categories of traits. A **[c]** _____ is a single characteristic that directs most of a person's activities. Most people do not have cardinal traits; instead, they have five to ten **[d]** _____ that define major characteristics. **[e]** _____ are characteristics that affect fewer situations and are less influential than cardinal or central traits. Preferences would be secondary traits.

The statistical technique called **[f]** _____, in which relationships among a large number of variables are summarized into smaller, more general patterns, has been used to identify fundamental patterns or combinations of traits. Raymond Cattell suggested that there are 46 *surface traits*, or clusters of related behaviors. Cattell then reduced this number to 16 *source traits* that represent the basic dimensions of personality. He then developed the Sixteen Personality Factor Questionnaire (16 PF).

Hans Eysenck used factor analysis to identify three major dimensions.

[g] _____ is the dimension marked by quiet and restrained individuals on one end and outgoing and sociable ones on the other. **[h]** _____ is the dimension marked by moody and sensitive behavior (neuroticism) on the one hand and calm, reliable, and even-tempered behavior (stability) on the other. **[i]** _____ refers to the degree to which reality is distorted. Recent research has suggested that there are five traits: *surgency, neuroticism, intellect, agreeableness,* and *conscientiousness.*

According to B. F. Skinner, personality is a collection of learned behavior patterns. Similarities across situations are caused by a similarity of reinforcements. Strict learning theorists are less interested in the consistency issue than they are in finding ways to modify behavior. In their view, humans are quite changeable.

[j] _____ *approaches* emphasize the role of a person's cognitions in determining personality. According to Albert Bandura, people are able to foresee the outcomes of behaviors before carrying them out by using the mechanism of **[k]** _____. Bandura considers **[l]** _____, the expectations of success, to be an important factor in determining the behaviors a person will display. The key to understanding behavior,

[m] _____, refers to the interaction between environment, behavior, and the individual.

Traditional learning theories have been criticized for ignoring internal processes and reducing behavior to stimuli and responses.

[n] _____ *approaches* to personality suggest that important components of personality are inherited. The study of **[o]** _____, the basic innate disposition that emerges early in life, is studied through the biological approach. Jerome Kagan's study of inhibited and uninhibited children suggests that *inhibited children* have an inborn characteristic of greater physiological reactivity.

[p] _____ *approaches to personality* emphasize the basic goodness of people and their tendency to grow to higher levels of functioning. Carl Rogers is a major representative of this approach. The positive regard others have for us makes us see and judge ourselves through the eyes of other people. The views others have of us may not match our own *self-concept.* If the difference is great, we may have problems with daily functioning. The discrepancy is overcome by support from another person in the form of **[q]** _____, defined as an attitude of acceptance and respect no matter what the person says or does. Rogers and Maslow (Chapter 10) view the ultimate goal of personality growth to be **[r]** _____.

The criticisms of humanistic theory are centered on the difficulty of verifying the basic assumptions of the theory. The assumption that all people are basically "good" is unverifiable and injects nonscientific values into scientific theories.

Evaluate

_____ 1.   cardinal trait

_____ 2.   central traits

_____ 3.   secondary traits

_____ 4.   surface traits

_____ 5.   source traits

a. A single trait that directs most of a person's activities.

b. The 16 basic dimensions of personality.

c. Clusters of a person's related behaviors that can be observed in a given situation.

d. Traits less important than central and cardinal traits.

e. A set of major characteristics that compose the core of a person's personality.

Rethink

32-1   If personality traits are merely descriptive and not explanatory, of what use are they? Can assigning a trait to a person be harmful—or helpful? Why or why not?

32-2   In what ways are Cattell's 16 source traits, Eysenck's three dimensions, and the "Big Five" factors similar, and in what ways are they different? Which traits seem to appear in all three schemes (under one name or another) and which are unique to one scheme? Is this significant?

Spotlight on Terminology and Language—ESL Pointers

Other Major Approaches to Personality: In Search of Human Uniqueness

Page 401 "He's just so **even-tempered**, no matter what's happening."

Even-tempered is calm. He is not likely to get flustered.

Page 401 "**Trait theorists** do not assume that some people have a trait and others do not; rather, they propose that all people possess certain traits, but that the degree to which a particular trait applies to a specific person varies and can be quantified."

Trait theory is an approach for analyzing the structure of personality by measuring, identifying, and classifying similarities and differences in distinguishing qualities or personality characteristics.

Page 402 "When personality psychologist Gordon Allport systematically **pored over** an **unabridged** dictionary, he came up with some 18,000 separate terms that could be used to describe personality."

To **pore over** something is to read it studiously or attentively.

The **unabridged** version is the complete version, the full-length document.

Page 402 "**Factor analysis** is a method of summarizing the relationships among a large number of variables into fewer, more general patterns."

Factor analysis is a statistical method that finds relationships among different or diverse items and allows them to be grouped together.

Page 402 "Trait approaches have several **virtues**."

A **virtue** is a beneficial quality.

Page 404 "However, trait approaches also have some **drawbacks**."

A **drawback** is the downside of this approach, the negative aspect or shortcomings of the trait approach.

Page 407 "Of course, some of these criticisms are **blunted** by social cognitive approaches, which explicitly consider the role of cognitive processes in personality."

These criticisms are weakened, or dulled. They are **blunted**.

Page 407 "The degree of success of these treatments is a **testimony** to the merits of learning theory approaches to personality."

The degree of success is **testimony**, or proof, supporting these treatments.

Module 33: Assessing Personality: Determining What Makes Us Special

Exploring Diversity: Should Race and Ethnicity Be Used to Establish Norms?

Self-Report Measures of Personality
Projective Methods
Behavioral Assessment

Becoming an Informed Consumer of Psychology:
Assessing Personality Assessments

- *How can we most accurately assess personality?*
- *What are the major types of personality measures?*

Assessing Personality: Determining What Makes Us Special

The intentionally vague statements that introduce the topic of assessment suggest that measuring different aspects of personality may require great care and precision. The assessment of personality requires discriminating the behavior of one person from that of another.
[a] _____ are standard measures that measure aspects of behavior objectively.

Psychological tests must have **[b]** _____, that is, they must measure something consistently from time to time. A reliable test will produce similar outcomes in similar conditions. The question of whether a test measures the characteristic it is supposed to is called

[c] _____. If a test is reliable, that does not mean it is valid.

[d] _____ are the standards of test performance that allow comparison of thescores of one test-taker to others who have taken it. The norm for a test is determined by calculating the average score for a particular group of people for whom the test is designed to be given.

Instead of conducting a comprehensive interview to determine aspects of childhood, social

relationships, and success and failures, the use of **[e]** _____ allows individuals to respond to a small sample of questions. The most frequently used self-report measure is the

[f] _____. Originally developed to distinguish people with psychological disturbances from people without disturbances, the MMPI scores have been shown to be good predictors of such things as whether college students will marry within 10 years and whether they will get an advanced degree. The test has 567 true-false items covering categories such as mood, opinions, and physical and psychological health. The interpretation of the responses is important, but there are no right or wrong answers. The test is scored on 10 scales and includes a lie scale for people trying to falsify their answers. The MMPI has undergone a procedure called

[g] _____ by which the test authors have determined which items best differentiate among groups of people, like differentiating those suffering depression from normal subjects.

[h] _____ *tests* require the subject to describe an ambiguous stimulus. The responses are considered to be projections of what the person is like. The best known is the

[i] _____ *test*, which consists of symmetrical stimuli. The **[j]** _____ consists of a series of pictures about which the person is asked to write a story. Inferences about the subject are then based on these stories. These tests are criticized because too much inference depends on the scorer.

In order to obtain an objective test based on observable behavior, a **[k]** _____ may be conducted either in a natural setting or in a laboratory under controlled conditions. The assessment requires quantifying behavior as much as possible.

Evaluate

____ 1.   Minnesota Multiphasic Personality Inventory-2 (MMPI-2)

____ 2.   test standardization

____ 3.   projective personality test

____ 4.   Rorschach test

____ 5.   Thematic Apperception Test (TAT)

a. Used to identify people with psychological difficulties.

b. Consists of a series of ambiguous pictures about which a person is asked to write a story.

c. Uses inkblots of indefinite shapes.

d. Uses ambiguous stimuli to determine personality.

e. Validates questions in personality tests by studying the responses of people with known diagnoses.

Rethink

33-1   What do you think are some of the problems that developers and interpreters of self-report personality tests must deal with in their effort to provide useful information about test-takers? Why is a "lie scale" included on such measures?

33-2   Should personality tests be used for personnel decisions? Should they be used for other social purposes, such as identifying individuals who are at risk for certain types of personality disorders? What sorts of policies would you devise to ensure that such tests were used ethically?

Spotlight on Terminology and Language—ESL Pointers

Assessing Personality: Determining What Makes Us Special

Page 413 "Although you have some personality weaknesses, you generally are able to **compensate** for them."

You **compensate** for your personality weaknesses by making up for these weaknesses in other ways or with other behaviors.

Page 413 "You prefer a certain amount of change and variety and become dissatisfied when **hemmed in** by restrictions and limitations."

When you're **hemmed in**, you're restricted or constrained. You can't respond or behave in the manner you would like.

Page 413 "You have found it unwise to be too **frank** in revealing yourself to others."

Frank is open and forthright. You may have found it unwise to be too honest when speaking with others.

Page 413 "Most college students think that the descriptions are **tailored** just to them."

Tailored is custom-made, personalized. Most college students identify very closely with these descriptions.

Page 413 "The ease with which we can agree with such **imprecise** statements **underscores** the difficulty in coming up with accurate and meaningful assessments of people's personalities (Johnson et al., 1985; Prince & Guastello, 1990)."

An **imprecise** statement is a vague statement.

Underscores means emphasizes or highlights.

Page 417 "For instance, employers who use it as a **screening tool** for job applicants may interpret the results improperly, relying too heavily on the results of individual scales instead of taking into account the overall patterns of results, which require skilled interpretation."

A job **screening tool** would be an assessment inventory or application process used to select or eliminate job applicants.

Test your knowledge of the modules by answering these questions. These questions have been placed in three Practice Tests. The first two tests consist of questions that will test your recall of factual knowledge. The third test contains questions that are challenging and primarily test for conceptual knowledge and your ability to apply that knowledge. Check your answers and review the feedback using the Answer Key in the following pages of the *Study Guide*.

PRACTICE TEST 1:

1. Sigmund Freud believed that the _____ harbors repressed emotions and thoughts as well as instinctual drives.
    a. unconscious
    b. collective unconscious
    c. conscience
    d. conscious

2. Which of the following is **least** likely to involve making unrealistic demands on the person?
    a. the id
    b. the ego
    c. the superego
    d. the pleasure principle

3. The most important mental factors in Freud's psychoanalytic theory were:
    a. those that the person consciously controls or manipulates.
    b. associated with the latency developmental stage.
    c. those about which the person is unaware.
    d. based on social learning and influence.

4. Freud's concept of the ego-ideal refers to:
    a. infantile wishes, desires, demands, and needs hidden from conscious awareness.
    b. the part of the superego that motivates us to do what is morally proper.
    c. the part of personality that provides a buffer between the id and the outside world.
    d. the part of the superego that prevents us from doing what is morally wrong.

5. A child who is in the midst of toilet training is probably in the:
    a. genital psychosexual stage.
    b. anal psychosexual stage.
    c. phallic psychosexual stage.
    d. oral psychosexual stage.

6. Which of the following defense mechanisms did Freud find most socially acceptable?
    a. repression
    b. sublimation
    c. rationalization
    d. projection

7. Unconscious strategies, called defense mechanisms, are what people use to:
    a. decrease their reliance on the reality principle.
    b. reduce anxiety.
    c. increase the superego's power to regulate behavior.
    d. prevent Freudian slips.

8. Trait theorists believe that:
    a. everyone has the same traits, but in different amounts.
    b. everyone has different traits that do not change with time.
    c. everyone has different traits, and they change with time.
    d. everyone has different traits, but they cannot be measured.

9. Which of the psychologists listed is **not** a trait theorist?
   a. Albert Bandura   c. Raymond B. Cattell
   b. Gordon Allport   d. Hans Eysenck

10. From the perspective of learning theorists such as B.F. Skinner, consistencies of behavior across situations relate to:
    a. stable individual characteristics called personality traits.
    b. the dynamics of unconscious forces.
    c. the rewards or punishments received by the person previously.
    d. any conflict between the person's experiences and his or her self-concept.

11. Factor analysis is:
    a. a method of recording data that requires sophisticated equipment.
    b. a method of understanding how the unconscious works.
    c. a statistical method of finding common traits.
    d. a sociometric method of determining personality traits in a group.

12. Carl Rogers would argue that prisons should offer rehabilitation programs because humanistic theories of personality assume that:
    a. man's basic goodness is contrasted with an evil unconscious.
    b. man is self-sufficient and that society corrupts the individual.
    c. man is basically good and desires to improve.
    d. man's fundamental depravity may be offset through education.

13. Alcoholics Anonymous relies on the conscious, self-motivated personal ability to improve, which is the core of:
    a. the learning theory of personality.
    b. the neo-Freudian psychoanalytic theory of personality.
    c. the humanistic theory of personality.
    d. the trait theory of personality.

14. Which one of the following tests is designed to uncover unconscious content?
    a. MMPI   c. California Psychological Inventory
    b. TAT   d. Edwards Personal Preference Schedule

15. A student retakes the SAT. Despite her claim that she did poorly the first time because she was very sleepy that day, her score is within 2 percent of her first score. This outcome supports the notion that the SAT is:
    a. a standardized assessment tool.   c. a reliable assessment tool.
    b. an academic ability assessment tool.   d. a valid assessment tool.

_____ 16. pleasure principle   a. Provides a buffer between the id and the outside world.

_____ 17. ego   b. The principle by which the id operates.

_____ 18. reality principle   c. Prevents us from doing what is morally wrong.

_____ 19. superego   d. Represents the morality of society as presented by parents, teachers, and others.

_____ 20. conscience

                                   e. The principle by which the ego operates.

21. The _____ provides a buffer between the id and the outside world.

284

22. A phenomenon whereby adults have continuing feelings of weakness and insecurity is referred to as having an _____.

23. _____ is when unpleasant id impulses are pushed back into the unconscious.

24. The refusal to accept anxiety-producing information is known as _____.

25. Allport suggests three basic categories of traits: cardinal, central, and _____.

26. Given that Freud's theory appears to be primarily focused on male development and thus on a male personality, identify the areas of Freud's theory that are the weakest with regard to female psychological issues. Defend your response with other points of view presented in the text.

PRACTICE TEST 2:

1. _____ suggests that a person's desire to improve is self-motivated behavior and is triggered largely by powerful forces found in the unconscious.
   a. Humanistic theory
   b. Learning theory
   c. Psychoanalytic theory
   d. Trait theory

2. Freud's structure of personality has three major parts. Which alternative is **not** one of them?
   a. libido
   b. id
   c. superego
   d. ego

3. In Freud's explanation of personality development, which of the following controls thought, solves problems, and makes decisions?
   a. id
   b. ego
   c. superego
   d. conscience

4. Freud's theory of psychosexual development illustrates that a child who is constantly putting things in its mouth is most likely at the:
   a. genital stage.
   b. anal stage.
   c. phallic stage.
   d. oral stage.

5. Freud's stages theory of mature sexual relationships begin to occur at which psychosexual stage?
   a. phallic
   b. oral
   c. genital
   d. anal

6. Defense mechanisms are:
   a. unconscious.
   b. instinctive.
   c. learned.
   d. reflexive.

7. Victims of child abuse, rape, or incest attacks might not recall the incident or may remember only scanty details. Freud suggested that the reason for this is that the defense mechanism of _____ was applied.
   a. sublimation
   b. repression
   c. denial
   d. projection

8. For Gordon Allport, _____ traits were so distinct that having only one of these traits will define a person's personality.
   - a. general
   - b. secondary
   - c. central
   - d. cardinal

9. What are the three important categories defined in Allport's theory of personality dimensions?
   - a. primary, secondary, and tertiary
   - b. factors, traits, and features
   - c. source, surface, and circumscript
   - d. cardinal, central, and secondary

10. The basic assumption shared by trait personality theorists is that:
    - a. the traits are consistent across situations.
    - b. the unconscious mind is the underlying source of the traits we have.
    - c. traits are learned habits that are modified by reinforcers.
    - d. people possess the traits to the same degree but differ in how they choose to apply them.

11. According to Bandura, we can modify our own personalities through the use of:
    - a. defense mechanisms.
    - b. drive reduction.
    - c. psychoanalysis.
    - d. self-reinforcement.

12. Temperament is presumed to originate from the child's:
    - a. personally chosen interests and ideas.
    - b. source traits.
    - c. early learning experiences with the primary caregiver or mother.
    - d. genetic predisposition.

13. If a test provides a consistent score for a particular individual over repeated administrations, the test is said to be:
    - a. accurate.
    - b. valid.
    - c. reliable.
    - d. statistical.

14. The MMPI was originally developed to:
    - a. identify personality disorders.
    - b. uncover unconscious thoughts.
    - c. locate traits.
    - d. conduct behavioral assessments.

15. Test stimuli are the most ambiguous on the:
    - a. TAT.
    - b. California Psychological Inventory.
    - c. Rorschach.
    - d. MMPI.

____ 16. oral stage

____ 17. anal stage

____ 18. phallic stage

____ 19. identification

____ 20. penis envy

a. A child's attempt to be similar to the same-sex parent.

b. An infant's center of pleasure is the mouth.

c. A child's interest focuses on the genitals.

d. A child's pleasure is centered on the anus.

e. A girl's wish that she had a penis.

21. According to Freud, children's sexual concerns are temporarily put aside during the

_____.

22. A defense mechanism identified by an unwanted feeling directed toward a weaker object is
_____.

23. When a person attributes his inadequacies or faults to someone else, it is known as
_____.

24. _____ is the diversion of unwanted impulses into acceptable thoughts, feelings, and behaviors.

25. _____ is defined as supportive behavior for another individual.

26. State one issue or situation that most adolescents tend to deal with during their high school years. Looking over Freud's defense mechanisms, describe how each of three of the mechanisms might be used by the adolescent to "protect one's psyche" from the anxiety produced by the stated situation.

PRACTICE TEST 3: Conceptual, Applied, and Challenging Questions

1. Listed below are four alternatives. Three of the four give pairs of items that are related. Which alternative below items that are **not** related?
   a. ego; reality principle
   b. Sigmund Freud; Viennese physician
   c. superego; "executive" of personality
   d. id; pleasure principle

2. Dr. Kasha viewed the thumb-sucking of 7-year-old Maureen as:
   a. behavior of a normal youngster.
   b. fixated at the oral stage of development.
   c. having been breastfed as an infant.
   d. ready to enter the phallic stage of development.

3. According to the psychoanalytic perspective, a rapist would be considered to have:
   a. unconditioned positive regard for his victim.
   b. a well-developed ego-ideal.
   c. a deficient superego.
   d. brain damage.

4. Rupert kept his clothes hung up and neatly pressed, whereas his roommate Renita rarely laundered or hung up his clothes. Freud might have suggested that both men were fixated at the:
   a. anal stage.
   b. oral stage.
   c. phallic stage.
   d. genital stage.

5. Tina accepted a date from a young man she greatly admired. At the time of the date, however, the man didn't show up. In response, she exclaimed, "I didn't want to go out with him anyway!" This illustrates:
   a. rationalization.
   b. denial.
   c. regression.
   d. repression.

6. Freud's stages of psychosexual development:
   a. emphasize adolescence as the key interval in personality development.
   b. designate the oral stage as the highest in the sequence.
   c. identify parts of the body that are biological pleasure zones toward which gratification is focused.
   d. relate to the same behaviors described in Piaget's theory.

7. The _____ approach emphasizes voluntary conscious aspects of personality, while the _____ approach emphasizes unconscious aspects.
   - a. biological; learning
   - b. trait; humanistic
   - c. humanistic; psychoanalytic
   - d. trait; humanistic

8. Listed below are four alternatives. Three of the four list pairs of items that are related. Which alternative contains items that are **not** related?
   - a. Jung; collective unconscious
   - b. Horney; women do not have penis envy
   - c. Adler; inferiority complex
   - d. Cattell; striving for superiority

9. A trait theorist would most likely make which of the following statements:
   - a. He really hurt her feelings, but he's rationalizing it away.
   - b. He really could have gone a long way, but his inferiority complex destroyed any confidence he had.
   - c. These are five stages in the process of his development toward fulfilling his highest potential.
   - d. He is a sensitive, warm, and considerate person.

10. Various approaches to personality have names and concepts uniquely associated with them. Three of the four alternatives below list pairs of items that are related. Which alternative contains items that are **not** related?
    - a. trait theory; assessment of traits that comprise personality
    - b. learning theory; experiences with situations in the environment
    - c. learning theory; Skinner
    - d. psychoanalytic theory; consistency of behavior across situations

11. Kate loves working with animals and wants to study veterinary science in college. Her boyfriend wants her to be a computer analyst and criticizes her for her love of animals. According to Carl Rogers, this conflict will lead to:
    - a. Kate learning to love being a computer analyst.
    - b. anxiety on Kate's part.
    - c. Kate becoming a fully functioning person.
    - d. unconditional positive regard.

12. Which of the following situations best illustrates reliability as a quality of psychological tests?
    - a. A prospective Air Force pilot takes a test, passes it, and becomes an excellent pilot.
    - b. A college student studies diligently for an important exam and receives an A on it.
    - c. A psychiatric patient takes a psychological test that yields the diagnosis the patient had suspected.
    - d. A mentally retarded patient takes an intelligence test on Monday and again on Tuesday, getting the same result on each administration.

13. Which of the following statements about the heritability of traits is most accurate?
    - a. The degree of heritability of traits is compromised by the important role of parents in shaping the environment.
    - b. Traditionalism and stress reaction were highly heritable, while achievement and social closeness were somewhat lower.
    - c. Alienation and absorption were low in heritability and social control is high.
    - d. Heritability plays about a 50 percent role in important traits and is lower in less important traits.

14. According to Kagan, inhibited children differ from uninhibited children:
   a.   because inhibited children are biologically disposed to have higher physiological reactivity.
   b.   because uninhibited children are biologically disposed to have higher physiological reactivity.
   c.   because inhibited children are genetically disposed to greater social closeness.
   d.   because uninhibited children are genetically disposed to greater social closeness.

15. Which of the following would be a confounding variable for studies that are attempting to demonstrate which traits parents pass on to their children genetically?
   a.   The fact that social traits like religiosity rate high in twin studies, even when this trait is entirely dependent on traditional cultural practices.
   b.   When twins are separated at birth, they always express similar traits.
   c.   The role of parents in shaping the environment.
   d.   Evidence that some traits appear more heritable than others.

____ 16.   anxiety

____ 17.   neurotic anxiety

____ 18.   defense mechanisms

____ 19.   collective unconscious

____ 20.   archetypes

   a.   The concept that we inherit certain personality characteristics from our ancestors and the human race.

   b.   Anxiety caused when irrational impulses from the id threaten to become uncontrollable.

   c.   Universal, symbolic representations of a particular person, object, or experience.

   d.   A feeling of apprehension or tension.

   e.   Unconscious strategies used to reduce anxiety by concealing its source from oneself and others.

21.   The _____ is defined by marked mature sexual behavior.

22.   A defense mechanism identified by the justification of a negative situation to protect one's self-esteem is called _____.

23.   Behavior that is reminiscent of an earlier stage of development is called _____.

24.   _____ is learning by viewing the actions of others.

25.   Psychologists refer to the realization of one's highest potential as _____.

26.   A major issue that will affect virtually everyone is the creation of norms for different minority and ethnic groups. Describe the issues involved and discuss whether the use of different norms will be helpful, harmful, or a mixture of both.

■ ANSWER KEY: MODULES 31, 32, AND 33

Module 31:	Module 32:	Module 33:
[a] personality	[a] trait theory	[a] Psychological tests
[b] Psychoanalysts	[b] Traits	[b] reliability
[c] psychoanalytic theory	[c] cardinal trait	[c] validity
[d] unconscious	[d] central traits	[d] Norms
[e] id	[e] Secondary traits	[e] self-report measures
[f] libido	[f] factor analysis	[f] Minnesota Multiphasic
[g] pleasure principle	[g] Introversion-extroversion	Personality Inventory-2
[h] ego	[h] Neuroticism-stability	(MMPI-2)
[i] reality principle	[i] Psychoticism	[g] test standardization
[j] superego	[j] Cognitive-social	[h] Projective personality
[k] conscience	[k] observational learning	[i] Rorschach
[l] ego-ideal	[l] self-efficacy	[j] Thematic Apperception Test
[m] oral	[m] reciprocal determinism	(TAT)
[n] Fixation	[n] Biological and evolutionary	[k] behavioral assessment
[o] anal	[o] temperament	
[p] phallic	[p] Humanistic approaches to	Evaluate
[q] latency	personality	1. a
[r] genital	[q] unconditional positive	2. e
[s] defense mechanisms	regard	3. d
	[r] self-actualization	4. c
Evaluate		5. b
1. c	Evaluate	
2. b	1. a	
3. d	2. e	
4. e	3. d	
5. a	4. c	
	5. b	

Selected Rethink Answers

32-1   Traits are enduring dimensions of personality characteristics along which people differ. Because each person probably possesses certain traits, what makes individuals different is the degree to which a given trait applies to a single person. Traits allow us to compare one person with another and provide an explanation for a person's behavioral consistency. Assigning certain negative traits to a person may cause a person to be stigmatized by others. Assigning other, more positive traits to a person may raise peoples' expectations of them and cause them undo pressure in many situations.

33-2   Personality tests might be useful to both the employer and the employee as one more source of information in trying to make employment decisions. Test should be used to find ways to include people and place them in appropriate work situations. In this way, both parties would gain. No single test should be used alone to exclude anyone from obtaining a position. Tests are helpful to distinguish personality disorders when they are one of several assessment tools. They are not accurate enough to make conclusive judgments on their own. Anyone who is going to be excluded from a job, placed in, or excluded from a program should have a means to appeal the decision and have other means of assessment available to determine if the decision is valid.

Practice Test 1:

1. a mod. 31 p. 393
*a. Correct. Repressed wishes, desires, anxiety, and conflict are found in the realm Freud called the unconscious.
b. Incorrect. This was a concept introduced by Freud's follower, Carl Jung.
c. Incorrect. The conscience is to be found in the superego.
d. Incorrect. The conscious contains our awareness of the world.

2. b mod. 31 p. 394
a. Incorrect. The id is always making demands on the person that are unrealistic, even sometimes dangerous.
*b. Correct. It is the ego's role to manage the competing demands of the id and the superego, and it responds according to the reality principle.
c. Incorrect. The superego's demands of moral perfection and ego-ideal are unrealistic and in conflict with the id.
d. Incorrect. The pleasure principle is the principle that animates the id, making its demands very unrealistic.

3. c mod. 31 p. 394
a. Incorrect. While important, they are not at the center of his theory.
b. Incorrect. More likely the earlier stages.
*c. Correct. The mental factors of which we are least aware can have the most grave effects on our personality.
d. Incorrect. This theory came long after Freud.

4. b mod. 31 p. 394
a. Incorrect. This describes the id.
*b. Correct. The ego-ideal represents the internalized expectations of our parents and others for us to do and be moral.
c. Incorrect. This is the role of the ego.
d. Incorrect. There is no part of the superego that does this.

5. b mod. 31 p. 395
a. Incorrect. The genital stage is the last stage in the sequence, and it occurs long after toilet training.
*b. Correct. During the anal stage, the child learns self-control, and one of the manifestations of self-control is toilet training.
c. Incorrect. The phallic stage is marked by the Oedipal conflict, and it occurs after the stage that includes toilet training.
d. Incorrect. The oral stage is the first stage, and it is marked by a focus on pleasure taken from the mouth.

6. b mod. 31 p. 397
a. Incorrect. Repression forces conflict into the unconscious.
*b. Correct. Sublimation converts repressed desire, especially sexual desire, into socially acceptable forms, like work.
c. Incorrect. Rationalization involves creating self-justifying reasons after the fact.
d. Incorrect. Projection places unacceptable impulses onto a safe object.

7. b mod. 31 p. 396
a. Incorrect. Probably just the opposite.
*b. Correct. Anxiety is a great threat to the ego, so the ego's defense mechanisms helps protect it.
c. Incorrect. The ego, at times, needs protection against the superego as well.
d. Incorrect. Sometimes, defense mechanisms cause Freudian slips.

8. a mod. 32 p. 402
*a. Correct. For most trait theorists, everyone has the major traits to some extent, and the amount of these traits tends to be stable through time.
b. Incorrect. See answer a.
c. Incorrect. See answer a.
d. Incorrect. See answer a.

9. a mod. 32 p. 405
*a. Correct. Albert Bandura is the leading social learning theorist.
b. Incorrect. Allport is known for the cardinal, central, and secondary traits.
c. Incorrect. Cattell is known for the 16 factor theory, distinguishing source from surface traits.
d. Incorrect. Eysenck proposed three main trait characteristics: extroversion, neuroticism, and psychoticism.

10. c mod. 32 p. 407
a. Incorrect. This terminology is that of the trait theorists.
b. Incorrect. This terminology is from the psychodynamic perspective.
*c. Correct. As Skinner is a behaviorist, "traits" are explained in behavioral terms.
d. Incorrect. This terminology is from the humanistic perspective.

11. c   mod. 32 p. 403
a. Incorrect. It is an analytic technique, and it requires no special equipment.
b. Incorrect. Used by trait theorists, this use is unlikely.
*c. Correct. Factor analysis identifies common patterns in data and was used by Cattell to identify the source traits in his theory.
d. Incorrect. While it might help identify personality traits in a group (if that is possible), it is only a statistical technique.

12. c   mod. 32 p. 410
a. Incorrect. Humanistic theories tend not to judge the unconscious as evil.
b. Incorrect. Society is not generally viewed by humanistic theories as a corrupting force.
*c. Correct. Humans have within themselves the ability to heal their own psychological disorders and resolve their conflicts.
d. Incorrect. No psychological view holds to this thesis of fundamental depravity.

13. c   mod. 32 p. 410
a. Incorrect. Learning theory depends on conditioning and reinforcement.
b. Incorrect. The psychodynamic theory focuses on unconscious forces.
*c. Correct. The humanistic approach focuses on the abilities of the individual to engage in self-actualization.
d. Incorrect. The trait theory searches for long-term, consistent behavior patterns.

14. b   mod. 33 p. 418
a. Incorrect. The MMPI asks the test-taker to respond to questions concerning items of which the test-taker has an awareness.
*b. Correct. The Thematic Apperception Test (TAT) asks that respondents tell a story about a picture and through that story, they may reveal unconscious concerns.
c. Incorrect. The California Psychological Inventory is a self-report test; thus it reveals only items about which the test-taker has awareness.
d. Incorrect. This is probably another self-report instrument.

15. c   mod. 33 p. 417
a. Incorrect. It is a standardized test, but the scenario does not support this notion.
b. Incorrect. It is supposed to be an academic ability assessment tool, but this scenario does not question that.
*c. Correct. Since it measured her performance and knowledge the same in both circumstances, the assessment is quite reliable.
d. Incorrect. It may be valid, but this story does not support that claim.

16. b   mod. 31 p. 394
17. a   mod. 31 p. 394
18. e   mod. 31 p. 394
19. d   mod. 31 p. 394
20. c   mod. 31 p. 394

21. ego-ideal   mod. 31 p. 394
22. inferiority complex mod. 31 p. 399
23. Repression   mod. 31 p. 397
24. denial   mod. 31 p. 397
25. secondary   mod. 32 p. 403

26.
■ The weakest area is Freud's developmental stages, particularly with the Oedipus complex. Freud's concept of penis envy is not well accepted by many.
■ Just as Gilligan contests Kohlberg's views of moral development, one could argue that Freud's concept of a genital stage rests on masculine norms.

Practice Test 2:
1. c   mod. 31 p. 393
a. Incorrect. Humanistic theory is concerned with the person recognizing his or her own potential and finding ways to achieve self-actualization.
b. Incorrect. Learning theory is concerned with the kinds of reinforcements and punishments that have contributed to the formation of the current patterns of behavior of an individual.
*c. Correct. Psychoanalytic theory considers the hidden contents of the unconscious to be powerful forces in the shaping of personality.
d. Incorrect. Trait theory seeks to identify and measure the consistent patterns of traits manifested by people.

2.	a	mod. 31 p. 394
*a.	Correct. The libido is psychic energy and not a part of Freud's structural model of the personality. The three parts of Freud's structural model of the personality are the id, ego, and superego.
b.	Incorrect. See answer a.
c.	Incorrect. See answer a.
d.	Incorrect. See answer a.

3.	b	mod. 31 p. 394
a.	Incorrect. The id seeks to satisfy the pleasure principle and is not concerned with thought, decisions, or solving problems.
*b.	Correct. The ego is responsible for balancing the demands of the id and the superego, and thus must solve problems, think, and make decisions.
c.	Incorrect. The superego seeks to present a moralistic, ego-ideal and a judgmental conscience to the ego.
d.	Incorrect. The conscience is one of the two components of the superego; the other is the ego-ideal.

4.	d	mod. 31 p. 395
a.	Incorrect. See answer d.
b.	Incorrect. See answer d.
c.	Incorrect. See answer d.
*d.	Correct. This child is seeking pleasure from the mouth, and is thus in the oral stage.

5.	c	mod. 31 p. 396
a.	Incorrect. The child is only about 6 years old during this stage, and thus unlikely to participate in mature sexual relations.
b.	Incorrect. The child is less than 2 years old during this stage, and thus will not be engaging in any mature sexual relations.
*c.	Correct. This was the name Freud gave to the stage in which sexual maturity develops.
d.	Incorrect. This stage occurs when the child is between 2 and 4 years of age, and thus mature sexual relations are unlikely.

6.	a	mod. 31 p. 396
*a.	Correct. Defense mechanisms operate below the level of awareness as part of their role in protecting the ego from anxiety and conflict.
b.	Incorrect. There are two instincts (drives) in Freud's view: eros (love) and the death drive.
c.	Incorrect. Freud did not describe whether the defense mechanisms were learned or innate.
d.	Incorrect. After they have been utilized, they may become reflexive, but they respond to complex stimuli rather than the simple stimuli typically associated with reflexes.

7.	b	mod. 31 p. 397
a.	Incorrect. Sublimation does not apply here.
*b.	Correct. Repression is a form of intentional forgetting.
c.	Incorrect. Denial is one means of dealing with this kind of trauma, but the core mechanism is repression.
d.	Incorrect. After repression, the victims of child abuse may project fears onto other people.

8.	d	mod. 32 p. 402
a.	Incorrect. Allport did not identify any traits as "general."
b.	Incorrect. Allport's concept of secondary traits is that people have many of these, and they govern such things as the style and preference of many everyday behaviors.
c.	Incorrect. In Allport's view, everyone has several central traits, but these do not dominate the personality.
*d.	Correct. Allport called these cardinal traits, and they dominate the personality of the individual.

9.	d	mod. 32 p. 402
a.	Incorrect. See answer d.
b.	Incorrect. See answer d.
c.	Incorrect. See answer d.
*d.	Correct. The cardinal trait controls and dominates the personality, while at the other end, secondary traits define style and preferences.

10.	a	mod. 32 p. 402
*a.	Correct. If traits exist, then by definition they need to persist.
b.	Incorrect. Trait theories did not commonly offer a theory for the existence of traits.
c.	Incorrect. To only a few are traits learned in the traditional operant conditioning approach.
d.	Incorrect. People do not chose to apply traits.

11.	d	mod. 32 p. 405
a.	Incorrect. This is Freud's idea.
b.	Incorrect. This belongs to other drive theorists, like Clark Hull.
c.	Incorrect. Bandura may agree that psychoanalysis will modify our personality, but not by using any of Bandura's concepts.
*d.	Correct. Self-reinforcement is an important component of the social learning theory of Bandura.

12. d mod. 32 p. 408
a. Incorrect. Since it appears long before the child has an opportunity to form interests, this answer is incorrect.
b. Incorrect. Temperament might be considered a source trait.
c. Incorrect. Temperament is present before the opportunity to have early learning experience.
*d. Correct. This is the current view of temperament, that it is genetically disposed.

13. c mod. 33 p. 413
a. Incorrect. If the test does not measure what it should, it would not be very accurate.
b. Incorrect. If the test made the same measure each time, it would still have to measure what it is supposed to measure to be considered valid.
*c. Correct. Even if the test failed to measure what it was supposed to measure, yet it made the same measurement each time, then the test would be reliable.
d. Incorrect. A statistical test would have to measure some kind of statistics, would it not?

14. a mod. 33 p. 415
*a. Correct. The MMPI measures tendencies toward psychological difficulties, but it can be taken by anyone and it does produce meaningful results for people who do not have psychological problems.
b. Incorrect. The MMPI is a self-report test, and thus unlikely to reveal many thoughts that are not within the awareness of the test-taker.
c. Incorrect. The MMPI does not locate "traits" and is not specific to any trait theory.
d. Incorrect. The MMPI is a self-report test, and thus it cannot be used for a behavioral assessment except for the selection of true or false on the test.

15. c mod. 33 p. 417
a. Incorrect. The TAT uses ambiguous pictures, but they are not as ambiguous as the inkblots used on the Rorschach.
b. Incorrect. The California Psychological Inventory and the MMPI both use statements that require a direct and unambiguous response to a rather unambiguous item.
*c. Correct. The Rorschach inkblots are probably the most ambiguous test stimuli used in this manner.
d. Incorrect. See answer b.

16. b mod. 31 p. 395
17. d mod. 31 p. 395
18. c mod. 31 p. 395
19. a mod. 31 p. 395
20. e mod. 31 p. 396

21. latency period   mod. 31 p. 396
22. displacement   mod. 31 p. 397
23. projection   mod. 31 p. 397
24. Sublimation   mod. 31 p. 397
25. Unconditional positive regard   mod. 32 p. 410

26. Adolescents want autonomy and attempt to negotiate with their parents for more freedom to make their own decisions:
   ▪ Regression allows them to scream and yell and carry on when they don't get their own way. They act as they did when they were younger in order to avoid the real conflict and get their way.
   ▪ Rationalization would involve creating self-justifying excuses after the fact.
   ▪ Projection places unacceptable impulses onto a safe object.

Practice Test 3:
1. c mod. 31 p. 394
a. Incorrect. The ego does operate on the reality principle as it tries to balance demands of the id and the superego.
b. Incorrect. Sigmund Freud was a Viennese physician.
*c. Correct. The ego is considered the executive of the personality, not the superego.
d. Incorrect. The id follows the pleasure principle as it seeks to satisfy desires and wishes.

2. b mod. 31 p. 395
a. Incorrect. This is unusual, yet not abnormal for a child of this age.
*b. Correct. Thumb sucking is an oral behavior, so the youngster must be fixated in the oral stage.
c. Incorrect. Breast feeding is not relevant to later thumb sucking.
d. Incorrect. The child is probably already in the phallic stage, but the fixation or regression to the oral stage is present.

3.   c   mod. 31 p. 394
a.   Incorrect. The concept of unconditioned positive regard is from humanistic theory, and the rapist is the last person who would have such regard for another person.
b.   Incorrect. Only if the ego-ideal was that of a rapist.
*c. Correct. The superego provides a sense of right and wrong, and a rapist is clearly missing this dimension of morality.
d.   Incorrect. A psychoanalyst would not attribute the behavior of a rapist to brain damage.

4.   a   mod. 31 p. 395
*a. Correct. The extremes of neatness and messiness have been associated with the anal stage, with the neat person overdoing anal retention and the messy person rejecting order.
b.   Incorrect. The messy person could be fixated in the oral stage, but not the neat one.
c.   Incorrect. Fixation in the phallic stage does not result in messiness or neatness.
d.   Incorrect. Freud did not describe what fixation would be like for stages in which we are currently occupied.

5.   b   mod. 31 p. 397
a.   Incorrect. Rationalization would involve making an explanation that would protect the self through after-the-fact justification.
*b. Correct. The young woman is denying that she had any interest in the young man in the first place.
c.   Incorrect. Regression would require that she regress to an earlier developmental stage.
d.   Incorrect. Repression requires that she force her anxiety and anger into the unconscious.

6.   c   mod. 31 p. 395
a.   Incorrect. Many researchers in addition to Freud saw earlier childhood as critical for the development of the personality.
b.   Incorrect. The first in the sequence, but highest only if you stand up.
*c. Correct. Infants, children, and adults seek physical pleasure.
d.   Incorrect. Piaget's sensorimotor stage is similar to Freud's oral stage, but the others differ.

7.   c   mod. 32 p. 410
a.   Incorrect. The biological view would not be that interested in conscious decisions.
b.   Incorrect. The trait approach does not consider traits within the person's ability to choose, and the humanistic approach certainly focuses on conscious behavior.
*c. Correct. The humanistic approach rests on the person's ability to be rational and self-motivated while the psychodynamic approach assumes the power of the irrational and unconscious forces in the person.
d.   Incorrect. The biological view would not be that interested in conscious decisions, and the humanistic approach certainly focuses on conscious behavior.

8.   d   mod. 32 p. 399
a.   Incorrect. Jung proposed the idea of a collective unconscious.
b.   Incorrect. Horney argued that women do not have penis envy.
c.   Incorrect. Adler did develop the idea of an inferiority complex.
*d. Correct. Striving for superiority is Adler's idea, not Cattell's.

9.   d   mod. 32 p. 402
a.   Incorrect. Sounds psychoanalytic.
b.   Incorrect. Sounds like Adler's idea of inferiority complex.
c.   Incorrect. Sounds like Maslow's hierarchy of needs.
*d. Correct. A trait theorist would describe someone in terms of traits, like warm and considerate.

10. d   mod. 32 p. 402
a.   Incorrect. Trait theory proposes that traits can be assessed and a picture of the person composed.
b.   Incorrect. Learning theory suggests that the environment is a major force in shaping the personality.
c.   Incorrect. Skinner is associated with learning theory.
*d. Correct. While psychoanalytic theory would suggest that behavior would be consistent across situations, this is a major issue for trait theorists.

11. b   mod. 32 p. 410
a.   Incorrect. This is unlikely, except if she compromises her own desires.
*b. Correct. The incongruency between Kate and her boyfriend could lead to anxiety.
c.   Incorrect. If this incongruency becomes a condition of worth, then Kate cannot become a fully functioning person.
d.   Incorrect. Unconditional positive regard requires more acceptance than this.

12. d   mod. 33 p. 413
a.   Incorrect. This suggests that the test was a valid measure of pilot potential.
b.   Incorrect. This suggests that studying is a valid means of preparing for an exam.
c.   Incorrect. The test has validated the suspicion.
*d. Correct. Repeating a test and getting the same or nearly the same score on each administration demonstrates reliability.

13. b   mod. 32 p. 409
a.   Incorrect. This statement cannot be made based on the evidence reported in the text.
*b. Correct. Believe it or not, the extent to which a person is traditional and the manner in which the person responds to stress are highly heritable.
c.   Incorrect. Alienation and absorption were moderately high.
d.   Incorrect. The research did not judge which traits were important and which were not.

14. a   mod. 32 p. 408
*a. Correct. Kagan has argued that the higher reactivity in children makes them be inhibited as a protection against the stimulation.
b.   Incorrect. This is reversed.
c.   Incorrect. They are genetically disposed to high physiological reactivity, not social closeness.
d.   Incorrect. Uninhibited children are not necessarily disposed to greater social closeness.

15. c   mod. 32 p. 409
a.   Incorrect. Traditionalism has been shown to be heritable.
b.   Incorrect. This would actually indicate something about the dependent variable, not a confounding variable.
*c. Correct. When trying to separate parental genes from environmental forces, one must accept the confounding aspect of the parent's role in shaping the environment.
d.   Incorrect. This is not a confounding element.

16. d   mod. 31 p. 396
17. b   mod. 31 p. 396
18. e   mod. 31 p. 397
19. a   mod. 31 p. 398
20. c   mod. 31 p. 399

21. genital stage   mod. 31 p. 396
22. rationalization   mod. 31 p. 397
23. regression   mod. 31 p. 397
24. Observational learning mod. 32 p. 406
25. self-actualization   mod. 32 p. 410

26.
- Some people argue that any kind of separation of a group from the larger society is detrimental.
- One major problem is the use of norms or averages to prepare job "profiles." These are still average and composite pictures of the individual and may unfairly discriminate against those who do not fit the profile. With these kinds of norms, negative reactions can and have occurred by those excluded from the special normed group. Recent court cases will change how this is viewed as well.

Health Psychology: Stress, Coping, and Well-Being

34: Stress and Coping
35: Psychological Aspects of Illness and Well-Being
36: Promoting Health and Wellness

Overview

This set of modules discusses the ways in which psychological factors affect one's health. Health psychology investigates the prevention, diagnosis, and treatment of medical problems.

Module 34 focuses on the causes and consequences of stress, as well as the means of coping with it. The consequences of stress are explained by Selye's general adaptation syndrome. Finally, classes of events that provoke stress, cataclysmic events, personal stressors, background stressors, and daily stressors are discussed.

Module 35 explores the psychological aspects of several major health problems, including heart disease, cancer, and smoking. The characteristics of happy people are also presented.

Module 36 offers insight into patient and physician interactions to see how they influence our health. Suggestions are offered for increasing patients' compliance with behavior that will improve their well-being.

To further investigate the topics covered in this chapter, you can visit the related Web sites by visiting the following link: www.mhhe.com/feldmanup6-15links.

Prologue: So Much to Do, So Little Time to Do It
Looking Ahead

Module 34:
Stress and Coping

Stress: Reacting to Threat and Challenge
Coping with Stress

Becoming an Informed Consumer of Psychology:
Effective Coping Strategies

- *How is health psychology a union between medicine and psychology?*
- *What is stress, how does it affect us, and how can we best cope with it?*

Stress and Coping

[a] _____ focuses on the application of psychology to the prevention, diagnosis, and treatment of medical problems. Health psychologists view the mind and the body as closely linked. Good health and the ability to stay healthy are affected by how a person manages stress and the person's health habits. The [b] _____ of the body is affected by attitudes and emotional state. Health psychology has changed the view of disease from a purely biological problem, and it has had to help people cope with the problems associated with adjustment to diseases that last for a long time. [c] _____ is the study of the relationship between psychological factors and the immune system.

The response to events that threaten or challenge a person is called [d] _____, and the events are called *stressors*. Stressors can be both pleasant and unpleasant events, although the negative events can be more detrimental. The class of medical problems called

[e] _____, caused by the interaction of psychological, emotional, and physiological problems, are also related to stress. High levels of stress interfere with people's ability to cope with current and new stressors.

Hans Selye proposed that everyone goes through the same set of physiological responses no matter what the cause is, and he called this the [f] _____. The first stage is the

[g]_____, during which the presence of a stressor is detected and the sympathetic nervous system is energized. The second stage is the [h] _____, during which the person attempts to cope with the stressor. If coping is inadequate, the person enters the

[i] _____. The person's ability to cope with stress declines and the negative consequences appear. These include illness, psychological symptoms like the inability to concentrate, and possibly disorientation and losing touch with reality.

GAS has provided a model that explains how stress leads to illness. The primary criticism has focused on the fact that the model suggests that every stress response is physiologically the same. If people are to consider an event stressful, they must perceive it to be threatening and must lack the ability to cope with it adequately. The same event may not be stressful for everyone. The perception of stress may depend on how one attributes the causes for events.

There are three classes of events that are considered stressors. The first is

[j] _____, strong stressors that affect many people at the same time. The stress of these events is usually dealt with well because so many people experience the event and share the problem. Some people experience prolonged problems caused by catastrophic events, and

this is called **[k]** _____. People may experience flashbacks or dreams during which they reexperience the event. The symptoms can include a numbing of emotional experience, sleep difficulties, problems relating to others, and drug problems, among others. The

second class of stressor is **[l]** _____, which include life events of a personal or individual nature, like the death of a parent or spouse, the loss of a job, or a major illness. Typically, personal stressors cause an immediate major reaction that tapers off. Sometimes, though, the effects can last for a long time, such as the effects of being raped. The third class of

stressors is called **[m]** _____, and they include standing in long lines, traffic jams,

and other **[n]** _____. Daily hassles can add up, causing unpleasant emotions and moods. A critical factor is the degree of control people have over the daily hassles. When they have control, the stress reactions are less. On the other side of daily hassles are

[o] _____, positive events that lead to pleasant feelings.

In an environment in which control is seen as impossible, one can experience

[p] _____. Victims of learned helplessness have decided that there is no link between the responses they make and the outcomes that occur. When elderly people in nursing homes were given control over simple aspects of their lives, they were less likely to experience an early death. Not everyone experiences helplessness.

Our efforts to control, reduce, or learn to tolerate stress are known as **[q]** _____.

Many of our responses are habitual. The **[r]** _____ are unconscious strategies that help control stress by distorting or denying the actual nature of the situation. Denying the

significance of a nearby geological fault is an example. **[s]** _____ is another example in which a person does not feel emotions at all. Another means of dealing with stress is the use of

direct and positive means. These include **[t]** _____, the conscious regulation of

emotions, and **[u]** _____, the management of the stressful stimulus. People use both strategies, but they are more likely to use the emotion-focused strategy when they perceive the problem as unchangeable.

People can be described as having coping styles. [v] _____ refers to the style associated with a low rate of stress-induced illness, consisting of three components: commitment, challenge, and control. *Commitment* is a tendency to be involved in whatever we are doing with a sense that it is important and meaningful. *Challenge* refers to the view that change is the standard condition of life. *Control* refers to the sense of being able to influence events. The hardy person is optimistic and approaches the problem directly.

Relationships with others help people cope with stress. The knowledge of a mutual network of concerned, interested people helping individuals experience lower levels of stress is called

[w] _____. Social support demonstrates the value of a person to others and provides a network of information and advice. Also, actual goods and services can be provided through social support networks. Even pets can contribute to this support.

Stress can be dealt with through several steps: Turn stress into a challenge, make the threatening situation less threatening by changing attitudes about it, change goals in order to remove oneself from an uncontrollable situation, and take physical action. The most successful approach requires that the person be prepared for stress. One method of preparation is called

[x] _____. With inoculation, stress is dealt with through preparation for both the nature of the possible stressors and developing or learning clear strategies for coping.

Evaluate

_____ 1. immune system

a. Circumstances that produce threats to well-being.

_____ 2. stressors

b. A person's initial awareness of the presence of a stressor.

_____ 3. psychophysiological disorders

c. The stage of coping with the stressor.

_____ 4. alarm and mobilization

d. Medical problems caused by an interaction of psychological, emotional, and physical difficulties.

_____ 5. resistance

e. The body's natural defenses that fight disease.

Rethink

34-1 Why are cataclysmic stressors less stressful in the long run than other types of stressors? Does the reason relate to the coping phenomenon known as social support? How?

34-2   Given what you know about coping strategies, how would you train people to avoid stress in their everyday lives? How would you use this information with a group of veterans from the war in Iraq suffering from posttraumatic stress disorder?

Spotlight on Terminology and Language—ESL Pointers

Stress and Coping

Page 425 "Stress can take its **toll** in many ways, producing both biological and psychological consequences."
There is damage sustained due to stress. How does stress take its **toll** on you?

Page 425 "On a biological level, the sympathetic nervous system becomes **energized**, helping a person cope initially with the stressor."
The sympathetic nervous system becomes active, or **energized**.

Page 427 "Selye's theory has not gone **unchallenged**."
Selye's theory has not always been accepted.

Page 427 "They believe that people's biological response is specific to the way they **appraise** a stressful event."
The way people evaluate or **appraise** a stressful event may be an important factor.

Page 428 "In normal circumstances, our bodies produce lymphocytes, specialized white blood cells that fight disease, at an extraordinary rate—some 10 million every few seconds—and it is possible that stress can **alter** this level of production (Ader, Felten, & Cohen, 2001; Miller & Cohen, 2001; Cohen et al., 2002)."
To **alter** is to change.

Page 429 "One reason is that natural disasters have a clear **resolution**."
When something has a clear **resolution**, it has a clear solution.

Page 430 "Typically, personal stressors produce an immediate major reaction that soon **tapers off**."
As the reaction **tapers off**, it is gradually reduced. It is becoming smaller in size or amount.

Page 430 "**Exemplified** by standing in a long line at a bank and getting stuck in a traffic jam, daily hassles are the minor irritations of life that we all face time and time again: delays, noisy cars and trucks, broken appliances, other people's irritating behavior, and so on."
When you **exemplify** something, you are giving an example in order to make something clearer.

Page 431 "Have you ever faced an **intolerable** situation that you just couldn't resolve, where you finally just gave up and accepted things the way they were?"
Intolerable is very unpleasant or annoying.

The A's and B's of Coronary Heart Disease
Psychological Aspects of Cancer
Smoking

Exploring Diversity: Hucksters of Death:
Promoting Smoking Throughout the World

- *How do psychological factors affect such health-related problems as coronary heart disease, cancer, and smoking?*

Psychological Aspects of Illness and Well-Being

Two characteristic behavior patterns have been identified that are associated with coronary heart disease. [a] _____ is seen in individuals who are competitive, have a sense of urgency about time, are aggressive, and are driven regarding their work. [b] _____ is seen in individuals who are less competitive, less time-oriented, and not aggressive, driven, or hostile. In an extensive study, people with Type A behavior developed heart disease twice as often as Type B individuals. One theory says that Type A individuals become excessively aroused when they are placed in stressful situations, and that this arousal increases the hormones epinephrine and norepinephrine, in turn leading to higher blood pressure and heart rate. Long-term damage then results. The evidence supporting the connection between Type A behavior and coronary heart disease is not conclusive. One study showed Type A individuals more likely to survive a second heart attack.

[c] _____ is the second leading cause of death after [d] _____. Although its causes remain unknown, the progress of cancer is from altered cell to tumor, and the tumor robs nutrients from healthy tissue, eventually impairing normal function. Evidence is growing that the emotional response to cancer influences the disease's progress. Fighters appear more likely to recover than pessimists. Survival rates for women with breast cancer were higher among those who fought the disease or even denied it than for those who stoically accepted the illness or who accepted their fate. Evidence suggests that the patient's immune system may be affected by [e] _____. Positive emotional responses may help increase the natural "killer" cells.

[f] _____ may suppress these kinds of cells. Other studies have found that positive emotional states improve longevity of cancer patients. Social support and cancer have also been linked. One study found that individuals who receive psychotherapy live longer than those who do not.

Although the link between smoking and cancer is well-established, millions of people continue to smoke. Most smokers agree that smoking damages their health, but they continue to smoke. Mostly caused by **[g]** _____, the habit of smoking moves through four stages that end in the habit:

- *Preparation*, during which a relatively positive attitude about smoking develops
- *Initiation*, when smoking a cigarette becomes a rite of passage and is seen as a sign of growing up
- *Becoming a smoker*, during which smoking becomes part of the self-concept and the body becomes tolerant of nicotine
- *Maintaining the smoking habit*, the stage in which the aspects of smoking become part of the routine

Quitting smoking is very difficult. Only about 15 percent of those trying to stop smoking will have long-term success. Behavioral strategies for quitting view smoking as a learned habit that needs to be unlearned. Social norms will also eventually lead to reduced smoking, as smoking is banned in more and more public places and society begins to change its attitude about those who smoke. Still more than one-quarter of the population smokes, and those who begin do so at an earlier age.

Cigarette manufacturers have turned to new markets as the number of smokers in the United States declines. The new markets include targeted campaigns toward teenagers, African-Americans, Chinese people, and people of Latin American countries.

Evaluate

_____ 1. emotion-focused coping

_____ 2. problem-focused coping

_____ 3. hardiness

_____ 4. Type A behavior pattern

_____ 5. Type B behavior pattern

a. The conscious regulation of emotion as a means of dealing with stress.

b. Characterized by noncompetitiveness, nonaggression, and patience in times of potential stress.

c. Characterized by competitiveness, impatience, a tendency toward frustration, and hostility.

d. Characterized by commitment, challenge, and control.

e. The management of a stressful stimulus as a way of dealing with stress.

Rethink

35-1 Do you think Type A or Type B behavior is more widely encouraged in the United States? Why?

35-2 Is there a danger of "blaming the victim" when we argue that the course of cancer can be improved if a person with the disease holds particular beneficial attitudes or beliefs? Why?

Spotlight on Terminology and Language—ESL Pointers

Psychological Aspects of Illness and Well-Being

Page 437 "They nod in **tacit understanding**, eight women sitting in a loose circle of chairs here in a small, sparely furnished room at Stanford University Medical Center."
Tacit understanding is unspoken understanding.

Page 437 "All of them have been diagnosed with **recurrent** breast cancer."
Recurrent breast cancer is breast cancer that has returned after treatment.

Page 437 "As recently as two decades ago, most psychologists and health-care providers would have **scoffed at** the notion that a discussion group could improve a cancer patient's chances of survival."
When you **scoff at** something, you make fun of it, you ridicule it.

Page 437 "How could the driver **dawdle** like that?"
To **dawdle** is to waste time.

Page 438 "Have you, like Tim, ever **seethed** impatiently at being caught behind a slow-moving vehicle, felt anger and frustration at not finding material you needed at the library, or experienced a sense of competitiveness with your classmates?"
When you **seethe** impatiently, you are furious, boiling with rage.

Page 438 "Many of us experience these sorts of feelings at one time or another, but for some people they represent a **pervasive**, characteristic set of personality traits known as the Type A behavior pattern."
They represent a **pervasive** or persistent, always present, personality characteristic.

Page 439 "Why are the hostility and anger behind the Type A behavior so **toxic**?"
Toxic is poisonous, deadly.

Page 439 "Although a diagnosis of cancer is not as **grim** as one might at first suspect—several kinds of cancer have a high cure rate if detected early enough—cancer remains the second leading cause of death after coronary heart disease."
When something is **grim**, it is bleak and dismal.

Page 439 "For example, one experiment found that people who adopt a fighting spirit are more likely to recover than are those who **pessimistically** suffer and resign themselves to death (Pettingale et al., 1985)."
Pessimistically is gloomily, negatively.

Page 440 "For example, psychologists specializing in **psychoneuroimmunology** (PNI) suggest that a patient's emotional state affects the immune system in the same way that stress affects it."
Psychoneuroimmunology is the study of the connection among the central nervous system, the endocrine system, and psychosocial factors such as cognitive reactions to stressful procedures, the individual's personality traits, and social pressures.

Module 36: Promoting Health and Wellness

Following Medical Advice
Well-Being and Happiness

Applying Psychology in the 21st Century: Happy Thoughts: Thinking Positively May Help You Live Longer

- *How do our interactions with physicians affect our health and compliance with medical treatment?*

- *What leads to a sense of well-being?*

Promoting Health and Wellness

How the patient and the physician communicate can influence the effectiveness of the diagnosis and medical treatment. Many patients are reluctant to tell their physicians their symptoms. The prestige and power of the physician intimidates many patients. On the other side, physicians have difficulties getting their patients to provide the proper information. The technical nature of their questions does not mesh with the personal nature of the individual's concerns. The reluctance can prevent the health-care giver from understanding the full nature of the problem, and often the patient sees the physician as all-knowing. Patients who do not understand their treatment cannot ask questions about it. Many patients do not know how long they should take their medication, and many do not know the purpose of the drug. The use of professional jargon to communicate technical information does not help the patient understand the treatment. Sometimes medical practitioners use "baby talk" and talk down to the patient. The number of patients seen makes it difficult for many physicians to determine how much each patient can understand. Patients often construct their own theories about their illnesses that have little to do with reality. The problem can be dealt with by training patients to ask more direct questions. Physicians who are taught simple rules of courtesy, like saying hello, addressing the patient by name, and saying goodbye, are better perceived by their patients.

One major consequence of the difficulties in communication between the physician and the patient is the lack of compliance with medical advice. Noncompliance can include failing to meet appointments, not following diets, discontinuing medication, and other behaviors. Patients may practice **[a]** _____, in which they adjust their treatments themselves.

Sometimes noncompliance results from **[b]** _____, a disagreeable emotional and cognitive reaction that results from the restriction of one's freedom and can be associated with medical regimens. Compliance is linked to the degree of satisfaction a patient has with the physician. Satisfied patients tend to comply better than dissatisfied patients.

Patients with a positive view of the physicians may also have a greater sense of control, and they perceive themselves as in a kind of partnership rather than merely following advice. Physicians may be motivated to keep the patient uninformed. Apparently, physicians avoid telling patients when they are terminally ill. On the other hand, almost every survey shows that people want to be informed about the details of their illnesses. Patients prefer to be well-informed, and their degree of satisfaction is linked to how well the physician is able to convey the nature of the illness. An increase in satisfaction tends to have a positive effect on recuperation.

Evaluate

_____ 1. creative nonadherence

_____ 2. reactance

_____ 3. subjective well-being

_____ 4. noncompliance

_____ 5. increase of compliance

a. Negative emotional and cognitive reaction that results from the restriction of one's freedom.

b. Patient discontinues medication, misses appointments, doesn't follow treatment.

c. Occurs when patient is friendly and satisfied with a physician.

d. Patient adjusts a treatment prescribed by a physician relying on their own medical judgment.

e. People evaluate their lives based on thoughts and emotions.

Rethink

36-1　Do you think stress plays a role in making communication between physicians and patients difficult? Why?

36-2　You are given the job of instructing a group of medical school students on "Physician-Patient Interactions." How would you set up your class, and what kind of information would you provide?

Spotlight on Terminology and Language—ESL Pointers

Promoting Health and Wellness

Page 445 "Let's take a closer look at two areas they have **tackled**: producing compliance with health-related advice and identifying the determinants of well-being and happiness."

To **tackle** something is to deal with it.

Page 445 "As many as 85 percent of patients do not fully **comply with** a physician's recommendations."

To **comply with** is to obey, or to meet the terms of. Do you comply 100% with your instructor's recommendations for academic success?

Page 446 "But as the surgeon diagrammed **incision** points on my chest with a felt-tip pen, my husband asked a question: 'Is it really necessary to transfer this back muscle?' (Halpert, 2003, p. 63)."

Incision points are the points where the surgeon will make the cuts.

Page 446 "But after a hurried consultation with her husband, the patient **opted for** the less invasive procedure."

The patient **opted for**, or chose, this procedure.

Page 446 "Furthermore, the relatively high **prestige** of physicians may intimidate patients."

In American society, we give a lot of prestige, or esteem, to persons in the medical profession. We hold these individuals in high regard.

Page 447 "Although **compliance** with medical advice does not guarantee that a patient's medical problems will go away, it does optimize the possibility that the patient's condition will improve."

Compliance with medical advice would be fulfilling the directions for treatment as prescribed by the physician.

Page 447 "One strategy is to provide clear instructions to patients regarding drug **regimens**."

A drug **regimen** is the schedule for the medication.

Page 448 "Patients generally prefer to be well informed—even if the news is bad—and their degree of satisfaction with their medical care is **linked** to how well and how accurately physicians are able to convey the nature of their medical problems and treatments (Hall, Roter, & Katz, 1988; Haley, Clair, & Saulsberry, 1992.)"

Their satisfaction is **linked**, or connected, to the honest and accurate delivery of information.

Page 448 "The way in which a message is **framed** also can result in more positive responses to health-related information."

The way a person uses language and examples will impact the way in which a message is **framed** or stated.

Test your knowledge of the material in this set of modules by answering these questions. These questions have been placed in three Practice Tests. The first two tests consist of questions that will test your recall of factual knowledge. The third test contains questions that are challenging and primarily test for conceptual knowledge and your ability to apply that knowledge. Check your answers and review the feedback using the Answer Key in the following pages of the *Study Guide*.

PRACTICE TEST 1:

1. The system of organs and glands that forms the body's natural defense against disease is called:
   a. the limbic system.
   b. the endocrine system.
   c. the immune system.
   d. the sympathetic system.

2. Which alternative is **not** a stage of Selye's general adaptation syndrome?
   a. resistance
   b. challenge
   c. alarm and mobilization
   d. exhaustion

3. _____is a circumstance that produces threats to people's well-being.
   a. A stressor.
   b. A mobilization state.
   c. A defense mechanism.
   d. An inoculation.

4. The alarm and mobilization stage of Selye's general adaptation syndrome is characterized by:
   a. preparing to react to the stressor.
   b. increased resistance to disease.
   c. emotional and physical collapse.
   d. becoming aware of the presence of a stressor.

5. Events that are strong stressors and that occur suddenly and affect many people simultaneously are called:
   a. cataclysmic stressors.
   b. background stressors.
   c. uplifts.
   d. personal stressors.

6. Uplifts are defined as:
   a. minor irritations of life that are encountered daily.
   b. minor positive events that make a person feel good.
   c. exhilarating experiences that leave a person in a dazed state.
   d. major positive life events.

7. High blood pressure, ulcers, or eczema are common:
   a. defense mechanism disorders.
   b. life-crisis disorders.
   c. hardiness disorders.
   d. psychophysiological disorders.

8. A person's ability to tolerate, control, or reduce threatening events is called:
   a. defense.
   b. arousal.
   c. coping.
   d. adaptation.

9. Michael has been classified as hardy. This means he is:
   a. unable to cope with stress at all.
   b. unlikely to develop stress-related disease.
   c. unlikely to view stress as a challenge.
   d. affected mostly by hard emotional choices.

10. Which personality type is most highly associated with heart disease, independent of other single factors?
    a. Type A
    b. Type B
    c. hardy personality
    d. cataclysmic

11. Which behavior or personality type is best described by the following traits: achievement, competitiveness, and commitment to completing a task?
    a. Type B behavior
    b. hardy personality
    c. helpless personality
    d. Type A behavior

12. Addiction to nicotine may first emerge in:
    a. the preparation stage.
    b. the maintenance stage.
    c. the initiation stage.
    d. the becoming-a-smoker stage.

13. Which of the following is **not** a reason for communication difficulties between doctor and patient?
    a. Physicians may ask patients questions that are highly technical.
    b. Physicians have difficulty encouraging patients to give helpful information.
    c. Physicians sometimes simplify things too much and talk down to patients.
    d. Patients have the primary responsibility for discussing their medical problems, and they are often unskilled in initiating discussions about their problems.

14. The accuracy with which physicians present information about the nature of medical problems is related to the degree of patient:
    a. suffering.
    b. anxiety.
    c. discontent.
    d. satisfaction.

15. What should a physician do to enhance the physician-patient relationship?
    a. Be courteous and supportive toward the patient.
    b. Use simplistic explanations.
    c. Explain the diagnosis in professional jargon.
    d. Encourage the patient to construct a personal theory to account for the reported symptoms.

____ 16. cataclysmic events

____ 17. personal stressors

____ 18. background stressors

____ 19. daily hassles

____ 20. uplifts

a. The same as background stressors.

b. Strong stressors that occur suddenly, affecting many people at once (e.g., natural disasters).

c. Events, such as the death of a family member, that have immediate negative consequences that generally fade with time.

d. Minor positive events that make one feel good.

e. Events such as being stuck in traffic that cause minor irritations but have no long-term ill effects unless they continue or are compounded by other stressful events.

21. Commitment, control, and challenge seem to make _____ people more resistant to negative stressors.

22. The fight-or-flight response is also known as the _____ stage.

23. Several months after his wife was diagnosed with Alzheimer's disease, Sam's own body lost its ability to respond or adjust. He had reached the _____ stage of GAS.

24. Lazarus, in his research, described stressors as _____, things like lost keys, rude sales clerks, and bad hair days.

25. Calculate the degree of stress in your life using the table in module 45. Interpret the results using the scoring information at the bottom of the table. What do the results say about the cause of illness and the role of stress in your health?

PRACTICE TEST 2:

1. The branch of psychology devoted to exploring psychological factors and principles in treatment, diagnosis, and prevention of physical illness is called:
   a. health psychology.
   b. physiological psychology.
   c. forensic psychology.
   d. organizational psychology.

2. _____ developed the general adaptation syndrome model.
   a. Martin Seligman
   b. Hans Selye
   c. B. F. Skinner
   d. Sigmund Freud

3. The general adaptation syndrome (Selye) states that:
   a. stress generates biological responses in animals that differ from those in humans.
   b. stressful situations produce many different responses in individuals.
   c. the same set of physiological reactions to stress occur regardless of the situation.
   d. immobilization happens when the organism confronts a stressor.

4. Myron has been coping with the death of his wife. He has been hospitalized for an acute respiratory infection, fatigue, and physical collapse. He is likely experiencing the _____ stage of the general adaptation syndrome.
   a. resistance
   b. alarm and mobilization
   c. exhaustion
   d. challenge

5. The best predictor of breast cancer victims' survival time was a factor of mental resilience and vigor, also labeled as:
   a. acceptance.
   b. hardiness.
   c. fatalism.
   d. joy.

6. Background stressors do not require much coping or response, but continued exposure to them may produce:
   a. an inability to use problem-focused techniques.
   b. as great a toll as a single, more stressful incident.
   c. as great a toll as a cataclysmic event.
   d. psychosomatic illness.

7. According to Seligman, _____ occurs when one concludes that unpleasant or annoying stimuli cannot be controlled.
   a. learned helplessness
   b. hysteria
   c. cataclysmic stress
   d. posttraumatic stress

8. What two types of strategies do people use when consciously attempting to regulate a stressful situation?
    a. control-oriented or defensive coping strategies
    b. emotion-focused or problem-focused coping strategies
    c. emotional insulation or denial coping strategies
    d. conscious or unconscious coping strategies

9. Which of the following traits is characteristic of a Type B personality?
    a. relaxed
    b. aggressive
    c. scheduled
    d. competitive

10. Frequently experiencing negative emotions has been linked to _____ and also to the _____ personality.
    a. hypertension; Type B
    b. lowered incidence of heart failure; Type A
    c. eczema; Type B
    d. coronary disease; Type A

11. Some evidence suggests that, rather than focusing on Type A behavior as the cause of heart disease, a more effective approach should concentrate on:
    a. Type A behaviors that affect the immune system.
    b. Type B behaviors that appear critical to the prevention of heart disease.
    c. Type A behaviors that can be altered instead of eliminated.
    d. Type B behaviors that work with the immune system.

12. Although about _____ of smokers agree that smoking is bad for your health, only about _____ are able to achieve long-term successes in their efforts to stop smoking.
    a. 95 percent; 40 percent
    b. 80 percent; 30 percent
    c. 70 percent; 15 percent
    d. 30 percent; 15 percent

13. Which behavior personality type would best be described as someone who is resilient to stress and does not get stress-related diseases?
    a. Type A behavior
    b. hardy personality
    c. helpless personality
    d. Type B behavior

14. Patients' erroneous theories about their own illnesses:
    a. reinforce their confidence in the physician's wisdom.
    b. lead them to disobey the doctor's prescribed course of treatment.
    c. are actually correct in an amazingly large number of cases.
    d. relate closely to their improvements from prior medical treatment.

15. Which of the following is **not** likely to bring you the best possible health care?
    a. Choose physicians who communicate well.
    b. Ask questions until you fully understand your treatment.
    c. Accept some responsibility for your treatment.
    d. Do anything necessary to gain the attention of the health-care providers.

____	16.	learned helplessness	a. Preparation for stress before it is encountered.
____	17.	coping	b. The efforts to control, reduce, or learn to tolerate the threats that lead to stress.
____	18.	defense mechanisms	
____	19.	social support	c. A learned belief that one has no control over the environment.
____	20.	inoculation	d. Unconscious strategies people use to reduce anxiety by concealing its source from themselves and others.
			e. Knowledge of being part of a mutual network of caring, interested others.

21. The _____ is the complex of organs, glands, and cells that make up our body's natural line of defense.

22. A state that occurs when an individual must choose between two or more competing goals is called _____.

23. The tendency to throw ourselves into whatever we are doing with a sense that the activity is important is called _____.

24. One characteristic of hardiness is the anticipation of change that serves as an incentive rather than a threat. This is called _____.

25. _____ is comfort provided by other humans as well as pets.

26. Smoking is a serious habit with both psychological and physiological addictions. Should smoking be banned in public places? Discuss the problems posed by such a ban and the benefits that should be expected by enforcing it.

PRACTICE TEST 3: Conceptual, Applied, and Challenging Questions

1. Which alternative about health psychology is **not** correct?
   a. Health psychology uses treatments such as prescription medications, surgery, and radiation therapy when indicated.
   b. Health psychology is concerned with changing people's habits and lifestyles to help them prevent disease.
   c. Health psychology recognizes that health is interwoven with psychological factors.
   d. Health psychology recognizes that psychological factors may affect the immune system and have beneficial or detrimental effects upon health.

2. Health psychologists take the position on the mind-brain problem that:
   a. the mind-brain problem is an eternal mystery that will never be solved.
   b. mind and brain are separate and operate independently.
   c. mind and brain are separate but work with perfect synchrony, like two clocks that are set to give synchronized time readings.
   d. mind and brain interact with each other.

3. Carlos realized that he had failed to reach his sales goals at the end of the year, so he set new goals for the following year. Carlos's behavior is typical for a person at the _____ stage of the general adaptation syndrome.
   - a. resistance
   - b. exhaustion
   - c. alarm and mobilization
   - d. repression

4. For those involved, the terrorist bombing of an office building is which type of stressor?
   - a. personal stressor
   - b. background stressor
   - c. daily hassle
   - d. cataclysmic event

5. Upon visiting the doctor's office and going through extensive testing, Michael finds out that he has a lung disease. Which type of stress is Michael likely to experience?
   - a. cataclysmic stress
   - b. personal stress
   - c. posttraumatic stress
   - d. background stress

6. A physician uses his assistants to regulate in-patients' every activity. By the end of their time in his clinic, the patients take no initiative. This demonstrates:
   - a. the general adaptation syndrome.
   - b. daily hassles.
   - c. the inferiority complex.
   - d. learned helplessness.

7. Your boss learns that he exhibits Type A behavior pattern, while attending a company-sponsored stress workshop. Which alternative is correct?
   - a. Nothing can be done to change your boss's Type A behavior pattern.
   - b. Your boss should remember that the relationship between the Type A behavior pattern and heart attacks or development of coronary heart disease is correlational.
   - c. There is little hope for your boss because the Type A behavior pattern has been found to cause heart attacks or development of heart disease.
   - d. Your boss is fortunate because women with Type A behavior patterns are at greater risk.

8. In a study that placed patients with advanced breast cancer in either psychotherapy or a control that did not receive psychotherapy, what were the results?
   - a. The psychotherapy group felt better, and they lived longer.
   - b. The psychotherapy group felt better, but there was no impact on their survival rate.
   - c. The psychotherapy group became more depressed because of their increased awareness of the cancer, but they also lived longer.
   - d. The study proved that psychotherapy increased the survival rate of cancer patients.

9. Aunt Nina, who is 87 years old, is in the hospital for minor surgery. However, because she is older, she realizes that even minor surgery can be risky. Her surgeon, apparently trying to calm her fears, says "We'll just pop right in there and sneak back out." The problem with his comments appears to be quite common in that:
   - a. they treat Nina as if she were either a child or senile.
   - b. they don't go far enough in minimizing the risk factors.
   - c. when spoken to in this manner, patients get an exaggerated sense of the surgeon's ability.
   - d. they reflect techniques taught in medical school.

10. Kiesha, who is 35 years old, has been smoking for 15 years. She knows it is extremely unhealthy for her and wants to stop but is having difficulty doing so. What may prove to be the most effective means to help Kiesha to stop smoking?
   - a. the "cold-turkey" method
   - b. banning smoking in all public places
   - c. behavior strategies that concentrate on changing the smoking response
   - d. changing societal norms and attitudes about smoking

11. The malfunction of the Three Mile Island plant in the early 1980s exposed people to a potential nuclear meltdown. This produced emotional, behavioral, and psychological consequences that lasted more than a year. This would be considered a:
   a. cataclysmic event.
   b. background stressor.
   c. uplift.
   d. personal stressor.

12. A patient decides that she will do better by maintaining her exercise and taking the rest of some medication she had been given earlier instead of carefully following the prescribed regimen of rest and antibiotics for an infection. This is an example of:
   a. reactance.
   b. Type A behavior.
   c. preventive medicine.
   d. creative nonadherence.

13. In a group therapy session with alcoholics, the counselor describes the range of personal issues that are aggravated by alcohol; this approach is meant to promote:
   a. hardiness.
   b. problem-focused coping.
   c. learned helplessness.
   d. stress inoculation.

14. Whenever Pablo measures his blood pressure at the drug store, where they have free blood-pressure checks, his pressure is always in the normal range. However, whenever he goes to his physician, he gets nervous and anxious, and his blood pressure usually measures in the high range. This could best be explained by:
   a. reactance.
   b. Type A behavior.
   c. Type B behavior.
   d. creative nonadherence.

15. Social support is an effective means of coping with all of the following types of stress. However, based on the descriptions in the text, in which one of the following is social support most likely to occur as a matter of the nature of the stressor?
   a. personal stressors
   b. events leading to posttraumatic stress disorder
   c. cataclysmic events
   d. uplifts

____ 16. general adaptation syndrome (GAS)

____ 17. posttraumatic stress disorder (PTSD)

____ 18. creative nonadherence

____ 19. reactance

a. When patients modify a physician's treatment.

b. A set of symptoms that occurs after disturbing events: trouble concentrating, anxiety, guilt, and sleep difficulties.

c. Typical series of responses to stressful situations that includes alarm, resistance, and exhaustion.

d. A negative emotional and cognitive reaction to a restriction of one's freedom.

20. Most people _____ agree with the statement, "Cigarette smoking frequently causes disease and death."

21. People smoke in an effort to regulate both emotional states and _____ in the blood.

22. Research on well-being shows that happy people have high _____.

23.   _____ helps individuals to persevere at tasks and ultimately to achieve more.

24.   One explanation for the stability of subjective well-being is that people may have a general _____ for happiness.

25.   Define the personality characteristic hardiness. Discuss how parents can encourage the development of hardiness in their children.

■ ANSWER KEY: MODULES 34, 35, AND 36

Module 34:	[p] learned	Module 35:	Module 36:
[a] Health psychology	helplessness	[a] Type A behavior	[a] creative nonadherence
[b] immune system	[q] coping	pattern	[b] reactance
[c] Psychoneuroimmunology	[r] defense	[b] Type B behavior	
[d] stress	mechanisms	pattern	Evaluate
[e] psychophysiological	[s] Emotional	[c] cancer	1. d
disorders	insulation	[d] coronary heart	2. a
[f] general adaptation	[t] emotion-focused	disease	3. e
syndrome (GAS)	coping	[e] emotional state	4. b
[g] alarm and mobilization	[u] problem-focused	[f] Negative response	5. c
stage	coping	[g] environmental	
[h] resistance stage	[v] Hardiness	factors	
[i] exhaustion stage	[w] social support		
[j] cataclysmic events	[x] inoculation	Evaluate	
[k] posttraumatic stress		1. a	
disorder, or PTSD	Evaluate	2. e	
[l] personal stressors	1. e	3. d	
[m] background stressors	2. a	4. c	
[n] daily hassles	3. d	5. b	
[o] uplifts	4. b		
	5. c		

Selected Rethink Answers

34-1   Cataclysmic stressors are strong stressors that occur suddenly and affect many people. They produce less stress in the long run because they have a clear resolution. Social support, the sharing of the event with others, helps reduce stress because there are others who know how you are feeling.

34-2   To avoid stress, people can be trained to identify and manage their emotions in the face of stress by getting support or reframing the situation to identify any positive aspects of a situation. People can develop strategies or plans of action to deal with stress such as planning, anticipating problems, and having preplanned solutions.

35-1   The United States is a highly competitive society. People who are aggressive and have drive in their personal and professional life are regarded positively; they can also be aggressive and hostile when things don't go their way. Our democratic society focuses largely on individual success, whereas other cultures focus on cooperation and community success.

Practice Test 1:

1. c   mod. 34 p. 424
a. Incorrect. The limbic system is part of the brain.
b. Incorrect. The endocrine system is the system of hormone-secreting organs, and it is part of the larger system that defends against disease.
*c. Correct. The immune system includes the endocrine system, the sympathetic system, and parts of the limbic system, as well as other organs.
d. Incorrect. The sympathetic system is part of the nervous system, and it is part of the larger immune system.

2. b   mod. 34 p. 427
a. Incorrect. See answer b.
*b. Correct. The stages of Selye's general adaptation syndrome are alarm and mobilization, resistance, and exhaustion.
c. Incorrect. See answer b.
d. Incorrect. See answer b.

3. a   mod. 34 p. 425
*a. Correct. Stressors present threats or challenges to a person and require some type of adaptive response.
b. Incorrect. A mobilization state is not a threat to a person's well-being.
c. Incorrect. A defense mechanism is used by the ego to protect against unconscious conflict.
d. Incorrect. An inoculation is a medical intervention that builds the immune system response.

4. d   mod. 34 p. 427
a. Incorrect. The stage is part of the reaction to a stressor, not just a preparation to react.
b. Incorrect. Increased resistance to the stressor occurs in the next stage, during which the ability to resist disease declines.
c. Incorrect. This describes the final stage of the general adaptation syndrome.
*d. Correct. The "alarm" involves the psychological awareness of the stressor.

5. a   mod. 34 p. 429
*a. Correct. Cataclysmic stressors include manmade and natural disasters, like earthquakes and terrorist attacks.
b. Incorrect. Background stressors are the ongoing demands made on the individual all the time.
c. Incorrect. Uplifts are the positive challenges that contribute to a sense of accomplishment or completion.
d. Incorrect. Personal stressors are the demands that are unique to the person and typically not shared with others (like being fired from a job).

6. b   mod. 34 p. 431
a. Incorrect. These are described as hassles.
*b. Correct. These minor positive events may be just as demanding and stressful on the individual as are hassles, but they leave the person feeling good rather than drained.
c. Incorrect. Uplifts, by definition, would not be exhilarating.
d. Incorrect. Uplifts, by definition, would not be major.

7. d   mod. 34 p. 426
a. Incorrect. These disorders can appear as a result of the extended operation of the resistance phase of the GAS and are sometimes called disorders of defense (but not of the psychodynamic ego defense mechanisms).
b. Incorrect. These do not immediately threaten life.
c. Incorrect. Hardy people appear to have fewer of these disorders than the less hardy.
*d. Correct. These disorders often have psychological origins in stress and are thus considered psychophysiological.

8. c   mod. 34 p. 433
a. Incorrect. In the psychoanalytic view, "defense" would apply to unconscious events that threaten the ego.
b. Incorrect. Arousal is not the appropriate adjective.
*c. Correct. "Coping" is used to describe the ability to deal with stress and the techniques used.
d. Incorrect. However, coping is a form of adaptation.

9. b   mod. 34 p. 434
a. Incorrect. Hardy individuals are quite capable of coping with stress.
*b. Correct. The hardy individual is resilient to stress and does not get stress-related diseases.
c. Incorrect. The hardy individual does recognize the challenge of stress.
d. Incorrect. Everyone is affected in some way by emotional choices, especially if they are difficult.

10. a   mod. 35 p. 438
*a. Correct. Type A behavior pattern is most associated with heart disease.
b. Incorrect. Type A, not Type B, is most associated with heart disease.
c. Incorrect. The hardy personality is actually more resistant to stress-related heart disease.
d. Incorrect. There is no personality type known as cataclysmic (although you may know someone who would fit such a description).

11. d   mod. 35 p. 438
a. Incorrect. Type B behavior is neither competitive nor driven by achievement.
b. Incorrect. The hardy individual is resistant to stress-related diseases.
c. Incorrect. A helpless person would not be competitive or focused on completion of tasks.
*d. Correct. These traits describe the Type A behavior pattern.

12. d   mod. 35 p. 441
a. Incorrect. This is the stage in which positive attitudes toward smoking are developed.
b. Incorrect. After becoming a smoker, maintenance of the habit requires making the behavior part of the routine.
c. Incorrect. This is the stage marked by first experimenting with cigarettes.
*d. Correct. The nicotine addiction marks the ascension to being a smoker.

13. b   mod. 36 p. 446
a. Incorrect. Physicians apparently have difficulty asking questions in such a way that the patient can answer them with information that is useful.
*b. Correct. Patients often begin the discussion, and when they do take responsibility, communication with the physician often improves.
c. Incorrect. A common response with the elderly is to act as if they are children and condescend to them.
d. Incorrect. Physicians often ask questions that patients have difficulty understanding, or they understand them in other ways.

14. d   mod. 36 p. 446
a. Incorrect. Suffering results from the disease.
b. Incorrect. See answer d.
c. Incorrect. See answer d.
d. Correct. The accuracy of the communication seems to improve the patient's satisfaction with treatment and lessens anxiety about the disease and discontent with the physician.

15. a   mod. 36 p. 446
*a. Correct. Simple courtesy goes a long way.
b. Incorrect. Simplistic answers and explanations make understanding the problem more difficult.
c. Incorrect. Professional jargon is the greatest barrier to improved communication.
d. Incorrect. Patients will do this if the explanation they receive is not well understood.

16. b   mod. 34 p. 429
17. c   mod. 34 p. 430
18. e   mod. 34 p. 430
19. a   mod. 34 p. 430
20. d   mod. 34 p. 431

21. hardy   mod. 34 p. 434
22. Alarm and mobilization   mod. 34 p. 427
23. resistance   mod. 34 p. 427
24. Hassles   mod. 34 p. 430

25.
- Tabulate your stress score using Table 15-1.
- Determine whether you are at risk or normal. Do the events that contribute to your score seem part of the normal course of life, or have you experienced an unusual number of stressful things recently?
- Identify any recent illnesses that would have been influenced by the stress.

Practice Test 2:
1. a   mod. 34 p. 424
*a. Correct. Health psychology includes all of the psychological aspects of health.
b. Incorrect. Physiological psychology is focused on the various psychological aspects of our biological organism.
c. Incorrect. Forensic psychology is the use of psychology in the legal system.
d. Incorrect. Organizational psychology attends to the study of behavior in organizations.

2. b   mod. 34 p. 427
a. Incorrect. Seligman is responsible for the concept of learned helplessness.
*b. Correct. A Canadian physician, Hans Selye proposed and researched this universal pattern of stress reaction.
c. Incorrect. Skinner is responsible for operant conditioning.
d. Incorrect. Freud developed psychoanalytic theory.

3. c   mod. 34 p. 427
a. Incorrect. See answer c.
b. Incorrect. The psychological responses vary considerably, but the physiological responses differ only by degree.
*c. Correct. Selye believed and demonstrated through his research that the physiological stress response pattern was pretty much universal.
d. Incorrect. This happens rarely and with extreme stressors.

4. c   mod. 34 p. 427
a. Incorrect. This is the middle stage, during which the individual puts up a fight.
b. Incorrect. This is the earliest stage of initial response, and it does not have these symptoms.
*c. Correct. The conditions described suggest that the man has reached the final stage of the GAS.
d. Incorrect. There is no "challenge" stage.

5. d   mod. 35 p. 440
a. Incorrect. Acceptance does not have an influence on survival of cancer.
b. Incorrect. Hardiness does not have an influence on survival of cancer.
c. Incorrect. Fatalism has a negative impact on survival of cancer.
*d. Correct. Researchers defined this as joy, and it was correlated to higher survival rates.

6. b   mod. 34 p. 430
a. Incorrect. This ability depends on factors other than the presence of background stressors.
*b. Correct. The effect of background stress, and any stress, can accumulate, with the sum of many small stressors having the same effect as one large one.
c. Incorrect. This would be difficult to judge.
d. Incorrect. Background stressors would be unlikely to cause a psychosomatic illness.

7.   a   mod. 34 p. 427
*a. Correct. Seligman applied this term to the perception that a situation was beyond the individual's control.
b.   Incorrect. Hysteria refers to a psychological disorder treated by Freud.
c.   Incorrect. Cataclysmic stress refers to major stressful events that affect many people.
d.   Incorrect. Posttraumatic stress disorder refers to the long-term effects of highly stressful events.

8.   b   mod. 34 p. 433
a.   Incorrect. See answer b.
*b. Correct. The two types are emotion-focused and problem-focused coping. Emotion-focused coping is used more in situations in which circumstances appear unchangeable.
c.   Incorrect. See answer b.
d.   Incorrect. See answer b.

9.   a   mod. 35 p. 438
*a. Correct. Of the traits given, relaxed best fits the Type B personality. Aggressive, scheduled, and competitive are Type A characteristics.
b.   Incorrect. See answer a.
c.   Incorrect. See answer a.
d.   Incorrect. See answer a.

10. d   mod. 35 p. 439
a.   Incorrect. Type B personalities tend to have less hypertension than Type A.
b.   Incorrect. This may be true only of second heart attacks.
c.   Incorrect. Eczema is not associated with Type A or B patterns.
*d. Correct. The Type A behavior that correlates most with CHD is negative emotions.

11. b   mod. 35 p. 439
a.   Incorrect. It appears that all Type A behaviors have an effect on the immune system.
*b. Correct. Those Type B behaviors that are associated with healthy results can be taught to the Type A person.
c.   Incorrect. This approach has not been successful.
d.   Incorrect. Rather than those that work with the immune system (if they can be isolated), the approach has been to focus on those that are successful with heart conditions.

12. c   mod. 35 p. 441
a.   Incorrect. See answer c.
b.   Incorrect. See answer c.
*c. Correct. Smoking is one of the most difficult habits to break.
d.   Incorrect. See answer c.

13. b   mod. 36 p. 446
a.   Incorrect. The need for achievement, competitiveness, and commitment sometimes leads to illness.
*b. Correct. The hardy individual is less affected by stress.
c.   Incorrect. An individual would not be competitive or driven but not protected from illness, still affected by stress.
d.   Incorrect. The person who is not competitive or driven may be less likely to get illness than a Type A person.

14. b   mod. 36 p. 440
a.   Incorrect. They probably did not receive any of their physician's wisdom.
*b. Correct. They become their own physicians and change their regime of treatment.
c.   Incorrect. Simply not true.
d.   Incorrect. Perhaps one accidental correct guess may lead them to think they know better.

15. d   mod. 36 p. 440
a.   Incorrect. Better communication reduces anxiety and improves recovery after surgery.
b.   Incorrect. Never give up, these answers make a difference in your health.
c.   Incorrect. The more responsibility you accept, they better your chances of recovery.
*d. Correct. This may result in some detrimental effects, including being ignored when a true emergency occurs.

16. c   mod. 34 p. 432
17. b   mod. 34 p. 433
18. d   mod. 34 p. 433
19. e   mod. 34 p. 435
20. a   mod. 34 p. 433

21. immune system   mod. 34 p. 428
22. conflict   mod. 34 p. 434
23. commitment   mod. 34 p. 434
24. challenge   mod. 34 p. 434
25. Social support   mod. 34 p. 435

26.
▪   Identify whether you believe that public places should ban smoking.
▪   Under which conditions should a person be allowed or not allowed to smoke in public.
▪   Describe the difficulties and problems that would be involved with enforcing a complete ban.

Practice Test 3:

1. a   mod. 34 p. 424
*a. Correct. Health psychology may promote the effective use of medical treatments, but it is not involved in using the treatments.
b. Incorrect. Health psychology can contribute to changing habits by implementing behavior modification strategies, among other strategies.
c. Incorrect. Some health psychologists have taken a holistic view of mind and body, suggesting that the two are inseparable.
d. Incorrect. The role of the immune system and the way psychological factors can affect it is a major interest for health psychology.

2. d   mod. 34 p. 424
a. Incorrect. The mind-brain problem is a mystery created by modern philosophy.
b. Incorrect. True only among philosophers.
c. Incorrect. This is a view reminiscent of the philosopher Leibniz.
*d. Correct. Without this basic assumption, attention to the physical health of the brain as an organ (and the rest of the body as well) would have no impact on the mind.

3. c   mod. 34 p. 427
a. Incorrect. This is a new stress, so Carlos is probably at the alarm and mobilization stage.
b. Incorrect. Exhaustion would only appear in this circumstance after many years of failing to meet goals.
*c. Correct. Because this is a new recognition, Carlos has mobilized his energies and already begun to cope with the stress of not meeting this year's goals.
d. Incorrect. In repression, Carlos would probably ignore his failure to meet this year's goals and make no effort to compensate for next year.

4. d   mod. 34 p. 429
a. Incorrect. Personal stressors are major life events like marriage or death.
b. Incorrect. Background stressors include everyday annoyances like traffic.
c. Incorrect. Daily hassles are also known as background stressors, and they include everyday annoyances like traffic.
*d. Correct. The traumatic experience would be classed as cataclysmic.

5. b   mod. 34 p. 430
a. Incorrect. Cataclysmic stress involves many people, such as during war, earthquakes, and terrorist attacks.
*b. Correct. This is considered a major personal stressor.
c. Incorrect. Posttraumatic stress disorder actually follows a significant period of traumatic stress.
d. Incorrect. Background stress includes the many small and insignificant worries and challenges one faces each day.

6. d   mod. 34 p. 431
a. Incorrect. This does not illustrate the GAS.
b. Incorrect. Daily hassles will not account for their not taking any initiative.
c. Incorrect. If they come to believe that they are inferior, then the answer would be "d" anyway.
*d. Correct. They have learned that they are totally under the control of the assistant coaches, thus helpless.

7. b   mod. 35 p. 439
a. Incorrect. Certainly, he can change a number of his behavior patterns or he can take measures to improve his health practices.
*b. Correct. The correlation does not mean that he will definitely develop coronary heart disease.
c. Incorrect. With precautions, he will have just as good an outlook as anyone else.
d. Incorrect. Women are not at greater risk with these patterns.

8. a   mod. 35 p. 440
*a. Correct. They had a more positive outlook, and in early studies, they extended their lives significantly.
b. Incorrect. There apparently was a link between how they felt and their survival rate.
c. Incorrect. They were less depressed.
d. Incorrect. The study did not prove the relationship; it only suggested that more study was necessary.

9. a   mod. 36 p. 446
*a. Correct. This condescending approach is extremely common among physicians.
b. Incorrect. They go too far in minimizing the risks involved.
c. Incorrect. If they are not entirely put off, patients may develop expectations of success that are not realistic.
d. Incorrect. They reflect that for many physicians, techniques for communicating with patients have not been taught at all.

10. c   mod. 35 p. 441
a.   Incorrect. The cold-turkey method is effective in only a few cases.
b.   Incorrect. Banning smoking in public places helps nonsmokers, but it does not help smokers.
*c. Correct. Behavior strategies have proven to be the most effective, but they still require perseverance.
d.   Incorrect. This will help others avoid starting the habit, but it will not help Kiesha.

11. d   mod. 34 p. 430
a.   Incorrect. Although they occur suddenly and affect many people, they usually have a clear resolution.
b.   Incorrect. Minor irritations that are sometimes called daily hassles. Require little coping.
c.   Incorrect. Positive events that make one feel good.
*d. Correct. Major life events where the effects produce an immediate major reaction but that can sometimes linger for long periods.

12. d   mod. 36 p. 445
a.   Incorrect. Reactance is the disagreeable emotional and cognitive reaction to being restricted to a medical regimen.
b.   Incorrect. Type A behavior does not predict compliance to medical prescriptions.
c.   Incorrect. It may prevent physicians from losing their jobs because she will probably have to visit them again.
*d. Correct. The term for her actions is creative nonadherence.

13. b   mod. 34 p. 433
a.   Incorrect. Hardiness may be improved by shifting to a problem-focused coping approach.
*b. Correct. Attention to problems that can be addressed and resolved.
c.   Incorrect. Therapists should not promote learned helplessness.
d.   Incorrect. Stress inoculation would focus more on what is about to happen, not what has already surfaced.

14. a   mod. 36 p. 445
*a. Correct. Reactance is the disagreeable emotional and cognitive reaction to being restricted to a medical regimen, and it can cause higher reading on blood pressure because of increased anxiety about the physician.
b.   Incorrect. Reactance is independent of Type A or Type B behavior.
c.   Incorrect. Reactance is independent of Type A or Type B behavior.
d.   Incorrect. Creative nonadherence occurs when a patient creates his or her own course of treatment, often ignoring the prescribed treatment.

15. c   mod. 34 p. 429
a.   Incorrect. Personal stressors are not shared unless someone seeks out support.
b.   Incorrect. One element of posttraumatic stress disorder is the failure of the support systems in the first place.
*c. Correct. Because many others have just experienced the same major stressor, the social support group is already defined.
d.   Incorrect. Uplifts are personal background stressors that result in the person feeling good.

16. c   mod. 34 p. 427
17. b   mod. 34 p. 430
18. a   mod. 34 p. 445
19. d   mod. 36 p. 445

20. smokers   mod. 35 p. 442
21. nicotine levels mod. 35 p. 443
22. self-esteem   mod. 36 p. 449
23. Optimism   mod. 34 p. 434
24. set point   mod. 36 p. 449

25.
- Hardiness is the coping style whose characteristics are associated with a lower rate of stress-related illness.
- Parents can encourage their children to be optimistic, to commit themselves to activities that are important and meaningful to them.
- Children should understand that change rather than stability is the standard condition of life.
- Parents can allow children a sense of control over the events in their lives.

Psychological Disorders

Overview

In this set of modules, you see that abnormality is difficult to define, and it is best to consider behavior as on a continuum from normal to abnormal.

Module 37 presents the contemporary perspectives that attempt to explain abnormal behavior. They are the medical perspective, the psychoanalytical perspective, the behavioral perspective, the cognitive perspective, the humanistic perspective, and the sociocultural perspective. The system used by most professionals to classify mental disorders is the *DSM-IV*.

Module 38 helps us identify the anxiety disorders, the somatoform disorders, and the dissociative disorders. Also included in this module are discussions on mood disorders and one of the most severe mental illnesses, schizophrenia. The personality disorders, those that cause little or no personal distress but do present difficulty in trying to function as a normal member of society, are also discussed. These include antisocial personality disorder, borderline personality disorder, and the narcissistic personality. This module finishes with a presentation of the major childhood disorders and includes major depression and attention-deficit hyperactivity disorder.

Module 39 explains that about half the people in the United States are likely to experience a disorder at some time in their lives. The signals that indicate a need for professional help are discussed. These include long-term feelings of psychological distress, inability to cope, phobias, compulsions, and the inability to interact with others.

To further investigate the topics covered in this chapter, you can visit the related Web sites by visiting the following link: www.mhhe.com/feldmanup6-16links.

Prologue: Chris Coles
Looking Ahead

Module 37: Normal Versus Abnormal: Making the Distinction

Defining Abnormality

| **Applying Psychology in the 21st Century:** |
| Suicide Bombers: Normal or Abnormal? |

Perspectives on Abnormality: From Superstition to Science
Classifying Abnormal Behavior: The ABCs of *DSM*

- *How can we distinguish normal from abnormal behavior?*
- *What are the major perspectives on psychological disorders used by mental health professionals?*
- *What classification system is used to categorize psychological disorders?*

Normal Versus Abnormal: Making the Distinction

A passage from James Joyce's *Ulysses* suggests that madness cannot be determined by a small sample of a person's behavior. The text examines the following approaches to the definition of abnormal behavior:

- *Abnormality as deviation from the average.* This definition uses the statistical definition of behavior to define "abnormal" as behavior that is statistically unusual or rare. The problem with this approach is that simply being unusual or rare does not define abnormal: Individuals with high IQs are rare, but they are not considered abnormal.
- *Abnormality as deviation from the ideal.* This definition classifies behavior as abnormal if it deviates from the ideal or standard behavior. However, society has very few standards on which everyone agrees.
- *Abnormality as a sense of subjective discomfort.* This approach focuses on the consequences of behavior that make a person feel discomfort. However, some people who engage in what others would consider abnormal behavior do not experience discomfort.
- *Abnormality as the inability to function effectively.* People who are unable to adjust to the demands of society and unable to function in daily life are considered abnormal in this view. An unemployed homeless woman would be classified as abnormal in this view even if the choice to live on the streets were her own.
- *Legal definitions of abnormality.* The legal system uses the concept of insanity to distinguish normal from abnormal behavior. Insanity refers generally to whether the defendant could understand the difference between right and wrong when the act was committed. The precise definition and how it is used varies from one jurisdiction to another.

None of the five approaches is broad enough to include all possibilities of abnormal behavior, and the line between normal and abnormal remains unclear. The best way to solve the problem is to consider normal and abnormal as on a continuum, or scale, of behavior rather than to consider them to be absolute states. In the past, abnormal behavior has been attributed to superstition, witchcraft, or demonic possession. The contemporary approach includes six major perspectives on abnormal behavior:

- The **[a]** _____ of abnormality views the cause of abnormal behavior to have a physical origin such as a hormone or chemical imbalance or a physical injury.

- The **[b]** _____ of abnormality maintains that abnormal behavior comes from childhood. The conflicts of childhood that remain unresolved can cause abnormal behavior in adulthood.

- The **[c]** _____ of abnormality views the behavior as the problem, understanding that behavior is a response to stimuli that one finds in one's environment.

- The **[d]** _____ of abnormality assumes that *cognitions* are central to a person's abnormal behavior, which can then be changed by learning new cognitions.

- The **[e]** _____ of abnormality emphasizes the control and responsibility people have for their own behavior. This model considers people to be basically rational, oriented to the social world, and motivated to get along with others.

- The **[f]** _____ of abnormality assumes that behavior is shaped by the family group, society, and culture. The stresses and conflicts people experience promote and maintain abnormal behavior.

One standard classification system has been accepted by most professionals for classifying mental disorders. Devised by the American Psychiatric Association, the system is known as the

[g] _____. The manual has more than 200 diagnostic categories. It evaluates behavior according to five dimensions called *axes*. The first three axes address the primary disorder exhibited, the nature of any personality disorders or developmental problems, and any physical disorders. The fourth and fifth axes address the severity of stressors and the general level of functioning. The *DSM-IV* attempts to be descriptive and to avoid suggestions of cause. The objective is to provide precise description and classification. Criticisms include the fact that it reflects categories that assume a physiological view of causes (arising from the fact that it was developed by physicians) and that the categories are inflexible. In other views, the labeling of an individual as deviant is seen as a lifelong, dehumanizing stigma. A classic study by Rosenhan illustrated how the stigma of being labeled mentally ill can linger. Eight people, including Rosenhan, presented themselves to mental hospitals complaining of only one symptom, hearing voices. Although they did not complain of the symptom again, they stayed for an average of 19 days and were released with labels like "schizophrenia in remission." None of the impostors was detected by the staff. Despite its drawbacks, the *DSM-IV* does provide a reliable and valid way to classify psychological disorders.

Evaluate

_____ 1. medical model

_____ 2. psychoanalytic model

_____ 3. behavioral model

_____ 4. cognitive model

_____ 5. humanistic model

_____ 6. sociocultural model

a. Suggests that abnormality stems from childhood conflicts over opposing desires regarding sex and aggression.

b. Suggests that people's behavior, both normal and abnormal, is shaped by family, society, and cultural influences.

c. Suggests that people's thoughts and beliefs are a central component to abnormal behavior.

d. Suggests that when an individual displays symptoms of abnormal behavior, the cause is physiological.

e. Suggests that abnormal behavior is the problem to be treated, rather than viewing behavior as a symptom of some underlying medical or psychological problem.

f. Suggests that abnormal behavior results from an inability to fulfill human needs and capabilities.

Rethink

37-1   Imagine that an acquaintance of yours was recently arrested for shoplifting a $3 pen. What sorts of questions and issues would be raised by proponents of *each* of these perspectives on abnormality: medical, psychoanalytic, behavioral, cognitive, humanistic, and sociocultural?

37-2   Do you agree or disagree that the *DSM* should be updated every several years? What makes abnormal behavior so variable? Why can't there be one definition of abnormal behavior?

Spotlight on Terminology and Language—ESL Pointers

Normal Versus Abnormal: Making the Distinction

Page 457 "It would be easy to conclude that these are the **musings** of a madman."

Musings are thoughts about something.

Page 457 "Actually this passage is from James Joyce's classic *Ulysses*, **hailed** as one of the major works of twentieth-century literature (Joyce, 1934, p. 377)."

Hailed is acclaimed and praised. This is one of the premier works of the 20th century.

Page 457 "To employ this statistically based approach, we simply observe what behaviors are rare or occur infrequently in a particular society or culture and label those **deviations** from the norm 'abnormal.'"

Deviation is a departure from the norm.

Page 457 "Similarly, such a concept of abnormality unreasonably labels a person who has an unusually high IQ as abnormal, simply because a high IQ is **statistically rare**."

Statistically rare would be unlikely, uncommon.

Page 458 "The definition of insanity varies from one **jurisdiction** to another."

Jurisdiction is the limits, or boundaries, within which authority exists.

Page 458 "Behavior should be evaluated in terms of **gradations**, ranging from completely normal functioning to extremely abnormal behavior."

Gradations are steps, or stages, of an activity. They are a series of gradual, successive stages.

Page 459 "Contemporary approaches take a more **enlightened** view."

These approaches take a more progressive, or tolerant, view. An **enlightened** view uses knowledge based on theoretical perspectives to understand psychological disorders.

Page 460 "Whereas the medical perspective suggests that biological causes are at the **root of** abnormal behavior, the psychoanalytic perspective hold that abnormal behavior stems from childhood conflicts over opposing wishes regarding sex and aggression."

At the **root of** means the cause or origin of.

Page 460 "To understand the roots of people's disordered behavior, the psychoanalytic perspective **scrutinizes** their early life history."

The psychoanalysts pore over, analyzing and **scrutinizing** the details of their childhood experiences. When you scrutinize something, you inspect and observe it carefully and critically.

Page 461 "For instance, suppose a student forms the **erroneous** belief that 'doing well on this exam is crucial to my entire future' whenever he or she takes an exam."

Erroneous is mistaken, wrong. Sometimes our cognitive thoughts are based on unrealistic, or **erroneous**, thinking.

Page 462 "Psychologists who **subscribe to** the humanistic perspective emphasize the responsibility people have for their own behavior, even when such behavior is seen as abnormal."

These psychologists **subscribe to**, or support, the humanistic perspective.

Module 38: The Major Psychological Disorders

Anxiety Disorders
Somatoform Disorders
Dissociative Disorders
Mood Disorders
Schizophrenia
Personality Disorders
Childhood Disorders
Other Disorders

- **What are the major psychological disorders?**

The Major Psychological Disorders

Everyone experiences *anxiety*, a feeling of apprehension or tension, at some time. When anxiety occurs without external reason and interferes with daily functioning, the problem is known as

anxiety. **[a]** _____ refers to the disorder in which an individual experiences long-term consistent anxiety without knowing why. The anxiety makes the person unable to

concentrate, and life becomes centered on the anxiety. **[b]** _____ is distinguished by attacks that may last a few seconds or several hours. In a panic attack, the individual feels anxiety rise to a peak and gets a sense of impending doom. Physical symptoms of increased heart rate, shortness of breath, sweating, faintness, and dizziness may be experienced.

[c] _____ has as its primary symptom a **[d]** _____, an irrational fear of specific objects or situations. Exposure to the stimulus may cause a full-blown panic attack. (A list of common phobias is given in Table 16-3.) Phobias may be minor, or they may cause extreme suffering.

[e] _____ is characterized by unwanted thoughts and the impulse to carry out

a certain action. **[f]** _____ are thoughts or ideas that keep recurring. Although everyone has some, when they continue for days and months and include bizarre images, they make it

difficult for the individual to function. **[g]** _____ are urges to repeat behaviors that seem strange and unreasonable even to the person who feels compelled to act. If they cannot carry out the action, extreme anxiety can be experienced. The cleaning ritual described in the text is a good example of a compulsion. Carrying out the action usually does not reduce the anxiety.

The causes of anxiety disorders are not fully understood. A tendency for both identical twins to have an anxiety disorder if one of them has the disorder suggests that there may be a biological cause. Some chemical deficiencies in the brain have also been linked to the disorder.

The behavioral approach suggests that anxiety is a learned response to stress and that the anxiety is reinforced by subsequent encounters with the stressor. The cognitive approach suggests that anxiety grows out of inappropriate and inaccurate cognitions.

[h]_____ involves a constant fear of illness, and physical sensations are misinterpreted as disease symptoms. The symptoms are not faked—hypochondriacs actually experience the symptoms. Hypochondriasis belongs to a class of disease known as

[i]_____, which are psychological difficulties that take physical form. There are no underlying physical problems to account for the symptoms, or if one does exist, the person's reaction exaggerates it. A major somatoform disorder is [j]_____, in which actual physical symptoms are caused by psychological problems. These disorders usually have a rapid onset—a person may awaken one morning totally blind or with a numb hand (called "glove anesthesia"). One characteristic is that individuals with conversion disorders seem relatively unconcerned with the symptoms. Generally, conversion disorders occur when an emotional stress can be reduced by having a physical symptom.

[k]_____ have been the most dramatized disorders, including the multiple-personality stories of *The Three Faces of Eve* and *Sybil*. The central factor is the dissociation, or splitting apart, of critical parts of the personality. There are three major dissociative disorders.

[l]_____ occurs when two or more distinct personalities are present in the same individual. Each personality is a separate person with desires and reactions to situations. Even vision can change when the personality changes. Because the personalities reside in only one body, they must take turns, causing what appears to be sometimes radically inconsistent behavior. [m]_____ is a failure or inability to remember past experiences. In psychogenic amnesia, information has not been forgotten, it simply cannot be recalled. In some cases, memory loss can be total, as illustrated in the case of Jane Doe, who had to go on television to have her identity discovered. [n]_____ is a state in which people may take an impulsive, sudden trip and assume a new identity. After a period of time, they realize they are in a strange place. They often do not recall what they did while wandering.

Changes in mood are a part of everyday life. However, mood changes can be extreme enough to cause life-threatening problems and to cause an individual to lose touch with reality. These situations result from [o]_____, disturbances in mood severe enough to interfere with daily life. Major depression is one of the more common mood disorders. As many as 14 to 15 million people experience major depression at any time. Twice as many women as men experience major depression, and one in four females will encounter it at some time. Depression is not merely sadness, but involves feelings of uselessness, worthlessness, loneliness, and despair. Major depression is distinguished by the severity of the symptoms.

[p]_____ refers to an extended state of intense euphoria and elation. Also, people experience a sense of happiness, power, invulnerability, and energy. They may be involved with wild schemes. When this is paired with bouts of depression, it is called a bipolar

disorder. The swings between highs and lows can occur every several days or can be over a period of years. Typically, the depression lasts longer than the mania.

Major depression and bipolar disorder may have a biological cause, and heredity may play a role in bipolar disorder. The cognitive approach draws on the experience of

[q]_____, a state in which people perceive that they cannot escape from or cope with stress. According to this view, depression is a response brought on by helplessness. Aaron Beck has suggested that depression involves faulty cognitions held by the sufferer about themselves. Theories about the cause of depression have not explained why twice as many women get it as men. One theory suggests that the stress for women is higher at certain times of life. Women are also more subject to physical and sexual abuse, earn less money than men, and report greater unhappiness with marriage.

Schizophrenia is a class of disorders in which severe distortion of reality occurs. Thinking, perception, and emotion deteriorate, there is a withdrawal from social interaction, and there may be bizarre behavior. (Classes of schizophrenia are listed in Table 16-5.) The characteristics of schizophrenia include:

- *Decline from a previous level of functioning.*
- *Disturbances of thought and language*, in which logic is peculiar, thoughts do not make sense, and linguistic rules are not followed.
- *Delusions* are unshakable beliefs that have no basis in reality, involving thoughts of control by others, persecution, or the belief that thoughts are being broadcast to others.
- *Perceptual disorders* occur in which schizophrenics do not perceive the world as everyone else does, and they may have [r] _____, the experience of perceiving things that do not actually exist.
- *Emotional disturbances* include a lack of emotion or highly inappropriate emotional responses.
- Schizophrenics tend to *withdraw* from contact with others.

The symptoms follow two courses: process schizophrenia develops symptoms early in life, with a gradual withdrawal from the world; and [s] _____ has a sudden and conspicuous onset of symptoms. Reactive schizophrenia responds well to treatment; process schizophrenia is more difficult to treat.

Schizophrenia is recognized to have both biological and psychological components at its root. The biological components are suggested by the fact that schizophrenia is more common in some families than others. This suggests a genetic link to the disease. Another biological explanation suggests the presence of a chemical imbalance or a structural defect. The [t] _____ suggests that schizophrenia occurs when there is an excess activity in the areas of the brain that use dopamine to transmit signals across nerve cells. Drugs that block dopamine action are effective in reducing symptoms. These drugs take effect immediately, but the symptoms linger for several weeks, suggesting that there must be other factors at work. Structural differences in the brains of schizophrenics have also been found.

330

Evaluate

_____ 1.   hypochondria   a.   Characterized by actual physical disturbances.

_____ 2.   somatoform disorder   b.   A failure to remember past experience.

_____ 3.   conversion disorder   c.   Characteristics of two or more distinct personalities.

_____ 4.   dissociative identity disorder   d.   A misinterpretation of normal aches and pains.

_____ 5.   dissociative amnesia   e.   Psychological difficulties that take on physical form.

Rethink

38-1   Do you think the behavioral perspective would be effective in dealing with dissociative disorders? Why or why not? Which perspective do you think would be the most promising for this type of disorder?

38-2   Do any of the explanations of schizophrenia offer the promise of a treatment or cure of the disorder? Do any of the explanations permit us to predict who will be affected by the disorder? How is explanation different from treatment and prediction?

38-3   Personality disorders are often not apparent to others, and many people with these problems seem to live basically normal lives and are not a threat to others. If these people can function well in society, why should they be considered psychologically disordered?

Spotlight on Terminology and Language—ESL Pointers

The Major Psychological Disorders

Page 469 "Instead, during an attack, such as the ones experienced by Sally in the case described earlier, anxiety suddenly—and often without warning—rises to a peak, and an individual feels a sense of **impending**, unavoidable doom."

The event is **impending**; it is imminent, approaching rapidly.

Page 469 "In other cases, though, people with the disorder feel that something dreadful is about to happen but can't identify the reason, experiencing 'free-floating' anxiety."

Free-floating anxiety is anxiety without an apparent or identifiable cause.

Page 469 "Because of heightened muscle tension and arousal, individuals with generalized anxiety disorder may develop headaches, dizziness, heart **palpitations**, or insomnia."

Heart **palpitations** are a fast or irregular heartbeat. Heart **palpitations** may occur in response to anxiety.

Page 469 "In obsessive-compulsive disorder, people are **plagued** by unwanted thoughts, called obsessions, or feel that they must carry out actions, termed compulsions, against their will."

These symptoms **plague** the recipient; they're very bothersome.

Page 469 "As part of an obsessive-compulsive disorder, people may also experience compulsions, **irresistible** urges to repeatedly carry out some act that seems strange and unreasonable, even to them."

Irresistible urges are overwhelming urges—a person plagued with **irresistible** urges finds they must carry out some compulsion.

Page 470 "She would then thoroughly scrub her body, starting at her feet and working **meticulously** up to the top of her head, using certain washcloths for certain areas of her body."

Meticulously is painstakingly carefully.

Page 471 "Although such **compulsive rituals** lead to some immediate reduction of anxiety, in the long term the anxiety returns."

A **compulsive ritual** is a habit or behavior that must be performed.

Page 471 "In fact people with severe cases lead lives filled with **unrelenting** tension (Goodman, Rudorfer, & Maser, 1999; Penzel, 2000)."

Unrelenting is insistent and merciless.

Page 472 "For instance, a person in good health who wakes up blind may react in a **bland**, matter-of-fact way."

They may react in a **bland** way; they may react very mildly to this symptom.

Page 473 "Their emotional **volatility** leads to impulsive and self-destructive behavior."

Because of their emotional **volatility**, their moods and tempers are unpredictable and changeable.

Module 39: Psychological Disorders in Perspective

The Prevalence of Psychological Disorders: The Mental State of the Union
The Social and Cultural Context of Psychological Disorders

Exploring Diversity: *DSM* and Culture—and the Culture of *DSM*

Becoming an Informed Consumer of Psychology: Deciding When You Need Help

- *How prevalent are psychological disorders?*
- *What indicators signal a need for the help of a mental-health practitioner?*

Psychological Disorders in Perspective

Other forms of abnormal behavior described by the DSM-IV include **[a]** _____,

[b] _____, and **[c]** _____. The disorders in the *DSM-IV*
reflect late-20th-century thinking. There was also significant controversy during its development.
One controversial disorder was "self-defeating personality disorder," which referred to people in
abusive relationships. This disorder was not placed in the *DSM-IV*. The other disorder was
"premenstrual dysphoric disorder," or premenstrual syndrome. This disorder was included. The
Exploring Diversity section discusses the differences between cultures in the nature of abnormal
behavior.

Determining the number of people with signs of psychological disorders is a difficult task. A
survey of 8,000 Americans found that 30 percent currently had a mental disorder, and a total of
48 percent had experienced a disorder at some time in their lives.

The decision concerning if and when to seek help for psychological disorders is difficult, but
several guidelines should help. If the following signals are present, help should be considered:
long-term feelings of distress that interfere with functioning, occasions when stress is
overwhelming, prolonged depression, withdrawal from others, chronic physical problems, a fear
or phobia that prevents normal functioning, feelings that other people are talking about the
person or are out to get the person, or the inability to interact effectively with others.

Evaluate

_____ 1. premenstrual disphoric disorder

_____ 2. anxiety disorder

_____ 3. *Diagnostic and Statistical Manual IV*

_____ 4. depression

_____ 5. self-defeating personality disorder

a. Directory where the specific nature of the disorders is a reflection of 20th-century Western values.

b. Removed from *DSM-IV*, applied to cause in which individuals in unpleasant or demeaning situations take no action.

c. Controversial inclusion to *DSM-IV*.

d. One of four categories found in all cultures includes schizophrenia, dipolar disorder, depression.

e. Most common of all psychological disorders.

Rethink

39-1   Why is inclusion in the *DSM-IV* of "borderline" disorders such as self-defeating personality disorder and premenstrual dysphoric disorder so controversial and political? What disadvantages does inclusion bring? Does inclusion bring any benefits?

39-2   What societal changes would have to occur for psychological disorders to be regarded as the equivalent of appendicitis or another treatable physical disorder? Would you have reservations voting for someone who has been treated for a major psychological disorder for president of the United States? Why?

Spotlight on Terminology and Language—ESL Pointers

Psychological Disorders in Perspective

Page 487 "That's the conclusion drawn from a **massive study** on the prevalence of psychological disorders."

A **massive study** would be a study based on a large population.

Page 487 "In addition, 30 percent experience a disorder in any particular year, and the number of people who experience **simultaneous** multiple disorders (known as comorbidity) is significant (Kessler et al., 1994; Welkowitz et al., 2000)."

Simultaneous disorders are problems occurring or existing at the same time.

Page 489 "Furthermore, some critics complained that use of the label had the effect of **condemning** targets of abuse for their **plight**—a blame-the-victim phenomenon—and as a result, the category was removed from the manual."

When you **condemn** someone, you consider them guilty. You blame that person for something.

Plight is a difficult or dangerous situation or predicament.

Page 490 "Most often, of course, your concerns will be **unwarranted**."

Unwarranted is uncalled-for, or unjustifiable.

Page 490 "On the other hand, many people do have problems that **merit** concern, and in such cases it is important to consider the possibility that professional help is warranted.

When something **merits** thinking about, it deserves more consideration.

Test your knowledge of the material in this set of modules by answering these questions. These questions have been placed in three Practice Tests. The first two tests consist of questions that will test your recall of factual knowledge. The third test contains questions that are challenging and primarily test for conceptual knowledge and your ability to apply that knowledge. Check your answers and review the feedback using the Answer Key in the following pages of the *Study Guide*.

PRACTICE TEST 1:

1. Mr. Smith reports that he suffers from the constant fear of illness, and he misinterprets normal aches and pains. He suffers from:
   a. conversion disorder.
   b. hypochondriasis.
   c. somatoform disorder.
   d. phobic disorder.

2. When the Titanic sank in 1912, some male passengers saved themselves at the expense of women and children, contrary to the Victorian standard of manly heroism. This behavior was abnormal because it was:
   a. very different from average.
   b. insane.
   c. opposed to an ideal.
   d. severely uncomfortable.

3. The therapists have assured his family that Kenneth's abnormal behavior is related to an endocrine system malfunction. His problem best fits the:
   a. medical model of abnormality.
   b. psychoanalytic model of abnormality.
   c. behavioral model of abnormality.
   d. sociocultural model of abnormality.

4. The _____ perspective of abnormality suggests that when an individual displays the symptoms of abnormal behavior, the diagnosed causes are physiological.
   a. humanistic
   b. medical
   c. psychoanalytic
   d. sociocultural

5. Which of the following approaches of abnormality is **least** likely to see the therapist as the expert who cures the patient?
   a. the behavioral approaches
   b. the humanistic approaches
   c. the medical approaches
   d. the psychoanalytic approaches

6. Tory and Dave Joshal, siblings who grew up in a very disruptive environment, have discovered that the sources of their strange beliefs or actions are hidden conflicts that are carried over from there childhood, according to:
   a. the psychoanalytic approaches.
   b. the humanistic approaches.
   c. the cognitive approaches.
   d. the behavioral approaches.

7. Many people with psychological disorders come from broken homes and low-income backgrounds. To understand the effects of these and similar conditions on abnormal behavior, a comprehensive diagnosis must include insights from the:
   a. behavioral approaches.
   b. psychoanalytic approaches.
   c. humanistic approaches.
   d. sociocultural approaches.

8. In the *DSM-IV,* there are approximately _____ different diagnostic categories.
   a. 50
   b. 100
   c. 200
   d. 500

9. Kirsten has been told by her therapist that her nervousness and fears that have no apparent justification and impair her normal daily functioning are symptoms of a:
   a. psychosomatic disorder.
   c. anxiety disorder.
   b. personality disorder.
   d. neurotic disorder.

10. The main character in the movie *Sybil* suffered from:
   a. schizophrenia.
   c. disordered personality.
   b. psychogenic personality.
   d. dissociative identity disorder.

11. Kiesha often has feelings of impending doom or even death paired with sudden and overwhelming bodily reactions. These are typical symptoms of:
   a. obsessive-compulsive disorder.
   c. personality disorder.
   b. panic attack.
   d. generalized anxiety disorder.

12. Isaiah, a Chicago native, was unable to account for his actions in the past three weeks or figure out how he arrived in Tucson, Arizona, but could recall memories before his amnesia. This description exemplifies:
   a. dissociative identity disorder.
   c. hypochondriasis.
   b. dissociative fugue.
   d. panic attack.

13. An individual who has a bipolar disorder is one who has:
   a. opposing phobias.
   c. a split personality.
   b. alternation of mania and depression.
   d. alternation of phobia and panic.

14. _____ schizophrenia is characterized by gradual onset, general withdrawal from the world, blunted emotions, and poor prognosis.
   a. Paranoid
   c. Process
   b. Catatonic
   d. Reactive

15. The belief that Bigfoot enters the house during the night and contaminates any food that has been left in the refrigerator would be regarded as a:
   a. compulsion.
   c. delusion.
   b. hallucination.
   d. early sign of narcissism.

____ 16. dissociative fugue

____ 17. anxiety

____ 18. mood disorder

____ 19. mania

____ 20. bipolar disorder

a. A disorder in which a person alternates between euphoric feelings of mania and bouts of depression.

b. Affective disturbance severe enough to interfere with normal living.

c. A condition in which people take sudden, impulsive trips, sometimes assuming a new identity.

d. An extended state of intense euphoria and elation.

e. A feeling of apprehension or tension.

21. A constant fear of illness and the misinterpretation of normal aches and pains would be considered _____.

22. The _____ study illustrated that placing labels on individuals influences how their actions are perceived and interpreted.

23. The intense but real fear Megan felt at just the thought of an airplane flight is known as a

_____.

24. Men and women whose lives seem to center around their worry may suffer from

_____. `

25. People experiencing _____ feel intense happiness, power, invulnerability, and
energy.

26. Discuss the implications of Rosenhan's study, in which he and seven other individuals faked
mental illness in order to test the ability of mental hospitals to distinguish abnormal from
normal behavior and the effects of labeling. What are the scientific issues related to his study?
Are there any ethical issues?

PRACTICE TEST 2:

1. "Mental illness" as a description of a person implies that:
   a. demons and devils exert their evil influence on the body through medical ailments,
      especially ailments of the nervous system.
   b. the target person suffers a lack of unconditional positive regard.
   c. the person has bizarre thoughts but not bizarre behavior.
   d. the speaker or writer accepts the medical model.

2. The main difference between panic disorder and generalized anxiety disorder is that generalized
   anxiety is:
   a. more intense than panic.
   b. continuous, whereas panic is short-term.
   c. triggered by alcohol, whereas panic is triggered by social events.
   d. dissociative, whereas panic is schizophrenic.

3. Which of the following approaches in the study of abnormality is likely to hold most strongly
   to the concept that the patient has little control over his or her actions?
   a. the medical approaches   c. the behavioral approaches
   b. the sociocultural approaches   d. the humanistic approaches

4. According to the psychoanalytic model of abnormality, abnormal behavior derives from:
   a. failure to develop logical thought processes.
   b. physiological malfunctions.
   c. unresolved childhood conflicts.
   d. confusion in the collective unconscious.

5. Which of the following models of abnormality is most likely to emphasize the patient's
   responsibility and participation in the treatment?
   a. the medical model   c. the behavioral model
   b. the psychoanalytic model   d. the humanistic model

6. Proponents of which therapeutic approach are most likely to take the position that there is no
   such thing as abnormal behavior?
   a. the sociocultural approach   c. the behavioral approach
   b. the psychoanalytic approach d. the medical approach

338

7. Dr. Gaipo uses the *DSM-IV* classifications primarily to:
   a. show the causes of and to treat abnormality.
   b. classify and identify causes of abnormality.
   c. classify and describe abnormality.
   d. describe and treat abnormality.

8. The Rosenhan (1973) study in which normal individuals were admitted to mental hospitals showed that:
   a. therapeutic techniques that improve disordered patients can be applied by normal people to make them even better adjusted than they were at first.
   b. mental patients served as models for each others' strange behaviors.
   c. the "mental patient" label affects how ordinary acts are perceived.
   d the *DSM-IV* categories are prone to stability and change.

9. Which of the following is **not** a reasonable criticism of the *DSM-IV* ?
   a. Mental disorders are classified into a "category" rather than along a continuum.
   b. The *DSM-IV* materials usually do not reflect changing views in society about mental disorders, since the manual is updated only every 15 years.
   c. The *DSM-IV* system of classification may be too heavily influenced by the medical model.
   d. A diagnosis may become an explanation for a problem.

10. Mr. Carney has been diagnosed with a disorder that shares a common feature with all other dissociative disorders in that:
    a. their hereditary basis is well-known and documented.
    b. an obsessive-compulsive disorder usually precedes the onset of any dissociative disorder.
    c. they tend to occur in persons who are poor and have large families.
    d. they allow the person to escape from anxiety-producing situations.

11. Hannah has been suffering from psychological difficulties that take on a physical form, but doctors have found no actual physical or physiological abnormality. These difficulties are called:
    a. somatoform disorders.   c. psychophysical disorders.
    b. psychological disorders.   d. freeform disorders.

12. Together, dissociative identity disorder, amnesia, and dissociative fugue are called:
    a. depressive disorders.   c. somatoform disorders.
    b. schizophrenic disorders.   d. dissociative disorders.

13. Mania and bipolar disorder differ mainly in:
    a. the sense that mania applies to both genders but bipolar applies to men.
    b. the fact that mania has a psychological origin but bipolar is biological.
    c. the stability of the emotional state.
    d. the sense that one is a personality disorder, whereas the other is a mood disorder.

14. Convicted murderers like Ted Bundy and John Wayne Gacy have been diagnosed as sociopaths. They were able to fool the lie detector test because they:
    a. feel stress or anxiety more or less continuously.
    b. are psychologically sophisticated; many have studied the *DSM-IV*.
    c. feel no guilt or remorse.
    d. have lost touch with reality.

15. Which mental disturbance is most likely to result in the afflicted person's using language in ways that do **not** follow conventional linguistic rules?
    a. schizophrenia
    b. dissociative identity disorder
    c. dissociative fugue
    d. depressive disorder

____ 16. learned helplessness

____ 17. process schizophrenia

____ 18. reactive schizophrenia

____ 19. dopamine hypothesis

____ 20. predisposition model of schizophrenia

a. Suggests that individuals may inherit tendencies that make them vulnerable to environmental stress factors.

b. Onset of symptoms is sudden and conspicuous.

c. Symptoms begin early in life and develop slowly.

d. Suggests that schizophrenia occurs when excess activity occurs in certain areas of the brain.

e. A state in which people give up fighting stress, believing it to be inescapable, leading to depression.

21. Together, dissociative identity disorder, amnesia, and dissociative fugue are called

_____.

22. Critics suggest that the _____ compartmentalizes people into inflexible all-or-nothing categories.

23. _____, which are brought about by specific objects or situations, can last from a few seconds to hours.

24. A person with _____ may actually carry several pairs of eyeglasses because vision changes with each personality.

25. One approach used to explain the disorder depression is the _____ approach, which suggests that depression is the result of feelings of loss.

26. What can research with groups of twins, some reared together and some reared apart, tell researchers about the causes of schizophrenia?

PRACTICE TEST 3: Conceptual, Applied, and Challenging Questions

1. Schizophrenia produces many dramatic and debilitating changes in a person affected with this disorder. Which alternative is **not** one of them?
    a. delusions
    b. dissociative identity disorder
    c. decline from an earlier level of functioning
    d. withdrawal

2. Which statement is **not** consistent with the sociocultural model of abnormality?
    a. Behavior is shaped by our family, by society, and by the culture in which we live.
    b. There is something wrong with a society that is unwilling to tolerate deviant behavior.
    c. Competing psychic forces within the troubled individual erode personal standards and values.
    d. Abnormal behaviors are more prevalent among some social classes than others.

3. Caroline was beginning her SAT exams when she suddenly became extremely anxious and felt a sense of impending, unavoidable doom. Her heart beat rapidly, she was short of breath, she became faint and dizzy, and she felt as if she might die. Caroline was experiencing:
   a. phobic disorder.
   b. panic disorder.
   c. generalized anxiety disorder.
   d. obsessive-compulsive disorder.

4. "The kinds of stresses and conflicts that people experience in their daily interactions with others can promote and maintain abnormal behavior." This statement is consistent with the _____ model of abnormality.
   a. sociocultural
   b. behavioral
   c. humanistic
   d. psychoanalytic

5. Dr. Keane, a psychiatrist, listened patiently as Myriah revealed a series of episodes involving irrational fears of snakes. Dr. Keane probably labeled Myriah's symptoms as:
   a. schizophrenic reactions.
   b. phobic reactions.
   c. organic reactions.
   d. obsessive-compulsive reactions.

6. Scott is terrified to ride in an elevator in any building. He is especially bothered by the small, confined space and the fact that he is "trapped" until the elevator doors open. Usually, he avoids this unpleasantness by refusing to ride in elevators. Scott is experiencing:
   a. phobic disorder.
   b. panic disorder.
   c. obsessive-compulsive disorder.
   d. tension disorder.

7. Mr. Lombardi, a lawyer in a large, prosperous law practice, finds that two or three hours before an important appearance in court, he cannot talk. The firm's doctor cannot find any medical reason for this problem. The doctor is also surprised that the lawyer seems unconcerned. If the lawyer's symptoms are the result of a psychological disorder, it would most likely be diagnosed as:
   a. somatoform disorder.
   b. conversion disorder.
   c. panic disorder.
   d. obsessive-compulsive disorder.

8. Marlane has been tense and anxious during her professors' lectures, and it is causing her to have a difficult time at college. She has been much better lately because she distracts herself by counting the number of times her professors say "the" during their lectures. Marlane's "counting" suggests she is experiencing:
   a. panic disorder
   b. phobic disorder.
   c. obsessive-compulsive disorder.
   d. generalized anxiety disorder.

9. The most frequent mental disorder in America after depression is:
   a. bipolar disorder.
   b. obsessive-compulsive disorder.
   c. paranoid schizophrenia.
   d. alcohol dependence.

10. What is one difference between dissociative fugue and dissociative amnesia?
   a. In fugue, memory can be restored with drugs.
   b. In amnesia, the memory loss is temporary.
   c. In fugue, past memory is eventually regained.
   d. In amnesia, the memories are physically lost.

11. Process schizophrenia is different from reactive schizophrenia because with reactive schizophrenia, the patient:
   a. experiences a sudden and conspicuous onset of symptoms.
   b. is less withdrawn.
   c. may be dangerously aggressive and abusive to others.
   d. is less likely to have a hereditary basis for the disorder.

12. When minor symptoms of schizophrenia follow a severe case or episode, the disorder is called:
    a. disorganized schizophrenia.
    c. paranoid schizophrenia.
    b. catatonic schizophrenia.
    d. residual schizophrenia.

13. Which of the following accounts of schizophrenia assumes that inappropriate behavior is learned by attending to stimuli that are not related to normal social interaction?
    a. learned helplessness hypothesis
    c. predisposition model
    b. dopamine hypothesis
    d. learned-inattention theory

14. Personality disorder is best characterized by:
    a. firmly held beliefs with little basis in reality.
    b. a mixture of symptoms of schizophrenia.
    c. a set of inflexible, maladaptive traits.
    d. an extended sense of euphoria and elation.

15. Tanisha is uncooperative, refuses to speak to her coworkers, and frequently disrupts meetings with distracting questions and irrelevant challenges. However, she is fully capable of doing all her work and maintains a reasonable family life. She uses her status as a female to threaten her superiors with "harassment" if they question what she is doing, and she exploits anyone who is unwitting enough to be caught in her self-promotion schemes. Because she believes she can do whatever she can get away with doing, which of the following categories best fits her?
    a. sociopathic personality disorder
    c. premenstrual dysphoric disorder
    b. self-defeating personality disorder
    d. dissociative identity disorder

_____ 16. personality disorder
_____ 17. antisocial or sociopathic personality disorder
_____ 18. narcissistic personality disorder
_____ 19. borderline personality disorder

a. Characterized by a set of inflexible, maladaptive traits that keep a person from functioning properly in society.

b. Inability to develop a secure sense of self.

c. Characterized by an exaggerated sense of self and an inability to experience empathy for others.

d. Individuals display no regard for moral and ethical rules or for the rights of others.

20. The _____ perspective suggests that when an individual displays symptoms of abnormal behavior, the cause will be found in a medical exam.

21. Nyringian feels apprehensive or tense every time he has to speak publicly; he is experiencing _____.

22. Big Joe suffers from _____, which often causes him such anxiety that he is unable to leave his home.

23. The term _____ is sometimes used to describe the last memories of dissociative amnesia.

24. The psychologist _____ has proposed that faulty cognitions underlie people's depressed feelings.

25. Describe the types of schizophrenia, its symptoms, and its causes. Compare the differing theories concerning the cause of schizophrenia.

■ ANSWER KEY: MODULES 37, 38, AND 39

Module 37:	Module 38:	[m] Dissociative amnesia	Module 39:
[a] medical model	[a] Generalized anxiety	[n] Dissociative fugue	[a] psychoactive
[b] psychoanalytic model	disorder	[o] mood disorders	substance-use
[c] behavioral model	[b] Panic disorder	[p] Mania	disorder
[d] cognitive model	[c] Phobic disorder	[q] learned helplessness	[b] sexual disorders
[e] humanistic model	[d] phobia	[r] hallucinations	[c] organic mental
[f] sociocultural model	[e] Obsessive-compulsive	[s] reactive schizophrenia	disorders
[g] *Diagnostic and*	disorder	[t] dopamine hypothesis	
Statistical Manual of	[f] Obsessions		Evaluate
Mental Disorders,	[g] Compulsions		1. c
Fourth Edition (DSM-	[h] Hypochondriasis	Evaluate	2. d
IV)	[i] somatoform disorders		3. a
	[j] conversion disorder	1. d	4. e
Evaluate	[k] Dissociative disorders	2. e	5. b
1. d	[l] Dissociative identity	3. a	
2. a	disorder	4. c	
3. e		5. b	
4. c			
5. f			
6. b			

Selected Rethink Answers

37-1   Proponents of each perspective on the topic of shoplifting:
Medical—might view shoplifting as arising from organic, physiological conditions.
Psychoanalytic—would view shoplifting as a conflict in the unconscious and the adequacy of ego development.
Cognitive—would focus on the irrational conscious thoughts that preceded the shoplifting.
Humanistic—would suggest that the individual take control and responsibility for the shoplifting.
Sociocultural—shoplifting was the result of sociocultural forces such as income or a broken home.

38-3   People who have personality disorders have maladaptive personality traits that do not permit them to function appropriately as members of society. They have no regard for the moral and ethical rules of society or the rights of others. They are manipulative and deceptive; have a lack of guilt or anxiety over wrong-doing; are often impulsively distrustful and controlling, demanding, eccentric, obnoxious, or difficult.

Practice Test 1:

1.   b   mod. 38 p. 471
a.   Incorrect. This is a form of somatoform disorder.
*b.   Correct. Hypochondriacs suffer every ache as a major disease.
c.   Incorrect. This is the disorder in which psychological problems are manifest as physical systems.
d.   Incorrect. Phobic disorder is a fear of a specific event or stimulus.

2.   c   mod. 37 p. 458
a.   Incorrect. It probably was not different from how people would behave on average.
b.   Incorrect. Such behavior is quite sane.
*c.   Correct. The ideal was for men to sacrifice themselves for their wives and children.
d.   Incorrect. Although many were probably uncomfortable after the fact, they were still alive.

3.   a   mod. 37 p. 460
*a.   Correct. The medical model views abnormal behavior as arising from organic, physiological conditions.
b.   Incorrect. The psychoanalytic view of abnormality depends on the extremes of conflict in the unconscious and the adequacy of ego development.
c.   Incorrect. The behavioral model of abnormality views abnormality as a result of inappropriate, learned behaviors.
d.   Incorrect. The sociocultural view of abnormality views abnormality as the result of sociocultural forces, often with the view that social systems are themselves abnormal.

4. b   mod. 37 p. 460
a. Incorrect. The humanistic view would understand abnormality as the self in conflict.
*b. Correct. The medical approach seeks to understand abnormality as a result of organic, physiological causes.
c. Incorrect. The psychoanalytic view of abnormality depends on the extremes of conflict in the unconscious and the adequacy of ego development.
d. Incorrect. The sociocultural view of abnormality views abnormality as the result of sociocultural forces, often with the view that social systems are themselves abnormal.

5. b   mod. 39 p. 462
a. Incorrect. The behavioral model utilizes a behavioral expert who can help modify behavior.
*b. Correct. The humanistic model views the client as the person capable of effecting a cure; the humanistic therapist is there to facilitate.
c. Incorrect. The medical model depends on a medical professional.
d. Incorrect. The psychoanalytic model requires a trained psychoanalyst.

6. a   mod. 37 p. 461
*a. Correct. Psychodynamic views depend on hidden or unconscious conflicts as the cause of most behavior.
b. Incorrect. The humanistic view would embrace the notion of "open" rather than hidden conflicts.
c. Incorrect. The cognitive model would accept the idea of strange beliefs, but it would focus on the irrational conscious thoughts.
d. Incorrect. The behavioral model would suggest that all strange behaviors were learned.

7. d   mod. 37 p. 462
a. Incorrect. However, a behaviorist should be able to identify the system of rewards and punishments that contribute to these patterns.
b. Incorrect. The psychoanalyst is unlikely to be concerned with the socioeconomic status in which the conditions occur.
c. Incorrect. The humanistic model would not be interested in the socioeconomic conditions in which the abnormality occurs.
*d. Correct. The sociocultural model emphasizes the contributions made by social and economic factors such as income and broken homes.

8. c   mod. 37 p. 463
a. Incorrect. Try 200.
b. Incorrect. Try 200.
*c. Correct. The 200 categories suggest an increasing attention to a wide range of diseases.
d. Incorrect. Try 200.

9. c   mod. 38 p. 467
a. Incorrect. A psychosomatic disorder involves a physical symptom with no apparent physical cause.
b. Incorrect. A personality disorder involves a long-standing, habitual, and maladaptive personality pattern.
*c. Correct. This describes an anxiety disorder.
d. Incorrect. The term "neurotic disorder" is no longer used.

10. d   mod. 38 p. 472
a. Incorrect. Schizophrenia involves disordered thought, not multiple personalities.
b. Incorrect. Not quite sure what this is, but Sybil did not have it.
c. Incorrect. This is not an official diagnostic category.
*d. Correct. Once called "multiple personality," this problem is increasingly common.

11. b   mod. 38 p. 468
a. Incorrect. In obsessive-compulsive disorder, the sufferer has uncontrollable thoughts and compulsions to act.
*b. Correct. The panic attack can be without warning and without apparent cause.
c. Incorrect. A personality disorder involves a long-standing, habitual, and maladaptive personality pattern.
d. Incorrect. A generalized anxiety disorder involves long-standing, consistent anxiety without an apparent cause or source.

12. b   mod. 38 p. 473
a. Incorrect. A dissociative identity disorder is marked by the presence of two or more personalities, not the dissociative fugue described.
*b. Correct. In dissociative fugue, the individual disappears, often just wondering off, and later reappears, without any knowledge of why he or she left.
c. Incorrect. Someone suffering hypochondriasis has symptoms without physical illness.
d. Incorrect. Panic attack is marked by feelings of impending doom or even death, paired with sudden and overwhelming bodily reactions.

13. b   mod. 38 p. 475
a. Incorrect. Or maybe, alternating fears of penguins and polar bears?
*b. Correct. The "bipolar" aspect is the swing from the high mood of mania to the depths of depression.
c. Incorrect. See answer b.
d. Incorrect. See answer b.

14. c   mod. 38 p. 478
a. Incorrect. Paranoid schizophrenia is characterized by delusions of persecution or grandeur.
b. Incorrect. Catatonic schizophrenia is characterized by waxy flexibility and autistic withdrawal.
*c. Correct. This statement describes process schizophrenia.
d. Incorrect. Reactive schizophrenia usually has a quicker onset and has a better prognosis than the process schizophrenia described in the item.

15. c   mod. 38 p. 479
a. Incorrect. A compulsion is an idea that seems to have a life of its own—the sufferer gets up every night to hide the remote.
b. Incorrect. The hallucination is just seeing Bigfoot.
*c. Correct. Very delusional. Everyone knows Bigfoot belongs in garages.
d. Incorrect. Only if you are Bigfoot.

16. c   mod. 38 p. 473
17. e   mod. 38 p. 467
18. b   mod. 38 p. 473
19. d   mod. 38 p. 474
20. a   mod. 38 p. 475
21. Hypochondriasis   mod. 38 p. 471
22. Rosenhan   mod. 37 p. 464
23. phobia   mod. 38 p. 468
24. generalized anxiety disorder   mod. 38 p. 469
25. Mania   mod. 38 p. 474

26.
▪ The Rosenhan study suggested that mental health workers label their clients with rather unshakable labels. The labels also lead to interpretations of behavior that continue to confirm the diagnosis (note that some stayed for many weeks even though they only complained of the symptom once on admission to the hospital).
▪ The issues of deception and the use of a subject who had not given consent are major problems.
▪ A brief examination of the study does not explain the contexts involved: Few people voluntarily walk into a mental hospital and complain of a major symptom. The sudden disappearance of the symptom could be considered abnormal as well.

Practice Test 2:
1. d   mod. 37 p. 460
a. Incorrect. Centuries ago, maybe.
b. Incorrect. Rogers never intended for this to be a meaning of his concept.
c. Incorrect. The person may have bizarre behavior as well.
*d. Correct. The notion of psychological disorders being an "illness" suggests the medical view.

2. b   mod. 38 p. 468
a. Incorrect. Panic is probably the more intense.
*b. Correct. Panic involves symptoms that last for a brief period and then disappear until the next incident.
c. Incorrect. Generalized anxiety disorder is not caused by alcohol.
d. Incorrect. Panic disorder is not schizophrenic, although persons suffering from schizophrenia may experience panic.

3. a   mod. 37 p. 460
*a. Correct. If the disease is organic and physiological, then abnormal behaviors are beyond the individual's control.
b. Incorrect. The sociocultural model would accept that the individual has control over his or her actions, even though those actions may be present partly because of sociocultural forces.
c. Incorrect. The behavioral model allows for the individual to take control of his or her actions through behavior modification and self-regulation.
d. Incorrect. The humanistic model suggests that the individual must ultimately take control and responsibility for his or her actions.

4. c   mod. 37 p. 461
a. Incorrect. This explanation is more consistent with a cognitive model.
b. Incorrect. This explanation is more consistent with the medical model.
*c. Correct. Unresolved childhood conflicts would be repressed in the unconscious, and their efforts to be expressed and the costs of keeping them repressed can lead to abnormalities.
d. Incorrect. The unconscious is confused and confusing for both healthy and psychologically disturbed individuals.

5. d   mod. 37 p. 462
a. Incorrect. The medical model is currently focused on treatment through medication, and the only role the patient has is to take the drugs.
b. Incorrect. The psychoanalyst directs the patient toward an understanding of the problem.
c. Incorrect. The behavioral model depends on the application of different reward systems to alter the problem.
*d. Correct. The humanistic model views the patient as capable of self-healing and control and having responsibility over his or her actions.

6. a   mod. 37 p. 462
*a. Correct. Some proponents of the sociocultural model claim that the society is sick, not the individual.
b. Incorrect. See answer a.
c. Incorrect. See answer a.
d. Incorrect. See answer a.

7. c   mod. 37 p. 463
a. Incorrect. Treatment is not part of the manual.
b. Incorrect. The causes of abnormality are identified with specific theories, so they have not been addressed in the manual.
*c. Correct. The purpose of the manual is classification and description without implied theories.
d. Incorrect. The manual does not offer treatment.

8. c   mod. 37 p. 464
a. Incorrect. While this may be true in some cases, it is not the conclusion of the Rosenhan study.
b. Incorrect. This may be true, but it was not addressed by the Rosenhan study.
*c. Correct. Labeling carries a stigma that is difficult to erase.
d. Incorrect. The *DSM-IV* categories have little to do with stability and change.

9. b   mod. 37 p. 463
a. Incorrect. Some prefer a continuum approach and are critical of the category approach.
*b. Correct. The manual is updated with greater frequency, and the update is highly sensitive to changing views of society about mental disorders.
c. Incorrect. This is a common complaint, especially among psychologists who prefer a less medical orientation.
d. Incorrect. Often, the diagnosis is viewed as if it provided an analysis of the cause of a disorder.

10. d   mod. 38 p. 472
a. Incorrect. The anxiety that gives rise to them is environmental, but the cause of the illness remains open.
b. Incorrect. Not so.
c. Incorrect. They are equal opportunity disorders.
*d. Correct. They all have some form of escape from anxiety.

11. a   mod. 38 p. 471
*a. Correct. These include hypochondriasis and conversion disorders.
b. Incorrect. The stem describes a psychological disorder known as somatoform disorder, and not all psychological disorders have these symptoms.
c. Incorrect. A disorder related to the study of psychophysics?
d. Incorrect. No such disorder has been recognized.

12. d   mod. 38 p. 472
a. Incorrect. Depressive disorders include major and minor depression.
b. Incorrect. Schizophrenia does not share these disorders with the dissociative category.
c. Incorrect. Somatoform disorders involve a physical symptom without a physical cause, not the dissociation of part of the personality.
*d. Correct. Each of these disorders involves the separation of some part of the personality or memory.

13. c   mod. 38 p. 474
a. Incorrect. Bipolar disorders appear in men and women.
b. Incorrect. Both can have either origin.
*c. Correct. In mania, the state remains high-pitched all the time.
d. Incorrect. Both are mood disorders.

14. c   mod. 38 p. 483
a. Incorrect. They feel stress and anxiety to the same extent that normal individuals experience stress and anxiety.
b. Incorrect. A rare sociopath has bothered to study the *DSM-IV.*
*c. Correct. Guilt or remorse are necessary to trigger the physiological reaction that the polygraph measures.
d. Incorrect. They are quite in touch with reality.

15. a   mod. 38 p. 478
*a. Correct. Some people with schizophrenia have their own private language.
b. Incorrect. People with dissociative identity disorder appear quite normal on the surface.
c. Incorrect. The fugue state results in wandering off, not incoherence.
d. Incorrect. Depressive individuals can become incoherent, but not because of unconventional language use.

16. e   mod. 38 p. 476
17. c   mod. 38 p. 480
18. b   mod. 38 p. 480
19. d   mod. 38 p. 480
20. a   mod. 38 p. 482

21. dissociative disorders   mod. 38 p. 472
22. *DSM-IV*   mod. 37 p. 463
23. Panic attacks   mod. 38 p. 468
24. dissociative identity disorder mod. 38 p. 472
25. Psychoanalytic   mod. 37 p. 461

26. Schizophrenia has both biological and environmental origins.
   • Being more common in families suggests genetic factors seem to be involved.
   • Biochemical or structural abnormality (dopamine hypothesis) or exposure to a virus during pregnancy are suggested causes.
   • Regression to earlier experiences and stages; lack of strong ego, id acts with no concern for reality—inability to cope.
   • Another theory suggests high levels of expressed emotion.
   • Genetic factors may become evident in twins who are reared apart if genetic factors held when environments changed.
   • Different family lifestyles may indicate certain factors that precipitate the condition in twins who have been identified with genetic factors that predispose them to schizophrenia.

Practice Test 3:
1. b   mod. 38 p. 472
a. Incorrect. This is one of the major symptoms.
*b. Correct. Dissociative identity disorder, also known as multiple personality disorder, is not associated with schizophrenia.
c. Incorrect. This is a common symptom of schizophrenia.
d. Incorrect. This is a common symptom of schizophrenia.

2. c   mod. 38 p. 462
a. Incorrect. This statement is consistent with the sociocultural model.
b. Incorrect. See answer a.
*c. Correct. The sociocultural model recognizes that many aspects of abnormal behavior arise from the conditions of society, even psychic forces within the individual would reflect conflicts in society.
d. Incorrect. See answer a.

3. b   mod. 38 p. 468
a. Incorrect. A phobic disorder is an irrational fear of a specific situation or object.
*b. Correct. This describes a panic attack.
c. Incorrect. Generalized anxiety disorder is very similar to this condition, but it occurs without the rapid heartbeat, shortness of breath, and becoming faint (that is, without the panic).
d. Incorrect. Obsessive-compulsive disorder is marked by uncontrollable thoughts and compulsions to carry out ritualistic behaviors, not by panic.

4. a   mod. 37 p. 462
*a. Correct. The sociocultural model of abnormality emphasizes the interactions between people as well as the conditions of society as contributors to abnormal behavior.
b. Incorrect. The behavioral model would attribute abnormal behavior to faulty learning.
c. Incorrect. The humanistic model would attribute abnormal behavior to conflicts within the self.
d. Incorrect. The psychoanalytic model would attribute abnormal behavior to inner psychic conflicts.

5. b   mod. 38 p. 468
a. Incorrect. It is possible for someone with schizophrenia to have irrational fears of snakes, but this kind of fear is more likely a phobia.
*b. Correct. A phobia is a persistent, irrational fear of an object or situation.
c. Incorrect. While the psychiatrist is more prone to using a medical model, the term "organic reactions" is not used to describe any known ailment.
d. Incorrect. Obsessive-compulsive disorder is marked by uncontrollable thoughts and compulsions to carry out ritualistic behaviors, not by panic.

6.   a   mod. 38 p. 468
*a.   Correct. A phobia is a persistent, irrational fear of an object or situation.
b.   Incorrect. Panic disorder involves extreme anxiety and a sense of impending, unavoidable doom accompanied by rapid heartbeat, shortness of breath, and becoming faint and dizzy.
c.   Incorrect. Obsessive-compulsive disorder is marked by uncontrollable thoughts and compulsions to carry out ritualistic behaviors, not by panic.
d.   Incorrect. There is no category called tension disorder.

7.   b   mod. 38 p. 471
a.   Incorrect. This falls in the class of somatoform disorders, but another choice offers the specific disorder.
*b.   Correct. In a conversion disorder, psychological problems are converted into physical problems, often without the sufferer showing the concern one might expect if the situation were a truly serious physical condition.
c.   Incorrect. Panic disorder involves extreme anxiety and a sense of impending, unavoidable doom accompanied by rapid heartbeat, shortness of breath, and becoming faint and dizzy.
d.   Incorrect. Obsessive-compulsive disorder is marked by uncontrollable thoughts and compulsions to carry out ritualistic behaviors, not by loss of voice.

8.   c   mod. 38 p. 469
a.   Incorrect. Panic disorder involves extreme anxiety and a sense of impending, unavoidable doom accompanied by rapid heartbeat, shortness of breath, and becoming faint and dizzy.
b.   Incorrect. A phobia is a persistent, irrational fear of an object or situation.
*c.   Correct. Obsessive-compulsive disorder is marked by uncontrollable thoughts and compulsions to carry out ritualistic behaviors, like counting the number of times the professor says "the" in the lecture.
d.   Incorrect. Generalized anxiety is the feeling that something bad is about to happen without any direct object causing the fear or anxiety.

9.   d   mod. 38 p. 487
a.   Incorrect. Less than 1 percent at any given time.
b.   Incorrect. Less than 1 percent at any given time.
c.   Incorrect. Less than 1 percent at any given time.
*d.   Correct. As many as 7 percent of the population may experience alcohol dependence each year.

10.   c   mod. 38 p. 472
a.   Incorrect. Drugs are not typically used in this state, because the condition is not typically recognized until the memory is recovered.
b.   Incorrect. In dissociative amnesia, the loss can be permanent.
*c.   Correct. The fugue state helps the person escape an anxiety-producing situation, and sometime after the escape, memory can be recovered.
d.   Incorrect. In dissociative amnesia, the memories are considered present, but psychologically blocked.

11.   a   mod. 38 p. 478
*a.   Correct. Reactive schizophrenia also has a better treatment outlook.
b.   Incorrect. Although process schizophrenia is marked by gradual withdrawal, reactive schizophrenia can be just as withdrawn.
c.   Incorrect. No type of schizophrenia is necessarily aggressive or abusive.
d.   Incorrect. Neither type has been shown to be more hereditary than the other.

12.   d   mod. 38 p. 478
a.   Incorrect. Disorganized schizophrenia involves inappropriate laughter and giggling, silliness, incoherent speech, infantile behavior, and strange behaviors.
b.   Incorrect. Catatonic schizophrenia involves disturbances of movement, sometimes a loss of all motion, sometimes with the opposite extreme of wild, violent movement.
c.   Incorrect. Paranoid schizophrenia is marked by delusions and hallucinations related to persecution or delusions of grandeur, loss of judgment, and unpredictable behavior.
*d.   Correct. Residual schizophrenia displays minor symptoms of schizophrenia after a stressful episode.

13.   d   mod. 38 p. 482
a.   Incorrect. Learned helplessness is used to explain other problems (like depression) more than it is used to explain schizophrenia.
b.   Incorrect. The dopamine hypothesis relates schizophrenia to an excess of dopamine.
c.   Incorrect. The predisposition model suggests that a genetic predisposition exists for developing schizophrenia.
*d.   Correct. This attention to inappropriate social stimuli is the foundation of the learned-inattention theory.

14. c   mod. 38 p. 483
a. Incorrect. This sounds like paranoia.
b. Incorrect. Personality disorder is not considered a mix of schizophrenic symptoms.
*c. Correct. Personality disorders are marked by inflexible, maladaptive personality traits, and these can take several forms.
d. Incorrect. An extended sense of euphoria and elation is found in the manic state of bipolar disorder.

15. a   mod. 38 p. 483
*a. Correct. Tanisha's apparent action without conscience and manipulation of the system are hallmarks of the antisocial or sociopathic personality disorder.
b. Incorrect. This does not describe someone who is self-defeating.
c. Incorrect. because this is not cyclic behavior, it could not be considered premenstrual dysphoric disorder.
d. Incorrect. While having multiple personalities is not ruled out, the condition is better described as sociopathic personality disorder.

16. a   mod. 38 p. 483
17. d   mod. 38 p. 483
18. c   mod. 38 p. 484
19. b   mod. 38 p. 483

20. medical   mod. 37 p. 460
21. anxiety   mod. 38 p. 467
22. agoraphobia   mod. 38 p. 468
23. repressed memories   mod. 38 p. 472
24. Aaron Beck   mod. 38 p. 476

25.
- Describe the major symptoms of schizophrenia.
- Distinguish process and reactive, and examine the list of types.
- Discuss the biological and psychological components.

Treatment of Psychological Disorders

40: Psychotherapy: Psychodynamic, Behavioral, and Cognitive Approaches to Treatment

41: Psychotherapy: Humanistic, Interpersonal, and Group Approaches to Treatment

42: Biomedical Therapy: Biological Approaches to Treatment

Overview

In this set of modules, the treatment of psychological disorders is discussed.

Module 40 presents the psychodynamic approach, which seeks to resolve unconscious conflicts. Also explained are the behavioral approaches, which suggest that the outward behavior must be changed, using behaviors such as aversive conditioning, systematic desensitization, observational learning, and contingency contracting. Cognitive approaches such as rational-emotive therapy and cognitive therapy suggest that the goal of therapy should be to help a person restructure his or her belief system to reflect a more logical, realistic view of the world.

Module 41 offers a discussion of the humanistic approach focusing on issues related to the person's taking responsibility for his or her own actions regarding the meaning of life. Interpersonal therapy focuses on the interpersonal relationships of the individual. Finally, a discussion regarding the benefits of both group and individual therapy is presented.

Module 42 presents the biomedical therapy for the treatment of psychological disorders. Drug therapy has made psychotic patients calmer, alleviated depression, and calmed anxiety. Also, the controversy surrounding electroconvulsive therapy and psychosurgery, treatments of last resort, is presented. Finally, a discussion presents the issues that the community health movement now must cope with in providing care for deinstitutionalized patients. This movement has led to the development of such services as hotlines and campus crisis centers.

To further investigate the topics covered in this chapter, you can visit the related Web sites by visiting the following link: www.mhhe.com/feldmanup6-17links.

Prologue: Conquering Schizophrenia
Looking Ahead

Module 40: Psychotherapy: Psychodynamic, Behavioral, and Cognitive Approaches to Treatment

Psychodynamic Approaches to Therapy
Behavioral Approaches to Therapy
Cognitive Approaches to Therapy

- *What are the goals of psychologically and biologically based treatment approaches?*
- *What are the basic kinds of psychotherapies?*

Psychotherapy: Psychodynamic, Behavioral, and Cognitive Approaches to Treatment

The common goal of therapy is relief of the psychological disorder and enabling individuals to achieve richer, more meaningful lives. Psychologically based therapy is called

[a] _____, a process in which a patient (client) and a professional work together to deal with psychological difficulties. [b] _____ depends on drugs and other medical procedures. Many therapists today draw on the large number of therapies for the approach most suited to the client, and this is considered an [c] _____ to therapy.

[d] _____ assumes that the primary causes of abnormal behavior are unresolved conflicts from the past and anxiety over unconscious impulses. The

[e] _____ that individuals use to guard against anxiety do not bury these anxieties completely, and they emerge in the form of *neurotic symptoms*. Freud said that the way to deal with the unwanted desires and past conflicts was to confront them, to make them conscious. The role of the [f] _____ is then to explore the unconscious conflicts and help the patient understand them. Techniques such as [g] _____ and

[h] _____ are used.

The principles of reinforcement are central to [i] _____, which suggests that both abnormal and normal behavior is learned. To modify abnormal behavior, new behaviors must be learned. Behavioral psychologists are not interested in the past history of the individual, focusing instead on the current behavior.

Classical conditioning principles are applied to behaviors like alcoholism, smoking, and drug abuse, with a technique known as [j] _____. In aversive conditioning, the unwanted behavior is linked with a stimulus that produces an unpleasant response, like a drug that produces vomiting when mixed with alcohol. The long-term effectiveness of the approach is

questionable. The most successful classical conditioning technique is called **[k]** _____,
in which a person is taught to relax and is then gradually exposed to an anxiety-provoking
stimulus. It has been successful with phobias, anxiety disorders, and impotence.

[l] _____ is used in therapy by **[m]** _____ appropriate behaviors.
People can be taught skills and ways of handling anxiety by observing a model cope with the
same situation.

Operant conditioning techniques are used in settings where rewards and punishments can be
controlled. Behavior therapy works well for phobias and compulsions; however, it is not very
effective for deep depression or personality disorders. One example is that of the

[n] _____, in which individuals are rewarded with tokens that can be exchanged for
desired objects or opportunities.

Cognitive approaches to therapy attempt to change faulty cognitions held by patients about
themselves and the world. The therapies are typically based on learning principles and thus are

often called **[o]** _____. **[p]** _____ is one of the best examples of the
cognitive approach. The therapist attempts to restructure the person's belief system into a more
realistic, rational, and logical set of views.

Evaluate

____ 1. biomedical therapy

____ 2. psychodynamic
therapy

____ 3. psychoanalysis

____ 4. behavioral treatment
approaches

____ 5. cognitive approaches to
therapy

a. Basic sources of abnormal behavior are unresolved
past conflicts and anxiety.

b. People's faulty cognitions about themselves and the
world are changed to more accurate ones.

c. Appropriate treatment consists of learning new
behavior or unlearning maladaptive behavior.

d. A form of psychodynamic therapy that often lasts
for many years.

e. Uses drugs and other medical procedures to
improve psychological functioning.

Rethink

40-1 In what ways are psychoanalysis and cognitive therapy similar, and how do they differ?

40-2 How might you examine the reliability of dream interpretation?

Spotlight on Terminology and Language—ESL Pointers

Psychotherapy: Psychodynamic, Behavioral, and Cognitive Approaches to Treatment

Page 497 "But therapy is also provided by people in fields **allied with** psychology, such as psychiatry and social work."

Allied with means related to. Can you identify any other field that might be associated with psychology?

Page 497 "Psychodynamic therapy is based on the **premise**, first suggested by Freud in his psychoanalytic approach to personality, that the primary sources of abnormal behavior are unresolved past conflicts and the possibility that unacceptable unconscious impulses will enter a person's consciousness."

Psychodynamic therapy is based on these basic principles.

Page 497 "How does one **rid oneself** of the anxiety produced by unconscious, unwanted impulses and drives?"

How does one **rid oneself**, or free oneself, of this anxiety?

Page 497 "To Freud, the answer was to **confront** the conflicts and impulses by bringing them out of the unconscious part of the mind and into the conscious part."

To **confront** is to face up to these impulses and conflicts.

Page 498 "They will then be able to 'work through'—understand and rectify—those difficulties.

To **rectify** is to correct, to cure.

Page 498 "Psychoanalysts tell patients to say aloud whatever comes to mind, regardless of its apparent **irrelevance** or senselessness, and the analysts attempt to recognize and label the connections between what a patient says and the patient's unconscious."

Irrelevance is insignificance or unimportance.

Page 499 "Moreover, no **conclusive** evidence shows that psychoanalysis, as originally conceived by Freud in the nineteenth century, works better than other, more recent versions of psychodynamic therapy."

No **conclusive** evidence means no definite, convincing, irrefutable evidence exists.

Page 500 "Furthermore, less **articulate** patients may not do as well as more verbal ones do."

Articulate persons are expressive and communicative. They speak clearly.

Page 500 "Behavioral psychologists do not need to **delve into** people's pasts or their psyches."

When you **delve into** something, you explore it further or verbally probe for more information.

Page 501 "Suppose you bite into your favorite candy bar and find that it is not only **infested** with ants but that you've swallowed a bunch of them?"

Infested with ants means it is bug-ridden.

Module 41: Psychotherapy: Humanistic, Interpersonal, and Group Approaches to Treatment

Humanistic Therapy
Interpersonal Therapy
Group Therapy
Evaluating Psychotherapy: Does Therapy Work?

> **Applying Psychology in the 21st Century:**
> Therapy Online: Is the Internet a Good Place to Get Treatment?

> **Exploring Diversity:** Racial and Ethnic Factors in Treatment: Should Therapists Be Color-Blind?

- *What are the humanistic approaches to treatment?*
- *What is interpersonal therapy?*
- *How does group therapy differ from individual types of therapy?*
- *How effective is therapy, and which kind of therapy works best in a given situation?*

Psychotherapy: Humanistic, Interpersonal, and Group Approaches to Treatment

[a] _____ depends on the perspective of self-responsibility as the basis for treatment. The view is that we control our own behavior, make choices about how to live, and it is up to us to solve our problems. Humanistic therapists see themselves as guides or facilitators.

[b] _____ refers to approaches that do not offer interpretations or answers to problems. First practiced by Carl Rogers, [c] _____ was founded on the nondirective approach providing [d] _____. Rogers attempted to establish a warm and accepting environment in order to enable the client to make realistic and constructive choices about life.

The goal of [e] _____ is to help the client come to grips with freedom, to find his or her place in the world, and to develop a system of values that gives meaning to life. The therapist is more directive, and probes and challenges the client's views.

[f] _____ has the goal of integrating the client's thoughts and feelings into a whole. The approach was developed by Fritz Perls to increase perspectives on a situation. He asked the client to go back and work on unfinished business, playing the part of the angry father and taking other roles in a conflict.

[g] _____ is a form of treatment that has several unrelated people meet with a therapist at the same time. Problems, usually one held in common with all group members, are discussed with the group, while members of the group provide social support.

[h] _____ is a specialized form of group therapy that involves two or more members of a family. Therapists focus on the entire family system rather than only on the family member with the problem, and each family member is expected to contribute to the solution. Family therapists assume that family members engage in set patterns of behavior, and the goal of therapy is to get the family to adopt more constructive behaviors.

Evaluate

_____ 1. rational-emotive therapy

_____ 2. cognitive therapy

_____ 3. client-centered therapy

_____ 4. humanistic therapy

_____ 5. existential therapy

a. Addresses the meaning of life, allowing a client to devise a system of values that gives purpose to his or her life.

b. The therapist reflects back the patient's statements in a way that helps the patient find solutions.

c. People have control of their behavior, can make choices about their lives, and are essentially responsible for solving their own problems.

d. Attempts to restructure one's belief into a more realistic, rational, and logical system.

e. People are taught to change illogical thoughts about themselves and the world.

Rethink

41-1 How can people be successfully treated in group therapy when individuals with the "same" problem are so different? What advantages might group therapy offer over individual therapy?

41-2 List some examples of behavior that might be considered abnormal among members of one cultural or economic group and normal by members of a different cultural or economic group. Suppose that most therapies had been developed by psychologists from minority-culture groups and lower socioeconomic status; how might they differ from current therapies?

Spotlight on Terminology and Language—ESL Pointers

Psychotherapy: Humanistic, Interpersonal, and Group Approaches to Treatment

Page 507 "The many types of therapy that fall into this category have a similar **rationale**: We have control of our own behavior, we can make choices about the kinds of lives we want to live, and it is up to us to solve the difficulties we encounter in our daily lives."

The therapies have a similar **rationale**; they have a similar underlying principle.

Page 508 "By providing a warm and accepting environment, therapists hope to motivate clients **to air** their problems and feelings."

In this client-centered environment, it is hoped patients will **air,** or discuss, their problems and feelings.

Page 508 "In turn, this enables clients to make realistic and **constructive** choices and decisions about the things that bother them in their current lives (Bozarth, Zimring, & Tausch, 2002)."

They will make **constructive** choices, productive and useful choices.

Page 508 "**Furnishing** unconditional positive regard does not mean that therapists must approve of everything their clients say or do."

Furnishing means providing.

Page 509 "The other members of the group provide emotional support and **dispense** advice on ways in which they have coped effectively with similar problems (Yalom, 1997; Free, 2000; Alonso, Alonso, & Piper, 2003)."

They **dispense** advice; other members of the group give out advice.

Page 510 "He is fairly skeptical of psychologists, thinking that a lot of what they say is just **mumbo jumbo**, but he's willing to put his doubts aside and try anything to feel better."

Mumbo jumbo is unnecessarily involved and incomprehensible language, also known as gibberish.

Page 510 "In fact, identifying the single most appropriate form of treatment is a controversial, and still **unresolved**, task for psychologists specializing in psychological disorders."

The issue remains unanswered and the resolution is unclear.

Page 510 "Although others quickly challenged Eysenck's conclusions, his review stimulated a continuing stream of better controlled, more carefully **crafted** studies on the effectiveness of psychotherapy, and today most psychologists agree: Therapy does work."

These studies were well-**crafted**; they were better designed.

Page 511 "Because no single type of psychotherapy is invariable effective, **eclectic** approaches to therapy have become increasingly popular."

An **eclectic** approach is an approach to therapy in which the psychotherapist combines techniques and ideas from many different schools of thought.

Module 42: Biomedical Therapy: Biological Approaches to Treatment

Drug Therapy
Electroconvulsive Therapy (ECT)
Psychosurgery
Biomedical Therapies in Perspective
Community Psychology: Focus on Prevention

Becoming an Informed Consumer of Psychology:
Choosing the Right Therapist

- *How are drug, electroconvulsive, and psychosurgical techniques used today in the treatment of psychological disorders?*

Biomedical Therapy: Biological Approaches to Treatment

Biomedical treatments that treat brain chemical imbalances and other neurological factors directly are regularly used for some problems. In **[a]** _____, drugs are given that alleviate symptoms for several psychological disturbances. In the mid-1950s, **[b]** _____ were introduced, causing a major change in the treatment of patients in mental hospitals. These drugs alleviate symptoms related to the patient's loss of touch with reality, agitation, and overactivity. **[c]** _____ are used to improve the moods of severely depressed patients. These drugs work by increasing the concentration of certain neurotransmitters.

[d] _____, a form of simple mineral salt, has been used to treat bipolar disorders. It ends manic episodes 70 percent of the time; though its success with depression is not as good.

[e] _____—Valium and Xanax—are the drugs most prescribed by physicians. These drugs reduce the anxiety level experienced by reducing excitability and increasing drowsiness.

Physicians in the 1930s found a way to induce convulsions using electric shocks.

[f] _____ is administered by passing an electric current of 70 to 150 volts through the head of a patient. The patient is usually sedated and given muscle relaxants to prevent violent contractions. ECT is controversial because of its side effects, which include disorientation, confusion, and memory loss, but it continues to be used because it does help severely depressed patients when other treatments are ineffective.

[g] _____ is brain surgery used to alleviate psychological symptoms. An early procedure was [h] _____, in which parts of the frontal lobes are removed or destroyed. The patients are then less subject to emotional impulses.

Evaluate

____ 1. antipsychotic drugs

____ 2. antidepressant drugs

____ 3. antianxiety drugs

____ 4. chlorpromazine

____ 5. lithium

a. Temporarily alleviate symptoms such as agitation and overactivity.

b. Used in the treatment of schizophrenia.

c. Improves a patient's mood and feeling of well-being.

d. Used in the treatment of bipolar disorders.

e. Alleviate stress and feelings of apprehension.

Rethink

42-1   One of the main criticisms of biological therapies is that they treat the symptoms of mental disorder without uncovering and treating the underlying problems from which people are suffering. Do you agree with this criticism or not? Why?

42-2   If a dangerously violent person could be "cured" of violence through a new psychosurgical technique, would you approve the use of this technique? Suppose the person agreed to—or requested—the technique? What sort of policy would you develop for the use of psychosurgery?

Spotlight on Terminology and Language—ESL Pointers

Biomedical Therapy: Biological Approaches to Treatment

Page 515 "Previously, the typical mental hospital fulfilled all the stereotypes of the nineteenth-century insane asylum, giving mainly **custodial care** to screaming, moaning, clawing patients who displayed the most bizarre behaviors."

Custodial care involves mostly watching and protecting patients, rather than seeking to cure them.

Page 517 "Does Prozac deserve its **acclaim**?"

Does this drug deserve its **acclaim**, its praise, its enthusiastic approval?

Page 518 "Often, people who have been subject to bipolar disorder episodes can take a daily dose of lithium that prevents a **recurrence** of their symptoms."

Lithium is used to prevent a **recurrence**, reappearance or return, of the symptoms.

Page 518 "But a more important issue concerns their use to **suppress** anxiety."

To **suppress** anxiety is to hold it back, to keep it in check or to block it out.

Page 518 "Although it did produce some memory loss and temporary headaches, the procedure also brought Manning back from the **brink of suicide**."

The treatment brought her back from being on the **brink**, or verge of suicide.

Page 518 "Usually health professionals **sedate** patients and give them muscle relaxants before administering the current, and this helps reduce the intensity of muscle contractions produced during ECT."

To be put under **sedation** is to anesthetize or to tranquilize.

Page 520 "In some respects, no greater **revolution** has occurred in the field of mental health than biological approaches to treatment."

There has been a transformation and modernization in this field.

Page 521 "This transfer of former mental patients out of institutions and into the community—a process known as deinstitutionalization—further **spurred** the community psychology movement."

The movement was **spurred**; it was stimulated and somewhat driven by these occurrences.

Practice Tests

Test your knowledge of the modules by answering these questions. These questions have been placed in three Practice Tests. The first two tests consist of questions that will test your recall of factual knowledge. The third test contains questions that are challenging and primarily test for conceptual knowledge and your ability to apply that knowledge. Check your answers and review the feedback using the Answer Key in the following pages of the *Study Guide*.

PRACTICE TEST 1:

1. Clients requiring some form of medical treatment are typically treated by a:
    a. psychiatric nurse.
    b. counseling psychologist.
    c. psychiatrist.
    d. clinical psychologist.

2. Therapy in which change is brought about through discussions and interactions between client and professional is called:
    a. eclectic therapy.
    b. semantic therapy
    c. psychotherapy.
    d. interpersonal therapy.

3. Freud believed that in order to protect our egos from the unwanted entry of unacceptable unconscious thoughts and desires, we all use:
    a. transference.
    b. aversive conditioning.
    c. systematic desensitization.
    d. defense mechanisms.

4. Which alternative is **not** a term associated with psychodynamic therapy?
    a. hierarchy of fears
    b. neurotic symptoms
    c. defense mechanisms
    d. transference

5. Katrina wants to reduce her anxiety and eliminate her phobia of "confined spaces"; a technique that is based on classical conditioning is called:
    a. biofeedback.
    b. behavior modification.
    c. systematic desensitization.
    d. aversive conditioning.

6. Which of the following approaches to therapy would be **least** concerned with the underlying causes of abnormal behavior?
    a. psychoanalytic
    b. behavioral
    c. eclectic
    d. humanistic

7. The goal of rational-emotive therapy is to restructure one's beliefs about oneself and the world into:
    a. a view that focuses on problems that arise only when events fail to turn out as expected.
    b. a realization that it is necessary for one to love and be approved by each significant person in one's life.
    c. a rational, realistic, and logical system.
    d. an understanding of the role of emotion in behavior.

8. The best known of the humanistic therapies assumes at the outset that a person's troubles reflect unfulfilled potential. The approach is called:
    a. rational-emotive therapy.
    b. gestalt therapy.
    c. systematic desensitization.
    d. client-centered therapy.

361

9. Which therapies emphasize establishing inner rather than outer control of behavior?
   a. psychodynamic and humanistic
   c. rational-emotive and behavioral
   b. psychodynamic and behavioral
   d. behavioral and humanistic

10. The goal of client-centered therapy is to enable people to reach their potential for:
    a. getting in touch with reality.
    c. taking control of their thoughts.
    b. understanding the unconscious.
    d. self-actualization.

11. Dr. Johnson said that his client, Mr. Keane, was experiencing a spontaneous remission. This is:
    a. an attack, either verbal or physical, by the therapist against the client when provoked repeatedly.
    b. disappearance of psychological symptoms even without therapy.
    c. an emotional outburst by the client during the therapy session.
    d. behavior by a family member (especially one's spouse) that worsens one's psychological symptoms.

12. Mrs. Walleran was given antipsychotic drugs to alleviate psychotic symptoms by:
    a. increasing neurotransmitter function.
    b. blocking the production of dopamine.
    c. slowing down the autonomic nervous system.
    d. sedating the patients.

13. The most widely applied biological approach to treatment is:
    a. psychosurgery.
    c. genetic engineering.
    b. electroconvulsive therapy.
    d. drug therapy.

14. Which medication would most likely be given to someone experiencing a manic episode?
    a. lithium
    c. chlorpromazine
    b. Valium
    d. Librium

15. A procedure by which areas of the brain are removed or destroyed in order to control severe abnormal behaviors is called:
    a. psychosurgery.
    c. electroconvulsive therapy.
    b. shock therapy.
    d. personality therapy.

_____ 16. free association

_____ 17. manifest content

_____ 18. latent content

_____ 19. resistance

_____ 20. transference

a. A patient's transfer of certain strong feelings for others to the analyst.

b. The "true" message hidden within dreams.

c. The patient says everything that comes to mind, providing insights into the patient's unconscious.

d. An inability or unwillingness to discuss or reveal particular memories, thoughts, or motivations.

e. The surface description and interpretation of dreams.

21. Freudian therapy is called _____.

22. Systematic desensitization uses a _____ of fears, where a patient is exposed to less threatening stimuli at first in order to treat phobias.

23. In Aaron Beck's _____, the therapist is less confrontive and more like a teacher.

24. Dr. Daly's training in psychotherapy gave him the skills to use a technique called _____, during which the patient will say anything that comes to mind.

25. _____ requires a written agreement between the therapist and the patient that specifies goals to be reached and consequences of reaching goals.

26. Describe the reasons why you think that psychotherapy works. Draw on the principles of psychology that have been discussed in previous chapters, such as learning principles, theories of development, and theories of personality, to explain why you think it is effective.

PRACTICE TEST 2:

1. Biomedical therapies:
    a. are the most common therapies used by clinical psychologists.
    b. are reserved for the less severe types of behavioral disorders.
    c. presume that many disorders result from improper nutrition, food additives, or exposure to toxic environmental chemicals.
    d. use drugs, shocks, or surgery to improve the client's functions.

2. With more and more information available, psychologists and psychiatrists often use an eclectic approach to therapy, which:
    a. first fragments the personality and then reconstructs it.
    b. is controversial because of its connection to the paranormal world of psychic phenomena.
    c. mixes techniques of various theoretical perspectives.
    d. is based on the teachings of Horatio Eclectic, a Danish therapist who promoted meditation as a therapeutic technique.

3. The basic premise of psychodynamic therapy is the notion that abnormal behavior is:
    a. repressing normal behaviors that need to be uncovered.
    b. the result of the ego repressing the superego.
    c. rooted in unresolved past conflicts, buried in the unconscious.
    d. the result of the ego failing to gain access to consciousness.

4. Psychoanalysts believe neurotic symptoms are caused by:
    a. defense mechanisms.   c. inappropriate choices.
    b. anxiety.   d. contingency contracting.

5. What technique is used in psychoanalysis to help the patient remember the experiences of a past relationship?
    a. transcendence   c. translation
    b. transference   d. transrotation

6. What happens to the reaction to alcohol following aversive conditioning for alcoholism?
    a. The reaction takes on that response associated with the aversion.
    b. There is no longer a craving for the alcohol.
    c. There is a fear of the alcohol.
    d. The alcohol becomes a source of anxiety.

7. Humanistic approaches to therapy emphasize:
    a. environmental control over actions.
    b. probing for unresolved hidden conflicts that arose long ago.
    c. discovering the unreasonableness of one's thoughts.
    d. personal choice and responsibility.

8. In rational-emotive therapy, the therapist challenges the client's:
    a. defensive views of the world.   c. paranoid views of the world.
    b. self-centered views of the world.   d. irrational views of the world.

9. Which of the following approaches to treatment takes the view that it is primarily the client's responsibility to make needed changes?
    a. behavioral therapy   c. humanistic therapy
    b. rational-emotive therapy   d. psychoanalytic therapy

10. In humanistic therapy, unconditional positive regard is provided to the client:
    a. as a reinforcement when goals have been met.
    b. as part of the contingency contract.
    c. no matter what the client says or does.
    d. to help resolve inner conflicts.

11. Which of the following therapies is most closely associated with the concepts of freedom, values, and the meaning of human existence?
    a. behavioral therapy   c. humanistic therapy
    b. rational-emotive therapy   d. existential therapy

12. As compared with individual therapy, group therapy gives the client:
    a. insight into his or her unconscious ideas.
    b. automatically performed fresh new habits.
    c. impressionistic feedback from others.
    d. logically correct thinking, free from delusions.

13. Chlorpromazine is most commonly used in the treatment of:
    a. mood disorders.   c. schizophrenia.
    b. anxiety disorders.   d. bipolar disorder.

14. Which drug is used to help prevent future occurrences of the behavioral disorder it is used to treat?
    a. Valium   c. chlorpromazine
    b. lithium   d. Librium

15. Antidepressant drugs improve the mood of depressed patients by:
    a. increasing the activity of the autonomic nervous system.
    b. suppressing the function of certain neurotransmitters.
    c. increasing the speed of neural transmission.
    d. increasing the concentration of certain neurotransmitters.

16. Which of the following types of treatment is rarely, if ever, still used?
    a. electroconvulsive shock therapy   c. psychotherapy
    b. antipsychotic drugs   d. psychosurgery

_____ 17. aversive conditioning   a. A person is rewarded for performing desired behaviors.

_____ 18. systematic desensitization   b. Breaks unwanted habits by associating the habits with very unpleasant stimuli.

_____ 19. token system   c. Requires a written contract between a therapist and a client that sets behavioral goals and rewards.

_____ 20. contingency contracting

d. A stimulus that evokes pleasant feelings is repeatedly paired with a stimulus that evokes anxiety.

21. In psychotherapy, the term _____ is used when a patient has the inability to discuss or reveal particular memories or thoughts.

22. _____ is a phenomenon in which the relationship between the analyst and the patient becomes emotionally charged and the analyst takes on the role of significant others in the patient's past.

23. An acceptance by the therapist of the individual, without conditions no matter what attitude is expressed by the client, is known as _____.

24. A method used by psychoanalyists of getting clues from the unconscious is _____.

25. Most therapists use a somewhat _____ to therapy, which provides several treatment techniques from which to select.

26. Describe the advantages and disadvantages of electroconvulsive therapy. Do you think that it should be banned from use? Explain your answer.

PRACTICE TEST 3: Conceptual, Applied, and Challenging Questions

1. If you were having trouble adjusting to the death of a friend, who would you be most likely to see?
   a. psychiatrist
   b. psychoanalyst
   c. psychiatric social worker
   d. counseling psychologist

2. Dr. Gaipo has clients explore their past by delving into the unconscious using dream interpretation and free association. Dr. Gaipo practices:
   a. existential therapy.
   b. cognitive therapy.
   c. behavioral therapy.
   d. psychodynamic therapy.

3. Professor Portis is the director of guidance at a student mental-health clinic. He holds a degree appropriate to his position, so he must hold a doctorate or master's degree in:
   a. psychiatric social work.
   b. counseling psychology.
   c. clinical psychology.
   d. educational psychology.

4. Which problem is **least** likely to be treated with aversive conditioning?
   a. substance (drug) abuse
   b. depression
   c. smoking
   d. alcoholism

5. _____ is the basis for behavioral approaches to therapy.
   a.   Removing negative self-perception   c.   Understanding the unconscious mind
   b.   Emphasizing personal responsibilities   d.   Training new habits

6. If a therapist asks you to act out some past conflict or difficulty in order to complete unfinished business, he or she most likely is using:
   a.   behavior therapy.   c.   rational-emotive therapy.
   b.   existential therapy.   d.   gestalt therapy.

7. Lane, a 17-year-old client of Dr. Griswald, explains, "I was uncomfortable and didn't interview well for a job I wanted and I made a perfect fool of myself." In response, Dr. Griswald says, "Is it important for you to be perfectly competent in every area of your life?" Dr. Griswald is using:
   a.   behavioral therapy.   c.   humanistic therapy.
   b.   rational-emotive therapy.   d.   existential therapy.

8. Betty is in therapy with a psychotherapist to work through her feelings about her recent broken engagement. She is telling her therapist that she really didn't love her fiancé and that she realized how different she and her fiancé are. Suddenly, her therapist says, "Betty, I heard the words that you just said, but they don't tell the same message that your facial expression and other nonverbal cues do. See if you can sense the differences." Betty's therapist is most likely:
   a.   a gestalt therapist.   c.   a client-centered therapist.
   b.   a psychoanalytic therapist.   d.   a behavioral therapist.

9. Generalizing from the discussion in the text, both humanistic and psychoanalytic approaches to therapy are more appropriate for clients who are:
   a.   highly verbal.   c.   experiencing sexually related disorders.
   b.   severely disordered.   d.   reluctant to converse with someone else.

10. Which of the following types of treatment appears to actually *cure* the disorder, so that when the treatment is discontinued, the symptoms tend not to recur?
   a.   antipsychotic drugs   c.   antianxiety drugs
   b.   antidepressant drugs   d.   chlorpromazine

11. Melanie, after being assaulted, is nervous, overreacts to ordinary stimuli, and has trouble getting to sleep. Her psychiatrist prescribes a drug for her, which most likely is:
   a.   an antianxiety drug.   c.   an antipsychotic drug.
   b.   an antidepressant drug.   d.   an analgesic drug.

12. Electroconvulsive shock treatment (ECT) is usually reserved for severe cases of:
   a.   mania.   c.   depression.
   b.   schizophrenia.   d.   panic attack.

13. Electroconvulsive therapy (ECT):
   a.   relieves the patient from severe depression.
   b.   has been used since about 1910.
   c.   is used in preference to drug therapy.
   d.   can be administered by clinical psychologists.

14. Juan and his therapist spend much of their time discussing issues arising from deep religious and philosophical questions. Often the question of the meaning of life comes up, and other concerns about the real meaning of human self-determination are discussed. Juan is working with:
   a.   a behavioral therapist.   c.   an existential therapist.
   b.   a psychoanalyst.   d.   a group therapist.

15. During a therapy session, Larry explores an image of his home that he had in a dream. The therapist asks him to say what the house feels, to express the unfinished business of the house. Larry's therapist is most likely:
    a. a psychoanalyst.
    b. a group therapist.
    c. an existential therapist.
    d. a gestalt therapist.

16. Bethany has prepared a list of experiences that run from the most frightening to the least frightening. She has prepared a _____, and her therapist is probably a _____.
    a. systematic desensitization; behavioral therapist
    b. hierarchy of fears; behavioral therapist
    c. systematic desensitization; humanistic therapist
    d. hierarchy of fears; humanistic therapist

_____ 17. gestalt therapy

_____ 18. group therapy

_____ 19. family therapy

_____ 20. community psychology

a. People discuss problems with others who have similar problems.

b. Movement aimed at preventing psychological disorders.

c. Attempts to integrate a client's thoughts, feelings, and behavior into a whole.

d. Family as a unit to which each member contributes.

21. The _____ of dreams is the actual description of the dream itself.

22. In Eysenck's study on the effectiveness of psychotherapy, clients sometimes had symptoms go away without treatment; this was called _____.

23. The _____ of dreams is the message of the dream.

24. Former mental patients who return to the community in a process called _____ often do not get their needs met, and the goals of the program have not been met in most communities.

25. _____ have made it possible to end the use of brain surgery to alleviate psychological symptoms.

26. What are some things the patient has to keep in mind when selecting and working with a therapist? What are the patients' responsibilities in therapy?

■ ANSWER KEY: MODULES 40, 41, AND 42

Module 40:	Evaluate	Module 41:	Module 42:
[a] psychotherapy	1. e	[a] Humanistic therapy	[a] drug therapy
[b] Biomedical therapy	2. a	[b] Nondirective counseling	[b] antipsychotic drugs
[c] eclectic approach	3. d	[c] client-centered therapy	[c] Antidepressant drugs
[d] Psychodynamic therapy	4. c	[d] unconditional positive	[d] Lithium
[e] defense mechanisms	5. b	regard	[e] Antianxiety drugs
[f] psychoanalysis		[e] existential therapy	[f] Electroconvulsive
[g] free association		[f] Gestalt therapy	therapy (ECT)
[h] dream interpretation		[g] Group therapy	[g] Psychosurgery
[i] behavioral treatment		[h] Family therapy	[h] prefrontal lobotomy
approaches			
[j] aversive conditioning		Evaluate	Evaluate
[k] systematic desensitization			1. a
[l] Observational learning		1. d	2. c
[m] modeling		2. e	3. e
[n] token system		3. b	4. b
[o] cognitive-behavioral		4. c	5. d
approaches		5. a	
[p] Rational-emotive therapy			

Selected Rethink Answers

41-1 Define group therapy. Because people are different and are dealing with similar issues, they may be able to provide a variety of coping mechanisms to one of the group members and to develop empathy for others with similar problems.

42-1 Biological therapies do treat symptoms. For some illnesses, the relief of the symptoms may be all that is required. Most successful therapies are a combination of the medical model with some type of therapy. When symptoms are somewhat relieved, a client may be better able to focus on the underlying problems associated with the illness.

Practice Test 1:

1. c   mod. 40 p. 498
a. Incorrect. A psychiatric nurse may provide some support in a nursing role, but the psychiatrist conducts the therapy in these cases.
b. Incorrect. A counseling psychologist is not involved in medical treatment.
*c. Correct. A psychiatrist is a medical doctor who administers medical treatment for psychological disorders.
d. Incorrect. A clinical psychologist does not administer medical treatments.

2. c   mod. 40 p. 498
a. Incorrect. Eclectic therapy may utilize approaches that do not involve discussions and interactions.
b. Incorrect. There is not a major therapy called semantic therapy.
*c. Correct. Psychotherapy specifically involves this kind of direct interaction and discussion between the client and the psychotherapist.
d. Incorrect. Also known as ITP, this approach does involve interaction, but psychotherapy is the larger category described by this item.

3. d   mod. 40 p. 497
a. Incorrect. Transference occurs in therapy, and it involves transferring emotional energy from other relationships into the therapy relationship.
b. Incorrect. Aversive conditioning utilizes behavioral techniques.
c. Incorrect. Systematic desensitization utilizes behavioral techniques.
*d. Correct. They are called defense mechanisms because they defend the ego from anxiety arising from unconscious conflicts.

4. a   mod. 40 p. 502
*a. Correct. A hierarchy of fears is used in the behavioral technique known as systematic desensitization.
b. Incorrect. Neurotic symptoms, defense mechanisms, and transference are all psychodynamic concepts.
c. Incorrect. See answer b.
d. Incorrect. See answer b.

5. c mod. 40 p. 501
a. Incorrect. Biofeedback uses signals from the body to help the person control physiological functions and achieve states of relaxation.
b. Incorrect. Behavior modification includes classical and operant conditioning techniques to change undesirable behaviors.
*c. Correct. Systematic desensitization utilizes classical conditioning techniques by having the person imagine a hierarchy of fears and gradually become desensitized to the frightening stimuli.
d. Incorrect. Aversive conditioning uses both classical and operant principles to get the subject to avoid certain responses.

6. b mod. 40 p. 500
a. Incorrect. The psychoanalytic approach is keyed to the problems caused by unconscious causes of abnormal behavior.
*b. Correct. The behavioral approach is only concerned with the observable causes of behavior, like the reinforcements or stimuli associated with learning.
c. Incorrect. An eclectic approach draws on the most appropriate technique for the problem being treated.
d. Incorrect. The humanistic approach is concerned with how the individual views him or herself, and this may include causes beyond the person's awareness.

7. c mod. 40 p. 504
a. Incorrect. This may be a rational approach to problem solving, but it is not the approach of rational-emotive therapy.
b. Incorrect. Love and approval are not part of rational-emotive therapy.
*c. Correct. This is the goal of rational-emotive therapy.
d. Incorrect. This may be part of the theory behind rational-emotive therapy, but it is not the therapeutic goal.

8. d mod. 41 p. 507
a. Incorrect. Rational-emotive therapy is a cognitive therapy, and thus it incorporates what the person thinks about themselves.
b. Incorrect. Gestalt therapy is a humanistic approach that requires the person to accept parts of him or herself that he or she has denied or rejected.
c. Incorrect. Systematic desensitization utilizes classical conditioning techniques by having the person imagine a hierarchy of fears and gradually become desensitized to the frightening stimuli.
*d. Correct. Client-centered therapy assumes that the client has the potential to handle his or her own problems.

9. a mod. 41 p. 499
*a. Correct. The psychodynamic approach focuses on control of unconscious impulses and the humanistic approach focuses on self-control and responsibility.
b. Incorrect. The behavioral approach is entirely focused on outer forces.
c. Incorrect. See answer b.
d. Incorrect. See answer b.

10. d mod. 41 p. 508
a. Incorrect. All therapies involve, in one way or another, helping the client get in touch with reality.
b. Incorrect. The psychoanalytic approach is focused on understanding the unconscious.
c. Incorrect. Cognitive therapies, like rational-emotive therapy, are focused on the person taking control of his or her thoughts.
*d. Correct. Humanistic therapy strives to help the client achieve some form of self-actualization, or at least move toward realizing his or her potential.

11. b mod. 41 p. 510
a. Incorrect. This would be called unethical.
*b. Correct. Sometimes, simply allowing time to pass cures a psychological disorder.
c. Incorrect. This may be a spontaneous emission, but not a remission.
d. Incorrect. This is not remission.

12. b mod. 42 p. 515
a. Incorrect. Antipsychotic drugs block the production of dopamine.
*b. Correct. Unfortunately, this is not a cure for the problem.
c. Incorrect. See answer a.
d. Incorrect. See answer a.

13. d mod. 42 p. 516
a. Incorrect. Psychosurgery has always been a method of last resort.
b. Incorrect. ECT has become less common than it once was, but even in its heyday it was not the most common.
c. Incorrect. Genetic engineering has not yet been applied to direct treatment of psychological disorders.
*d. Correct. Even general practitioners will prescribe psychoactive drug therapies.

14. a   mod. 42 p. 517
*a. Correct. How this mineral salt works remains a mystery.
b. Incorrect. Valium is an antianxiety drug.
c. Incorrect. Chlorpromazine is an antipsychotic drug.
d. Incorrect. Librium is an antianxiety drug.

15. a   mod. 42 p. 519
*a. Correct. The original psychosurgery was the prefrontal lobotomy, where the frontal lobes are destroyed.
b. Incorrect. Electroconvulsive therapy, also known as shock therapy, does not destroy any tissue.
c. Incorrect. See answer b.
d. Incorrect. There is not a group of therapies or an approach to therapy known as "personality" therapy.

16. c   mod. 40 p. 497
17. e   mod. 40 p. 497
18. b   mod. 40 p. 497
19. d   mod. 40 p. 497
20. a   mod. 40 p. 497

21. psychoanalysis   mod. 40 p. 497
22. hierarchy   mod. 40 p. 502
23. cognitive therapy   mod. 40 p. 503
24. free association   mod. 40 p. 497
25. Contingency contracting mod. 40 p. 502

26.
▪ Identify the reasons you think psychotherapy works. These may include (1) psychotherapy offers a chance to reflect on life's problems in a safe environment; (2) it offers a sense of control over one's problems; and (3) it provides new ways of coping with and understanding stress.
▪ Select at least two of the previously discussed concepts and describe their roles in depth.
▪ Remember, Eysenck's early study that suggested that psychotherapy was no more effective than being on a waiting list.

Practice Test 2:
1. d   mod. 40 p. 515
a. Incorrect. Clinical psychologists cannot prescribe drugs.
b. Incorrect. Drug therapy is used for almost every disorder.
c. Incorrect. This may be part of the view, but the predominant view is that the disorders are medical in nature.
*d. Correct. Biomedical therapy uses medical interventions.

2. c   mod. 40 p. 511
a. Incorrect. That is not what eclectic means.
b. Incorrect. It is not connected to the paranormal.
*c. Correct. The therapist chooses the technique best matched to the client's needs.
d. Incorrect. It was actually his long-lost brother, Homer Simpson.

3. c   mod. 40 p. 499
a. Incorrect. In the psychoanalytic view, abnormal behaviors do not suppress normal behaviors.
b. Incorrect. The ego does not repress the superego.
*c. Correct. The focus in psychodynamic therapy is on past, unresolved conflicts, often going back to childhood.
d. Incorrect. The ego always has access to consciousness.

4. b   mod. 40 p. 515
a. Incorrect. Defense mechanisms may play a role when they fail to protect the ego from anxiety.
*b. Correct. Anxiety is the main cause of neurotic symptoms, and the anxiety arises because of undesirable motives or repressed conflicts.
c. Incorrect. Inappropriate choices would be the cause of symptoms, as viewed by humanistic theory.
d. Incorrect. Contingency contracting might be found in behavior therapy, but not as the cause for neurotic symptoms in Freud's view.

5. b   mod. 40 p. 499
a. Incorrect. See answer b.
*b. Correct. Transference brings the emotional energy of the past relationship into the current therapeutic relationship.
c. Incorrect. See answer b.
d. Incorrect. See answer b.

6. a   mod. 40 p. 501
*a. Correct. The response to alcohol after successful aversion therapy is to avoid alcohol because it is linked to the aversive stimulus.
b. Incorrect. The craving is probably still there.
c. Incorrect. No fear of alcohol should develop.
d. Incorrect. Properly undertaken, alcohol should not become a source of anxiety.

7. d   mod. 41 p. 507
a. Incorrect. This is the behavioral approach.
b. Incorrect. This is the psychodynamic approach.
c. Incorrect. This is the cognitive approach.
*d. Correct. Humanistic approaches focus on personal responsibility and self healing.

8. d   mod. 40 p. 504
a. Incorrect. The views may be defensive, but those challenged are the irrational views held by the client.
b. Incorrect. The views may be self-centered, but those challenged are the irrational views held by the client.
c. Incorrect. The views may be paranoid, but those challenged are the irrational views held by the client.
*d. Correct. The therapist attempts to get the client to eliminate faulty ideas about the world and himself or herself.

9. c   mod. 41 p. 507
a. Incorrect. The therapist is primarily responsible for establishing a program of stimuli or reinforcement that will retrain the client in behavioral therapy.
b. Incorrect. The rational-emotive therapist attempts to get the client to eliminate faulty ideas about the world and him or herself.
*c. Correct. Humanistic therapy attempts to help the client gain insight into his or her responsibility for the need to make changes.
d. Incorrect. The psychoanalytic approach seeks to understand the unconscious forces at work.

10. c   mod. 41 p. 508
a. Incorrect. Reinforcement would be used in behavioral therapy, not humanistic therapy.
b. Incorrect. A contingency contract is used in behavioral therapy, not humanistic therapy.
*c. Correct. Unconditional positive regard is the basis of any therapeutic relationship in the humanistic view.
d. Incorrect. The psychoanalytic approach is aimed more at inner conflicts.

11. d   mod. 41 p. 507
a. Incorrect. Behavioral therapy is not interested in human freedom and other concepts related to existence and the meaning of life.
b. Incorrect. Rational-emotive therapy is focused on changing the client's way of thinking about the world.
c. Incorrect. Humanistic therapy is focused on helping the client take responsibility for his or her actions.
*d. Correct. This describes the goals of existential therapy, a type of humanistic therapy.

12. c   mod. 41 p. 508
a. Incorrect. Psychodynamic group therapy will focus on this aspect of the client.
b. Incorrect. This is not possible in any kind of therapy.
*c. Correct. Others in the group have had similar experiences, and the client learns that he or she is not alone.
d. Incorrect. Only in cognitive group therapy.

13. c   mod. 42 p. 515
a. Incorrect. Antidepressant drugs are used for many mood disorders.
b. Incorrect. Antianxiety drugs, like Valium and Xanax, are used for anxiety disorders.
*c. Correct. Chlorpromazine is an antipsychotic drug used to treat schizophrenia.
d. Incorrect. Lithium is used to treat the mania of bipolar disorders.

14. b   mod. 42 p. 517
a. Incorrect. Valium is an antianxiety drug without any preventive characteristics.
*b. Correct. Lithium is one of the few drugs that appears to provide a degree of cure.
c. Incorrect. Chlorpromazine does not cure schizophrenia or any of the other disorders it is used to treat.
d. Incorrect. Librium is an antianxiety drug without any preventive or curative characteristics.

15. d   mod. 42 p. 516
a. Incorrect. Antidepressants do not increase the activity of the autonomic system.
b. Incorrect. Antipsychotics decrease the production of dopamine, but antidepressants actually increase the concentrations of some neurotransmitters.
c. Incorrect. Drugs do not increase the speed of neural transmission.
*d. Correct. Antidepressants, like Prozac and tricyclics, increase the concentration of neurotransmitters.

16. d   mod. 42 p. 519
a. Incorrect. Electroconvulsive shock therapy is commonly used today.
b. Incorrect. Antipsychotic drugs continue to be relied upon by the medical community.
c. Incorrect. Psychotherapy is very common.
*d. Correct. The use of psychosurgery, especially the lobotomy, is used less and less for treatment of psychological disorders.

17. b   mod. 40 p. 501
18. d   mod. 40 p. 501
19. a   mod. 40 p. 502
20. c   mod. 40 p. 502

21. resistance   mod. 40 p. 500
22. Transference   mod. 40 p. 499
23. unconditional positive regard   mod. 41 p. 508
24. dream interpretation   mod. 40 p. 499
25. eclectic approach   mod. 41 p. 511

26.
- Describe your response to the idea of electrical shock being passed through your brain as a means of therapy. Would you want this to be done?
- What assumptions are made about the harm or benefit of using ECT? Do we assume that it must have some unseen long-term effect?

Practice Test 3:
1. d   mod. 40 p. 498
a. Incorrect. A psychiatrist would probably be inappropriate for this kind of short-term problem.
b. Incorrect. A psychoanalyst would probably be inappropriate for this kind of short-term problem.
c. Incorrect. A psychiatric social worker is trained to deal with other kinds of problems and would probably be inappropriate for this kind of short-term problem.
*d. Correct. A counseling psychologist is especially prepared for dealing with problems of adjustment such as this one.

2. d   mod. 40 p. 498
a. Incorrect. Some, but not all, existential therapists use psychodynamic techniques.
b. Incorrect. Cognitive therapy would have the client explore conscious thoughts.
c. Incorrect. Behavioral therapy would not have the client think much at all.
*d. Correct. Dream interpretation is a core technique for psychodynamic therapy.

3. b   mod. 40 p. 498
a. Incorrect. Someone with a degree in psychiatric social work would be more appropriately placed in a community health center.
*b. Correct. This is the most appropriate degree for this kind of position.
c. Incorrect. A clinical psychologist could hold this position, but a counseling degree would be more suitable.
d. Incorrect. An educational psychologist would not be suitable for this position.

4. b   mod. 40 p. 501
a. Incorrect. See answer b.
*b. Correct. Aversive conditioning works well with habits that are being broken, like drug habits, smoking, and alcoholism, but not with psychological problems like depression.
c. Incorrect. See answer b.
d. Incorrect. See answer b.

5. d   mod. 40 p. 500
a. Incorrect. Behaviorists are not that interested in self-perception.
b. Incorrect. Humanistic approaches focus on personal responsibilities.
c. Incorrect. Psychodynamic approaches focus on the unconscious mind.
*d. Correct. These new habits are meant to replace the old, malfunctioning ones.

6. d   mod. 41 p. 508
a. Incorrect. Behavior therapy does not ask clients to act out past conflicts.
b. Incorrect. Existential therapy is much more focused on the meaning of life than on past conflicts.
c. Incorrect. Rational-emotive therapy is focused more on the client's irrational ideas about the world.
*d. Correct. Gestalt therapy seeks to have clients integrate and "own" these conflicts to be able to resolve the issues for themselves.

7. b   mod. 40 p. 504
a. Incorrect. In behavior therapy, other avenues would be explored, like the reinforcements that were being sought.
*b. Correct. In rational-emotive therapy, this expectation of perfection would be viewed as irrational and thus in need of being altered.
c. Incorrect. In humanistic theory, the concern would be more about the issue of personal responsibility rather than thoughts about how others would view one.
d. Incorrect. In existential therapy, Dr. Griswald might have asked Lane to consider what it means to be perfect in such an imperfect world.

8. a   mod. 41 p. 508
*a. Correct. The gestalt therapist tries to integrate the nonverbal message with the verbal message and thus reduce Betty's conflict.
b. Incorrect. A psychoanalytic therapist might be interested in the nonverbal cues as efforts of the unconscious to get a message across.
c. Incorrect. A client-centered therapist would attempt to mirror Betty's concerns back to her so she could hear what she was saying.
d. Incorrect. A behavioral therapist might suggest that there is something reinforcing about Betty's breaking the engagement that she is failing to recognize.

9. a   mod. 41 p. 507
*a. Correct. These two approaches require much discussion and insight, so a verbal client will do well in these approaches.
b. Incorrect. Severely disordered patients should probably be treated with drugs and some psychotherapy.
c. Incorrect. People with sexual disorders would be best served if they sought a sex therapist.
d. Incorrect. People who are reluctant to converse with others would have difficulty talking to a psychoanalytic or humanistic therapist.

10. b   mod. 42 p. 516
a. Incorrect. Antipsychotic drugs only suppress the symptoms.
*b. Correct. After taking a regimen of antidepressant drugs, depression tends not to return.
c. Incorrect. Antianxiety drugs suppress the response, but they do not remove the cause.
d. Incorrect. Chlorpromazine is an antipsychotic drug and it suppresses psychotic symptoms, but they return if the drug is stopped.

11. a   mod. 42 p. 518
*a. Correct. These are symptoms of anxiety.
b. Incorrect. She is not depressed.
c. Incorrect. She is not psychotic.
d. Incorrect. She does not need an aspirin.

12. c   mod. 42 p. 518
a. Incorrect. See answer c.
b. Incorrect. See answer c.
*c. Correct. ECT is used for severe depression when other treatments do not work.
d. Incorrect. See answer c.

13. a   mod. 42 p. 518
*a. Correct. It does seem to relieve depression.
b. Incorrect. It was introduced in the 1930s.
c. Incorrect. Drug therapy is much preferred.
d. Incorrect. Clinical psychologists are not licensed to administer drugs or ECT.

14. c   mod. 41 p. 507
a. Incorrect. These are not the concerns of a behavioral therapist.
b. Incorrect. These are not the concerns of a psychoanalyst.
*c. Correct. Existential psychotherapy is concerned with important religious and philosophical issues, especially the meaning and purpose of life.
d. Incorrect. A group therapist would probably not bring these kinds of issues to a group.

15. d   mod. 41 p. 507
a. Incorrect. A psychoanalyst would be interested in what the house symbolized for Larry, not the unfinished business it entails.
b. Incorrect. A group therapist would not likely be conducting individual dream therapy.
c. Incorrect. An existential therapist might be interested in the dream as it provides insight into the client's concerns about life and existence.
*d. Correct. The gestalt therapist attempts to get Larry to recognize and integrate the unfinished business that his dream home represents.

16. b   mod. 40 p. 502
a. Incorrect. See answer b.
*b. Correct. This list is called a hierarchy of fears, and the behavioral approach is based on classical conditioning principles.
c. Incorrect. See answer b.
d. Incorrect. See answer b.

17. c   mod. 41 p. 508
18. a   mod. 41 p. 508
19. d   mod. 41 p. 509
20. b   mod. 42 p. 507

21. manifest content   mod. 40 p. 499
22. spontaneous remission   mod. 42 p. 510
23. latent content   mod. 40 p. 499
24. Deinstitutionalization   mod. 42 p. 521
25. Biomedical therapies   mod. 42 p. 515

26. Patients should:
▪ Make sure therapists have appropriate training, credentials, and licensing.
▪ Feel comfortable with the therapist, not intimidated.
▪ Feel that they are making progress with the therapy.
▪ Be committed to making therapy work.
▪ Patients, not therapists, must do the work to resolve issues.

Social Psychology

Overview

This set of modules illustrates how people's thoughts, feelings, and actions are affected by others. Both the nature and the causes of individual behavior in social situations are studied.

Module 43 explains how attitudes are composed of affective, behavioral, and cognitive components. People show consistency between their attitudes and behavior, and we form schemas to help us categorize people and events in the world around us. This helps us predict the actions of others.

Module 44 explores the effects that social influence has on an individual. These behaviors include behaviors that result from the actions of others, as found in conformity, compliance, and obedience.

Module 45 addresses the issue of prejudice as a consequence of stereotyping and how both of these create challenges for people living in a diverse society. How prejudice originates and its relationship to stereotyping and discrimination are discussed.

Module 46 presents a discussion on social behaviors. These behaviors include the study of liking and loving, the influence of friendship between people, and the behavior involved in helping others.

To further investigate the topics covered in this chapter, you can visit the related Web sites by visiting the following link: www.mhhe.com/feldmanup6-18links.

Prologue: Everyday Heroes
Looking Ahead

Module 43: Attitudes and Social Cognition

Persuasion: Changing Attitudes
Social Cognition: Understanding Others

> **Exploring Diversity:** Attributions in a Cultural
> Context: How Fundamental Is the Fundamental
> Attribution Error?

- *What are attitudes, and how are they formed, maintained, and changed?*
- *How do we form impressions of what others are like and of the causes of their behavior?*
- *What are the biases that influence the ways in which we view others' behavior?*

Attitudes and Social Cognition

[a] _____ is the study of how people's thoughts, feelings, and actions are affected by others. Attempts to persuade people to purchase specific products involves principles derived from the study of attitudes. [b] _____ are learned predispositions to respond in a favorable or unfavorable manner to a particular person, behavior, belief, or object.

The formation of attitudes follows classical and operant learning principles. Attitudes can be formed by association. They can also be reinforced positively or punished by the responses others may have to them, and a person may develop an attitude through [c] _____. This type of learning occurs when a person learns something through observation of others. Children learn prejudices through others by hearing or seeing others express prejudicial attitudes.

Another important component consists of the characteristics of the recipient. The intelligence of the recipient influences the ability to remember and recall the message, yet intelligent people are more certain of their opinions. Highly intelligent people tend to be more difficult to persuade. A small difference in persuadability exists between men and women, with women being slightly easier to persuade. The means by which the information is processed also has an influence on the persuasion. [d] _____ occurs when the recipient considers the arguments involved. [e] _____ occurs when the recipient uses information that requires less thought. Advertisers are using demographic information about people to help target their advertisements. [f] _____ is a technique for dividing people into lifestyle profiles that are related to purchasing patterns.

Attitudes influence behavior, but the strength of the relationship varies. People do try to keep behavior and attitudes consistent. Sometimes, in order to maintain the consistency, behavior can influence attitudes. **[g]** _____ occurs when a person holds two *cognitions* (attitudes or thoughts) that are contradictory. In cases where dissonance is aroused, the prediction is that behavior or attitudes will change in order to reduce the dissonance.

The area of social psychology called **[h]** _____ refers to the processes that underlie our understanding of the world. Individuals have highly developed **[i]** _____, or sets of cognitions, about people and experiences. Schemas are important because they organize how we recall, recognize, and categorize information about others. They also help us make predictions about others.

[j]_____ refers to the process by which an individual organizes information about another person, forming an overall impression of that person. Information given to people before meeting them can have dramatic effects on how the person is perceived. Research has focused on how people pay attention to unusually important traits, called **[k]** _____, as they form impressions of others.

Evaluate

____ 1.   attitudes

____ 2.   central-route processing

____ 3.   peripheral-route processing

a.   Characterized by consideration of the source and related general information rather than of the message.

b.   Characterized by thoughtful consideration of the issues.

c.   Learned predispositions to respond in a favorable or unfavorable manner to a particular object.

Rethink

43-1   Suppose you were assigned to develop a full advertising campaign for a product, including television, radio, and print ads. How might the theories in this chapter guide your strategy to suit the different media?

43-2   Joan sees Annette, a new coworker, act in a way that seems abrupt and curt. Joan concludes that Annette is unkind and unsociable. The next day, Joan sees Annette acting kindly to another worker. Is Joan likely to change her impression of Annette? Why or why not? Finally, Joan sees several friends of hers laughing and joking with Annette, treating her in a friendly fashion. Is Joan likely to change her impression of Annette? Why or why not?

Spotlight on Terminology and Language—ESL Pointers

Attitudes and Social Cognition

Page 530 "Instead, factors that are irrelevant or **extraneous** to the issue, such as who is providing the message and how long the arguments are, influence them (Petty, Cacioppo, Strathman, & Priester, 1994; Petty, Wheeler, & Tormala, 2003)."

Extraneous to the issue would be off the point of the main issue. **Extraneous** is something that comes from the outside and is not vital or essential.

Page 530 "However, if a person is uninvolved, unmotivated, bored, or distracted, the nature of the message becomes less important, and **peripheral** factors become more critical."

Peripheral factors are minor factors or secondary factors.

Page 530 "People who have a high need for cognition, a person's habitual level of thoughtfulness and cognitive activity, are more likely to employ central route processing."

Habitual is usual or customary.

Page 532 "These two thoughts should arouse **dissonance**."

Dissonance implies conflict or a difference of opinion. **Cognitive dissonance** is the unpleasant psychological tension that motivates us to reduce our cognitive inconsistencies by making our beliefs more consistent with one another.

Page 532 "The reasoning behind this condition was that $20 was so much money that participants in this condition had a good reason to be **conveying** incorrect information; dissonance would not be aroused, and less attitude change would be expected."

Conveying is communicating.

Page 533 "Regardless of Bill Clinton's personal **transgressions** and impeachment trial, many Americans genuinely liked him when he was president, and his popularity remained high throughout his term in office."

Transgressions suggest a lack of discretion, seen often in reckless behavior. A **transgression** is a behavior that goes beyond a boundary.

Page 533 "Our schema for 'teacher,' for instance, generally consists of a number of characteristics: knowledge of the subject matter he or she is teaching, a desire to **impart** that knowledge, and an awareness of the student's need to understand what is being said."

Teachers want to **impart** their knowledge; they want to pass it on. When you **impart** knowledge, you communicate it and make it known to others.

Page 535 "But from a logical standpoint, it is equally **plausible** that something about the situation caused the behavior."

It is equally believable, or conceivable.

Module 44:
Social Influence

Conformity: Following What Others Do
Compliance: Submitting to Direct Social Pressure
Obedience: Following Direct Orders

- **What are the major sources and tactics of social influence?**

Social Influence

The area called **[a]** _____ is concerned with how the actions of an individual affect the behavior of others. In uncertain situations, we tend to look to the behavior of others to guide our own behavior. **[b]** _____ is the change in behavior or attitudes that results from a desire to follow the beliefs or standards of other people. **[c]** _____ is a type of thinking in which group members share strong motivation to achieve consensus, which leads them to lose the ability to critically evaluate alternatives. The group overrates its ability to solve problems and underrates contradictory information.

The behavior that occurs in response to direct, explicit pressure to endorse a particular view or to behave in a certain way is called **[d]** _____. Several techniques are used by salespersons to get customers to comply with purchase requests. One is called the

[e] _____ technique, in which a person agrees to a small request and is then asked to comply with a bigger request. Compliance increases when the person first agrees to the smaller request. The **[f]** _____ technique is the opposite of the foot-in-the-door technique. The door-in-the-face technique follows a large request with a smaller one, making the second request appear more reasonable. The **[g]** _____ technique presents a

deal at an inflated price, then a number of incentives are added. The **[h]** _____ is another method that creates a psychic cost by giving "free" samples. These samples instigate a _norm of reciprocity_, leading people to buy as a matter of reciprocation.

Compliance follows a request, but obedience follows direct orders. **[i]** _____ is defined as a change in behavior resulting from the commands of others. Obedience occurs in situations involving a boss, teacher, parent, or someone who has power over us.

Evaluate

_____ 1. cognitive dissonance

_____ 2. foot-in-the-door technique

_____ 3. door-in-the-face technique

_____ 4. obedience

_____ 5. compliance

a. Behavior that occurs in response to direct social pressure.

b. Going along with an important request is more likely if it follows compliance with a smaller previous request.

c. A change in behavior resulting from the commands of others.

d. A large request, refusal of which is expected, is followed by a smaller request.

e. The conflict resulting from contrasting cognitions.

Rethink

44-1 Because persuasive techniques like those described in this section are so powerful, should the use of such techniques be outlawed? Should people be taught defenses against such techniques? Is the use of such techniques ethically and morally defensible? Why?

44-2 Why do you think the Milgram experiment is so controversial? What sorts of effects might the experiment have had on participants? Do you think the experiment would have had similar results if it had been conducted not in a laboratory setting, but among members of a social group (such as a fraternity or sorority) with strong pressures to conform?

Spotlight on Terminology and Language—ESL Pointers

Social Influence

Page 539 "As you undoubtedly know from your own experience, pressures to **conform** can be painfully strong, and can bring about changes in behavior that otherwise never would have occurred."

    Conformity is any behavior you perform because of group pressure, even though that pressure might not involve direct requests. The social pressure may be subtle or indirect to be in agreement or harmony with the group. What circumstances existed when you last felt the need to **conform**?

Page 539 "The task was seemingly **straightforward**: Each of the participants had to announce aloud which of the first three lines was identical in length to the 'standard' line on the second card."

    Straightforward means uncomplicated. In this case, the task appeared simple and clear-cut.

Page 539 "As you might have guessed, this experiment was more **contrived** than it appeared."

    When something is **contrived**, there's a scheme involved; it is not what it seemed.

Page 539 "The first six participants were actually confederates (paid employees of the experimenter) who had been instructed to give unanimously **erroneous** answers in many of the trials."

    Erroneous is wrong; the confederates gave the incorrect answer on purpose.

Page 540 "Furthermore, we understand that not adhering to group norms can result in **retaliation** from other group members, ranging from being ignored to being **overtly derided** or even being rejected or excluded by the group.

    When someone seeks **retaliation,** they seek to get revenge. An **overt** act is an open and blatant act. To **deride** is to ridicule.

Page 542 "For one reason, involvement with the small request leads to an interest in an issue, and taking an action—any action—makes the individual more committed to the issue, thereby increasing the likelihood of future **compliance**."

    Compliance is a kind of conformity in which we give in to social pressure in our public responses but do not change our personal values.

Module 45: Prejudice and Discrimination

Applying Psychology in the 21st Century:
Discrimination in the Workplace: Can Your Name
(or Hat) Cost You a Job?

The Foundations of Prejudice
Reducing the Consequences of Prejudice and Discrimination

- *What is the distinction among stereotypes, prejudice, and discrimination?*
- *How can we reduce prejudice and discrimination?*

Prejudice and Discrimination

[a] _____ are the beliefs and expectations about members of groups held simply because of membership in the group. Stereotypes can lead to [b] _____, the negative evaluation of group members that is based primarily on membership in the group rather than on the behavior of a particular individual. When negative stereotypes lead to negative action against a group or group members, the behavior is called [c] _____. Stereotypes can actually cause members of stereotyped groups to behave according to the stereotype, a phenomenon known as [d] _____. Expectations about a future event increase the likelihood that the event will occur. People are also primed to interpret behaviors according to stereotypes.

The [e] _____ say that people's feelings about various groups are shaped by the behavior of parents, other adults, and peers and the mass media. According to [f] _____, we use membership in groups as a source of pride and self-worth. We then inflate the positive aspects of our own group and devalue groups to which we do not belong.

Evaluate

_____ 1. self-fulfilling prophecy

_____ 2. prejudice

_____ 3. stereotype

_____ 4. social identity theory

_____ 5. discrimination

a. Negative behavior toward members of a particular group.

b. Negative or positive judgments of members of a group that are based on membership in the group.

c. The expectation of an event or behavior results in the event or behavior actually occurring.

d. Beliefs and expectations about members of a group are held simply on the basis of membership in that group.

e. The view that people use group membership as a source of pride and self-worth.

Rethink

45-1 How are stereotypes, prejudice, and discrimination related? In a society committed to equality, which of the three should be changed first? Why? Will changing one of the components lead to changes in the other two?

45-2 Do you think women can be victims of stereotype vulnerability? In what topical areas might this occur? Can men be victims of stereotype vulnerability? Why?

Spotlight on Terminology and Language—ESL Pointers

Prejudice and Discrimination

Page 547 "**Stereotypes** can lead to **prejudice**, negative (or positive) evaluations of groups and their members."

Stereotypes are widely held beliefs that people have certain traits because they belong to a particular group.

Prejudice is an unfair, biased, or intolerant attitude toward another group of people.

Page 547 "Even today, despite major progress toward reducing **legally sanctioned** forms of prejudice such as school segregation, stereotypes remain (Johnston, 1996; Madon et al., 2001)."

Legally sanctioned means permitted by law.

Page 549 "For instance, **bigoted** parents may commend their children for expressing prejudiced attitudes."

A **bigoted** person is someone who is prejudiced, intolerant, or narrow-minded.

Page 549 "Other explanations of prejudice and discrimination focus on how being a member of a particular group helps to **magnify** one's sense of self-esteem."

Your sense of self-esteem is expanded when it is **magnified**.

Page 549 "**Slogans** such as 'gay-pride' and 'black is beautiful' illustrate that the groups to which we belong **furnish** us with a sense of self-respect (Tajfel, 1982; Rowley et al., 1998)."

Slogans are a brief, attention-getting phrase.

The groups may **furnish** us, or provide us, with a sense of self-respect.

Page 550 "Consequently, we **inflate** the positive aspects of our ingroup—and, at the same time, **devalue** outgroups."

We **inflate**, or exaggerate and overstate, aspects of our ingroup.

We may **devalue**, or diminish, the value of outgroups.

Page 550 "Making values and norms against prejudice more **conspicuous**."

When you make something more **conspicuous**, you make it more noticeable or prominent."

Page 550 "Similarly, people who hear others making strong, **vehement** antiracist statements are subsequently more likely to strongly condemn racism (Blanchard, Lilly, & Vaughn, 1991; Dovidio, Kawakami, & Gaertner, 2000)."

Vehement arguments are intense and passionate.

Page 551 "He argues that African American students who receive instruction from teachers who may doubt their abilities and set up special remedial programs to assist them may come to accept society's stereotypes and believe that they are **prone to fail** (Steele, 1992, 1997; Steele, Spencer, & Aronson, 2002)."

Prone to fail is having a tendency or inclination toward failure.

Page 551 "Members of minority groups, convinced that they have the potential to be academically successful, may become immune to the potentially **treacherous** consequences of negative stereotypes."

Treacherous is unsafe, dangerous.

Module 46:
Positive and Negative Social Behavior

Liking and Loving: Interpersonal Attraction and the Development of Relationships
Aggression and Prosocial Behavior: Hurting and Helping Others

Becoming an Informed Consumer of Psychology:
Dealing Effectively with Anger

- *Why are we attracted to certain people, and what progression do social relationships follow?*
- *What factors underlie aggression and prosocial behavior?*

Positive and Negative Social Behavior

Another area of social influence is called **[a]** _____, which encompasses the factors that lead to positive feelings about others. Research on liking has identified the following factors as important in the development of attraction between people. **[b]** _____ refers to physical nearness or geographical closeness as a factor in development of friendship. Proximity leads to liking. **[c]** _____ also leads to liking. The more often one is exposed to any stimulus, the more the stimulus is liked. Familiarity with a stimulus can evoke positive feelings. **[d]** _____ influences attraction because we assume that people with similar backgrounds will evaluate us positively. This is called the **[e]** _____. We also assume that when we like someone, that person likes us in return.

[f] _____ refers to attraction that is based on the needs that the partner can fulfill. We may then be attracted to the person who fulfills the greatest number of needs. It does appear that people with complimentary abilities are attracted to one another. More

[g] _____ tends to be more popular. Physical attractiveness may be the single most important factor in college dating.

Several kinds of love have been hypothesized, one being **[h]** _____ love, which is an intense state of absorption in another person. Another is **[i]** _____ love, which is strong affection that we have for someone with whom our lives are deeply involved. Robert Sternberg has proposed that love is made of three components.

The [j] _____ component includes feelings of closeness and connectedness; the [k] _____ component is made of the motivational drives related to sex, physical closeness, and romance; and the [l] _____ component encompasses the initial cognition that one loves someone and the long-term feelings of commitment to maintain love.

Drive-by shootings, car-jackings, and abductions give a pessimistic impression of human behavior. The helping behavior of many people, however, counteracts this impression. Social psychology seeks to explain these extremes.

[m] _____ occurs at societal and individual levels, and the basic questions concern whether aggression is inevitable or whether it results from particular circumstances. Aggression is defined as the intentional injury of or harm to another person.

Instinct theories explain aggression as the result of innate urges. Konrad Lorenz suggested that aggressive energy is built up through the instinct of aggression and that its release is necessary. The discharge of this energy is called [n] _____. Lorenz suggested that society should provide an acceptable means of achieving catharsis, like sports. There is no way to test this theory experimentally.

The frustration-aggression theory says that the frustration of a goal *always* leads to aggression. [o] _____ is defined as the thwarting of a goal-directed behavior. More recently, the theory has been modified to suggest that frustration creates a *readiness* to act aggressively.

The observational-learning view suggests that we learn to act aggressively by observing others. Observational-learning theory also suggests that the rewards and punishments received by a model are important in the learning of aggression. This formulation has wide support.

[p] _____ refers to helping behavior. The prosocial behavior studied most by psychologists is bystander intervention. When more than one person witnesses an emergency, [q] _____, the tendency for people to feel that responsibility is shared among those present, increases. In some cases, people act altruistically. [r] _____ is helping behavior that is beneficial to others but may require self-sacrifice. People high in *empathy* may be more likely to respond than others. Situational factors and mood may also affect helping behavior. Both good and bad moods appear to increase helping behavior.

Evaluate

_____ 1. passionate (or romantic) love

_____ 2. compassionate love

_____ 3. intimacy component

_____ 4. passion component

_____ 5. decision/commitment component

a. The motivational drives relating to sex, physical closeness, and romance.

b. Feelings of closeness and connectedness.

c. The initial cognition that one loves someone, and the longer-term feelings of commitment.

d. The strong affection we have for those with whom our lives are deeply involved.

e. A state of intense absorption in someone that is characterized by physiological arousal, psychological interest, and caring for another's needs.

Rethink

46-1 Can love be studied scientifically? Is there an elusive quality to love that makes it at least partially unknowable? How would you define "falling in love"? How would you study it?

46-2 How would the aggression of a Timothy McVeigh, convicted of blowing up a federal building in Oklahoma City, be interpreted by the three main approaches to the study of aggression: instinct approaches, frustration-aggression approaches, and observational-learning approaches? Do you think any of these approaches fits the McVeigh case more closely than the others?

Spotlight on Terminology and Language—ESL Pointers

Positive and Negative Social Behavior

Page 553 "Like **philosophers** and theologians, social psychologists have pondered the basic nature of humanity."

A **philosopher** is a scholar who seeks wisdom and enlightenment.

Page 553 "By far the greatest amount of research has focused on liking, probably because it is easier for investigators conducting short-term experiments to produce states of liking in strangers who have just met than to **instigate** and observe loving relationships over long periods."

To **instigate** some behavior is to prompt or to set off this behavior.

Page 555 "Psychologist Robert Sternberg makes an even **finer** differentiation between types of love."

A **finer** distinction is a more sensitive, or discriminating, distinction.

Page 557 "The difficulty of answering such **knotty** questions becomes apparent as soon as we consider how best to define the term aggression."

A **knotty** question is a tough question; as you think about it, the question becomes more complex and difficult to answer.

Page 557 "If you have ever punched an **adversary** in the nose, you may have experienced a certain satisfaction, despite your better judgment."

An **adversary** is an opponent or an enemy.

Page 558 "In fact, some studies **flatly** contradict the notion of catharsis, leading psychologists to look to other explanations for aggression (Anderson & Bushman, 2001; Bushman, Baumeister, & Phillips, 2001; Bushman, 2002)."

Some studies **flatly** and completely contradict this notion.

Page 559 "Whereas instinct theory would suggest that the aggression had been **pent up** and was now being discharged, and frustration-aggression theory would examine the girl's frustration at no longer being able to use her new toy, observational learning theory would look to previous situations in which the girl had viewed others being rewarded for their aggression."

Pent-up feelings are confined or repressed feelings.

Page 560 "Still, most social psychologists agree that no single set of **attributes** differentiates helpers from nonhelpers."

An **attribute** is an inherent characteristic, a trait or feature of that person.

Practice Tests

Test your knowledge of the modules by answering these questions. These questions have been placed in three Practice Tests. The first two tests consist of questions that will test your recall of factual knowledge. The third test contains questions that are challenging and primarily test for conceptual knowledge and your ability to apply that knowledge. Check your answers and review the feedback using the Answer Key in the following pages of the *Study Guide*.

PRACTICE TEST 1:

1. When advertisers hired Michael Jordan to sell men's underwear, their intent was to link a product they want consumers to buy to a:
    a. positive feeling or event.
    b. cognition.
    c. peripheral route.
    d. dissonant stimulus.

2. Sets of cognitions known as schemas serve as _____ for social cognitions.
    a. organizing frameworks
    b. defenses against stereotypes
    c. feeling-communicators
    d. insincerity whistle-blowers

3. People rely heavily on _____ when forming an impression of another person.
    a. central tendencies
    b. central traits
    c. primary traits
    d. schematic tendencies

4. The tendency for people to attribute others' behavior to dispositional causes and their own behavior to situational causes is known as:
    a. ingroup versus outgroup error.
    b. fundamental attribution error
    c. dispositional attribution error.
    d. stereotypic attribution error.

5. The classic demonstration of pressure to conform comes from a series of studies carried out in the 1950s by:
    a. B. F. Skinner.
    b. Solomon Asch.
    c. Philip Zimbardo.
    d. Stanley Milgram.

6. People working on tasks and questions that are ambiguous are more susceptible to:
    a. inoculation.
    b. obedience.
    c. forewarning.
    d. social pressure.

7. The classic experiment performed by _____ demonstrated the power of authority to produce obedience.
    a. Albert Bandura
    b. Solomon Asch
    c. Stanley Milgram
    d. B. F. Skinner

8. The Bosnian concept of "ethnic cleansing" that resulted in genocide of unwanted groups reflects:
    a. reverse discrimination.
    b. individualism.
    c. prejudice and discrimination.
    d. deterrence.

9. Beliefs and expectations about group members held simply on the basis of their group membership are called:
    a. self-fulfilling prophecies.
    b. culture.
    c. stereotypes.
    d. contingencies.

389

10. Which of the following is **not** a strong influence on the formation of friendships?
    a. others who are like them
    b. others who live nearby
    c. others whom they see frequently
    d. others who are exceptionally attractive

11. Which of the following elements does love have that liking does not?
    a. proximity
    b. complementarity
    c. similarity
    d. physical arousal

12. Sternberg found that different types of love are made up of different quantities of:
    a. liking, loving, and commitment.
    b. passion, compassion, and attraction.
    c. emotion, motivation, and attraction.
    d. intimacy, passion, and commitment.

13. Tanya has been trying to quit smoking since her mother was diagnosed with lung cancer. Although she knows the risks, it is very difficult to refrain from smoking when she finds herself in situations where she normally would have a cigarette. Festinger calls this:
    a. cathartic interference.
    b. tension reduction.
    c. cognitive dissonance.
    d. frustration aggression.

14. Prosocial is a more formal way of describing behavior that is:
    a. helping.
    b. cathartic.
    c. innate.
    d. aggressive.

_____ 15. impression formation

_____ 16. central traits

_____ 17. fundamental attribution error

_____ 18. halo effect

_____ 19. assumed-similarity bias

a. Tendency to think of people as being similar to oneself.

b. Major traits considered in forming impressions of others.

c. Organizing information about another individual to form an overall impression of that person.

d. A tendency to overattribute others' behavior to dispositional causes but to underattribute one's own behavior to situational causes.

e. An initial understanding that a person has positive traits is used to infer other uniformly positive characteristics.

20. Cognitive dissonance occurs when a person holds two _____ of thoughts that are contradictory.

21. The halo effect reflects _____ theories that indicate how we think traits are inferred.

22. An experiment by _____ demonstrated the power of the judgments of others on the perceptual judgments of an individual participant.

23. When people act on negative stereotypes, this _____ can lead to exclusion from jobs, neighborhoods, or educational opportunities.

24. Expectations that increase the likelihood that an event or behavior will occur are

_____.

25. Much has been made of attitudes and behavior and how they may or may not be consistent. Describe a situation in which your attitudes and behavior may not have been consistent, and then compare the cognitive-dissonance explanation and the self-perception explanation of the situation.

PRACTICE TEST 2:

1. One of the basic processes that underlies the formation and development of attitudes relates to learning principles. Which of the following learning methods best explains how attitudes are acquired?
   a. peripheral-route processing
   b. classical and operant conditioning
   c. central-route processing
   d. punishment

2. The advertising industry draws on findings from _____ regarding persuasion.
   a. experimental psychology
   b. psychometrics
   c. abnormal psychology
   d. social psychology

3. Katrina is seriously training to earn a place on the Olympic swim team. When she sees a piece of cake, Katrina wants to eat it, but knows that she shouldn't. Festinger called this:
   a. cognitive dissonance.
   b. cathartic interference.
   c. tension reduction.
   d. frustration-aggression.

4. The processes that underlie our understanding of the social world are called:
   a. social cognitions.
   b. schemas.
   c. central traits.
   d. stereotypes.

5. The task of _____ is to explain how people understand the causes of behavior.
   a. discrimination theory
   b. social cognition
   c. attribution theory
   d. directive-behavior theory

6. Conformity is a change in behavior or attitude brought about by:
   a. an increase of knowledge.
   b. a desire to follow the beliefs or standards of others.
   c. intense pressure to be a distinct individual.
   d. an insecure self-image.

7. A change in behavior that results from direct, explicit social pressure to behave in a certain way is called:
   a. conformity.
   b. congruence.
   c. commission.
   d. compliance.

8. What is the correct term for the technique in which a large request is asked, followed by expected refusal and later a smaller request?
   a. obedience
   b. social compliance
   c. door-in-the-face technique
   d. foot-in-the-door technique

9. The negative behavior toward an individual because of his or her membership in a particular group is known as:
   a. stereotyping.
   b. discrimination.
   c. prejudice.
   d. self-fulfilling prophecy.

10. Proximity is defined as:
    a. nearness to another person. c. a tendency of those whom we like to like us.
    b. a tendency to like those who like us. d. distance from another.

11. _____ love is a state of intense absorption in someone, with bodily arousal, mental interest, and care for the other's needs.
    a. The intimacy component of c. Compassionate
    b. The decision/commitment component of d. Passionate (romantic)

12. Advertisers who design a fear-evoking advertising campaign know that messages are most effective when:
    a. they frighten people into buying the product.
    b. they reach a small and indifferent audience.
    c. viewers' cognitive defense mechanisms are activated.
    d. they include advice for steps to avoid the described danger.

13. When stereotypes are attributed to a particular group, they may induce members of that group to act in ways that confirm the stereotype. This is known as:
    a. the ingroup-outgroup bias. c. a self-fulfilling prophecy.
    b. reverse discrimination. d. the interdependent view of the self.

14. Being unable to read has led to a great deal of frustration for Manuel. This frustration is most likely to lead to aggression:
    a. in the presence of aggressive cues. c. during late adolescence.
    b. immediately after being frustrated. d. several hours after being frustrated.

____ 15. proximity   a. Any helping behavior.

____ 16. reciprocity-of-liking effect   b. The hypothesis that people are attracted to others who have common interests and lifestyles.

____ 17. similarity

                                          c. Nearness to another, one cause for liking.
____ 18. prosocial behavior

                                          d. The tendency to like those who like us.
____ 19. diffusion of responsibility

                                          e. The tendency for people to feel that responsibility for helping is shared among those present.

20. Research in social psychology has demonstrated that children as young as _____ years of age begin to show preferences for members of their own race.

21. Often, inaccurate portrayals are the primary source of information about a group, and they can lead to the maintenance of unfavorable _____.

22. People may come to think that their own group is better than others in an effort to maximize our own _____.

23. Some psychologists argue that _____ results when there is perceived competition for scarce resources.

24. Geographic closeness or _____ is one of the most important factors in establishing personal relationships.

25. What factors would be at work when prejudices erupt into violence against racial groups? Analyze the factors of conformity, obedience, and stereotyping, including ingroup and outgroup biases.

PRACTICE TEST 3: Conceptual, Applied, and Challenging Questions

1. A 12-year-old boy who overhears his father tell his mother that "children are worthless" may grow up to believe this opinion and adopt it as an attitude as a result of the process of:
    a. direct reinforcement.
    b. vicarious learning.
    c. cognitive dissonance.
    d. persuasive communication.

2. If a target audience pays more attention to the celebrity doing the commercial than to the advertisement message, which processing route is being used the most by the audience?
    a. central-route processing
    b. circumference-route processing
    c. peripheral-route processing
    d. The message is not being processed.

3. Many variables influence the effectiveness of a communication to create attitude change. In which of the following situations will the impact be the greatest?
    a. The recipient appraises the message with central-route processing.
    b. The recipient of the message is male.
    c. The recipient appraises the message with peripheral-route processing.
    d. The recipient is very intelligent.

4. According to Festinger's theory of cognitive dissonance, if a smoker holds the cognitions "I smoke" and "Smoking causes cancer," he or she should be motivated to do all of the following *except*:
    a. modify one or both cognitions.
    b. enter a stop-smoking program.
    c. make the attitudes consistent.
    d. change the importance of one cognition.

5. The best example of cognitive dissonance is:
    a. stating that women should earn less money than men for doing the same job.
    b. exaggerating the merits of a product in order to promote sales.
    c. knowing that cigarette smoking is harmful, but doing it anyway.
    d. believing that people who are disabled cannot hold good jobs and therefore not recommending them.

6. Which one of the following statements is the best example of dispositional-attribution bias?
    a. John is being good because the teacher is watching.
    b. Even though I am not feeling sociable, I will go to the party if you do.
    c. I become very anxious when criticized.
    d. Sue is staying up all night to study because she is a conscientious student.

7. Which of the following situations best describes a situational cause for the described behavior?
    a. Tina straightens the guest room, which is normally a messy sewing room, because relatives will be staying at her house for a week.
    b. Barbara helps an old lady across the street because she is always thoughtful.
    c. Danny, who is normally grumpy, frowns about an exam as he walks down the hall.
    d. Mary is a punctual person who is on time for school every morning.

8. What measure may be most effective for reducing the tendency of people to conform in a group situation?
    a. Make sure all members value the group highly.
    b. Include lots of members in the group.
    c. Use a show of hands when voting.
    d. Use a secret ballot when voting.

9. Stereotypes differ from prejudices in that:
    a. stereotypes are beliefs that lead to prejudices, which are judgments.
    b. stereotypes must involve action against a group.
    c. prejudices must involve action against a group.
    d. prejudices are beliefs that lead to stereotypes, which are judgments.

10. Which of the following factors is the best predictor of whether two people will be initially attracted to each other?
    a. similarity   c. proximity
    b. mere exposure   d. complementarity

11. Which of the following is **not** a component of Sternberg's theory of love?
    a. intimacy   c. decision/commitment
    b. passion   d. individuation/separation.

12. Instinct theorist Konrad Lorenz would argue that opportunities to exercise and play sports ought to be given to prisoners because they:
    a. provide models of prosocial behavior.
    b. present violent models to be seen and imitated by prisoners.
    c. enable natural aggressive energy to be released harmlessly.
    d. reduce the frustration that causes aggression.

13. What measure may be most effective for reducing the tendency of people to conform in a group situation?
    a. Use a secret ballot when voting.
    b. Use a show of hands when voting.
    c. Include lots of members in the group.
    d. Make sure all of the members value the group highly.

14. Following the destruction of the Twin Towers in New York City, thousands of unpaid volunteers assisted at the site, thereby demonstrating:
    a. the fundamental attribution error.   c. altruism.
    b. diffusion of responsibility.   d. the halo effect.

_____ 15. rewards-costs approach

_____ 16. altruism

_____ 17. empathy

_____ 18. schemas

_____ 19. status

a. Helping behavior that is beneficial to others while requiring sacrifice on the part of the helper.

b. Sets of cognitions about people and social experiences.

c. One person's experiencing of another's emotions, in turn increasing the likelihood of responding to the other's needs.

d. The social rank held within a group.

e. The notion that, in a situation requiring help, a bystander's perceived rewards must outweigh the costs if helping is to occur.

20. While some might argue that opposites attract, other researchers believe we tend to like people who are _____ to us.

21. People who are _____ attractive are more popular than those who are not, other factors being equal.

22. Researchers believe that liking someone is qualitatively different than _____ someone.

23. Mutual attraction and love are the most important characteristics desired in a mate by men and women in the United States, whereas men in China rank _____ as most important.

24. _____ approaches propose that aggression is primarily the outcome of innate or inborn urges.

25. In the United States, the idea of arranged marriages often is seen with disdain. Our culture, for the most part, has always encouraged our freedom to select mates based on the notion of romantic love. Explain then the elements that may be present in arranged marriages that make them as successful as those partnerships we personally choose.

■ ANSWER KEY: MODULES 43, 44, 45, AND 46

Module 43:	Module 44:	Module 45:	Module 46:
[a] Social psychology	[a] social influence	[a] Stereotypes	[a] interpersonal attraction
[b] Attitudes	[b] Conformity	[b] prejudice	[b] Proximity
[c] vicarious learning	[c] Groupthink	[c] discrimination	[c] Mere exposure
[d] Central-route processing	[d] compliance	[d] self-fulfilling prophecy	[d] Similarity
[e] Peripheral-route processing	[e] foot-in-the-door	[e] social learning approaches	[e] reciprocity-of-liking effect
[f] Psychographics	[f] door-in-the-face	[f] social identity theory	[f] Need-complimentarity hypothesis
[g] Cognitive dissonance	[g] that's-not-all		[g] physical attractiveness
[h] social cognition	[h] not-so-free sample	Evaluate	[h] passionate (or romantic)
[i] schemas	[i] Obedience	1. c	[i] compassionate love
[j] Impression formation		2. b	[j] intimacy
[k] central traits	Evaluate	3. d	[k] passion
	1. e	4. e	[l] decision/commitment
	2. b	5. a	[m] Aggression
Evaluate	3. d		[n] catharsis
1. c	4. c		[o] Frustration
2. d	5. a		[p] Prosocial behavior
3. a			[q] diffusion of responsibility
			[r] Altruism
			Evaluate
			1. e
			2. d
			3. b
			4. a
			5. c

Selected Rethink Answers

43-2   Joan first experiences cognitive dissonance because her initial thoughts and attitudes about Annette were contradictory. Finally, with friends of Joan's treating Annette well, she was able to add positive cognitions, which enabled her to change her impression of Annette.

46-2   Define each approach to aggression. The observational-learning approach seems appropriate here. The social and environmental conditions is supported by McVeigh's past experiences (his military background, access to guns, etc., taught him, or supported his aggression). One of the consequences for him was fame and notoriety; the other was that he will give up his life.

Practice Test 1:

1.   a   mod. 43 p. 529
*a. Correct. Linking the product to a positive event originates with classical conditioning.
b.   Incorrect. They seek to link the product to a pleasant stimuli, like a feeling or event.
c.   Incorrect. The peripheral-route is one of the methods of communicating in persuasive communication.
d.   Incorrect. A dissonant stimulus might be one that does not fit with the others or causes some kind of conflict.

2.   a   mod. 43 p. 533
*a. Correct. A schema is an organizing framework.
b.   Incorrect. Schemas actually serve as the foundation for stereotypes.
c.   Incorrect. Schemas are not communicators.
d.   Incorrect. Schemers maybe, but not schemas.

3.   b   mod. 43 p. 533
a.   Incorrect. Central tendencies are the measures like mean, median, and mode that are produced using statistics.
*b. Correct. Apparently we utilize major, evident traits that are central to the personality of the individual we are forming impressions about.
c.   Incorrect. The term is central traits.
d.   Incorrect. The concept "schematic tendencies" is yet to be developed.

4. b   mod. 43 p. 537
a. Incorrect. The ingroup-outgroup bias (not error) may follow the fundamental attribution error, but its role is in determining the boundaries between groups and strengthening the sense of identity within the ingroup.
*b. Correct. The fundamental attribution error is common and may be understood in that we do tend to see the person's behavior more than the environment in which it occurs, and we see our own environment and not so much our own behavior.
c. Incorrect. There is no dispositional attribution error.
d. Incorrect. There is no stereotypic attribution error.

5. b   mod. 44 p. 539
a. Incorrect. Skinner did not conduct conformity experiments.
*b. Correct. Solomon Asch performed several experiments on conformity throughout the 1950s.
c. Incorrect. Zimbardo conducted experiments on compliance and obedience.
d. Incorrect. Milgram conducted a now-famous experiment on obedience.

6. d   mod. 44 p. 541
a. Incorrect. Inoculation occurs when the person is deliberately exposed to conformity pressures in order to be better at avoiding conformity.
b. Incorrect. Obedience requires more direct pressure.
c. Incorrect. Forewarning is a technique for developing the ability to resist pressures to conform.
*d. Correct. In ambiguous circumstances, social pressure is more likely to have an effect on conformity.

7. c   mod. 44 p. 544
a. Incorrect. Albert Bandura is known for his study of violence and the Bobo clown doll.
b. Incorrect. Solomon Asch is known for his experiments on conformity.
*c. Correct. Stanley Milgram asked subject to give an electric shock to other subjects, and he was able to get most to comply to the point of the highest shock level.
d. Incorrect. Skinner did not perform any human conformity studies.

8. c   mod. 44 p. 548
a. Incorrect. This discrimination is not reverse but is instead quite direct.
b. Incorrect. Individualism is not a concept relevant to active genocide.
*c. Correct. This is a manifestation not only of extreme prejudice but also of extreme discrimination.
d. Incorrect. Deterrence is a concept that would prevent the actions of open group by threatening retaliation.

9. c   mod. 46 p. 547
a. Incorrect. These are stereotypes, and stereotypes can become self-fulfilling prophecies.
b. Incorrect. Culture is the shared beliefs and practices of a group.
*c. Correct. This defines stereotypes.
d. Incorrect. These are not called contingencies, they are called stereotypes.

10. d   mod. 46 p. 553
a. Incorrect. See answer d.
b. Incorrect. See answer d.
c. Incorrect. See answer d.
*d. Correct. Living nearby, similarity, and frequent contact are the foundations of friendship, and exceptional attractiveness is not.

11. d   mod. 46 p. 554
a. Incorrect. See answer d.
b. Incorrect. See answer d.
c. Incorrect. See answer d.
*d. Correct. To being nearby, sharing interests, and being similar, love adds the component of physical attraction and arousal.

12. d   mod. 46 p. 555
a. Incorrect. See answer d.
b. Incorrect. See answer d.
c. Incorrect. See answer d.
*d. Correct. Sternberg's triarchic theory of love has three components, intimacy, passion, and commitment, which can be combined in different ways.

13. c   mod. 43 p. 532
a. Incorrect. No such thing.
b. Incorrect. If anything, it would heighten tension.
*c. Correct
d. Incorrect. It might lead to frustration, but not aggression.

14. a   mod. 46 p. 560
*a. Correct. Prosocial behavior is altruistic, helping behavior.
b. Incorrect. Insofar as helping another is cathartic, this could be a good answer, but the term prosocial typically refers to helping behavior.
c. Incorrect. Some biosociologists argue that prosocial behavior is innate because it promotes the survival of the species.
d. Incorrect. Prosocial behavior is altruistic, helping behavior.

15. c   mod. 43 p. 533
16. b   mod. 43 p. 533
17. d   mod. 43 p. 537
18. e   mod. 43 p. 536
19. a   mod. 43 p. 536

20. cognitions   mod. 43 p. 532
21. implicit personality   mod. 43 p. 536
22. Asch   mod. 43 p. 539
23. discrimination   mod. 45 p. 547
24. self-fulfilling prophecies   mod. 45 p. 547

25.
▪ Situations that might be relevant are those in which you did something, like go on a date with someone, that you really were not that interested in doing. The mismatch between the attitude (lack of interest) and behavior (going out), while not that great, does illustrate the problem.
▪ Describe how you felt after the specific incident or act and whether you changed your attitudes (she/he is actually pleasant to be with). Or perhaps, you wait until after the behavior to form your attitude (consistent with the self-perception theory).

Practice Test 2:
1. b   mod. 43 p. 529
a. Incorrect. Peripheral-route processing is not a learning principle.
*b. Correct. Both classical and operant conditioning principles are involved in the formation of attitudes.
c. Incorrect. Central-route processing is not a learning principle.
d. Incorrect. Punishment on its own cannot account for the richness and variety of our attitudes.

2. d   mod. 43 p. 530
a. Incorrect. See answer d.
b. Incorrect. Psychometrics is an important technique that probably was used by social psychologists as they developed key ideas that are now being used in the advertising industry.
c. Incorrect. Of all the branches of psychology, abnormal psychology has probably made the smallest contribution to the advertising industry.
*d. Correct. Social psychologists, some of whom are experimental psychologists as well, have made contributions that are useful to the advertising industry.

3. a   mod. 43 p. 532
*a. Correct. The conflict between two cognitions becomes cognitive dissonance when this conflict is accompanied by an affective state.
b. Incorrect. No such thing.
c. Incorrect. If anything, it would heighten tension.
d. Incorrect. It may lead to frustration, but probably not aggression.

4. a   mod. 43 p. 533
*a. Correct. Social cognitions refer to the thoughts we have about other people and the causes of their behavior.
b. Incorrect. Social cognitions are schemas, but schemas, the cognitive units of organization, refer to other cognitive categories as well.
c. Incorrect. Central traits are the traits we chose to make early impressions about people, and they may be included in our social cognitions.
d. Incorrect. Stereotypes are forms of social cognitions (but not all social cognitions are stereotypes).

5. c   mod. 43 p. 534
a. Incorrect. There is not "discrimination theory" that applies to this issue.
b. Incorrect. In the broadest sense this is true, but another alternative is more specific and thus a better choice.
*c. Correct. Attribution theory involves the efforts people make to understand the causes of their and others' behavior.
d. Incorrect. There is not a "directive-behavior" theory.

6.   b   mod. 44 p. 539
a.   Incorrect. More knowledge would not necessarily lead to conformity; it could just as well lead to nonconformity.
*b. Correct. Conformity is to the pressures of the group, and it is accomplished by accepting the attitudes and behaviors of the group.
c.   Incorrect. The intense pressure to be an individual would be counter to the pressure to conform.
d.   Incorrect. People with secure self-images may be highly conforming individuals.

7.   d   mod. 44 p. 542
a.   Incorrect. Conformity results from indirect social pressure and a desire to be part of the group.
b.   Incorrect. Congruence is a concept used in humanistic psychotherapy to describe different aspects of the self concept.
c.   Incorrect. A commission is an amount of money received for a specific task, like a sales commission.
*d. Correct. This is the definition of compliance.

8.   c   mod. 44 p. 542
a.   Incorrect. This is called the door-in-the-face technique; it is the opposite of the foot-in-the-door technique.
b.   Incorrect. But it is a form of social compliance.
*c. Correct. This technique is the opposite of the foot-in-the-door technique.
d.   Incorrect. It is the opposite of this, and called the door-in-the-face technique.

9.   b   mod. 45 p. 547
a.   Incorrect. Stereotyping applies to attitudes, not behaviors.
*b. Correct. Discrimination is the negative action toward another person based on group membership.
c.   Incorrect. Prejudice is positive or negative attitudes toward a group or member of a group.
d.   Incorrect. A self-fulfilling prophecy is an expectation that the occurrence of an event or behavior increases the likelihood that the event or behavior will occur.

10. a   mod. 46 p. 553
*a. Correct. Physical proximity is nearness to another person, and it is a major factor in both friendship and love relationships.
b.   Incorrect. This defines the effect of reciprocity on us.
c.   Incorrect. See answer b.
d.   Incorrect. Distance is the opposite of proximity.

11. d   mod. 46 p. 555
a.   Incorrect. This is from Sternberg's theory, and is separate from passion.
b.   Incorrect. See answer b.
c.   Incorrect. This type of love is seen in contrast to passionate love.
*d. Correct. Sounds like "romance."

12. d   mod. 46 p. 559
a.   Incorrect. This would be the measure of their effectiveness.
b.   Incorrect. Indifferent audiences are no more receptive to fear-based messages than any other audience.
c.   Incorrect. Defense mechanisms may make them ignore the warnings.
*d. Correct. Otherwise they are simply frightening.

13. c   mod. 45 p. 547
a.   Incorrect. In this bias, stereotypes are applied to help differentiate the two groups.
b.   Incorrect. Reverse discrimination occurs when one is making efforts to avoid the stereotype.
*c. Correct. Self-fulfilling prophecies are a danger to underprivileged groups because they sustain the circumstances.
d.   Incorrect. We are all interdependent.

14. a   mod. 46 p. 558
*a. Correct. Aggressive cues increase the likelihood of aggression (which initially creates a readiness to act).
b.   Incorrect. See answer a.
c.   Incorrect. See answer a.
d.   Incorrect. See answer a.

15. c   mod. 46 p. 553
16. d   mod. 46 p. 554
17. b   mod. 46 p. 553
18. a   mod. 46 p. 559
19. e   mod. 46 p. 559
20. 3   mod. 46 p. 559

21. stereotypes   mod. 45 p. 548
22. self-esteem   mod. 45 p. 547
23. prejudice   mod. 45 p. 547
24. Proximity   mod. 46 p. 553

25.
▪   Provide an example of recent violence against an ethnic group (or even an episode identified with a particular group).
▪   Gang violence is a clear application of the ingroup-outgroup bias. The riots in Los Angeles suggest that many people have very strong stereotypes about the groups represented in the violence, including African American, Hispanic, and Asian.

- Describe how each of the factors conformity, compliance, and obedience could work toward increasing prejudice and following group behavior.

Practice Test 3:

1. b   mod. 46 p. 558
a. Incorrect. Direct reinforcement would require that he express the attitude and then be reinforced for doing so.
*b. Correct. This is an example of learning through observation, or learning vicariously.
c. Incorrect. Cognitive dissonance involves contradictory thoughts or beliefs that then cause tension (of course, the 5-year-old may have a friend who is a southerner).
d. Incorrect. Persuasive communication usually involves a more direct message.

2. c   mod. 45 p. 530
a. Incorrect. The approach known as peripheral-route processing is being used.
b. Incorrect. This applies only to well-rounded messages.
*c. Correct. The peripheral route avoids presenting much reasoning or detail about the product.
d. Incorrect. But it is!

3. a   mod. 43 p. 530
*a. Correct. When the recipient puts effort into cognitively analyzing the message, as required in central-route processing, the change in attitude will be the greatest for the situations given here.
b. Incorrect. Being male does not make the message any more or less effective.
c. Incorrect. The recipient will do little work in appraising a message that is peripheral.
d. Incorrect. Intelligence does not affect attitude change.

4. b   mod. 43 p. 532
a. Incorrect. See answer b.
*b. Correct. Cognitive dissonance would lead to modifying one of the cognitions, making them consistent, or revaluing them, but it is unlikely to make the person enter a program to stop smoking (this requires additional pressures).
c. Incorrect. See answer b.
d. Incorrect. See answer b.

5. c   mod. 45 p. 532
a. Incorrect. This is simply a sexist position.
b. Incorrect. This is simply typical of salespersons.
*c. Correct. Here, two thoughts are opposed to each other and will certainly result in tension.
d. Incorrect. This is simply being prejudicial.

6. d   mod. 43 p. 535
a. Incorrect. John's behavior is explained according to the situation.
b. Incorrect. The decision to attend the party comes from dispositional forces.
c. Incorrect. Anxiety is explained in terms of what others do (thus situational).
*d. Correct. The disposition of conscientiousness is used to account for staying up all night.

7. a   mod. 43 p. 535
*a. Correct. Tiffany is engaging in a behavior because of the situation, not her disposition to keep the room messy.
b. Incorrect. Thoughtfulness is Robbie's disposition.
c. Incorrect. Grumpiness is Donny's disposition.
d. Incorrect. Punctuality is Debbie's disposition.

8. d   mod. 44 p. 539
a. Incorrect. The more the group members value the group, the stronger will be the pressures to conform.
b. Incorrect. The larger the group, the more likely conformity becomes.
c. Incorrect. Public statements increase the pressure to conform.
*d. Correct. Secret ballots remove pressure to conform because other members will be unaware of how the individual votes are cast.

9. a   mod. 45 p. 547
*a. Correct. Stereotypes are applications of category knowledge and prejudices involve using stereotypes to make judgments about people.
b. Incorrect. Neither require action.
c. Incorrect. Neither require action.
d. Incorrect. This is reversed.

10. a   mod. 46 p. 555
*a. Correct. Similarity is the best early predictor of attraction.
b. Incorrect. Mere exposure is probably the weakest predictor of attraction.
c. Incorrect. Similarity is the strongest predictor.
d. Incorrect. Need complimentarity is an inconsistent predictor of attraction.

11. d   mod. 46 p. 555
a. Incorrect. See answer d.
b. Incorrect. See answer d.
c. Incorrect. See answer d.
*d. Correct. Sternberg's triarchic theory of love has three components, intimacy, passion, and commitment, which can be combined in different ways.

12. c   mod. 46 p. 557
a.   Incorrect. Sports are not considered prosocial.
b.   Incorrect. Lorenz was referring to civilized, game-oriented sports like football.
*c. Correct. Because aggression arises from an instinct, in his view, it needs some form of release.
d.   Incorrect. This is from a different aspect of the frustration-aggression hypothesis.

13. a   mod. 44 p. 539
*a. Correct. Secret ballots remove pressure to conform because other members will be unaware of how the individual votes are cast.
b.   Incorrect. Public statements increase the pressure to conform.
c.   Incorrect. The larger the group, the more likely conformity becomes.
d.   Incorrect. The more the group members value the group, the stronger will be the pressure to conform.

14. c   mod. 46 p. 559
a.   Incorrect. Fundamental attribution error accounts for attributing the bombers' acts to their own evil nature.
b.   Incorrect. Diffusion of responsibility would have left many people standing by and watching.
*c. Correct. This prosocial behavior demonstrates that more must be involved than mere rewards.
d.   Incorrect. Only if they were angels.

15. e   mod. 46 p. 560
16. a   mod. 46 p. 560
17. c   mod. 46 p. 560
18. b   mod. 43 p. 533
19. d   mod. 44 p. 540

20. similar   mod. 46 p. 554
21. physically   mod. 46 p. 554
22. loving   mod. 46 p. 554
23. health   mod. 46 p. 556
24. Biological   mod. 46 p. 555

25. Often partners are chosen because of their proximity to each other. Selections are often made based on similarities in terms of values, attitudes, and traits. Knowing someone has evaluated us positively has a reciprocity-of-liking effect. Once commitments are made, intimacy and passion often follow.